67.50

7 - 50

Seventeenth-century Norwich

SEVENTEENTH-CENTURY NORWICH

Politics, Religion, and Government, 1620–1690

BY

JOHN T. EVANS

CLARENDON PRESS · OXFORD
1979

Oxford University Press, Walton Street, Oxford OX2 6DP

OXFORD   LONDON   GLASGOW
NEW YORK   TORONTO   MELBOURNE   WELLINGTON
KUALA LUMPUR   SINGAPORE   JAKARTA   HONG KONG   TOKYO
DELHI   BOMBAY   CALCUTTA   MADRAS   KARACHI
NAIROBI   DAR ES SALAAM   CAPE TOWN

British Library Cataloguing in Publication Data
Evans, John T
   Seventeenth-century Norwich.
   1. Norwich, Eng.—Politics and government
   I. Title
   320.9'426'1506   DA690.N88   79–40416
   ISBN 0–19–822476–1

*Set, printed and bound in Great Britain by
Fakenham Press Limited, Fakenham, Norfolk*

To
Father, Mother,
Mary and Shannon

Preface

During the reign of the Stuarts, Norwich was the largest provincial city in England and the economic, social, and religious capital of East Anglia. Thriving on the revival of its worsted industry and prospering as the axis of conspicuous consumption for the surrounding countryside, the city was famous for the affluence of its leading citizens. Renowned by contemporaries for heated religious and political controversies, Norwich was also a city in which men fought over issues which elsewhere in England were dividing Puritans and Anglicans, Roundheads and Royalists, Whigs and Tories. Given the increasing importance of urban studies, especially for the Civil War period and the years leading up to the Revolution of 1688, a political and religious history of seventeenth-century Norwich is overdue.

That the history of Norwich during this period sheds light on the disruptive impact which national affairs can have on local politics might seem surprising. A prevailing theme in recent research on provincial England, heavily stressed by Professors A. M. Everitt and Roger Howell, concerns the insularity of local communities. Even in the midst of the Civil War, the political perceptions of the men in most towns rarely extended beyond their city walls. This does not mean that provincial urban life may be characterized as tranquil, but rather that the faction and conflict which did exist stemmed invariably from local social and economic issues or from family and personal feuds. Norwich, however, was an exception. As intensely politicized as any other English city outside London, Norwich serves as a partial corrective to the notion that provincial towns were for the most part disinterested in and only minimally affected by national issues and events.

A second theme stressed in this book is that in Norwich the period from 1620 to 1690 possesses a unity. It was a period of continuing constitutional and political instability in which factions fought for control of the corporation, popular opinion was frequently channelled into petitions and mobilized for elections and, in moments of crisis, mob activity was stirred into frenzy. The two major sources of instability throughout the century were the impact of religious nonconformity on civic politics and the intervention of state, church, and county authorities in city affairs. Thus the history of Norwich suggests that the fashionable tendency of historians to adopt 1640 or 1660 as terminal dates for local studies may obscure important elements of continuity which connect the Civil War with the Revolution of 1688.

In the production of this work I owe a great deal of gratitude to many institutions and people. A grant from the Leverhulme Foundation, administered by the University of London, made research in England possible. The staffs of the Norfolk and Norwich Record Office and the Local History Department of the Norwich Central Library were extremely helpful and courteous. I am especially thankful to archivist Jean M. Kennedy, who has helped make the Norfolk and Norwich Record Office a model for county archives. I am also grateful to other depositories which provided materials for this study, especially the Public Record Office, the British Museum, Somerset House in London, the Bodleian Library, and the Stanford University Library. While I was in England, Dr. Roger Lockyer, Dr. A. Hassell Smith, and Professor J. R. Jones offered useful direction; and J. F. Pound kindly shared his experience with Norwich documents and his extensive knowledge of the city's social and economic life. In the preparation of my doctoral dissertation for Stanford University, of which this book is a revision, I benefited from the considerable assistance of Professor Philip Dawson and Professor Peter Stansky. My appreciation also extends to my loving wife Mary, who helped in the editing and typing of the revised manuscript.

Above all, I am now and shall always remain deeply indebted to Professor Paul Seaver, who provided the initial inspiration for this study and who gave patient guidance throughout its development. No student could be more fortunate in his apprenticeship than I, for surely Paul Seaver is a paragon as a friend, a mentor, and a scholar.

JTE

Contents

List of Figures

List of Tables

List of Abbreviations and Notes on Citations

A.B.	Norwich Assembly Book of Proceedings
Add. MSS.	Additional Manuscripts
A. & O.	*Acts and Ordinances of the Interregnum*
A.P.C.	*Acts of the Privy Council*
Brit. Lib.	British Library
C.C.R.	*Calendar of Charter Rolls*
C.J.	*Journal of the House of Commons*
C.S.P.D.	*Calendar of State Papers, Domestic Series*
D.N.B.	*Dictionary of National Biography*
H.M.C.	*Royal Commission on Historical Manuscripts, Reports and Calendars*
L.J.	*Journal of the House of Lords*
M.C.B.	Norwich Mayor's Court Book of Proceedings
N.C.C.	Norwich Consistory Court
N.N.R.O.	Norfolk and Norwich Record Office
P.C.C.	Prerogative Court of Canterbury
P.R.O.	Public Record Office
S.P.Dom.	State Papers, Domestic Series
V.C.H.	*Victoria County History*

Modernized spelling and punctuation have been used for all seventeenth-century documents. Names of persons and locations are spelt consistently, despite variants in the documents. The 'Old Style' dating has been used throughout, but dates between 1 January and 25 March are listed with both years. For example, 20 February 1649/50 is 20 February 1649 Old Style (year beginning 25 March) and 20 February 1650 New Style (year beginning 1 January).

I

The Political Community in Tradition and Transition

Seventeenth-century Norwich was a dynamic city undergoing considerable and frequently dramatic transformation. It was also a community imbued with and embedded in tradition. The central purpose of this study is to focus on elements of change and permanence in the political and religious arena, where after 1640 faction and conflict become the constant theme. These struggles, however, cannot be fully appreciated away from the backdrop of the social and economic life of the town.[1] Here the major developments were population growth, growing dependence on the textile industry, and increasing interaction between the city and neighbouring countryside. Although some of the six or seven major provincial centres were stagnating or even declining in the seventeenth century, Norwich experienced a period of expansion and solidified its position as the social and economic as well as the political and religious centre of Norfolk.[2] Its claim to be the premier provincial capital of England was strengthened.[3] Significant as these developments were, the political community continued to consist of only a portion of the population, and the traditional social structure with its hierarchy of status and sharp gradations of wealth remained intact.

The importance of tradition in structuring the life of sixteenth-

[1] The social and economic history of seventeenth-century Norwich is currently being written by John F. Pound. This chapter provides only an overview and its central concern is the political community and not society as a whole. For a full discussion of the urban society see Pound, 'Government and Society in Tudor and Stuart Norwich, 1525–1675' (unpublished Ph.D. thesis, University of Leicester, 1975).

[2] In addition to Norwich, the leading provincial towns included Bristol, Exeter, York, Newcastle-upon-Tyne, and perhaps Hull. As a group they are described in Peter Clark and Paul Slack, eds., *Crisis and Order in English Towns 1500–1700* (London, 1972), pp. 5 ff.

[3] On the basis of the 1523–7 subsidy and the number of hearths taxed in 1662, Norwich may be ranked second only to London. W. G. Hoskins, *Local History in England* (London, 1959), p. 177. See also Thomas Babington Macaulay, *History of England* (London, 1850), I. 336–8.

and seventeenth-century urban communities cannot be over-emphasized.[1] Norwich was no exception. The mentality of its citizens and the patterns of daily life were fashioned in large measure by this omnipresent force. In dealing with day-to-day civic problems, Norwich magistrates invariably preferred policies of preservation and restoration to innovation. In their attitude towards both politics and society, they were neither visionaries nor reformers. Radical reconstruction of urban life in any of its facets was aceptable to them only under the most critical of conditions or in response to the most formidable pressures. In particular, they revered tradition as the surest means of maintaining social stability and ensuring prosperity. Their conservatism, of course, did not prevent significant modification in the social and economic structures, yet it did dictate that change occurred slowly and resulted mainly from larger and uncontrolled factors. Consequently, the Civil War, Restoration, and Whig–Tory controversy, which so inflamed the political and religious passions of townsmen, had at best a minimal impact on gradually evolving social and economic trends.

Visible reminders of the city's deep roots in the past were to be seen everywhere. These enduring edifices, which had figured so prominently in the city's earlier history, continued to be the focal points of town activity and provided the setting for the political and religious conflicts. Like spokes from a wheel, the roads of Norfolk flowed into the city through the ancient gates. Except for a few suburbs which dotted the surrounding countryside, the inhabitants of the city and county of Norwich were still enclosed within the old medieval walls which, with the meandering River Wensum, circumscribed the city. The walls were constantly in need of repair, but they had not lost their usefulness and provided the first line of defence against anticipated Royalist attacks during the Civil War. The aged and neglected Norman Keep still sat majestically on a hill in the middle of town, and it continued to serve as a meeting place for county deputy-lieutenants. The centre of civic activity, however, had long since shifted to the still-flourishing market-place and the adjacent guild-hall.[2] Within its sombre

---

[1] See Wallace T. MacCaffrey, *Exeter, 1540–1640* (Cambridge, Mass., 1958), pp. 5–6.

[2] For a description of the market in the late seventeenth century, see *H.M.C.*, Portland MSS. II. 269; Penelope Corfield, 'A Provincial Capital in the Late Seventeenth Century: The Case of Norwich', in Clark and Slack, eds., *Crisis and Order*, pp. 288–9.

FIGURE 1: Norwich Parishes. From J. F. Pound, 'An Elizabethan Census of the Poor', *University of Birmingham Historical Journal*, VIII, 2 (1962), 161 and Cleer's Map of Norwich (1696)

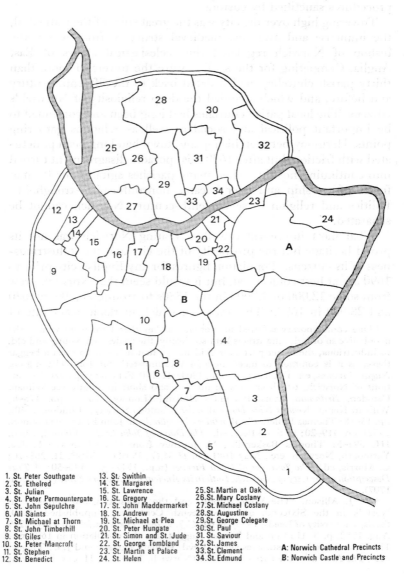

1. St. Peter Southgate	13. St. Swithin	
2. St. Ethelred	14. St. Margaret	
3. St. Julian	15. St. Lawrence	25. St. Martin at Oak
4. St. Peter Permountergate	16. St. Gregory	26. St. Mary Coslany
5. St. John Sepulchre	17. St. John Maddermarket	27. St. Michael Coslany
6. All Saints	18. St. Andrew	28. St. Augustine
7. St. Michael at Thorn	19. St. Michael at Plea	29. St. George Colegate
8. St. John Timberhill	20. St. Peter Hungate	30. St. Paul
9. St. Giles	21. St. Simon and St. Jude	31. St. Saviour
10. St. Peter Mancroft	22. St. George Tombland	32. St. James
11. St. Stephen	23. St. Martin at Palace	33. St. Clement
12. St. Benedict	24. St. Helen	34. St. Edmund

A: Norwich Cathedral Precincts
B: Norwich Castle and Precincts

chambers generation after generation of mayors and aldermen, clothed in resplendent robes and enveloped in pomp and ceremony, had conducted the routine of city business in accordance with procedures sanctified by custom.

Towering high over the city was the great spire of the Cathedral, the immense and awesome medieval structure from which the bishop of Norwich regulated the ecclesiastical affairs of East Anglia. Competing for the skyline were the towers of more than thirty parish churches, which dated back to the fifteenth century and before, and which signified the deep religiosity of Norwich's citizens. The local parish churches had long been and continued to be important political and social as well as religious gathering points. Harmony between bishop and town had long been punctuated with friction, but after 1620 this sporadic disagreement turned into continuing hostility when many parishes agitated for Puritan forms of worship and later became nonconformist strongholds. Politics and religion in seventeenth-century Norwich cannot be separated.

What most impressed travellers visiting Norwich was not its proud heritage but the prosperity of the city and the industriousness of its citizens.[1] Population figures for any English city prior to 1690 are at best conjectural, but it would seem that Norwich grew from some 12,000 or 13,000 in the 1580s to around 20,000 in 1620 and 28,000 in 1690.[2] This increase, which marks a faster rate of

[1] One contemporary referred to Norwich as 'another Utopia' in which 'the people live so orderly, the streets kept so cleanly, the tradesmen, young and old, so industrious; the better part so provident . . . that it is rare to meet a beggar there, as it is common to meet them in Westminster'. Sir John Harrington, *Nugae Antiquae*, ed. T. Clark (London, 1804), II. 170. For contemporary descriptions of Norwich, which are few in number and short in length, see William Camden, *Britannia*, trans. Philemon Holland (London, 1637), pp. 475–6; William Kemp, *Kemp's Nine Daies Wonder* [Camden Society] (London, 1840), pp. 15–18; Thomas Fuller, *The Worthies of England*, ed. John Freeman (London, 1952), pp. 419–20; E. S. de Beer, ed., *The Diary of John Evelyn* (Oxford, 1955), III. 593–5; Thomas Baskerville, 'A Journey from Oxford to Cambridge, Yarmouth, Norwich, etc., May 1681', in *H.M.C.*, Portland MSS. II. 268–70; C. Morris, ed., *The Journeys of Celia Fiennes* (n.p., 1947), pp. 146–50; *A True Description of the City of Norwich, Both in its Ancient and Modern State* (Norwich, 1707).

[2] K. J. Allison, 'The Wool Supply and the Worsted Cloth Industry in Norfolk in the Sixteenth and Seventeenth Centuries' (unpublished Ph.D. thesis, University of Leeds, 1955), p. 62; *C.J.* I. 784; *The Norwich Mercury*, 22–9 Aug. 1752, p. 3. Hudson and Tingey suggest that the population in 1600 was 15,000, and two later estimates agree. Revd. William Hudson and J. C. Tingey, eds., *The Records of the City of Norwich* (Norwich, 1906–10), II. cxxvii–cxxviii;

growth than that registered by most other provincial cities, was not continuous: severe plagues and trade slumps, especially during the 1620s and mid-1660s, resulted in demographic fluctuations and economic dislocation. Thus it is probable that the population levelled off at 20,000 in 1630, remained there for forty years, and then rose quickly to about 30,000 by 1700.[1] Although the population had more than doubled from 1590 to 1690, almost all the growth had taken place within the walls and the city must have been crowded.[2] Norwich may have been the largest provincial capital, slightly ahead of Bristol, York and Newcastle-upon-Tyne, but it was dwarfed by the comparative monstrosity of London, which had twenty times as many inhabitants.[3]

The townsmen of Norwich were separated into several clearly differentiated groups, each with its own status, function, and carefully defined niche in the social hierarchy. The essential feature of this hierarchy, which had persisted for centuries and remained unchallenged during the seventeenth century, was a basic correspondence between wealth, status, and political power. On the top were the wealthy citizens, who made their fortunes in the more prestigious trades and dominated civic officeholding. Beneath them were the lesser tradesmen, who together with the affluent élite formed the politically active and economically determinant segment of the community. Further down the social ladder were the apprentices and journeymen, who aspired to join the ranks of prosperous citizens by becoming freemen, and to improve their

[1] Penelope Corfield offers the best and most recent discussion of population change and the factors which account for fluctuation in seventeenth-century Norwich in 'A Provincial Capital', pp. 263–310. See also Pound, 'Tudor and Stuart Norwich', pp. 1–6. The population of Norfolk grew from about 215,000 in 1630 to about 230,000 in 1670. Gary Lynn Owens, 'Norfolk, 1620–1640: Local Government and Central Authority in an East Anglian County' (unpublished Ph.D. thesis, University of Wisconsin, 1970), p. 30.

[2] See Cleer's Map of the City of Norwich, 1696, in the Local History Collection of the Norwich Central Library. By the census of 1693, over 90 per cent of the population lived within the walls.

[3] Estimates of London population are about 200,000 in 1600, 400,000 in 1650, and 575,000 in 1700. E. A. Wrigley, 'A Simple Model of London's Importance in Changing English Society and Economy, 1650–1750', *Past and Present*, 37 (July 1967), 44.

John F. Pound, 'The Elizabethan Corporation of Norwich' (unpublished M.A. thesis, University of Birmingham, 1962), p. 11; Bruce Halliday Allen, 'The Administrative and Social Structure of the Norwich Merchant Class, 1485–1660' (unpublished Ph.D. thesis, Harvard University, 1951), pp. 41–2.

social position by means of a favourable marriage. If many of these men were motivated by high social expectations, the same cannot be said of the servant class. On the bottom were the poor. There is evidence that the gap between rich and poor widened during the seventeenth century. With recurrent economic crisis and plague, the number of indigent swelled. Hearth tax returns of 1671 show that some 60 per cent of the households were exempt owing to poverty.[1] The Norwich magistrates, in their concern for social order, were preoccupied with the preservation of the legal and social barriers which set these groups apart. Tudor and Stuart government on all levels was determined to retain traditional social distinctions. Upward social mobility was possible for an enterprising man, but group mobility involving social reconstruction was intolerable and even unthinkable.

Two urban groups lay outside this hierarchy. As a large and thriving provincial centre, Norwich was a gathering point and a source of fashionable goods for the county gentry. In this capacity the city served an extramural function similar to that of London, although on a much-reduced scale. Gentry town houses were built in the most fashionable areas in the city and doctors, lawyers, and clerks, whose professions depended upon contact with the county society, took up residence in the same parishes. A tax roll of 1660 lists twenty-one esquires and forty-one gentlemen together with fourteen lawyers living in Norwich.[2] Apart from but interacting with the higher levels of the hierarchy, their interests were frequently directed towards county affairs; but they did not hold elective office and did not participate in the administration of civic government. Less affluent, but more influential in local politico-religious matters, were the ministers and preachers who catered for the spiritual needs of the numerous parishes. Excluding the Cathedral clergy, at least twenty-nine clerics were in Norwich during the 1630s. The second group outside the hierarchy consisted of women. Wealthy widows and the daughters of affluent citizens were highly-desired commodities on the marriage market. For an ambitious townsman, a propitious marriage could develop valuable social contacts, enhance or restore financial status, and

[1] Pound, 'Tudor and Stuart Norwich', pp. 45–8. See also John F. Pound, 'An Elizabethan Census of the Poor', *University of Birmingham Historical Journal*, VIII (1962), 135–61.
[2] N.N.R.O., Assessment for Disbanding the King's Forces, 1660.

thus improve prospects for a political career. However, direct involvement of women in politics was minimal and thus they remain outside the scope of this study.[1]

The all-important dividing line among townsmen was between freemen and non-freemen. Freedom of the city involved both privileges and obligations as set down in local ordinances and enforced in the Mayor's Court. The effect of these ordinances was to provide the freemen, or citizenry, with a virtual monopoly over both political and economic affairs in Norwich.[2] Only freemen could hold civic office and only freemen could vote in municipal and parliamentary elections. Non-freemen and 'foreigners' were prohibited from taking on apprentices. Before 1616 they could keep shop in the city for only two years after which they had to choose between taking up the freedom or closing business.[3] An ordinance of 1616 was even more rigid: non-freemen were prohibited from keeping shop or practising any trade whatsoever in Norwich upon penalty of 40*s*. Moreover, non-freemen who merely bought or sold wares or merchandise in the city were to be fined 40*s*.[4] A city charter granted in 1662/3 expressly forbade freemen to take on foreigners as business partners.[5] Consequently, every householder in Norwich who wished to practise a trade was not only expected to become a freeman but in reality had little alternative. Whether the laws discriminating against foreigners were rigidly enforced throughout the century can never be fully known, but periodic attempts by the city government to pass additional legislation

[1] The widow of a craftsman could carry on her deceased husband's business, but single women could not set up shop without the sanction of the authorities. Women are also included in the tax rolls. Nevertheless, females were not permitted to obtain freedom to the city and permission to trade did not entitle them to the franchise. Percy Millican, ed., *The Register of the Freemen of Norwich 1548–1713: A Transcript* (Norwich, 1934), p. xv.

[2] A full discussion of the political aspects of freedom to the city is provided in Chapter II. The status of 'freeman' varied from town to town; for a general discussion see Derek Hirst, *The Representative of the People?* (Cambridge, 1975), pp. 92–6.

[3] Percy Millican and Winifred M. Rising, eds., *An Index of Indentures of Norwich Apprentices enrolled with the Norwich Assembly, Henry VII to George II* [Norfolk Record Society, XXIX] (Norwich, 1959), p. xii. For the pre-1600 ordinances governing freedom see Millican, ed., *Freemen*, pp. xvii–xx.

[4] N.N.R.O., A.B. (1613–42), 3 June 1616, 50^v–51^v. Nevertheless, Millican and Rising doubt that these fines were severe enough to prevent foreigners from practising their trades in Norwich. Millican and Rising, eds., *Index of Indentures*, p. xii.

[5] N.N.R.O., Norwich Charter of 1662/3.

suggests continued determination to preserve the status of freedom.[1]

Admission to the freedom could be obtained in one of four ways.[2] First, the legitimate and freeborn sons of Norwich freemen were granted their freedom gratis at the minimum age of sixteen but usually in their twenties; if not already apprenticed in a trade they were enrolled in the craft of their fathers. Secondly, an apprentice of a Norwich freeman could take up his freedom if he had served a term of at least seven years, had proved himself to be a competent workman, and had become a householder.[3] Thirdly, a foreigner could purchase freedom on the condition that he was enrolled in a craft and was approved by the master of that craft. Fees for freedom acquired by service as an apprentice were minimal,[4] but those who purchased their freedom did so at a higher price in proportion to their financial means. Customarily all qualified inhabitants and interested foreigners were encouraged to become freemen of the city, but occasionally the city corporation was not above assessing wealthy merchants for outrageous sums as the price of obtaining freedom.[5] Lastly, the Norwich Assembly was empowered to bestow admission on any person who in their opinion would benefit the community.[6] Just as the Assembly had the power to grant the freedom, so they could revoke it if there was sufficient reason, although this was rare.[7] Freemen were expected

---

[1] See, for example, N.N.R.O., M.C.B. (1666–77), 2 Oct. 1667, 46ᵛ; 20 June 1675, 318ʳ; A.B. (1668–1707), 3 May 1675, 48ᵛ; 16 Mar. 1676/7, 58ʳ.

[2] Millican, ed., *Freemen*, p. xv.

[3] In 1615 the Norwich Assembly, acknowledging that enforcement of this rule had been lax, passed an ordinance requiring apprenticeship indentures to be enrolled so that it could be proved that men desiring to become freemen had in fact been apprenticed for seven years. A.B. (1613–42), 16 May 1615, 35ᵛ.

[4] Fines of 4s. 10d. for apprentices were established in a craft ordinance of 1622. A.B. (1613–42), 29 July 1622, 143ᵛ–147ʳ. See also Millican, ed., *Freemen*, p. xx.

[5] The freemen register reveals that few foreigners paid more than £5 for their freedom, yet in March of 1601/2 James Dehem, merchant, consented to pay £50. Millican, ed., *Freemen*, p. 104.

[6] By a decision of 1621/2, the Assembly granted to itself the authority to bestow freedom on up to four foreigners in one year. A.B. (1613–42), 25 Feb. 1621/2, 137ᵛ. In 1627 the Assembly enlarged their prerogative to create as many freemen as they desired because the wardens of the trades were charging excessive fees. ibid., 3 May 1627, 232ᵛ–233ʳ.

[7] One example is the declaration of the Assembly on 11 December 1609: 'It is ordered and assented that John Cockshead being known to be a notorious drunkard and of late charged with blasphemy, shall be utterly discommuned and disfranchised forever.' A.B. cited in Millican, ed., *Freemen*, p. 35.

to reside within the town and, since 1554, citizens who moved outside the city and county of Norwich became foreigners and forfeited their privileged status.[1]

Upon admission to the freedom, new citizens were required to swear to the ancient freeman's oath. The purpose of the oath was to alert the freemen to their civic responsibilities as well as to maintain the economic privileges of the group. New freemen pledged to be loyal to the monarch and the royal heirs, to be obedient to the mayor, to maintain faithfully the customs and ordinances of the city, to pay all taxes, to refuse to do business or associate with a foreigner, to report any conspiracy against the Crown or the city to the municipal authorities, and to serve any office elected to.[2] The overthrow of monarchy in 1648/9 led to a revised oath which pointedly omitted references to the Crown, but the ancient oath was restored in 1662.[3] To the extent that citizens took the oath seriously, diligent enforcement of the ordinances encouraging townsmen to take up the freedom made a contribution to civic order and peaceful governance.

The size of the freeman populace at any one time cannot be determined with accuracy. Estimates, however, can be computed from the number of admissions to the freedom, given in Table 1.

TABLE 1: *Admissions to the Freedom of Norwich, 1590–1690**

1590–1599:	434	1640–1649:	620
1600–1609:	456	1650–1659:	642
1610–1619:	630	1660–1669:	886
1620–1629:	672	1670–1679:	886
1630–1639:	654	1680–1689:	559

*Figures are computed from Percy Millican, ed., *The Register of the Freemen of Norwich, 1548–1713: A Transcript* (Norwich, 1934). Dates used are new calendar style.

The sons of Norwich citizens were admitted by patrimony at an average age of 23·2, the apprentices by service at an average age of 26·6, and the foreigners by purchase at at average age of 31·9.[4]

[1] ibid., p. xv.
[2] ibid., pp. xi–xii. See also Hudson and Tingey, eds., *Records*, I. cix.
[3] Millican, ed., *Freemen*, p. xii.
[4] These figures are based on twenty-five instances of each case. Parish register entries have been compared with entries of admitted freemen which listed both father and son for freemen admitted by patrimony. For those who obtained their freedom through purchase, birth dates were determined by funeral monuments

There was also a significant change between 1590 and 1690 in the percentage of freemen admitted by each of these three methods.[1] Taking these factors into consideration, the average age of becoming a freeman in the fifty years up to 1640 is estimated to have been 27·3 and for the following fifty years the average was 25·5. If the life expectancy of a new freeman admitted before 1640 is accepted to be twenty-nine years, and of a freeman admitted after 1640 to be twenty-seven years,[2] an estimate of the number of freemen in the city at the beginning of each decade may be calculated by either of two methods and is provided in Table 2.

The freeman populace, which in the 1520s and 1570s had numbered some 705 and 1,250 men respectively,[3] increased considerably to about 1,800 in 1640, tapered off until 1660, and then rose again to about 2,300 in 1680. The drop in the number of freemen admitted during the 1640s and 1650s may have been caused by plague in the mid-1620s, a decline in the cloth industry,

---

[1] The number and percentage of 'foreigners' purchasing freedom was significantly lower in the half-century after 1640 than during the fifty years prior to 1640. From 1590 to 1640 the percentage of freedoms gained by patrimony, service, and purchase were 22·7, 46·4, and 30·4 respectively, whereas during the period 1640 to 1690 the percentage of freedoms gained by patrimony, service, and purchase were 36·1, 50·5, and 11·7 respectively. A complete tabulation of the number of freemen admitted by these three methods may be found in John T. Evans, 'The Political Elite of Norwich, 1620–1690: Patterns of Recruitment and the Impact of National Affairs' (unpublished Ph.D. thesis, Stanford University, 1971), p. 356. A shift in the recruitment of freemen from outside the city to sons of freemen after 1650 also occurred in other cities. Lawrence Stone, 'Social Mobility in England, 1500–1700', *Past and Present*, 33 (Apr. 1966), 47–8.

[2] Professor Wrigley has demonstrated that in Colyton the mortality of married men and women marrying under the age of thirty-five between 1538 and 1624 was 56·2 for those men and women whose date of death is known. The same figure for the years 1625 to 1699 is 52·2. E. A. Wrigley, 'Mortality in Pre-Industrial England: the Example of Colyton, Devon, Over Three Centuries', *Daedalus* (Spring 1968), 560. These figures are close to the estimates of Edmund Halley in the 1690s: he listed the life expectancy of men and women at age twenty to be 33·93 years and at age thirty to be 27·64 years. Peter Laslett, *The World We Have Lost* (New York, 1965), p. 93. Using Wrigley's figures, the life expectancy of a citizen on the date of becoming a freeman between 1590 and 1640 is taken to be about twenty-nine years (56·2 minus 27·3) and between 1640 and 1690 the life expectancy of a new freeman is taken to be about twenty-seven years (52·2 minus 25·5).

[3] John F. Pound, 'The Social and Trade Structure of Norwich, 1525–1575', *Past and Present*, 34 (July 1966), 59.

---

which listed date of death and age at death. For the apprentices a combination of both methods was used. Freedom to the city could also be granted by the Assembly, but these freemen are omitted because there were only fifteen men in this category over the century.

TABLE 2: *Estimated Freemou Electorate, 1620–1690*

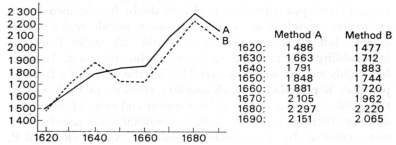

	Method A	Method B
1620:	1 486	1 477
1630:	1 663	1 712
1640:	1 791	1 883
1650:	1 848	1 744
1660:	1 881	1 720
1670:	2 105	1 962
1680:	2 297	2 220
1690:	2 151	2 065

Method A:
One approach for determining the freeman populace at the beginning of each decade is based on the survival statistics provided by E. A. Wrigley, 'Mortality in Pre-Industrial England', *Daedalus* (Spring 1968), p. 561. Professor Wrigley has calculated the number of married persons aged twenty-five who survived to different ages during the period 1625–99 in Colyton: age 25 = 100·0 %, age 40 = 79·5 %, age 50 = 60·3 %, age 60 = 41·5 %, age 70 = 18·4 %, and age 80 = 4·6 %. If we assume that approximately ninety per cent of the freemen admitted during a ten-year period survived the tenth year of that period, then the estimated freeman populace at the beginning of each decade may be calculated. For example, in 1650 the number of freemen = 0·90 × 620 (number of freemen admitted in the 1640s) + 0·795 × 654 + 0·603 × 672 + 0·415 × 630 + 0·184 × 456 + 0·046 × 434. The number of freemen admitted in the 1560s, 1570s, and 1580s was 426, 522, and 502 respectively.

Method B:
A second method is based on average life expectancy rather than survival. If the average life expectancy before 1640 was twenty-nine years and after 1640 was twenty-seven years, then the total number of freemen in 1620 = 630 (number of freemen admitted in the 1610s) + 456 + 0·9 × 434 or 1,477; for 1650 the calculation would be 620 + 654 + 0·7 × 672 = 1,744.

emigration produced by religious persecution, and economic dislocation arising from the Civil War. During the last years of the Interregnum the city is known to have suffered a severe economic slump.[1] The sudden drop in admissions during the 1680s was in large part due to non-economic factors: in 1677/8 the mayor prematurely granted freedom to 362 men for political reasons. Nevertheless, the period from 1670 to 1690 does exhibit a drop in the average number of freemen admitted each year compared to the 1660s, and this suggests that the city may have been undergoing a recession.[2] Admittedly the above methods of determining

[1] A.B. (1642–68), 13 Dec. 1659, 110ᵛ.

[2] There is reason to believe, however, that the freeman register does not accurately reflect the actual number of town-dwellers who were absorbed into the cloth industry, and thus that the city possibly did not experience a recession after 1670. See Corfield, 'A Provincial Capital', pp. 274 ff.

the estimated number of freemen in a given year is open to criticism. Better approximations could no doubt be obtained by an exhaustive examination of the numerous parish registers still extant,[1] but these approximations would still suffer from the impossibility of numbering the freemen who emigrated. Another, but highly suspect source for establishing the size of the freeman populace is provided by parliamentary election totals. However, the number of citizens who did not appear and vote is indeterminable and there was also the definite possibility that non-freemen were counted by indiscriminate sheriffs. Nevertheless, M.P. election returns do support the marked growth in the freeman populace suggested in Table 2. In 1640 three candidates received a total of 2,270 votes, which implies that 1,135 freemen were present.[2] In another contested election in 1679, four candidates received 4,428 votes from 2,214 freemen, almost twice as many as in 1640.[3]

The freemen, who monopolized the wealth of the city and constituted the economic and political community, were only a minority of the adult male populace. A parochial census taken in 1693 gives the total population of the city and suburbs as 28,876. Slightly more than half of these inhabitants were presumably females. If the median age of males is accepted to be about twenty-five, which is the same as the average age at which townsmen were granted freedom to the city, then approximately 7,000 adult males over the age of twenty-five were in the city and suburbs in 1693.[4] Table 2 gives a figure of slightly more than 2,000 freemen in the early 1690s, and thus the freemen formed about 30 per cent of the

[1] The N.N.R.O. presently possesses twenty-three parish registers which are complete for the period 1620 to 1690 and two other registers which cover large segments of this period. Only one register has been published: George Branwhite Jay, transcriber, *The First Parish Register of St. George Tombland, 1538–1707* (Norwich, 1891).

[2] M. F. Keeler, *The Long Parliament 1640–1641, A Biographical Study* (Philadelphia, 1954), pp. 56, 57n.

[3] *H.M.C., 7th Report*, Frere MSS., Edward L'estrange to Lady Yarmouth, 3 Sept. 1679, 532b.

[4] Gregory King put the average age of Englishmen at twenty-seven and a half and separate studies have established the average age in Linchfield and Stoke in the 1690s at about twenty-six. The median age at Buckfastleigh, Devon, in 1698 was 25·1 and at Linchfield in 1695 it was 23·6. Laslett, *World*, p. 103. My calculations are based solely on the median as distinct from the average age.

adult male population.[1] Some of the non-freemen were resident gentry and professional men and others were servants, but by far the largest number were the poor.

Norwich was considered to be a wealthy town during the seventeenth century and the fortunes amassed by its most affluent citizens were widely known. Thomas Wilson asserted in 1600 that the aldermen were worth £20,000 each and another estimate from the early 1680s claimed that the vast majority of magistrates were worth £10,000.[2] The numerous problems involved in ascertaining the real wealth of seventeenth-century townsmen makes it impossible to verify either of these figures.[3] The wills of deceased mayors, aldermen, and sheriffs leave the impression that the estates of the wealthy magistrates were at least equal to those of leading citizens of other provincial capitals but could not compare with the great estates built up by some London merchants.[4] Stranger's Hall in the parish of St. John Maddermarket and other still-standing seventeenth-century mansions in Norwich testify to

[1] The ratio of freemen to non-freemen in Norwich is apparently somewhat low with respect to other cities. MacCaffrey estimates that in Exeter between 1620 and 1640 the freemen constituted a substantial minority of the population, but Hirst estimates that in early seventeenth-century York and Bristol the freemen were about 75 and 50 per cent of the adult male populace respectively. MacCaffrey, *Exeter*, pp. 73, 164; Hirst, *Representative of the People?*, pp. 94–5.

[2] Thomas Wilson, *The State of England anno Dom. 1600*, ed. F. J. Fisher [Camden Misc., XVI, 3rd ser. LII] (London, 1936), p. 20; Brit. Lib., Add. MSS., 27448, fo. 151, John Fawcett to ——, 1683.

[3] See Richard Grassby, 'The Personal Wealth of the Business Community in Seventeenth-Century England', *Economic History Review*, 2nd ser. XXIII. 2 (Aug. 1970), 220–34.

[4] A search of the probate records in the P.C.C. (Somerset House, London), the N.C.C., the Peculiar Court of the Dean and Chapter of Norwich, and the Norwich Archdeaconry Court (N.N.R.O.) uncovered the wills of 127 of the 191 men who served as mayor, sheriff, or alderman between 1620 and 1690. Administrations for twelve more magistrates are also in the records of the courts. Evidence gleaned from wills defies statistical analysis and is highly suspect as a measure of real wealth. Personal belongings, business inventory, and, most important, investments in land and estates are not given monetary values. Moreover, wills were often drawn up long before a man died and thus provide only what the deceased hoped were realizable assets which his executor would employ towards carrying out his will and bequest. Lastly, the ratio of cash to other assets varied according to each man's investment policy. Probate inventories are the best indication of wealth, but the inventories in Somerset House were inaccessible at the time of this study. For London see R. G. Lang, 'Social Origins and Social Aspirations of Jacobean London Merchants', *Economic History Review*, 2nd ser. XXVII. I. 30.

14   *The Political Community in Tradition and Transition*

the sumptuous life-style of the most prominent men.[1] According to contributions to a loan to the King in 1611 and 1612, the wealthier magistrates considered themselves on a financial par with most knights and esquires in the county and nothing indicates that this parity was lost during the remainder of the century.[2]

Inequality of wealth was the normal pattern in Tudor and Stuart society, and this was especially true in the towns. City tax rolls provide an indication of the vast gulf between the very rich and the majority of townsmen (Table 3). Only a minority of the inhabitants were obligated to contribute even to the most minor of taxes, such as

TABLE 3: *Distribution of Taxpayers, 1645 and 1660**

Assessment for Sir Thomas Fairfax, 1645			Assessment for disbanding the King's forces, 1660		
sums assessed (s.)	number of ratepayers	percentage of total	sums assessed (s)	number of ratepayers	percentage of total
less than 1	4	0·57	2 to 3/11d.	389	35·46
1 to 1/11d.	146	20·71	4 to 7/11d.	259	23·61
2 to 3/11d.	226	32·06	8 to 15/11d.	185	16·86
4 to 7/11d.	187	26·52	16 to 31/11d.	134	12·22
8 to 15/11d.	107	15·18	32 to 63/11d.	61	5·56
16 to 31/11d.	30	4·26	64 to 127/11d.	27	2·46
32 to 51	5	0·71	128 to 540	42	3·83
	705	100·01		1,097	100·00

*Widows and unmarried females are excluded. Suburbs are included, as are gentry and professional men. The 1645 rates provided are assessments on personal estate only, whereas the 1660 lists combine personal and real estate. The 1660 assessment established set rates for knights, esquires, professional men, and magistrates. For further details on the assessments, both of which are in the N.N.R.O., see John T. Evans, 'The Political Elite of Norwich, 1620–1690: Patterns of Recruitment and the Impact of National Affairs' (unpublished Ph.D. thesis, Stanford University, 1971), pp. 415–20.

[1] See R. M. R. Young, *Guide to Stranger's Hall, Museum of Domestic Life*, issued by Norwich Museum Committee, 1967.
[2] Norfolk Contributions to a Loan for the King, 1611–12 printed in R. H. Mason, *History of Norfolk* (London, 1882–5), I. 240–4. 14 of the 21 knights, 24 of the 40 esquires, and 13 of the 24 Norwich aldermen donated £20 or more. A statistical breakdown of the loan may be found in Evans, 'Political Elite of Norwich', p. 440.

the poor rate and the collection for the river and streets.¹ In the parliamentary subsidy collected in 1660, the compiler included the names of only those town-dwellers rated 2s. or more; individuals assessed less than 2s. were grouped together at the end of each parochial list with the desgination 'in single polls'.² The more than £245 attributed to 'single polls', or roughly one-sixth of the total of £1,495.19s.10d., gives some indication of the several thousands of taxpayers who paid less than 2s. The distribution of wealth in early modern English society has traditionally been presented in terms of a stepped pyramid model, but this does not give an adequate picture of the overwhelming number who comprised the base in comparison with the relatively few men of vastly greater wealth who formed the middle and top of society.³ A graphical representation of Table 3 would take the form of an Eiffel Tower or an inverted funnel.⁴ The hierarchy of wealth in the 1660 assessment was not significantly different from what it had been in Henrician and Elizabethan Norwich.⁵

As there were vast differences in the wealth of freemen, so also there were some parishes which possessed far greater wealth *per capita* and many more wealthy citizens than other parishes. The average wealth per inhabitant in the 1690s may be calculated by combining a 1696 parliamentary subsidy with the 1693 population census.⁶ The most prosperous area of Norwich was a contiguous group of parishes in the centre of the city on both sides of the river (Figure 2). The parishes with the most conspicuous concentration of wealth were St. Peter Mancroft and St. Andrew. If parochial returns for an assessment of 1644 are compared with the 1696

¹ In 1633–4 some 844 townsmen paid a poor rate and in 1649 some 950 townsmen were assessed for a collection for the river and streets. These figures do not include the suburbs. Both tax lists are located in the N.N.R.O. and the former has been published in Walter Rye, ed., *The Norwich Rate Book, Easter 1633 to Easter 1634* (n.p., 1903).

² According to the provisions of the act, all single persons over the age of sixteen were taxed at least 12d. and all other inhabitants over the age of sixteen at least 6d. *Statutes of the Realm* (London, 1963), V, An Act for the speedy provision of money for disbanding and paying off the forces of this kingdom both by land and sea, 12 Car. II, c. IX, pp. 207–25.

³ See Stone, 'Social Mobility', pp. 16–55.

⁴ If the resident gentry and professional men were removed from Table 3, the stem of the graphical representation would be even narrower.

⁵ Cf. Pound, 'Social and Trade Structure', pp. 49–69.

⁶ The N.N.R.O. possesses a 1696 parliamentary subsidy listing sums collected in each parish, but it does not include rates for individuals.

subsidy, it would seem that the city's wealth was gradually being
dispersed away from the parishes with the highest *per capita*
wealth and into those areas which were relatively undeveloped
earlier in the century and in which the number of taxpayers had
increased, that is, primarily into the parishes north of the river and
south of the castle (Figure 3).[1] Whereas St. Peter Mancroft and St.
Andrew contributed 25·8 per cent of the 1644 assessment, they
accounted for only 19·4 per cent of the 1696 subsidy.[2] The parochial distribution of wealth as measured by tax liability did not
change appreciably during the century, however, and only two
parishes increased their tax portion by more than 1 per cent. The
most significant growth in wealth was in St. George Colegate,
which by the 1690s had moved from the seventh to the third
wealthiest parish. Although less than half as wealthy as St. Andrew
in 1644, St. George Colegate and St. Andrew had reached a near
parity by 1696.[3]

Norwich had been known as a cloth town for centuries, but
during the Elizabethan period the economic fortunes of the city
were based increasingly on its role as a supplier to the neighbouring
gentry and as a centre of conspicuous consumption.[4] The influx of
Walloons and other refugees from the continent in the late sixteenth century began a gradual reversal of this trend. Most of the
'strangers' were weavers and they introduced new types of cloth
and new techniques to the Norwich craftsmen.[5] Although most
Stuart towns depended more and more on their function as social
centres for county society,[6] the prosperity of seventeenth-century
Norwich was closely linked to the textile industry and related

[1] Complete data on the parochial distribution of the tax burden in 1644 and
1696 and the wealth *per capita* in the 1690s may be found in Evans, 'Political
Elite of Norwich', pp. 367–8.

[2] The percentage assessment for St. Peter Mancroft and St. Andrew dropped
from 15·8 to 13·9 and 7·0 to 5·5 respectively. In 1644 only one other parish,
St. Stephen, paid more than 4 per cent of the total assessment. The 1644 tax list
may be found in Add. MSS. 22619, fo. 204.

[3] The percentage of the city tax paid by St. George increased from 2·9 to
5·4.

[4] Pound, 'Social and Trade Structure', pp. 57–8.

[5] See W. J. C. Moens, *The Walloons and their Church at Norwich* [Huguenot
Soc. Pub., I] (1888); E. T. Blakely, *History of the Manufactures of Norwich*
(Norwich, [188?]); D. C. Coleman, 'An Innovation and its Diffusion:
"The New Draperies"', *Economic History Review*, 2nd ser. XXII (1969), 417–
29.

[6] Clark and Slack, eds., *Crisis and Order*, pp. 14–15.

FIGURE 3: Parochial Tax in Shillings per Inhabitant, 1696

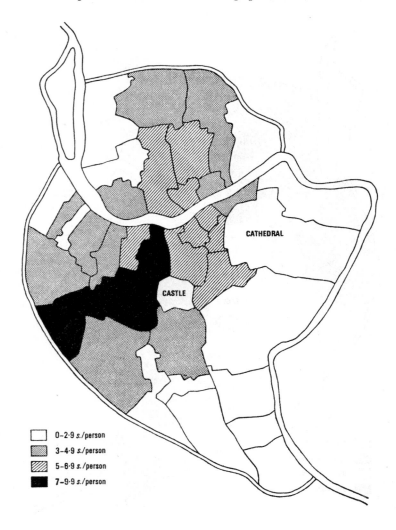

CATHEDRAL

CASTLE

☐ 0–2·9 *s.*/person

▨ 3–4·9 *s.*/person

▨ 5–6·9 *s.*/person

■ 7–9·9 *s.*/person

FIGURE 3: Percentage Change in Parochial Tax Liability, 1644–1696

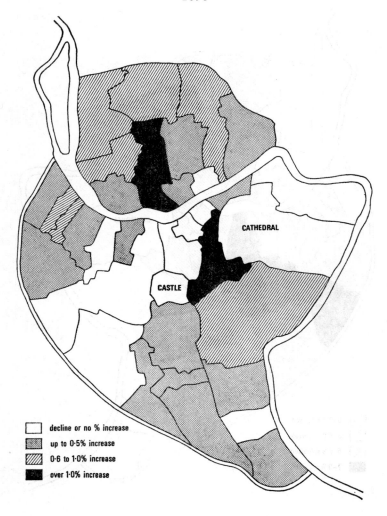

CATHEDRAL

CASTLE

☐ decline or no % increase

▨ up to 0·5% increase

▧ 0·6 to 1·0% increase

■ over 1·0% increase

trades in general, and to the worsted production in particular.[1] As
the sudden growth of Norwich in the first decades of the 1600s is
attributable to a revival of the cloth industry, so also the spurt
in population and prosperity after 1670 was connected with a
resurgence in this economic sector. Travelling through Norwich
in 1681, Thomas Baskerville noted: 'The chief trade of this
famous town consists mostly in making stuffs, and worsted
stockings, they in these sorts of manufactures excelling all other
places.'[2]

The dimensions of the growth of cloth manufacture are revealed
by the freeman register. From the 1590s to the 1670s the number of
freemen admitted annually to trades associated with the textile
industry rose 592 per cent (Table 4). Whereas only one in seven
new freemen of the 1590s was connected to a textile trade, in the
1620s the proportion had risen to one in three and in the 1670s to
nearly half. After 1650 there were more worsted weavers admitted
to the freedom than the next ten trades combined.[3] Norwich
undoubtedly continued to be a centre of conspicuous consumption,
a lesser London for the county landed classes, but the distributive
trades which catered for this business declined relative to other
occupational sectors. Almost 20 per cent of the freemen admitted
throughout the sixteenth century were associated with distributive
trades;[4] this percentage was maintained until 1620, but then
dropped to 15 per cent by the 1630s, 10 per cent by the 1660s, and
7 to 8 per cent from 1670 to 1690. The population doubled from
1590 to 1690, yet the number of drapers, grocers, haberdashers,
mercers, and merchants recruited per decade remained fairly

[1] K. J. Allison, 'The Norfolk Worsted Industry in the Sixteenth and Seventeenth Centuries', *Yorkshire Bulletin*, XII and XIII (1960 and 1961), 73–83,
61–77; Allison, 'Wool Supply and Worsted Cloth Industry'; Corfield, 'A
Provincial Capital', pp. 278–87; John James, *History of the Worsted Manufacture in England* (London, 1857), pp. 121–66; E. Lipson, *The History of the
Woollen and Worsted Industries* (London, 1921).
[2] Baskerville, 'Journey from Oxford . . .', in *H.M.C.*, Portland MSS. II. 270.
[3] From 1590 to 1609 the five most heavily recruited trades were the tailors,
worsted weavers, cordwainers, grocers, and carpenters with 125, 73, 67, 60, and
30 new freemen respectively. From 1670 to 1689 the five most popular trades
were the worsted weavers, tailors, cordwainers, bakers, and carpenters with 562,
147, 107, 65, and 48 new freemen respectively. A list of the leading trades from
1590 to 1690 in terms of the number of freemen admitted in twenty-year periods
may be found in Evans, 'Political Elite of Norwich', p. 559.
[4] Figures on sixteenth-century trade statistics are taken from Pound, 'Social
and Trade Structure', pp. 67–9.

TABLE 4: *Freemen Admitted to the Occupations of Norwich by decade, 1590–1690**

	1590s	1600s	1610s	1620s	1630s	1640s	1650s	1660s	1670s	1680s	Totals
Food and Drink	52 / 12·0%	41 / 9·0%	62 / 9·9%	84 / 12·5%	66 / 10·1%	53 / 8·5%	48 / 7·5%	59 / 6·7%	61 / 6·9%	69 / 12·4%	595 / 9·3%
Clothing	74 / 17·0%	66 / 14·2%	100 / 16·0%	78 / 11·6%	92 / 14·0%	77 / 12·4%	78 / 12·1%	122 / 13·8%	96 / 10·9%	70 / 12·5%	853 / 13·2%
Textiles	62 / 14·3%	91 / 19·9%	163 / 25·9%	219 / 32·6%	215 / 32·9%	204 / 32·9%	262 / 40·8%	370 / 41·8%	429 / 48·5%	216 / 38·8%	2231 / 34·6%
Metals	34 / 7·8%	35 / 7·7%	40 / 6·4%	54 / 8·0%	39 / 6·0%	42 / 6·8%	38 / 5·9%	46 / 5·2%	44 / 5·0%	15 / 2·7%	387 / 6·0%
Woodwork	6 / 1·3%	5 / 1·1%	6 / 1·0%	10 / 1·5%	8 / 1·2%	8 / 1·3%	15 / 2·3%	21 / 2·4%	16 / 1·8%	9 / 1·6%	104 / 1·6%
Building and Allied	40 / 9·2%	46 / 10·1%	33 / 5·2%	44 / 6·5%	52 / 8·0%	29 / 4·7%	45 / 7·1%	70 / 8·0%	65 / 7·3%	67 / 11·9%	491 / 7·6%
Distributive	86 / 19·8%	80 / 17·6%	123 / 19·5%	102 / 15·2%	98 / 15·0%	105 / 16·9%	86 / 13·4%	89 / 10·1%	56 / 6·2%	47 / 8·4%	872 / 13·5%
Leather and Allied	66 / 15·2%	66 / 14·2%	72 / 11·4%	63 / 9·2%	66 / 10·1%	85 / 13·4%	56 / 8·7%	78 / 8·8%	83 / 9·4%	43 / 7·7%	678 / 10·5%
Transport	3 / 0·7%		7 / 1·1%	2 / 0·3%	3 / 0·5%			2 / 0·2%	4 / 0·4%		21 / 0·3%
Professional	5 / 1·1%	10 / 2·2%	15 / 2·4%	7 / 1·0%	6 / 0·9%	10 / 1·6%	8 / 1·2%	12 / 1·4%	16 / 1·8%	10 / 1·8%	99 / 1·5%
Miscellaneous	1 / 0·2%	2 / 0·4%	2 / 0·3%	8 / 1·2%	2 / 0·3%	3 / 0·5%	5 / 0·8%	10 / 1·1%	9 / 1·0%	1 / 0·2%	43 / 0·7%
Trades Not Given	5 / 1·1%	14 / 3·1%	7 / 1·1%	1 / 0·1%	7 / 1·1%	4 / 0·6%	1 / 0·1%	7 / 0·8%	7 / 0·8%	12 / 2·2%	65 / 1·0%

* Occupational data on freemen taken from Millican, ed. *Freemen*. In assigning trades to different groups the system of classification used by J. F. Pound, 'The Social and Trade Structure of Norwich, 1525–1575', *Past and Present*, 34 (July 1966), 67–9 has been followed to allow for comparison. Pound has already detailed problems with this classification and no further comment is necessary. The trades which comprised the occupational sectors are given below; a decade by decade listing for individual trades may be found in Evans, 'Political Elite of Norwich', pp. 552–7. New Style calendar dates are used.

Food and Drink: bakers, brewers, brewers of beer, butchers, comfit makers, cooks, fishermen, fishmongers, gingerbread makers, innholders, innkeepers, maltsters, mealsellers, milleners, millers, poulterers, sugar bakers, victuallers, vintners

Clothing: body makers, hatbond makers, hatters, hosiers, point makers, tailors, upperbody makers

Textiles: bay weavers, calendrers, clothiers, clothshearmen, cloth workers, combers, dornix weavers, dyers, embroiderers, feltmakers, fringe makers, hair makers, hotpressers, lace weavers, linen and woollen weavers, ribbon weavers, say weavers, shermen, silk rasers, silk weavers, slay makers, slay wrights, starch makers, twisterers, upholsterers, waterers of stuffs, weavers, wool chapmen, wool combers, worsted shermen, worsted weavers

Metals: armourers, blacksmiths, bladesmiths, braziers, clasp makers, clock makers, cutlers, goldsmiths, gunsmiths, ironmongers, latten founders, locksmiths, pewterers, pin makers, plate workers, plumbers, sieve makers, smiths, spurriers, watch makers, white-plate makers, whiteplate workers

Woodwork: basket makers, card makers, chair makers, chair menders, coopers, instrument makers, shop carpenters, trunk makers, turners, wheelwrights, wine coopers

Building and Allied: bricklayers, brick makers, carpenters, glaziers, joiners, masons, painters, reeders, reed layers, rough masons, tilers

Distributive: apothecaries, barbers, chapmen, chemists, drapers, grocers, haberdashers, haberdashers of hats, haberdashers of small wares, kyddyers, linen drapers, map makers, mercers, merchants, merchants of coal, parchment makers, raffmen, reed merchants, stationers, woollen drapers

Leather and Allied: cobblers, collar makers, cordwainers, curriers, glovers, heel makers, jack makers, leather dressers, saddlers, skinners, tanners

Transport: carriers, kelemen, mariners, watermen

Professional: barber surgeons, musicians, schoolmasters, scriveners, surgeons, swordbearers, translators constant from 1560 to 1650 and then fell sharply.[1] The number of freemen to enter the other major trade groups (food and drink, clothing, metals, building and allied, leather and allied) rose gradually amid periodic fluctuation and generally reflects the increase in population. Each of them, however, declined in terms of its percentage of all new freemen admitted per decade with the exception of the building and allied group.

Wealth was not confined to a few prestigious trades, although the most affluent citizens were likely to be grocers, worsted weavers, hosiers, merchants, and drapers. At least 21 trades were represented among the 95 wealthiest townsmen in 1645; at least 30 trades were represented among the 203 wealthiest men (Table 5). The 1665 wall assessment indicates at least 18 trades among the 74 wealthiest men, and 37 trades among the 217 wealthiest. The grocers were clearly the most affluent men of Elizabethan Norwich,[2] and they continued to be the most numerous group among the 95 wealthiest townsmen of 1645. Their pre-eminence, however, was eroding as they were gradually eclipsed by the worsted weavers. In 1645 the grocers, hosiers, mercers, drapers, and merchants accounted for 39 per cent of the 203 wealthiest men; in 1665 the same trades accounted for 30 per cent of the 217 wealthiest men. As a proportion of these wealthiest men, the worsted weavers rose from 14 per cent in 1645 to 23 per cent in 1665. This corresponds to the fact that twice as many worsted weavers became freemen in the 1660s as in the 1640s. Even so, the probability of becoming a very rich man was small for a worsted weaver. That probability was three or four times as great for a grocer, five to seven times as great for a draper, and similarly favourable for mercers, merchants, hosiers, and brewers.[3]

The close economic and social interaction between the city and the county of Norfolk established during the sixteenth century did not diminish despite the increasing importance of the textile

---

[1] From 1558 to 1603 there was an average of 75 drapers, grocers, haberdashers, mercers, and merchants admitted to the freedom per decade. In the 1610s this figure rose to 101 and then dropped gradually to 73 in the 1640s, 57 in the 1650s and 1660s, and 30 in the 1670s and 1680s.

[2] Pound, 'Elizabethan Corporation of Norwich', p. 128.

[3] This implies that the grocers, merchants, mercers, drapers, and hosiers maintained their prestige in the face of a stagnant or perhaps declining market by admitting fewer and fewer freemen.

TABLE 5: *The Most Lucrative Trades, 1645 and 1665**

	9s. or more tax on personal estate, 1645	5s. or more tax on personal estate, 1645
grocers	16	28
worsted weavers	13	39
hosiers	11	19
mercers	8	13
drapers	6	11
merchants	5	8
brewers	4	5
ironmongers	3	4
apothecaries	2	3
tailors	2	7
others	11	31
unknown	14	35
	95	203

	16s. or more tax, 1665	10s. or more tax, 1665
worsted weavers	18	51
grocers	11	24
hosiers	9	18
merchants	6	9
drapers	4	7
mercers	3	8
brewers	3	7
pin makers	2	3
haberdashers	1	9
ironmongers	1	5
cordwainers	1	5
others	7	45
unknown	8	26
	74	217

*Figures compiled from N.N.R.O., Assessment for Maintaining Forces of Sir Thomas Fairfax, 1645; Rate for Repair of the Walls, 1665; Millican, ed., *Freemen.*

industry.[1] Despite their considerable wealth, townsmen had always been and continued to be the social inferiors of the county gentry.[2] Yet both groups recognized and profited from their symbiotic relationship.[3] The typical interactions between wealthy citizens and rural gentry in Tudor and Stuart England are to be found in Norwich as readily as elsewhere. The ranks of Norwich apprentices included the younger sons of some of the most prominent county families and the widows and daughters of affluent citizens were eagerly pursued by gentry in marriage deliberations. To the prosperous Norwich citizens, the lure of gentry status was almost overpowering and few wealthy families remained in the city for more than several generations. The wills of Norwich magistrates attest to the attraction of county land investment; indeed, it was the magistrate who did not possess lands and houses outside Norwich who was the exception.[4] Intermarriage between sons and daughters of gentry and townsmen as well as the movement of townsmen into the gentry through land purchases was not a new phenomenon in the seventeenth century, but it was significantly greater than in earlier periods.[5] The highly-cherished pedigrees of county families detailed in the visitation lists compiled by itinerant

[1] For details see Corfield, 'A Provincial Capital', pp. 287–95; A. Hassell Smith, *County and Court: Government and Politics in Norfolk, 1558–1603* (Oxford, 1974), pp. 14–15.

[2] Edward Chamberlayne commented in 1669 that 'tradesmen in all ages and nations have been reputed ignoble'. Stone, 'Social Mobility', p. 18. Stone also draws attention to the pre-Civil War pamphlet controversy on the topic of whether the son of a gentleman lost his gentle status by becoming an apprentice; he concludes that the older notion was disappearing after 1650. See also Perez Zagorin, *The Court and the Country* (London, 1969), pp. 121–5; W. A. Speck, 'Social Status in Late Stuart England', *Past and Present*, 34 (July 1966), 127–9.

[3] For recent conclusions on this topic see Stone, 'Social Mobility', *passim*.

[4] Of the 127 wills of magistrates which have been found, eighty-six specifically mention lands and tenements outside the city. More than the eighty-six wills would probably have mentioned estates and rural investments had there been need to do so. Many magistrates died leaving only one heir to whom they gave everything without further description of their estates. There are also numerous instances of a magistrate leaving all his lands, chattels, messuages, tenements, etc., to an heir without mention of whether these investments were confined to Norwich. Only fourteen of the wills may be interpreted as revealing no rural landholdings whatsoever, and even here it is possible that a magistrate had previously disposed of his properties through marriage portions for his children.

[5] Allen, 'Norwich Merchant Class', pp. 272–377.

heralds include many of the names of previous generations of Norwich mayors and aldermen.[1]

In brief, the political community of freemen grew in size, increased in geographical mobility, and came to rely heavily on the all-important textile industry. Yet the old social structure absorbed these changes and survived plague, religious transformation, and political upheaval as well. From the cradle to the grave, the pattern of daily life so long and deeply ingrained in the citizenry continued without interruption. As in medieval and Tudor times, the poor sought food, shelter, and charity, the women sought socially appropriate husbands, apprentices sought influential masters, young tradesmen industriously and opportunistically sought wealth, and affluent citizens sought a niche in the county gentry. The traditional rules and conventions which dictated almost every phase of social life for the different levels in the hierarchy also defined limitations in status and wealth for the respective sectors. Policing the entire mechanism and highly sensitive to even the smallest breach in established social customs, the magistrates stood as a bulwark against radical change. As they protected the traditional social structure of which they were the apex, so also they vigorously and, in large measure, successfully preserved a political system which bore the same stamp of honoured tradition.

[1] Visitations were held in 1563, 1589, 1613, and 1664. See Revd. G. H. Dashwood, *The Visitation of Norfolk in the Year 1563* (2 vols., Norwich, 1878); Walter Rye, *The Visitations of Norfolk, 1563, 1589, and 1613* [Harleian Soc. Pub., 32] (London, 1891); Arthur Campling and A. W. Hughes Clark, eds., *The Visitation of Norfolk, anno domini 1664* [Norfolk Rec. Soc., iv and v] (Norwich, 1934); Revd. G. H. Holley, *Observations and Comments on the Visitation of Norfolk, 1664* [Norfolk Rec. Soc., xxvii] (Norwich, 1956).

II

The Structure of Politics

Norwich citizens of the early seventeenth century inherited a governmental structure which was already two centuries old. During the reign of Henry IV, a struggle for supremacy between the social élite and the rest of the citizens resulted in a new constitutional accommodation, set down in the Composition of 1415 and ratified by royal charter in 1417, which survived with only minor alteration into the 1600s. The major officeholders and the regulations which governed their eligibility, election, and tenure were established in 1415; the duties attached to these offices had evolved over many years and were safeguarded by ancient royal charters. A system which had been functioning for so long and with so little change must have assumed a sense of permanance which seventeenth-century, tradition-oriented magistrates and townsmen were desirous of preserving in even the most critical of circumstances. The strife and crises which characterized Norwich politics after 1640 involved efforts by contending factions to gain control of the corporation by manipulating elections and adding religious and political criteria for officeholding, but no serious attempt was made to create a new system or even redistribute power and responsibility among the traditional offices and electorates. Since the local conflicts thus centred on the personnel and not the structure of government, the constitution of the city in 1690 differed in only minor ways from what it had been in 1600.

The most conspicuous feature of the political system was the predominant role played by the freeman citizenry in the election of officeholders. They nominated and elected all of the sixty common councilmen, one of the two sheriffs, and all of the twenty-four aldermen; and they nominated the two candidates for the mayoralty. It is noteworthy that the historical roots of this large measure of freeman participation went back to the early 1400s. The general trend in towns during the fifteenth century was the almost complete elimination of earlier elements of democratic process in favour of the establishment of political hegemony by the social élite.[1] Norwich, therefore, was an anomaly. This may be attributed to the socio-political conflict of the early fourteenth century and the need for compromise which arose out of it.

After years of expedient arrangements and experiments in revising the political structure, the rival factions, in a spirit of mutual distrust, worked out the Composition of 1415 in the hope that it would restore peace within the city. The urgency for some type of solution was apparent. According to the framers of this document, there had been 'dissensions, trauerses, variaunces, and discordes uppon diuers articles of longe tyme hangying [that] the Cite hath be diuided, dissoyled, and poynt to [have] been distroyed'.[2] The long and detailed Composition, with its intricate safeguards, elaborate electoral procedures, and meticulously prescribed distribution of authority, reflects the cautious negotiations for a political compromise. The new constitution was not the final step in a process whereby a once self-governing city of democratic foundations was reduced to a political oligarchy.[3] Contrary to creating a political separation of estates, the Composition was designed to 'make pees, unite, and acord [between] poore and ryche to be oon in herte, loue and charity neuermore fro this tyme forth to ben disseuered . . .' by bringing all citizens into the body politic.[4] The basis of the agreement was that the freemen were given the decisive power of election, but they would restrict their selection to wealthy and prominent citizens. Once elected, these magistrates would be supreme in nearly all matters of civic life: legislative initiative, in addition to complete executive and judicial authority, was placed in their hands.

*   *   *

Neither London nor any of the other seventeenth-century provincial capitals possessed such a strong constitutional heritage of

[1] Martin Weinbaum, *British Borough Charters, 1307–1660* (Cambridge, 1943), p. xiii; James Tait, 'The Common Council of the Borough', *English Historical Review*, 46 (Jan. 1931), 1–29; E. F. Jacob, *The Fifteenth Century, 1399–1485* (Oxford, 1961), pp. 385–405.

[2] The 'Composition of 1415', in Hudson and Tingey, eds., Records I. 94. The Charter of 1417 also makes reference to the 'many suits and dissensions [which] have arisen in the said city between the citizens and inhabitants . . .', *C.C.R.* V. 485.

[3] This is the interpretation presented in Hudson and Tingey, eds., *Records*, I. lviii–lx, lxxi–lxxii. This is the standard work on the early constitutional history of Norwich. For a conflicting interpretation see R. L. Storey, *The End of the House of Lancaster* (London, 1966), p. 217.

[4] 'Composition of 1415', in Hudson and Tingey, eds., *Records*, I. 94.

freeman political participation as Norwich. In addition, in none of the other major cities were the freemen as politically active. In consequence, the political history of seventeenth-century Norwich has a unique character and is both significant and interesting.

The government of Norwich was similar to that of London in many respects. Both cities were administered by a mayor, aldermen, sheriffs, and common councilmen and in both cities these elective offices were similar in jurisdiction and tenure. This was not coincidental, for the prototype for the Composition of 1415 had been the government of London.[1] Although the two governments had much in common, there were fundamental differences between them on the vital matter of freeman electoral involvement.[2] Constitutional control over the city government of London was so firmly in the grip of the magistrates that the Privy Council recommended the London election system to the aldermen of Norwich in 1619, when the latter were trying to cope with a rebellious freeman electorate.[3]

Compared to Norwich, the electorates of London were more limited in membership, had less control over the election process, and were restricted in their consideration of candidates by stringent eligibility requirements. The councilmen of London were to be chosen by the wardmotes, which theoretically included all freemen in the ward.[4] In practice, aldermen intervened regularly and frequently controlled the elections in favour of their own nominees. Moreover, only livery men were eligible for election and councilmen served life terms whereas in Norwich they were elected annually. Lastly, the London Common Council was usually called only five or six times a year, and sometimes only once. London aldermen were not elected directly by the ward electorates as in Norwich: the wardmote nominated four candidates from which the Court of

[1] In describing the new political accommodation in Norwich, the Charter of 1417 makes constant reference to similar practices in London that are being followed. *C.C.R.* V. 485–6. See also Hudson and Tingey, eds., *Records*, I. lxx; Tait, 'Common Council', pp. 12–16.

[2] Pearl has already observed that 'popular opinion in the city [London] was only to a small extent reflected in the municipality' and that the Lord Mayor and aldermen were 'oligarchic and self perpetuating'. In contrast, she points to Norwich as 'one of the few corporations where the citizens as a whole still exercised substantial influence'. Valerie Pearl, *London and the Outbreak of the Puritan Revolution* (London, 1961), pp. 60, 67.

[3] *A.P.C.*, James I, 1618–19: Privy Council to Norwich, 27 June 1619, p. 484.

[4] Details on the London government are taken from Pearl, *London*, pp. 50–68. See also Zagorin, *Court and Country* (London, 1969), pp. 127–8.

Aldermen chose one. If the aldermen disapproved of the nominees, the wardmote was given two additional opportunities to come up with acceptable nominees. If they failed to do so the Court chose its own candidate. It is not known for certain that the freemen were permitted to vote, and possibly the aldermanic nominees were made only by the councilmen and liverymen in the respective wards. In addition, a property qualification of £10,000 was needed to be eligible for election, and aldermen could not be recalled from office by their wardmote. The sheriffs and Lord Mayor were elected by the Common Hall, which in the mid-seventeenth century was composed of some 4,000 liverymen in a city with a population estimated at 400,000.[1] In contrast, the freeman electorate of Norwich was almost half as large and the population was only one-twentieth that of London. Theoretically the Common Hall nominated two men for the mayoralty from which the aldermen chose one, but it was customary for the Common Hall to nominate the senior alderman under the chair, who was normally elected.

In the other provincial capitals, the freemen were even less involved. Usually the magistrates had either the exclusive privilege of filling vacancies in their own body or the ability to manipulate the mechanism of political recruitment involving a wider electorate so that their own candidates were nominated and elected. This was true of Bristol, Exeter, Newcastle-upon-Tyne, and York.[2] For example, a self-perpetuating oligarchy of twenty-four men dominated every aspect of civic government in Exeter, a town slightly smaller than Norwich.[3] All political offices, including the mayor, justices of the peace, receiver, and sheriff, were reserved for members of the twenty-four. These twenty-four possessed the sole authority to dismiss one of their members, and in the event of discharge or death the remaining members met privately and co-opted a successor. There was no Common Council responsible to and yearly elected by the freemen. Only in the annual election of the mayor did the freeman electorate exercise a vote and even here its authority was carefully circumscribed: the twenty-four nominated two candidates from among themselves and the freemen chose one

[1] Pearl, *London*, p. 50 and Wrigley, 'A Simple Model', p. 44. The Lord Mayor of London personally hand-picked one of the two sheriffs.

[2] See John T. Evans, 'The Decline of Oligarchy in Seventeenth-Century Norwich', *Journal of British Studies* XIV (Nov. 1974), 47–8.

[3] MacCaffrey, *Exeter*, pp. 21, 26–53.

to be the mayor-elect. Thus the rights of the freemen of Exeter were primarily economic and their only influence on recruitment procedures was their meagre share in mayoral elections.

*   *   *

Political oligarchy was pervasive in the towns of Tudor and Stuart England. The most prominent feature of these oligarchies was the domination of important civic offices by urban dynasties whose members were engaged in the most influential and lucrative trades, were the most affluent citizens, and were linked by close family ties.[1] The largest provincial capitals (Bristol, Exeter, Newcastle-upon-Tyne, and York) conform in varying degrees with this pattern. Although the Norwich magistrates (defined here to include the mayor, aldermen, and sheriffs) had little constitutional control over the election of officeholders, the presence of a large electorate does not preclude the emergence of oligarchy if this electorate permits the imposition of either written or tacit social criteria as prerequisites for officeholding. Apparently this had occurred in Norwich by the end of the fifteenth century and the city may have been one of the more oligarchic of Elizabethan provincial towns. In the seventeenth century, however, oligarchy declined steadily. As a consequence, the door to political office was open to men of diverse social backgrounds and occupations to a greater extent than during the sixteenth century and apparently much more so than in the other large provincial capitals.

In a typical sixteenth-century urban oligarchy, the vast majority of town magistrates were recruited either from the families of previous magistrates or from foreigners who came to the city and established a connection with the ruling families through either apprenticeship or marriage, or both. As part of a tightly controlled and occasionally close social élite, the magistrates were subsequently bound to each other by kinship, apprenticeship, and alliance ties. This was true of Elizabethan Norwich. During the first decades of the seventeenth century, however, there was a marked decline in the number of these bonds between the magistrates, and this trend continued for the remainder of the century. More gradually there was a weakening of the Elizabethan recruit-

---

[1] The following discussion on urban oligarchy is taken from Evans, 'Decline of Oligarchy'. Only the major points are presented here. The article should be consulted for details, citations, and substantiation as well as for contrasts between Norwich and other provincial capitals.

ment pattern which stipulated tacitly that eligibility for the magistracy should include a kinship, apprenticeship, or alliance link with the magistracy prior to election. By 1620 the tight family structure of the Court of Aldermen was relaxing and the ruling class was becoming less exclusive socially. Kinship, apprenticeship, and alliance connections appear to have had little influence in political recruitment by the mid-seventeenth century. There was some measure of upward social mobility in which the son of a lesser tradesman could rise to the top, but the great majority of magistrates were the sons of the county gentry and yeomanry or traced their background to the upper levels of Norwich society. The importance of apprenticeship and marriage should not be underestimated, not because they placed a man in an exclusive group from which magistrates were chosen, but because they helped to establish a position in the community, improve business contacts, and enhance prospects of a successful and profitable business career. Money, not connection, was the key to political preferment.

The requirement of affluence as an indispensable ingredient in political eligibility has already received attention. Whereas the prospective alderman of London needed to meet the rigid minimum requirement of £10,000, the Composition of 1415 called only for 'suffisaunt' sheriffs and aldermen, which allows for considerable flexibility and interpretation.[1] By the Elizabethan period an understanding existed concerning the comparative level of wealth desired for officeholding eligibility and this continued into the Restoration with little alteration. In 1576 all of the city's aldermen and the richest third of the councilmen were among the 101 highest taxpayers. In 1645 all but six of the magistrates were among the eighty-four highest-taxed citizens for personal estate; similarly, all but two of the magistrates were among the seventy-one wealthiest citizens in 1665. Including the sitting magistrates, between 120 and 150 citizens (7 or 8 per cent of the freeman populace) possessed the minimum level of wealth expected of magisterial recruits in the mid-seventeenth century.

The ruling oligarchs of most of the provincial centres were business associates. The key political offices were dominated by a few select trades and in some cities a candidate's occupation was the

---

[1] The N.N.R.O. Norwich Charter of 1662/3 used the same language in calling for an 'able and sufficient man' for the shrievalty and 'most worthy and sufficient citizens and freemen' for the Court of Aldermen.

first consideration in appointment. In Elizabethan Norwich, a greater variety of trades were represented in the magistracy than in most other cities and this occupational diversity increased after 1600 despite the city's increasing dependence on the textile industry. As a consequence, political office was open to any man who possessed adequate wealth regardless of the trade he practised. Many trades provided enough wealth to satisfy this qualification. The 156 townsmen recruited to the magistracy from 1620 to 1690 represented twenty-seven different trades and in each decade townsmen of at least eight trades were promoted to the Court of Aldermen (Table 6). A correlation pattern is detectable: the trades which produced the greatest number of wealthy men provided proportionally the most new magistrates. Therefore, the trades of

TABLE 6: *Occupations of Recruited Magistrates by decade, 1620– 1690*

Trades	1620s	1630s	1640s	1650s	1660s	1670s	1680s	Total
apothecaries	–	1	1	2	–	–	–	4
bakers	2	–	–	–	–	–	–	2
barbers	–	–	–	–	–	1	–	1
bladesmiths	–	–	–	1	–	–	–	1
brewers	1	2	1	1	2	4	3	14
carpenters	–	–	–	–	–	1	–	1
dornix weavers	1	–	–	1	–	–	–	2
drapers	2	1	–	2	–	1	–	6
dyers	–	1	–	1	–	–	–	2
goldsmiths	–	–	–	–	1	1	–	2
grocers	5	4	7	3	3	3	4	29
haberdashers	–	–	–	–	–	2	1	3
hosiers	2	1	3	2	1	–	2	11
ironmongers	–	1	–	1	–	1	2	5
linen drapers	–	–	–	–	1	1	–	2
maltsters	–	–	–	–	1	–	–	1
mercers	–	2	2	1	–	2	1	8
merchants	5	3	5	–	3	–	–	16
milleners	–	–	–	–	–	–	1	1
scriveners	2	–	–	–	–	–	1	3
tailors	–	–	–	–	–	1	–	1
tanners	–	–	–	–	1	–	–	1
vintners	–	1	–	–	–	–	–	1
whiteplate makers	–	–	–	–	–	–	1	1
wine merchants	–	–	–	–	–	–	1	1
wool combers	–	–	1	–	–	–	1	2
worsted weavers	–	3	3	7	11	8	3	35
TOTAL	20	20	23	22	24	26	21	156
DIFFERENT TRADES	8	11	8	11	9	12	12	27

new magistrates reflected economic trends in the city. The most evident sign of the decline of certain trades was a drop in the number of freemen admitted to these trades often accompanied by a decline in individual incomes produced. As trades ceased to produce wealthy men, they ceased to provide magistrates. Conversely, the growing prosperity of other trades was reflected in the rising number of its members who joined the magistracy. Thus the major development during the century was the drop in the number of magistrates drawn from the distributive trades in general and the grocer-merchants in particular in contrast to a rise in the number of worsted weavers and other townsmen who became magistrates.

Although it is difficult to pinpoint the causes of this decline of oligarchy in the 1600s, it is clear that national and local political upheaval did not significantly affect developing trends. The decline was a slow process which had commenced in the early decades of the century. The importance of family and apprenticeship connections had diminished gradually and were relatively insignificant by 1640: they did not revive thereafter. Changes in the occupations of recruited magistrates were gradual and came as a consequence of changing economic conditions rather than from abrupt political or social dislocation. The gradual transition from oligarchy to plutocracy seemingly stems from local social factors, in particular, the high degree of geographical mobility among the élite. Successful families apparently left the city for the countryside so rapidly that there was little time for a group of leading families to intermarry and form deep roots in the fabric of town life. Hence, the magistracy was increasingly open to the economically successful of each generation. The factor of wealth in magisterial eligibility remained constant with respect to what it had been in the Elizabethan period and did not fluctuate in either the 1640s or 1660s. This, coupled with the preservation of the basic components of the political system, provided an element of stability and continuity in otherwise disjointed times.

* * *

A description of the electorates and offices might well begin with the wards. In accordance with the Composition of 1415, the entire freeman citizenry was assembled twice each year to elect one sheriff and nominate two men for the mayoralty. For purposes of electing councilmen and aldermen, however, the parishes of the city and suburbs were divided into four wards, which were segmented further into three lesser or sub wards.[1] Each ward was represented by a proportional number of councilmen: Conesford had twelve, Mancroft was served by sixteen, and Wymer and Over-the-Water possessed twenty and twelve respectively. This allocation probably corresponded with the demographic and social realities of the early 1400s. The city grew considerably in the following three centuries without reapportionment and, although the expansion did result in inequalities in representation, there is no evidence that an adjustment was ever contemplated. The precise number of freemen in each ward during the seventeenth century is not known, but an estimate can be made on the assumption that the geographical distribution of taxpayers was similar to the distribution of freemen. Tables 7 and 8 indicate that throughout the century the ward of Mancroft was over-represented in the Council and Over-the-Water was heavily under-represented.

TABLE 7: *Number and Distribution of Taxpayers Within the Walls at three dates**

	1633–1634		1649		1665	
Conesford	97	11·5%	138	14·5%	185	14·9%
Mancroft	200	23·7%	224	23·6%	271	21·8%
Wymer	306	36·2%	318	33·5%	395	31·7%
Over-the-Water	241	28·6%	270	28·4%	391	31·6%
	884	100·0%	950	100·0%	1242	100·0%

*The tax lists used are the poor rate lists for 1633–4, the collection for the river and streets of 1649, and the collection for the repair of the walls in 1665. All of these are presently located in manuscript form in the N.N.R.O. The poor rate lists for 1633–4 have been published in Walter Rye, ed., *The Norwich Rate Book, Easter 1633 to Easter 1634* (n.p., 1903). Widows, unmarried females, and the suburbs have been omitted from the above computations, the latter because not all the suburbs were included in the 1649 rate and none of them were assessed in the 1665 tax. The 1649 river and streets collection is complete except for the parish of St. Lawrence, Wymer; the total for Wymer in 1649 assumes that the number of taxpayers in St. Lawrence was proportionate to what it had been in 1633–4. The 1665 repair of the walls rate includes numerous individuals in Conesford and Mancroft taxed at 6*d.*, but they have been discounted since there were no persons taxed at 6*d.* in Wymer and Over-the-Water. All the resident taxpayers of St. George Tombland have been included in the ward of Wymer, even though part of the parish was in Conesford.

[1] The four great municipal divisions go back to at least the early thirteenth century. St. George Tombland was the only parish which fell into two wards. The suburbs of Trowse, Carrow, Lakenham, and Bracondale were associated with Conesford, Eaton with Mancroft, Christ Church, Earlham, and Heigham with Wymer, and Hellesdon and Pockthorpe with Over-the-Water.

FIGURE 4: The Wards of Norwich

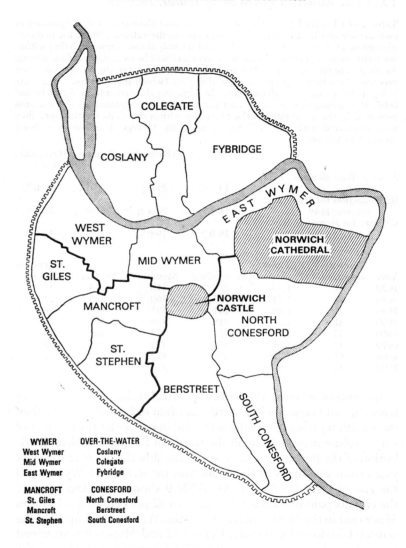

WYMER	OVER-THE-WATER
West Wymer	Coslany
Mid Wymer	Colegate
East Wymer	Fybridge
MANCROFT	**CONESFORD**
St. Giles	North Conesford
Mancroft	Berstreet
St. Stephen	South Conesford

TABLE 8: *Estimated Electorate of Wards, 1620–1690*

Table 2 of Chapter I provides the estimated total electorate at the beginning of each decade and thus includes freemen living in the suburbs. Since the percentages given in Table 7 of Chapter II consider only those taxpayers living within the walls, some adjustment in these percentages will be necessary in determining the electorate for each ward. The suburbs were included in the 1633–4 poor rate lists and the adjusted percentage for that year (which includes male taxpayers living in the suburbs) is given below. In adjusting the percentages for 1649 and 1665, the assumption is made that the number of taxpayers in the suburbs increased in the same ratio as the taxpayers within the walls for the ward they were associated with. As in Table 7, all of St. George Tombland has been assigned to Wymer.

	Conesford	Mancroft	Wymer	Over-the-Water
A: Poor Rate Returns, 1633–1634	14·9%	21·0%	34·1%	30·0%
B: Collection for River and Streets, 1649	18·3%	20·4%	32·4%	28·9%
C: Rate for Repair of the Walls, 1665	19·0%	19·0%	29·4%	32·6%

Year	Percentages Used	Total Estimated Freemen	Conesford	Mancroft	Wymer	Over-the-Water
1620	A	1,477	210	310	504	443
1630	A	1,712	255	360	583	514
1640	A	1,883	281	395	642	565
1650	B	1,744	319	356	565	504
1660	C	1,720	327	327	505	561
1670	C	1,962	373	373	577	639
1680	C	2,220	422	422	652	724
1690	C	2,065	392	392	608	673

In terms of seventeenth-century political realities, the number of freemen and taxpayers in a ward was often of less importance than the wealth represented by the ward and in particular the number of very wealthy men residing in the ward. In the geographical distribution of the tax burden, the most noticeable change over the sixty years from the 1630s to the 1690s was the decline of Wymer and the rise of Over-the-Water. As Table 9 shows, the percentage of the city tax paid by Wymer shrank from 42 per cent in the 1630s to 35per cent in the 1690s whereas Over-the-Water picked up all of the burden laid down by Wymer. Conesford and Mancroft maintained their share of the town's wealth. The comparative wealth of the wards corresponds roughly with the location of the wealthiest citizens (Table 10) and it was from this group that the magistrates were invariably chosen.

TABLE 9: *Returns on Taxes, Assessments, and Subsidies by Wards at four dates, 1637–1696*

	1637		1644		1662/63		1696	
	£	%	£	%	£	%	£	%
Conesford	54.11.6	13.1	63. 9.8	13.6	31. 3.2	16.7	870.19.9	13.7
Mancroft	91. 4.4	22.0	113. 6.8	24.6	39. 0.0	20.7	1,379. 5.6	21.6
Wymer	177. 7.2	42.6	174.16.4	38.0	69. 9.1	37.2	2,239. 9.9	35.0
Over-the-Water	92.13.9	22.3	109.12.0	23.8	47.10.2	25.4	1,899. 2.3	29.7
Total	415.16.9	100.0	461. 4.8	100.0	187. 2.5	100.0	6,388.17.3	100.0

1637: ship-money returns listed by parish but not by individual, now in the N.N.R.O.

1644: two month assessment dated 7 Aug. 1644 listed by parish but not by individual, now in Brit. Lib., Add. MSS. 22619, fo. 204.

1662/63: one month assessment dated 14 Jan. 1662/3 listed by parish but not by individual, now in N.N.R.O., Lieutenancy Order Book, 4ᵛ, 5ʳ.

1696: parliamentary subsidy listed by parish but not by individual, now in the N.N.R.O.

Note: In some cases the sums collected for parishes do not equal the total ward assessment given by the original compiler, and where this occurs the total assessment has been corrected.

TABLE 10: *Ward Residence of Wealthy Men, 1660*

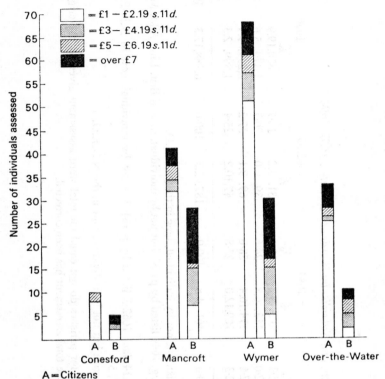

A = Citizens
B = Gentry and professional men (lawyers, physicians, clerks, ministers,
and army officers)

The above graph is based on a tax taken in 1660 for a parliamentary act for the
speedy provision of money for disbanding and payment of the forces of the
kingdom both by land and sea. Parliament ordered that a copy of the assessments
be made giving the name, degree, and sum assessed for each individual and
parish. The compiler supplied the names and ranks of all persons assessed 2s. or
more and all tax payers assessed less than 2s. were grouped together 'in single
polls' at the end of each parish. Thus the total number of taxpayers in each parish
is unknown and for this reason this tax is not included in Table 7. A copy of the
tax lists is in the N.N.R.O.

For the seventeenth century as a whole, Conesford possessed the smallest freeman electorate, the least total wealth, the lowest wealth *per capita*, and by far the fewest wealthy citizens.[1] Over-the-Water was growing in both population and wealth in relation to the rest of the city. Although this ward may have had more freemen than Wymer and its percentage of the city's wealth was increasing at the expense of Wymer, it nevertheless contained only half as many wealthy citizens. Mancroft and Wymer were the élite sections of the city and most of the resident gentry, physicians, and lawyers settled in the fashionable areas of these wards.[2] The number of wealthy citizens in Mancroft was far out of proportion to the estimated number of freemen in the ward: with roughly the same electorate as Conesford and only six-tenths the electorate of Over-the-Water, Mancroft had four times as many wealthy citizens as the former and slightly more than the latter. The wealth *per capita* in Wymer was lower than in Mancroft, at least in the 1690s, but Wymer possessed by far the greatest total wealth and number of very wealthy residents. This, together with its large number of freemen, made Wymer the most important ward politically and socially.

Each year, in the week following Passion Sunday (the fifth Sunday in Lent) the ward electorates were summoned to the guild-hall to elect sixty councilmen. On Monday the freemen of Conesford gathered at eight o'clock in the morning and were charged by the mayor to select twelve 'suffisaunt' men who were residents of the ward. The newly-elected councilmen were then sworn into office.[3] The Composition had stipulated that proportional representation should be extended within each ward so that the lesser or sub wards had a fixed allotment of the great ward. However, a comparison of lists of councilmen with their residences, as provided in tax rolls, reveals that this additional apportionment was not

[1] In the 1690s, Conesford had a tax *per capita* (in shillings) of 2·9, whereas for Over-the-Water, Wymer, and Mancroft it was 4·2, 4·9, and 5·9 respectively. The average for the city was 4·4.

[2] All but one of the twenty-two doctors, lawyers, captains, clerks, and wealthy ministers taxed in 1660 resided in Mancroft or Wymer, and so did eighteen of the twenty-one esquires. See Evans, 'The Political Elite', p. 422.

[3] The procedure for the election of councilmen is set down in the 'Composition of 1415', in Hudson and Tingey, eds., *Records*, I. 98–9.

operative in the seventeenth century.[1] On the next day, the same
procedure was followed for Mancroft, and on Wednesday and
Thursday the freemen of the wards of Wymer and Over-the-
Water assembled respectively. Strict adherence to the residence
qualification suggests that the councilmen were intended to reflect
the opinions of the freemen of their wards. If a councilman moved
to another ward, he was ineligible for re-election by his former
ward, although he could be returned to the Council by his new
ward. Lionel Claxton, for example, was admitted a freeman in 1592
and elected to the Council in 1596 by the freemen of Mancroft.
After eleven years of service, he moved to Wymer and was four
times chosen councilman for that ward. In 1611, he again changed
residence, this time to Over-the-Water, and represented this ward
until 1617.

The Composition clearly stated that all freemen should be
permitted to vote, but not that all freemen should be eligible for
election. 'Suffisaunt' to the seventeenth-century townsman, as to
his counterpart in 1415, suggested a measure of financial stability
and social position and the one usually accompanied the other. By
the 1600s nearly all freemen were deemed sufficiently 'suffisaunt'
in lieu of being householders and qualified craftsmen; some
citizens of limited resources were elected councilmen. The subsidies of 1645 and 1660 affirm that the Common Council was not a
very exclusive body. If the number of electable citizens is defined
to include the freemen in each ward who were taxed the same as or
more than the lowest taxed councilman in their ward, then all 622
citizens assessed for personal estate in 1645 and 733 of the 1,012
citizens taxed in 1660 fall into the electable category.[2] Most of the
councilmen were much more affluent. If the number of townsmen

[1] The list of councilmen in 1648, provided in the N.N.R.O., A.B. (1642–68),
11–14 Mar. 1647/8, 75ʳ, when compared with the rate for the river and streets of
the same year, reveals that each ward chose councilmen only from their own
ward, but that the 1415 allotments for sub wards within the major wards were
not being complied with. N.N.R.O., Norwich Parochial Collections for the
River and Streets, 1648.

[2] N.N.R.O., Assessment for Disbanding the King's Forces, 1660; Assessment for Sir Thomas Fairfax, 1645. Six of the councilmen of 1645 were not taxed
for personal estate; four of the councilmen of 1660 were not listed in the tax
assessment. The figures of 622 and 733 for 1645 and 1660 include taxpayers in
the suburbs but exclude resident gentry, professional men, and females. A complete analysis of the rates paid by councilmen in comparison with the other taxpayers in 1645 and 1660 may be found in Evans, 'Political Elite of Norwich',
pp. 534–48.

who had a reasonable expectation of election to the Council be defined as those whose wealth equalled or surpassed the median wealth of the councilmen for their ward, then the pool of potential councilmen would consist of 94 men in 1645 and 141 men in 1660.[1] As might be expected, a resident of Wymer, Mancroft, and Over-the-Water needed to be wealthier than a resident of Conesford to have the same expectation of election.[2]

The freemen were under no obligation to re-elect the same men to the Council year after year, except for the brief period from 1683 to 1688 when councilmen enjoyed a life tenure. Nevertheless, lengthy tenures were not uncommon. From 1590 to 1620 over 90 per cent of the Council was composed of citizens who had served before, although not necessarily the year preceding.[3] On average, five new councilmen with no prior tenure were added to the Council each spring, and never were more than ten new councilmen chosen during one election week. The continuity of personnel should not obscure the fact that 203 men held seats on the Council during this thirty-year period and that, except for a handful of veterans, a nearly complete turnover of membership occurred every fifteen years. From 1620 to 1690, 536 men sat in the Council and the number of recruits varied from 45 and 43 in the 1620s and 1630s to 80 and 98 in the 1640s and 1680s respectively. Tenure varied considerably. Of the 378 councilmen who held office from 1620 to 1670, 116 served five years or less and 26 men held the office for only one year. On the other hand, 41 men served for more than twenty years and 4 councilmen served terms in excess of thirty years. The median tenure was nine years.[4] The terms of some councilmen were split by years of absence, but usually a councilman's tenure was consecutive.

[1] These figures are arrived at by counting the number of citizens in each ward who were assessed the same as or more than the median assessment of the councilmen elected to serve that ward. The magistrates, who were ineligible for election to the Council, have been omitted from these calculations. The total of 94 in 1645 consisted of 11 in Conesford, 34 in Mancroft, 33 in Wymer, and 16 in Over-the-Water. In 1660 the total of 141 consisted of 27 in Conesford, 31 in Mancroft, 55 in Wymer, and 28 in Over-the-Water.

[2] The median assessment for Conesford, Mancroft, Wymer, and Over-the-Water councilmen in 1645 was 4s., 6s., 10s., and 9s. respectively; in 1660 it was 8s. 6d., £1. 1s. 6d., £1. 0s. 6d., and 18s. 3d. respectively.

[3] These statistics are computed from the lists of officeholders entered in the Assembly Book after the annual elections.

[4] A complete breakdown of councilman tenures may be found in Evans, 'Political Elite of Norwich', p. 374.

The most common causes for the departure of men from the Council were death and elevation to higher office, and thus the election of new men was limited and gradual. From 1620 to 1690, 476 citizens entered the Council for the first time, an average of 6·8 new men per year (Table 11). An exception must be made for

TABLE 11: *Election of New Men to the Council, 1620–1690*

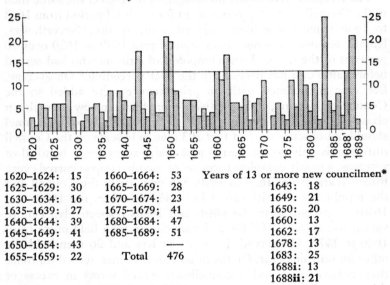

				Years of 13 or more new councilmen*
1620–1624:	15	1660–1664:	53	
1625–1629:	30	1665–1669:	28	1643: 18
1630–1634:	16	1670–1674:	23	1649: 21
1635–1639:	27	1675–1679;	41	1650: 20
1640–1644:	39	1680–1684:	47	1660: 13
1645–1649:	41	1685–1689:	51	1662: 17
1650–1654:	43		—	1678: 13
1655–1659:	22	Total	476	1683: 25
				1688i: 13
				1688ii: 21

* There were two elections in 1688

years of political turmoil. During periods of civic stability such as from 1620 to 1640, 1655 to 1659, and 1665 to 1675, an average of fewer than five new men per year were chosen. But during the Civil War, the early years of the Interregnum and Restoration, and the decade of the 1680s, the average was more than twice as high. Each of the nine elections in which thirteen or more new councilmen were elected can be associated with an urban crisis related to national affairs and issues. Another indicator which illustrates the impact of political conflict on council tenure is the lack of experience of the councilmen in 1645, 1650, 1665, 1680, 1685, and 1690: a majority had served four years or less. In 1650 only six of the sixty councilmen dated their entrance into the Council prior to

1640. In less turbulent times, the median number of years of previous experience averaged seven years.[1]

On at least four occasions in the year, the mayor was required to call the councilmen to a meeting of the Norwich Assembly, in which they met with the magistrates to deliberate upon municipal affairs.[2] Since the mayor, at his discretion, could and generally did summon the Assembly whenever important business or emergencies arose, the Assembly was convened quite frequently. From 1620 to 1690, 772 meetings of the Assembly took place, or an average of eleven sessions per year. In years of civic turmoil the Assembly met even more often.[3] The spokesman for the councilmen was their elected common speaker, a person of some dignity but little influence. The common clerk recorded the minutes of each session in the Assembly Book. In an effort to ensure that councilmen did not shirk their responsibility, an ordinance was passed in 1615 to enforce attendance at Assembly meetings and it carried a 2s. fine for absence without reasonable excuse.[4] Other ordinances to the same effect had been passed before, and more followed in the future. Meetings of great consequence were well attended, but fines were either insufficiently severe or too irregularly collected to induce many councilmen to abandon their business transactions for routine meetings. In 1644 the fine was raised to 2s. 6d. and in 1650 the mayor was empowered to imprison delinquents who refused to pay.[5] A majority of the aldermen and thirty-one councilmen constituted a quorum.[6] Apart from his duties as a member of the Assembly, the councilman exercised neither influence nor responsibility in city government.

The Assembly attended to a variety of political and fiscal matters: it elected administrative officials,[7] directed monetary affairs and audited city accounts; it administered municipal

[1] A table listing the prior years of tenure at five-year intervals from 1620 to 1690 may be found in Evans, 'Political Elite of Norwich', p. 377.

[2] These days were 21 September (St. Matthew), 24 February (St. Mathias), 3 May, and the day before swearing in the mayor in early summer.

[3] In the troubled years of 1620, 1642, 1649, 1660, and 1688 the Assembly was convened on 20, 18, 19, 17, and 13 occasions respectively.

[4] A.B. (1613–42), 15 Sept. 1615, 37r–v.

[5] ibid. (1642–68), 11 Sept. 1644, 23r; 31 Jan. 1650/1, 107r; see also 26 Feb. 1661/2, 225r; 8 Aug. 1662, 231r.

[6] ibid. (1613–42), 15 Sept. 1615, 37r–v.

[7] They included the recorder, steward, common clerk, coroners, and clavers; the election results were entered in the Assembly Book.

property, ordered collection, and granted citizenship.[1] The principal function of the Assembly, however, was the ratification of legislation and the interchange of points of view between the councilmen and the magistrates. The Assembly had no power to initiate legislation: it merely deliberated and voted on what the magistrates had prepared in advance for consideration. On the other hand, ordinances and alterations in the constitution needed the consent of the councilmen.[2] Harmony between the Council and the Court of Aldermen was necessary to the normal transaction of civic affairs and before 1600 their relationship had been one of co-operation. The only dispute between the Council and the magistracy in the forty-four-year reign of Elizabeth was a minor disagreement over the election of a town clerk in 1579.[3] Yet at critical moments during the seventeenth century an intractable Common Council, voicing the opinions of an agitated community, differed from the mayor and aldermen on decisive issues and threatened an open rupture within the corporation.

Election to the Common Council must have seemed an undesired burden to some men who, once elected, were obliged to accept office.[4] Of the three greatest benefits of officeholding in Tudor and Stuart England (status, power, and money) the Council had little to offer. Until 1654 the councilmen had no special designation to distinguish themselves from the rest of the townsmen, but after this date and for the remainder of the century the Assembly Book listed all councilmen as 'Mr.'. Although the Assembly was a very important body in times of crisis, the individual councilman was only one of sixty and wielded little personal power by virtue of his office. Routine meetings were often an

---

[1] William L. Sachse, ed., *Minutes of the Norwich Court of Mayoralty, 1630–1631* [Norfolk Record Society, xv] (Norwich, 1942), pp. 13–15. See also Allen, 'Norwich Merchant Class', pp. 129–31. Both Sachse and Allen discuss the authority of the Assembly, but a reading of the Assembly Books for the seventeenth century reveals that the jurisdiction of the Assembly could cover any municipal concern excluding strictly judicial and ecclesiastical matters.

[2] Before 1415, the mayor and aldermen often made binding contracts for the city. One of the concessions they made in the Composition was that they would do nothing 'that may bynde or charge the Cite wit owte the assent of the Commonaunte . . .'. The 'Composition of 1415', in Hudson and Tingey, eds., *Records*, I. 98, 100.

[3] Pound, 'Elizabethan Corporation of Norwich', p. 17.

[4] The 1662/3 Charter established a fine of up to £20 for refusal of an elected councilman to take office.

unwanted distraction from daily business activities. A clear indication that councilmen often tired of their legislative and administrative duties was that ordinances were passed in 1615 and 1662 forbidding the councilmen from leaving their seats until the Assembly had concluded.[1] The yearly compensation of 26s. 8d.[2] cannot have been much of an incentive to seek office, especially when election to the Council might entail sharing the cost of the annual Mayor's Feast.[3] Moreover, there is no indication that the councilmen profited from any hidden monetary fruits of office. There was, however, one major benefit: the Common Council was the customary office from which the aspiring citizen could launch a political career. Of the 149 sheriffs and 130 aldermen elected from 1620 to 1690, all but twenty-nine of the former and eleven of the latter had sat on the Council before their elevation.

The sheriffs, aldermen, and mayor constituted the magistracy of Norwich. Unlike the Council, which was ordered in advance to convene for a specific purpose, the magistrates met frequently and regularly for the day-to-day management of municipal affairs. These twenty-six men, recognized throughout the city as the governing estate, directed administration, dispensed justice, enforced parliamentary statutes, carried on official correspondence, and drafted legislation. Their civic authority, defined by the liberties granted by royal charters, was restricted only by the limited powers of the Council.

The sheriffs took precedence in civic ceremonies over all officeholders except the mayor and justices of the peace. Yet the days of the sheriffs' great prestige, influence, and profit had declined just as assuredly in Norwich as in rural England. Moreover, they remained in office for just one year and were not eligible for re-election. Until the Restoration, both sheriffs were elected on 8 September, one by the freemen and councilmen and the other by the mayor, existing sheriffs, and aldermen, and were sworn into

---

[1] A.B. (1613–42), 15 Sept. 1615, 37r–v; (1642–68), 29 Aug. 1662, 232v. The oath administered to councilmen required them to attend all Assembly meetings and remain in their seats until dismissed by the mayor, but was not very effective. N.N.R.O., Norwich Mayor's Book MSS., p. 137.

[2] A.B. (1642–68), 21 Nov. 1660, 212v.

[3] In 1650 the Assembly agreed that six councilmen should pay for the Mayor's Feast, which could easily come to more than £30. ibid., 12 June 1650, 98r, and 31 Jan. 1650/1, 106r.

office thirteen days later.[1] After 1662/3 the election date for the commons' sheriff was set for the last Tuesday in August and the magistrates were free to choose their sheriff at any time from 24 June to 1 September.[2] Participation of the freemen was voluntary, but failure to appear without adequate excuse could cost the alderman 2s. and the councilman 10d. Once the freemen had assembled, the magistrates withdrew into the mayor's chamber and, by majority vote, elected one sheriff.[3] The mayor would cast an additional deciding ballot if the vote were tied, but usually the magistrates had decided on their candidate well in advance, as letters to prospective candidates indicate.[4] The magistrates then returned to the hall and announced their choice to the freemen. The commons proceeded to elect their sheriff, but not until the magistrates had left the hall. Although all citizens living in the city and suburbs who had not previously borne the office were eligible for election, the freemen invariably chose a councilman. In the event that a decision could not be reached, the final determination rested with the councilmen alone.

Responsible for serving the king's writ and the mayor's warrant, holding their own court, attending the Mayor's Court and Assembly, and presiding over parliamentary elections, the sheriffs were important town figures. The Sheriffs' Court, which met on Wednesdays and Fridays, tried actions of debt, trespass, and other misdemeanours: more important cases were taken directly to the more prestigious Mayor's Court or the Quarter Sessions. The sheriff was not expected to be either experienced or competent in law: hence, he was provided with a special legal adviser, the steward, and a number of attorneys. An undersheriff and serjeants

---

[1] The procedure for the election of sheriffs is provided in the 'Composition of 1415', in Hudson and Tingey, eds., *Records*, I. 96–7. A description of the sheriffs' elections of 1627 is found in P.R.O., S.P. Dom., Chas I, LXXVIII, no. 53: Mayor and others of Norwich to Privy Council, 18 Sept. 1627.

[2] Norwich Charter of 1662/3.

[3] The Composition does not mention the participation of the sheriffs in these elections, but since 1452 it was common practice for them to be present.

[4] On 10 August 1616, for example, four different individuals were sent letters from the Mayor's Court to the effect that they would be made sheriffs unless they could show cause why not. N.N.R.O., M.C.B. (1615–24), 10 Aug. 1616, 84r. This practice continued throughout the century. In 1658, for example, the Assembly Book records that 'the mayor and aldermen have written a letter to Mr. William Steward that they intend to choose him sheriff unless he can give them good reasons to the contrary.' A.B. (1642–68), 3 Sept. 1658, 194r.

assisted him with routine duties, such as serving warrants and
summoning juries.

An accurate balance sheet of the expenses and profits reaped by
the sheriffs in performing their one-year tenure cannot be drawn
up, but certainly they suffered a considerable personal loss. The
first expense was the elaborate feast to celebrate the sheriffs'
election: the sheriff elected by the magistrates played host and paid
the bill.[1] Its actual cost is unknown, but it was probably in excess
of £10.[2] A second immediate expenditure of several pounds was the
purchase of a sheriff's violet robe worn on ceremonial occasions.[3]
After 1640 the corporation provided the sheriffs with their own
office at a cost to the latter of £20 and this was raised to £30 in the
1660s. During the Restoration the sheriffs also picked up the £20
tab for the prison.[4] By far the biggest outlay, however, was the
annual fee farm rent of £128. 2s. 4d. paid out of the sheriffs' pockets
to the receipt of the exchequer. In 1650 the corporation purchased
this ancient fee farm rent for £650, but it was restored to the
Crown after Charles's return to England in 1660.[5] There may well
have been additional entertainment costs and it is difficult to place
a monetary value on the time which the sheriffs devoted to their
duties, to the detriment of personal business activities. Between
Assembly meetings, Mayor's Court and Sheriffs' Court sessions,
and other functions, the sheriffs were the busiest city officeholders.

The sheriffs' salary of £30 was not nearly adequate in meeting
expenses. Indeed, it was little more than a token contribution to the
fee farm rent. In 1643 the two sheriffs flatly refused to pay the fee
farm even though they accepted their £30 remuneration.[6] The
Assembly debated the matter in 1644 and in 1645 it increased the
sheriffs' salary to £80 while retaining the fee farm.[7] The following

[1] M.C.B. (1624–34), 22 Sept. 1632, 405ʳ.
[2] In the plague year of 1625 Sheriff Nicholas Osborne was spared giving the
feast upon agreement that he donate £10 to the poor of the city and 40s. to the
poor prisoners. ibid., 17 Sept. 1625, 68ʳ. Under similar circumstances in 1666
Henry Crowe gave £15 to the infected poor rather than provide St. Michael's
Day entertainment. A.B. (1642–68), 21 Sept. 1666, 277ʳ.
[3] Civic gowns were a prominent feature of inventories. Roger Gaywood left
gowns valued at £32 in his inventory and a single gown was worth about £3.
N.N.R.O., N.C.C., Inventories, 1621, no. 115 and 1628, no. 156.
[4] A.B. (1603–42), 21 Sept. 1640, 363ᵛ; (1642–68), 21 Sept. 1664, 259ᵛ. and
21 Sept. 1666, 277ʳ.
[5] ibid. (1642–68), 1 May and 8 Sept. 1650, 97, 101ʳ; 25 June 1660, 209ᵛ.
[6] N.N.R.O., Certificate of Mayor, etc. concerning the fee farm rent, 1650.
[7] A.B. (1642–68), 25 Oct. 1644, 24ᵛ; 5 Sept. and 19 Nov. 1645, 33ʳ, 36ʳ.

year a provision was made allowing the sheriffs £30 out of the amercements, after the first £40 of amercements had been turned over to the corporation.[1] Therefore, the city treasury was already supporting the sheriffs to the tune of £120 when the corporation purchased the fee farm rent in 1650. In the first years of the Restoration the Assembly renounced the past ordinances which had increased the sheriffs' pay, yet the sheriffs were granted an additional £30.[2] Although the hidden profits of justice cannot be measured, the sheriffs' expenses after 1662 approached £200 compared to a yearly income of only £60.[3] An indication of the expense involved is revealed in an election to replace Sheriff Francis Norris, who died in August 1666. With no obligation to pay the fee farm rent and with only one month's duties to perform before the election of new sheriffs, two aldermen desiring the office each promised to donate £100 towards poor relief if the freemen would elect him.[4] The financial burden of office was a continuous source of complaint for sheriffs and they bickered with the corporation throughout the 1660s to no avail. The most imaginative solution was tried by the sheriffs of 1670; they decided to forgo their £60 allowance and tax the citizens for the fee farm, a procedure which the other magistrates condemned. An appeal to Whitehall, however, was needed to force the sheriffs to make a refund to the citizens.[5]

The freeman's oath required citizens to accept any office to which they were elected, but a procedure existed whereby men could avoid the shrievalty and the personal liability which it entailed. If a citizen anticipated election, he could negotiate with the corporation to be discharged either for a prescribed number of years, or for ever, for a fee set by the corporation. Fines for compounding from the shrievalty varied: up to 1660 a discharge for ever could cost from £20 to £50 and after the Restoration the

[1] ibid., 23 Sept. 1646, 45ᵛ.

[2] ibid., 31 Jan. 1661/2, 225ʳ; 22 Sept. 233ᵛ.

[3] Sachse has suggested that the sheriffs derived profits from certain business transactions in the Mayor's Court, but he does not indicate what business this was or how much money was involved. He does conclude, however, that the total amounts were very small in comparison with the costs of office. Sachse, ed., *Minutes*, p. 19.

[4] M.C.B. (1666–77), 25 Aug. 1666, 9ᵛ. This election took place when the plague was rampant in Norwich.

[5] ibid., 10 Dec. 1670, 10 Mar. 1670/1, and 15 Apr. 1671, 160ʳ, 169ʳ, 172ʳ; Mayor's Book MSS., pp. 42–4.

fines varied from £50 to £100.[1] A 1620 ordinance stipulated that
discharges would not be permitted after the elections had actually
taken place and if a sheriff-elect refused to assume office he was to
be assessed an extremely high penalty.[2] Despite the time-consum-
ing duties, the expense, and the short tenure, the shrievalty was
nevertheless a highly sought-after prize for many citizens. This
was not because the office itself was desirable, but because it was
the gateway to higher preferment. Throughout the century the
ex-sheriffs were the most eligible candidates in aldermanic
elections and no citizen who had not been sheriff could become
mayor.[3]

The sheriffs chosen from 1620 to 1690 were usually elder citizens
of long standing in the community and with previous political
experience. About 90 per cent were the sons of Norwich freemen
or had gone through the apprenticeship system.[4] Of those who had
learned their trade elsewhere and migrated to Norwich, all had
purchased their freedom at least ten years before their election.
Fully 85 per cent of the sheriffs had previously served on the
Council. Prior council experience was more prevalent before 1650
than after: 11 per cent of the sheriffs from 1620 to 1650 had not
been councilmen, whereas this was the case with 25 per cent of the
sheriffs from 1650 to 1690.[5] The average interval between confer-
ment of freedom and election to the shrievalty was 21·1 years and
only ten sheriffs were elected within ten years of the date they
became freemen. The ward residences of the sheriffs also bear a
close relationship to the number of wealthy men and the size of the
freeman populace in the different wards: Wymer provided the

[1] Applications for compounding were made to the Assembly and Mayor's
Courts, and they are included in the official records of these two bodies.
[2] A.B. (1613–42), 4 Aug. 1620, 120ʳ. In 1661/2 the corporation decided that
refusal to accept office could result in a fine of up to £300. ibid. (1642–68),
16 Feb. 1661/2, 255ʳ.
[3] A total of 131 men held the office of sheriff between 1628 and 1688. All but
twenty-five of these sheriffs were elected aldermen from 1628 to 1690. Of these
twenty-five, one compounded out of additional offices, four died in office, and
five died within three years of the date of their election.
[4] Statistics concerning the methods whereby seventeenth-century sheriffs
became freemen, the interval between date of freedom and election to shrievalty,
the previous Council experience of sheriffs, and the residence of sheriffs for each
decade from 1620 to 1690 are provided in Evans, 'Political Elite of Norwich',
pp. 393–5.
[5] All but two of the forty sheriffs from 1600 to 1620 were councilmen at the
time of their election.

most sheriffs and Conesford the least.[1] There is remarkable similarity between the sheriffs elected by the magistrates and the sheriffs chosen by the freemen. This was true of the method by which they had become freemen, the interval between their dates of freedom and election, their previous experience on the Common Council, and their residence.[2] There were no radical departures from established patterns in these factors from one decade to the next. However, in times of urban crisis (1640s, 1650s, 1660s, 1680s) the sheriffs seem to have been older by four to six years on the average than in periods of relative tranquillity (1620s, 1630s, 1670s).[3] Given this continuity, the 'typical' sheriff of the seventeenth century had learned his trade in the city, had served six terms in the Common Council, was in his middle or late forties, and lived in the better sections of town. In addition, he was invariably a member of the wealthy élite.

In carrying out their judicial functions, the sheriffs had to command the respect of their fellow townsmen. Moreover, as the stepping-stone to the highest levels of civic government and as an office of great dignity and considerable though brief power, the shrievalty needed to be filled by men of stature and civic responsibility. The Composition called for a 'suffisaunt' citizen and the cost of office helped to guarantee that this would be true in practice. A firm reminder to the magistrates and freemen that they were expected to select men of means was that if a sheriff went bankrupt during his term of office, the outstanding debts fell on the shoulders of the body that elected him.[4] Certainly the magistrates could be counted on to choose an affluent man from their own social level, but there was always the possibility that the freemen might select a man of lower social rank who would be objectionable to the magistrates. There was, however, only one recorded instance during the

[1] Conesford, Mancroft, Wymer, and Over-the-Water provided 5·6 per cent, 22·9 per cent, 37·5 per cent, and 34·0 per cent of the sheriffs respectively.

[2] The most noticeable difference was that after 1650 the magistrates were more inclined than the freemen to discount tenure in the Council as a factor in recruitment.

[3] In the 1650s the average interval between date of obtaining freedom and election to the shrievalty was higher than in any other decade (24·5 years cf. 21·1 years for all sheriffs from 1620 to 1690), yet the average years of prior Council experience were significantly lower (3·9 years cf. 6·6 years for all sheriffs from 1620 to 1690).

[4] 'Composition of 1415', in Hudson and Tingey, eds., *Records*, I. 96. There is no evidence that after 1615 either the commons or the magistrates had to rescue financially the sheriff at any time.

1600s when the magistrates challenged the credentials of the commons' nominee.[1] An analysis of tax assessments of the 1640s and 1660s reveals that in both periods only 100 to 120 freemen possessed the minimum level of wealth to be eligible for election.[2] Only one-fourth of the councilmen could match the wealth of the average sheriff. Therefore, up to 1650 the sheriffs were chosen with few exceptions from the ten to fifteen wealthiest councilmen and after 1650 from about 100 of the wealthiest citizens, with the non-sheriff aldermen and the wealthiest councilmen remaining the most likely contenders.

After serving his one-year term, the sheriff was usually re-elected to the Common Council, where he awaited promotion to higher office. The number of ex-sheriff councilmen varied from year to year, but the presence of six to twelve of these men in the Council added social and political prestige to its deliberations.[3] It also underscores the fact that the councilmen were not a group of socially inferior citizens in contrast to the magistrates, even though many of the former were lesser tradesmen. Thus some of the councilmen would later become magistrates, some of the councilmen had already been sheriffs, and almost all the aldermen and mayors had once been councilmen. The range of social backgrounds of the participants in the Common Council encouraged communication between various social levels in reaching peaceful solutions to civic problems. This arrangement also contributed to the unlikelihood that social discontent would be channelled into competitive political bodies.

Following the shrievalty, the next step in the *cursus honorum* was election to a life tenure in the Court of Aldermen. Like the sheriffs, the aldermen were officially listed as 'Mr.' and addressed as gentlemen once they had obtained office. After 1660 most aldermen preferred to style themselves as 'armigerous' if they possessed a coat of arms, perhaps in an effort to distinguish themselves from the councilmen who had recently been elevated to the status of 'Mr.'. In conjunction with the mayor, the aldermen regulated almost all aspects of town life, but they performed few duties individually. Each alderman was elected by and associated with the

[1] This occurred in 1627 and is discussed in depth in Chapter III.

[2] The criterion of wealth in shrievalty elections is explored fully in Evans, 'Decline of Oligarchy', pp. 59–67.

[3] A.B. (1585–1613 and 1613–42). An average of 9·85 ex-sheriffs were in the Common Council each year over the period 1600 to 1620.

freemen of one of the four wards; but, until the Restoration, he had only a minor supervisory responsibility in his ward.[1] Only in the regulation of crafts did the alderman provide an important service independent from his brethren. Craft guilds had never been a strong force in Norwich politics and by the seventeenth century they were completely dominated by the corporation.[2] In 1622 the trades were divided into twelve Grand Companies with two aldermen serving as masters of each company.[3] Petitions to be discharged from the aldermanry were exceedingly rare, which suggests that sheriffs and other citizens welcomed election.[4] Unlike the sheriffs, the aldermen received no official salaries. As the major politicians of the city and the custodians of city revenues and policies, the aldermen were well positioned to line their pockets. There was only one accusation during the century, however, that the aldermen exploited or abused office for private gain and this claim was not supported with evidence.[5] Most likely it was the lure of status and power and possibly a sense of civic responsibility rather than monetary gain which made the office attractive.

Each ward chose six aldermen. When a vacancy arose, the mayor called together the freemen of the ward involved and charged them to nominate and elect a replacement.[6] The ancient charters clearly intended that the Court of Aldermen be reserved for the social élite and provided a safety clause in the otherwise democratic process. If the freemen were to elect a man who, in the opinion of the mayor, was not one of the 'worthiest and more sufficient', the mayor could challenge the election and prevent the alderman-elect from being sworn in.[7] The objective was to maintain the social

---

[1] The Charter of 1662/3 made every alderman a justice of the peace in the ward which had elected him.

[2] The enrolment of apprentices, admission of freemen, and enactment of trade ordinances had fallen under the jurisdiction of the corporation and the final arbiter in all disputes was the Mayor's Court.

[3] A.B. (1613–42), 29 July 1622, 143ᵛ–147ʳ.

[4] Three instances are recorded. John Dethick requested a discharge in 1640, John Salter obtained a discharge for seven years in 1642, and Roger Hawes offered £100 for a discharge in 1665 after he was elected alderman, but his request was denied.

[5] M.C.B. (1615–24), 26 May 1624, 531ᵛ.

[6] 'Charter of 1417', in *C.C.R.* V. 486. See also *C.C.R.* VI (1462/3), 146. The form for the election of aldermen is described in the 'Composition of 1415', in Hudson and Tingey, eds., *Records*, I. 97–8. A description of an aldermanic election in 1632 may be found in S.P. Dom., Chas. I, 225/46: Mayor and others of Norwich to Privy Council, 20 Nov. 1632.

[7] *C.C.R.* V (1417), 486.

prestige of the office rather than to allow the mayor to reject a prospective alderman who was unacceptable to him personally. Hence, the veto power was reserved for exceptional cases, and there was only one instance in the Elizabethan period when the mayor utilized his prerogative.[1] Apparently seventeenth-century mayors never exercised this power. A dispute of 1704/5 strongly implies that they did not. An election controversy in that year resulted in the formation of a committee to investigate charters and all ancient records concerning the election of aldermen, and they reported that 'there is an original right in the mayor and Court of Aldermen, or the majority of them, of approving or disapproving of any person elected an alderman of this city by the freemen being householders in the ward'.[2] However, of the few precedents cited by the committee, only one dated from the seventeenth century and it involved a candidate's failure to have served as sheriff rather than an insufficiency in his social credentials.[3]

There were no officeholding prerequisites for election to the Court of Aldermen until 1620, when an ordinance was passed limiting the eligible candidates to men who had been or were sheriffs. Although this requirement was waived after 1662, nearly three-fourths of the aldermen chosen in the 1660s and 1670s were men who had previously served as sheriffs.[4] Moreover, when the freemen ward electorates did not elect a past or present sheriff, they almost always turned to a councilman and usually one from their own ward.[5] Since these councilmen were, in terms of wealth, in the upper one-sixth of the Council, no more than fifteen or twenty men were in contention in any aldermanic contest. As a result, the new aldermen were invariably wealthy citizens with political

[1] Pound, 'Elizabethan Corporation of Norwich', pp. 16–17. A narrative of this event may also be found in Allen, 'Norwich Merchant Class', pp. 210–13.

[2] N.N.R.O., Papers Concerning Various Norwich Offices MSS., 21 and 22 Mar. 1704/5.

[3] In 1642/3 Bernard Church, who had not been elected sheriff, was chosen alderman by Over-the-Water and the mayor disallowed the election. In 1644 Church was elected sheriff and in 1647 he was elevated to the aldermanry. ibid.; M.C.B. (1634–46), 26 Jan. 1642/3, 374v-375r.

[4] An exception must be made for the first years of the Interregnum when, in the midst of a political crisis and a chronic shortage of available sheriffs, eight councilmen were elevated directly to the Court. For the remainder of the Interregnum only sheriffs were eligible candidates.

[5] Eleven of the forty aldermen from 1660 to 1680 had never been sheriff; nine of these eleven were councilmen at the time of their election.

experience.[1] Whereas the freemen had to choose residents of their own ward to represent them in the Council, they could select an alderman from anywhere in the city. Before 1620 they frequently did so.[2] During the later 1620s and the 1630s the ward electorates clearly preferred to elevate an alderman residing in their own ward, but this predisposition lapsed during the 1640s and was not restored after 1660. Less than half of the aldermen elected from 1670 to 1690 lived in the ward which promoted them.

The aldermen were elected for life, but they were subject to both recall by their ward and dismissal from office by their peers. The Composition had forseen the possibility that an alderman would become objectionable to his ward and allowed provision for his removal.[3] The freemen first registered their complaint with the mayor. At a subsequent meeting convened by the mayor, the freemen, acting as judge and jury, tried the case against the accused alderman and, if he were found unacceptable, elected a new man in his place. An agreement of 1424 extended to the majority of aldermen the power of excluding one of their own members.[4] Before 1620 the citizenry removed aldermen from office only under the most exceptional of circumstances; the most recent instance of a dismissal from office had taken place in 1598 for reasons of inadequate service and refusal to pay scot and lot.[5] This changed dramatically in the politically charged atmosphere after 1640. As rival political parties vied for control of the corporation, expulsions from the Court of Aldermen initiated by the freemen and the magistrates became common, and increasingly a new force in urban politics, the national government, forced aldermen from office. After 1640 no alderman enjoyed complete security of tenure.

Political purges and a high mortality rate contributed to a rapid turnover in the Court of Alderman. A total of 130 men were chosen

---

[1] The aldermen who had not been sheriffs could expect election to the shrievalty within several years after they had become aldermen. Only eleven of the 130 aldermen elected from 1620 to 1690 had never been councilmen.

[2] In 1621, for example, only eleven of the twenty-four aldermen were residents of the ward for which they stood. N.N.R.O., Norwich Muster Rolls and Assessments for Maintaining Forces (17th century) MSS., 1621.

[3] 'Composition of 1415', in Hudson and Tingey, eds., *Records*, I. 98.

[4] "Tripartite Indenture of 1424', in Mayor's Book MSS., pp. 117–20.

[5] Pound, 'Elizabethan Corporation of Norwich', p. 26; Allen, 'Norwich Merchant Class', pp. 176–7. See also *C.S.P.D.*, James I, 1623–25, p. 534: Petition of Thomas Lane to Privy Council, date unknown.

to fill this office between 1620 and 1690 and, since some aldermen were re-elected following dismissals, the elections actually numbered 139 (Table 12). On average, then, about two elections were

TABLE 12: *Elections and Turnover of Aldermen, 1620–1690*

	number of elections*	number of turnovers
1620s	14	14
1630s	18	18
1640s	26	26
1650s	12	12
1660s	22	26
1670s	18	18
1680s	29	48
Total	139	162

*The figures for number of elections have omitted the aldermen named by the commission to enforce the Corporation Act in 1662, the aldermen appointed by Charles II in the 1682/3 charter, and the aldermen automatically restored to office in October 1688 when James II declared the 1682/3 charter void. Three aldermen returned to office during the Restoration have been included because they were restored by popular election before the Corporation Bill was passed; the aldermen imposed on the corporation by James II in April 1688 have also been included since they were confirmed by ward elections. The controversial first election of 1678 has not been included. The number of turnovers includes the appointments of 1662, 1682/3, and 1688.

held yearly. Few young citizens could hope to become aldermen. Up to the Restoration, this was a necessary consequence of the shrievalty as a prerequisite for election, but even after 1680 there was no appreciable decline in the interval between obtaining freedom and promotion to the Court. On average, the alderman-elect was forty-eight or forty-nine years old and could expect to live fifteen or sixteen years following election.[1] The impact of politically-motivated dismissals is manifest. Ten aldermen in the

[1] The median span from obtaining freedom to aldermanic election was twenty-three years. If the average age of obtaining freedom was about twenty-five, the newly-elected aldermen would average forty-eight years of age. Of the 130 aldermen elected from 1620 to 1690, eighteen died within five years of their election and sixteen died within ten years. Thirty-four aldermen lived more than twenty years following their election. The median was fifteen years. The date of death for twenty-three aldermen is not known. On this basis, the alderman forty-eight years old had a lifetime expectancy of fifteen years. This is slightly lower than the figure given by Edmund Halley in the 1690s of 17·05 years expectancy for a man of fifty, which Peter Laslett has suggested was a little high. Laslett, *World*, pp. 93–4.

1640s and ten in the 1660s lost their seats because they were connected to the wrong political faction. A total of forty-five displacements occurred from 1678 to 1690. Aldermen were in and out of office so frequently in the years leading up to 1688 that stability of tenure was practically non-existent.

One important consequence of the rapid turnover was that the ward electorates were provided with a greater opportunity to determine the composition of the Court of Aldermen and more citizens were able to serve than a system of life tenure would seem to imply. A comparison of the membership of the Court at the beginning of each decade with what it had been ten years before reveals the potential of the freemen to influence the opinion of the magistracy (Table 13). Numerous vacancies occasioned by death

TABLE 13: *Aldermanic Continuity of Tenure, 1630–1690*

	number of aldermen with ten or more years' tenure
1630	13
1640	7
1650	2
1660	17
1670	5
1680	11
1690	11

and ejection meant that in periods of political crisis the magistrates in power were for the most part the recently-elected representatives of the freemen. This must have contributed greatly to maintaining harmony between the citizenry and the magistracy, which was especially important during the Civil War and Restoration. Equally important was that rival factions could vie for control at the guild-hall elections and this diminished the dangerous prospect of political 'ins' opposed by indefinitely excluded 'outs'.

The mayor occupied the pinnacle of status and power. Supreme in all civic affairs, he was responsible for maintaining the laws and liberties of the city, keeping the general peace and order, directing the aldermen in the preparation of legislation, presiding over all elections and city functions, carrying out the regulations with respect to food, and dispensing justice as the 'chief justice of the peace in the city' in his Mayor's Court.[1] He was also, from old

[1] 'Composition of 1415', in Hudson and Tingey, eds., *Records*, I. 101.

times, the King's Escheator, and in this capacity it was his duty to protect the rights of the Crown and report to the Privy Council any danger of loss or dishonour.[1] After 1660 the mayoralty conferred the title of 'Esquire', which was then retained for life by all ex-mayors. For his services the mayor received a salary of £100.[2]

The annual election of the mayor on the first day of May and his entry into office in June were the most celebrated civic occasions of the year.[3] In consideration of his pre-eminent authority, the procedures regulating the mayor's election were drawn up with the utmost care. On May Day the mayor, aldermen, sheriffs and councilmen gathered at the guild-hall together with the freemen of the city.[4] Once assembled, the recorder declared the cause for assembly and the magistrates retired to their chamber. The councilmen and freemen were then instructed by the common speaker to nominate two aldermen who had previously been sheriff.[5] Thus the mayoral candidates had spent many years in Norwich politics and were venerable men; a typical mayor was sixty-five years old and many were in their seventies.[6] Ex-mayors were eligible for nomination until 1620, but an ordinance of that

[1] *C.C.R.* VI (1462/3), 145–6.

[2] In 1615 the Assembly agreed to provide the mayor £100, which was increased to £140 for Mayor Thomas Hyrne in 1616. This figure was maintained until 1620, although in 1619 the Assembly granted the mayor the right of granting one freedom. In 1620 the Assembly retracted the mayor's privilege of making one freeman, but gave him an additional £13. 6s. 8d., bringing his total salary to £153. 6s. 8d. Apparently the Assembly then decided that this was too much, for in 1622 they struck up a bargain with mayor-elect Francis Smallpiece whereby Smallpiece would receive only £100, but if any future mayor received more than this amount the Assembly would pay £100 to either Smallpiece or his executor. As might be expected, the aldermen under the chair made an unsuccessful effort to prevent this agreement. A.B. (1613–42), 3 May 1615, 28 June 1616, 3 May 1617, 8 May 1618, 3 May 1619, 3 May 1620, 3 May 1621, 16 June 1622, 34, 52ᵛ, 60ᵛ, 90ᵛ, 101ᵛ, 114ᵛ, 116ᵛ, 133ʳ, 142ᵛ.

[3] The day of swearing in the new mayor was a civic holiday complete with pageants, music, dancing, and feasting. Not surprisingly, the ceremony attracted large crowds from Norfolk.

[4] 'Composition of 1415', in Hudson and Tingey, eds., *Records*, I. 94. See also *C.C.R.* VI (1462/3), 145. There are no detailed descriptions of a mayor's election dating from the early seventeenth century.

[5] The Composition did not require the mayor to be an alderman, but this requirement is clearly stated in the charters of 1417 and 1462. *C.C.R.* V. 485; VI. 145.

[6] The median interval between date of freedom and date of election was thirty-one years. The interval was less than twenty years for eight mayors and more than forty years for twelve mayors. See Evans, 'Political Elite of Norwich', p. 408.

year restricted eligibility to aldermen under the chair and this provision remained in effect for the rest of the century.[1] After 1620 the freemen rarely had more than a dozen men amongst whom to choose, and in some years considerably less. The two aldermen with the most votes became the official nominees. Their names were then carried up to the mayor's chamber where the aldermen and sheriffs, voting individually by secret ballot, picked one of the two nominees to be the mayor-elect.[2] As in the sheriffs' election, the present mayor had the deciding vote if the election were deadlocked. The only departure from this formula was the automatic elevation of the senior alderman under the chair from 1620 to the early 1640s and again during the 1670s.

Assisting the mayor were a number of officials.[3] First and foremost were the other twenty-three aldermen who aided the mayor in his manifold duties. The mayor's serjeants presented his summons and supervised ordinances concerning the market and victuals. The ward constables, sworn subordinates of the mayor, were the seventeenth-century equivalent of policemen. They preserved peace and order in the wards, stopped unlawful assembly and arrested offenders. A very influential figure in city affairs was the recorder, who was the special legal adviser to the mayor and aldermen, as the steward was to the sheriff. Elected by the Assembly to an indefinite tenure, the recorder was *ex officio* a justice of the peace in the Mayor's Court.[4] His advice was cherished, especially on the legal aspects of political matters encountered by the corporation, and often during the seventeenth century the recorder became a controversial official.

Meeting several times each month, the Mayor's Court was the most important judicial body in the city. A court of equity, it handled its own cases and served also as a court of appeals for cases heard previously in the Sheriff's Court. The Court dealt

---

[1] Ancient charters permitted the nomination of ex-mayors as long as they had not served as mayors during the previous three years. A decree of 1599 established a nine-year rather than a three-year interval. Pound, 'Elizabethan Corporation of Norwich', p. 23. There was only one exception after 1620 to the rule that mayors should not serve a second term.

[2] If a man was simultaneously both sheriff and alderman, he had only one vote in elections and in the Mayor's Court. M.C.B. (1615–24), 5 Sept. 1618, 205ᵛ.

[3] The best listing of the various municipal officials and their duties is provided in Hudson and Tingey, eds., *Records*, I. cvi–cix.

[4] *C.C.R.* VI (1452), 115.

regularly with public nuisances, defective weights and measures, market offences, assaults, fraudulent manufacture and trade, and breaches of the Common Law.[1] It also arbitrated private disputes, dealt with swearers and wife beaters, enforced laws on drunkards, alehouses and gaming, and punished beggars and vagabonds. The Mayor's Court differed in jurisdiction from the Quarter Sessions only in its inability to try cases of manslaughter, murder, and accidental death. The justices of the peace who sat on the Court were presided over by the mayor and included the recorder and all aldermen who had previously been mayor.[2] The city also had its own Quarter Sessions Court, yet a case brought before the Sessions was presented to the same adjudicators, the mayor and his associate justices. Hence there were three different official bodies carrying out three different functions but containing much the same personnel: the assembly of all aldermen, the Mayor's Court, and the Quarter Sessions. In an extraordinary mingling of powers, the mayor and aldermen were a judicial bench, an administrative board, and a legislative committee.[3]

The necessity of preserving peaceful co-operation among the aldermen was imperative. To prevent friction, the aldermen were bound by their oath of obedience to uphold the Tripartite Indenture of 1424, which regulated their conduct in relation to each other.[4] Aldermen were not permitted to speak scandalous words of a fellow alderman, rejoice at his distress or loss, harm him in any way, or support any other person who scandalously abused another alderman. Further, if two aldermen had a serious dispute, neither could bring suit against the other until the grievances had been aired privately by the other aldermen and attempts at reconciliation by the mayor had proved fruitless. The aldermen were also forbidden to promote the candidacy of any man to any political office; the freemen were not supposed to be subjected to pressure, influence, or interference by the magistrates during elections. Above all, the aldermen were required to give attendance,

[1] Sachse, ed., *Minutes*, p. 16. This is the best account of the municipal judicial system of Norwich.

[2] *C.C.R.* VI (1452), 115.

[3] Referring to the scope of their activities, Sachse has commented that they 'brought the business transactions, family life, moral lapses, religious scruples, sanitary practices, modes of amusement, and personal health of the individual under close surveillance; which bound his tongue, controlled his thirst, and even affected his diet'. Sachse, ed., *Minutes*, p. 52.

[4] 'Tripartite Indenture of 1424', in Mayor's Book MSS., pp. 117–20.

counsel, and support to the mayor whenever requested. If an alderman was found to be guilty of violating any of the terms of the Indenture, he could be removed from the Court of Aldermen.

The Constitutional structure hammered out in 1415 survived the political storms of the seventeenth century with remarkably little alteration. Throughout this period the city was governed by the mayor, twenty-four aldermen, two sheriffs, and sixty councilmen, who performed their traditional duties and who, with the exception of the aldermen, served one-year terms. In addition, the traditional political ladder, commencing with the Common Council and, after the shrievalty and aldermanry, culminating in the mayoralty, remained unchanged apart from a minority of aldermen elected after 1660 who had not yet been sheriffs. Rapid promotion up this ladder was never guaranteed and depended more on the rate of aldermanic turnover and the availability of other candidates than on the personal credentials of individuals.[1] Usually those citizens with the proper credentials could expect to move up one rung of the ladder as space became available at the top, with two additional but all-important qualifications. First their political career could be indefinitely set back or even terminated by dismissal from office resulting from the struggle of competing factions or the intervention of an increasingly concerned national government. Second, at each stage of elevation they needed to satisfy the demands of a large, active, and at times ideologically-motivated electorate.

*   *   *

The Composition of 1415, the Tripartite Indenture of 1424, and the royal charters granted to Norwich in the fifteenth century were first and foremost concerned with the establishment of an effective and efficient government which could rule Norwich with a minimum of dissension. Internal harmony and co-operation within the city and corporation was the central objective. A second goal was the protection of the corporation from external interference. By royal charter of 1404, Norwich was proclaimed a city and county

---

[1] Thus rapid promotion occurred in the 1640s, early 1650s, early 1660s, and after 1677. On the other hand, progression from the shrievalty to the mayoralty between 1665 and 1678 was very slow because there were few aldermanic vacancies and during the 1670s seniority was used in selecting mayors. An ideal candidate might be revealed by the early age he was elected sheriff or alderman, whichever came first, but not by a rapid rise within the magistracy itself.

unto itself and separate from Norfolk.[1] Thirteen years later another royal charter confirmed a constitution designed to promote complete self-governance. The Composition explicitly forbade the election of outsiders to high civic office and similarly prohibited major officeholders from becoming the agent of an external magnate.[2] A system in which offices were elective and were filled by a large electorate consisting of resident freemen helped to preserve autonomy from county influence. Moreover, almost all officeholders were required to be residents as well as freemen in order to be eligible for election. The one exception was the sheriff chosen by the magistrates, but this sheriff, who might live outside the city before election, was required to become a resident during his one-year tenure.[3] It was not likely that many men would move family, household, and business, or leave them all behind, to occupy a political office which could cost him money and guarantee him nothing in terms of additional preferment.

The major problem in the early seventeenth century was not in preventing 'foreigners' from interfering in elections, but in preventing properly elected magistrates from moving to the countryside and in effect becoming gentry. There was a growing tendency for successful citizens to invest their fortunes in the land market, but the corporation acted decisively if any of its members retired to the country. In 1590 two aldermen were dismissed because they were living outside the city to the annoyance of their respective wards.[4] Throughout the seventeenth century, the Assembly and Mayor's Court sent letters to non-residents pointedly informing them that they could choose between returning to the city or forfeiting office.[5] The extent of corporation concern is evidenced in a case which arose in 1622. Shortly after his election as sheriff, Nicholas Emms requested permission from the Assembly to live in the suburb of Pockthorpe outside the wall, but the Assembly withheld authorization, at least until Emm's pregnant wife gave birth.[6]

The controversies, hostilities, and factional strife which dominated the political landscape of Norwich in the seventeenth century

---

[1] *C.C.R.* V (1404), 421.

[2] 'Composition of 1415', in Hudson and Tingey, eds., *Records*, I. 98.

[3] Sachse, ed., *Minutes*, p. 19.

[4] Pound, 'Elizabethan Corporation of Norwich', p. 26.

[5] For example, A.B. (1613–42), 18 Aug. 1620, 120ᵛ; M.C.B. (1624–36), 7 Feb. 1626/7, 127ᵛ.

[6] A.B. (1613–42), 21 Sept. 1622, 148ᵛ.

put a considerable strain on the political fabric. This was especially true in the 1640s and 1680s. Throughout it all the city continued to be regulated by a constitutional framework constructed more than two hundred years before. But it was a constitution which had been forged in similarly heated times and was well designed to survive local turmoil. Up to 1660 the citizens were free to work out their political problems without unwanted external pressure or intervention. This changed after the Restoration. While partisan politics racked the city from within, the meddling of county magnates and the forceful claims of the state threatened the independence of the corporation from without. The Achilles' heel of the Norwich political system, and of all urban corporations, was that the Crown, which had originally granted charters guaranteeing liberties and jurisdictions, could also revoke them and assert its own control.

III

The Breakdown of Harmony
and the Puritan Crisis, 1620-1640

The maintenance of order and stability, the principal concern of both central and local government, rested on respect for and obedience to the decisions and dictates of established authority. In Norwich this, in turn, depended upon harmony within the establishment itself: amicable relations among the magistrates, between the magistracy and the Assembly, the corporation and the Cathedral, and the city government and Whitehall were essential in preventing dissension and restoring stability. Challenges to civic authority arising out of municipal election controversies from 1618 to 1632 exhibit the reliance of the corporation on Crown intervention to maintain order. Similarly, co-operation between the city government and the bishop of Norwich was necessary to carry on peacefully the religious life of the community. In a city with strong Puritan leanings, friction between the magistrates and the bishops was inevitable and had led to confrontations in both the 1610s and 1620s. With the arrival of Bishop Wren in Norwich in early 1636 and his subsequent efforts to stamp out Puritanism, however, urban dissension seriously increased and the fabric of government and authority on all levels became unravelled. By 1641 the magistrates had split into bickering factions, the magistracy and the Assembly had come into sharp conflict, the relations between the city and the church had deteriorated into unprecedented and undisguised hostility, and large numbers of townsmen had lost confidence in the Crown.

In periods of urban tranquillity and prosperity there was little need for the Norwich magistrates to appeal to national government for assistance or, conversely, for the Privy Council to intervene in local affairs. Such was the case during most of Elizabeth's and the first part of James's reign. During these years Norwich was a world in itself: urban unrest was limited, the city was capable of handling its own affairs, and communications to and from either

Westminster or Whitehall were infrequent.[1] Even so, an important and symbiotic relationship between national and local urban government continued to exist, in Norwich as elsewhere. As the Privy Council was aware, the acts and decrees of the state were useless unless implemented by local authorities. Moreover, local authorities acted as the eyes and ears of the Crown. In 1621, for example, Thomas and John Woodhouse, in the middle of a drunken fit, uttered words disrespectful to the King. Despite the extenuating circumstances and the apparent triviality of the offence, the mayor and aldermen ordered the hapless men to appear at the next Sessions and provided the Privy Council with a complete account of their indiscretion.[2] The Crown was as concerned as the local magistrates for the preservation of order on the local level. In the midst of an election controversy in 1627, for example, the Council wrote to the Norwich corporation that the affair was 'a matter that his Majesty especially careth for, that the orderly government of city and corporation should be maintained, and that popular and factious humors that trouble the same should be suppressed and punished'.[3] In addition, the municipal authorities were responsible for collecting the loans and subsidies which the Stuart state so frequently and desperately needed.

The magistrates of Norwich and other towns benefited in turn from close ties with the Crown.[4] In a strict legal sense the town government received its authority and jurisdiction by royal charter, and an extension of local power vested in the corporation or any of its members required the assent of the Crown. More important, perhaps, was the magistrates' dependence on the Crown whenever they were confronted with the threat or reality of a major upheaval or violence. Relatively minor and uncontroversial issues, or contumacy limited at most to a few townsmen, were routinely dealt with by the Assembly and the Mayor's Court. If, however, the corporation was confronted with the necessity of introducing controversial measures or reacting to the spectre of public disturbance on a larger scale, as was frequently the case after 1618, the magistrates proved very reluctant to take measures on

[1] Pound, 'Elizabethan Corporation of Norwich', p. 340.
[2] P.R.O., S.P. Dom., James I, CXXII, no. 145: Mayor and aldermen of Norwich to Earl Marshall Arundel, 26 Sept. 1621. See also ibid. 123/20 and *A.P.C.*, James I, 1621–23, p. 56: 10 Oct. 1621.
[3] *A.P.C.*, Chas I, 1627–28, pp. 140–1: 15 Nov. 1627.
[4] See Zagorin, *Court and Country*, p. 130.

their own, even though they possessed the legislative and judicial powers to do so. Rather, they turned to the Privy Council for advice and support and invariably they accepted and implemented Whitehall's instructions. If violence or upheaval remained a threat or actually occurred, the magistrates could imprison or disfranchise or both. Nevertheless, they usually preferred to issue public threats while privately they rushed an urgent appeal to Whitehall for further backing and advice.[1]

The involvement of the Crown in local crises was an effective means of maintaining civic stability. The intervention of the Privy Council freed the corporation from assuming complete responsibility for compelling submission to their own decrees, which might otherwise have created friction within the city or the corporation itself. Moreover, disobedience to the Crown was a far more serious political sin than refusal to obey local magistrates, and frequently led to severe punishment. Hence a mandate from the Privy Council was a potent weapon in the magistrates' arsenal for intimidating culprits and diminishing the prospect of further disruption. Since the magistrates knew in advance that they could count on a sympathetic ear at Whitehall whenever popular disturbance or a challenge to established authority arose, the temptation to solicit Crown intervention was strong.

The election controversies which occurred in the 1610s and the 1620s reveal a consistent pattern in magisterial response to urban conflict. They also draw attention to discontent within the town and corporation similar to that experienced in numerous other towns. Challenges to oligarchical corporations mounted by local insurgent groups were a widespread phenomenon in early Stuart towns; the conflicts invariably focused on civic election procedures.[2] In Norwich an ambitious freeman electorate promoted candidates to office who were a challenge to tradition and repugnant to the magistrates. The latter, with the approval and under the watchful eye of the Privy Council, countered with a series of adjustments in election procedures, the first alterations in 200 years. Political oligarchy, however, was not established. Elections were henceforth determined by an inflexible seniority principle which greatly

[1] For the limitations of disfranchisement, see Allen, 'Norwich Merchant Class', pp. 175–80.

[2] Provincial urban discontent prior to 1640 has only recently received attention. For a provocative discussion of this topic see Hirst, *Representative of the People?*, Chap. 3 and App. II.

reduced both freeman and magisterial participation in choosing the town's governors, and proved to be a major obstacle to the Puritans in their ascendancy to power in the 1640s.

*   *   *

The first confrontation over elections did not reach serious proportions until 1619, although it had been building up for over a decade. The freemen were theoretically unrestricted in the nomination of two aldermen for the mayoralty, yet the magistrates had grown accustomed to and favoured a process of promotion which took seniority of tenure into consideration. For all civic occasions and official correspondence each alderman recognized his place in the hierarchy. First came the mayor, followed by the alderman-justices in the order in which they had been elected to the mayoralty, and they were followed by the aldermen under the chair according to the date of their admission to the aldermanry.[1] Acceptance of seniority as an electoral principle stipulated that the freemen limit their mayoral nominations to the senior aldermen. The freeman electorate, however, was eager to take the initiative in the choice of mayors and had persistently ignored seniority in ever bolder ways in the years before 1619. Since there was nothing in the charters which recognized, much less sanctioned, seniority, the magistrates, however irritated they became, were constitutionally impotent to prevent the electors from ignoring it.

An example of the practices that troubled many of the magistrates occurred in 1617. The year before, Sir Thomas Hyrne, twice mayor and member of Parliament, and John Mingay, alderman for twelve years and high on the seniority list, were nominated; and the aldermen elected Hyrne to serve a third term.[2] No complaint could be made about this. In 1617, however, the freemen again nominated Mingay, but this time with Richard Goldman, who had been sheriff in 1610, had been elevated to the aldermanry at the first opportunity in 1612, and who was eighth in seniority among the ten aldermen under the chair. Mingay was elected, but in the process some magistrates must have experienced distaste: for they had the choice of electing Goldman, a grave transgression of the seniority principle, or accepting Mingay. By this method of

---

[1] See N.N.R.O., Norwich Charter of 1662/3. Knighthood made an exception: a knighted alderman was elevated to a position second only to the mayor.

[2] The mayoral nominees are listed in N.N.R.O., A.B. under 1 May for each year.

nominating aldermen from the top and the bottom of the seniority list, the freeman electorate was quite capable of coercing the magistracy into electing a mayor objectionable to the majority of them. Indeed, the freemen had found this tactic quite useful in manipulating the elections of mayors, and had resorted to it in 1605, 1610, 1611, and 1613. The process was as simple as it was effective: in 1605, for example, the commonalty nominated Roger Gaywood when he was serving only his second year in the aldermanry, but it would seem that they merely utilized his candidacy to have their other nominee, Thomas Sotherton, elected, since they neglected to nominate Gaywood in any of the following fifteen years.

The freemen went one step further in 1618: both nominees, Richard Rosse and Henry Fawcett, were junior aldermen. Both had been members of the Common Council for more than fifteen years and both were over fifty years old. But tenure in the Council had nothing to do with seniority in the aldermanry, which in 1618 consisted of ten alderman-justices, twelve aldermen under the chair eligible to be chosen mayor, and two aldermen who had not completed service as sheriff.[1] Of the twelve eligible aldermen, Fawcett and Rosse ranked seventh and tenth in seniority. Nor was this the first time the magistrates were forced to consent to the promotion of a fresh recruit. Indeed, it was the fourth time in the past seven years.[2]

Altogether, the freemen had selected junior aldermen as one or both of their nominees in seven of the ten mayoral elections prior to 1618. For their part, the magistrates had never once failed to name the senior of the two nominees to be the mayor-elect. However, in 1618 they sacrificed the principle of seniority and picked Rosse. Apparently the freemen had been trying to impose Fawcett, now in nomination for the third time in four years, on a reluctant magistracy; but the latter were not inclined to accept him this time either, even though their only alternative was Rosse with his lone year on the aldermanic bench.

The elections of aldermen in 1617 and 1618 also testify to a defiant electorate exerting its constitutional prerogative. There

[1] A listing of the Court of Aldermen on 1 May 1618 together with the dates they were admitted freemen, their tenure in the Council, and the dates of their election to the shrievalty and aldermanry may be found in Evans, 'The Political Elite of Norwich', p. 51.

[2] The other years were 1612, 1614, and 1615.

were five ex-sheriffs on the Common Council in 1618, most of whom anticipated and later held higher office. The freemen of three different wards, however, elected as alderman one man who had completed the shrievalty the previous year, one who was currently sheriff, and one who had never been sheriff. What made the actions of the freemen even more exceptional was the political inexperience and youth of the three men. The aldermen sitting on the Court had been freemen on the average more than seventeen years before advancing to the aldermanry; the three recruits of 1618 averaged six years for the same interval. Moreover, since all of the recruits, Thomas Cory, Alexander Anguish, and Hamond Thurston, had received their freedom by patrimony since 1608, it is possible that some of them may have been under the age of thirty. Such rapid promotion was not lacking precedent, but for all three to be so inexperienced and elected in lieu of so many other eligible candidates was bound to cause antagonism.[1]

Absence of contemporary commentary makes it impossible to gauge the seriousness of election disturbances before 1619 or the factors which had prompted the freemen to disregard seniority and defy the magistracy. As with much of the internal disorder within the city, the Assembly Book and the Mayor's Court Book are disappointingly silent.[2] What is clear is that by 1619 many of the magistrates were considerably agitated and were prepared to do whatever was necessary to counter the freeman electorate. Some of the aldermen with mayoral aspirations were no doubt disgruntled by the realization that their elevation could be delayed indefinitely and even prevented by the freemen's behaviour. Others may have believed that disrespect for seniority was a breach of social propriety, a matter sure to arouse the sensitivities of most magis-

---

[1] Millican, ed., *Freemen*, pp. 90, 104. Hamond Thurston, the son of Nicholas Thurston of St. Peter Mancroft, was born on 10 April 1582, and was thirty-five in 1618. N.N.R.O., St. Peter Mancroft parish register. Sir Thomas Hyrne and Thomas Blosse, who were alderman-justices in 1618, were both promoted rapidly. Hyrne was admitted to the freedom in 1596, never served in the Council, and was elected both sheriff and alderman in 1597. Blosse became a freeman in 1604, served several months in the Council in 1606 before being elected sheriff in the same year and alderman in 1607.

[2] Derek Hirst has argued that adverse economic conditions in the 1590s and 1620s led many town oligarchs to consolidate their position and exploit their strength. This, in turn, created resentment among less privileged townsmen. Friction built up and led ultimately to challenges to corporations in civic elections. Hirst, *Representative of the People?*, pp. 46 ff. Norwich may conform to this model.

trates.[1] Or they may have realized that observance of seniority prevented personality conflicts and jealousy within the Court of Aldermen, and thus contributed to the harmonious functioning of the Court. Certainly the political élite as a socially prominent body was acutely aware that each election was a potential source of disorder and that in the process the commonalty was capturing control of the magistracy through its control of elections. This, above all, was insufferable.

There was little the magistrates could do to resolve the situation in their favour without risking considerable civic turmoil.[2] Outside intervention was needed. The affair was brought to the attention of the Crown before the next elections in 1619.[3] Less than a week before the election of a new mayor on 1 May, the King wrote to Mayor Richard Rosse that the promotion of young men above their seniors in the election of mayors and principal officers had caused disturbances which could no longer be tolerated.[4] Consequently, the memorandum continued, future elections must conform to the good custom of London, and the senior alderman under the chair must be promoted even though this would eliminate popular elections as prescribed by charter.[5] Here, as elsewhere in England, the early Stuart monarchy exhibited little respect for democratic processes when domestic order and stability were at stake.[6]

The letter from the King was received by the corporation and proclaimed throughout the city on the eve of the election.[7] The

[1] N.N.R.O., M.C.B. (1615–24), 6 Aug. 1617, 146ʳ⁻ᵛ, records a dispute between the sheriffs of Norwich and the sheriff of Norfolk over whether the justice on tour should sit on the right or the left of the mayor. Such a trivial matter as this was enough to create an altercation.

[2] In early 1619 the Assembly did discharge a common councilman for circulating a petition requesting that the charters should be renewed in point of elections. A.B. (1613–42), 8 Jan. 1618/19, 97ᵛ.

[3] Neither the Mayor's Court Book nor the Privy Council Register record any correspondence between the two bodies which would shed light on how Whitehall was informed and by whom. It is possible that individual members of the Court of Aldermen either directly or through contacts in London requested the Crown to intercede.

[4] *C.S.P.D.*, James I, 1619–23, p. 40: King James to Mayor et. al. of Norwich, 26 Apr. 1619.

[5] In London the Common Hall nominated two men and the magistrates chose one for mayor-elect. By tradition these nominations included the senior alderman under the chair who was then elected. Pearl, *London*, p. 51.

[6] See Lawrence Stone, *The Crisis of the Aristocracy, 1558–1641* (Oxford, 1965), p. 31; Hirst describes the policy of the Crown as a 'high-flying line in support of oligarchy'. Hirst, *Representative of the People?*, p. 47.

[7] M.C.B. (1615–24), 31 Apr. 1619, 234ʳ.

following day Aldermen Roger Gaywood and George Birch were nominated, which complied with the spirit of the King's demand.[1] The election did not pass without incident, however, and some of the aldermen dispatched news to Whitehall of the disruptions which had occurred. The Privy Council was alarmed: public disorder was serious enough, but flagrant disobedience to royal instructions was inexcusable.[2] Such contempt deserved a complete examination, and thus the Council directed the Justices of the Assize for Norfolk to look into the matter during their next circuit and provide a complete written report. Apparently no less a figure than Mayor Rosse had opposed the nomination of senior aldermen; and he and three others were bound over to appear before the Privy Council as 'disturbers of orders and contemners of the King's directions'.[3]

The King's letter was not law, but the Privy Council fully expected the city to legislate his order into the by-laws of the city. Legislation, however, required the consent of the Common Council and the councilmen were intractable. On 11 October 1619, the magistrates presented a draft by-law governing elections; the councilmen demanded time to consider the proposal, as was their constitutional right; and a committee was set up to study the matter.[4] The Mayor's Court, during the delay, sent a delegation to London to explore further the establishment of an election law.[5] By December, the Lord Chief Justice and the Justices of the Assize were actively agitating for a decision, as it was becoming apparent that deliberations had reached stalemate.[6] The Common Council had not considered the proposed law because the committee had failed to present any recommendations to the Assembly. Despite pressure from the justices, the negotiations dragged on with no progress.

Clearly the corporation was not about to resolve its own difficulties. By March 1620, the justices had stepped up their efforts

---

[1] Technically, Richard Rosse was the senior alderman under the chair, but Gaywood and Birch were second and third respectively.

[2] *A.P.C.*, James I, 1618–19, p. 484: 27 June 1619.

[3] Francis Blomefield, *An Essay Towards a Topographical History of the County of Norfolk* (London, 1805), III. 368. The others with Rosse included Richard Wyth, Thomas Claxton, and John Lyng, and they were all councilmen. Lyng was elected sheriff by the freemen in 1621.

[4] A.B. (1613–42), 11 Oct. 1619, 107^r.

[5] M.C.B. (1615–24), 6 and 8 Nov. 1619, 265^v, 266^r.

[6] ibid., 17 Dec. 1619, 270^r.

and presented their own draft for an election law.[1] Nevertheless, no resolution could be reached in time to prevent additional election disturbances in May.[2] The matter came to a head on 29 May. Mayor Gaywood and several associate aldermen expounded the justices' scheme to the Assembly and debate commenced immediately.[3] Eventually a vote was taken of the fifteen aldermen and thirty-three councilmen present and by twenty-five to twenty-three the proposed legislation was carried. It was a short-lived victory. Many councilmen were enraged because fourteen of the fifteen aldermen endorsed the legislation, but twenty-two of the thirty-three councilmen did not, 'and it was thereupon alleged by some of the Common Council that the aldermen ought not by charter to give their voice with the commons in the establishment of law'.[4] It was a point well taken. The magistrates hardly needed an additional source of friction and dispute. Once again the matter was postponed. Three weeks later, a second attempt was made to pass the justices' scheme into law, but this time the majority of councilmen present refused to debate the issue until the next assize when the justices would appear in person.[5]

On 4 August, the Chief Justice of the Common Pleas and two associate justices met in the guild-hall with the mayor, eighteen aldermen, both sheriffs, and forty-eight councilmen. James had instructed the justices to settle the difficulties 'with as little innovation as may be',[6] and, in a phrase, the King carried the day. The object of the by-law passed by the Assembly was declared to be the prevention of disturbances at elections and dissensions growing out of them. To accomplish this end, the very essence of election itself was eliminated: seniority alone would in the future determine the selection of mayors and aldermen. The little innovation desired by the King, however, had a profound impact on the election of magistrates without removing the potential for future election controversies.

The election ordinance concerned solely the election of mayors,

---

[1] ibid., 25 Mar. and 22 May 1620, 283ᵛ, 291ᵛ.
[2] Alderman Michael Parker, Councilman Thomas Seaman, and Roger Sedgewicke were the culprits. Blomefield, *Norfolk*, III. 368. See also M.C.B. (1615–24), 23 Dec. 1620, 326ʳ.
[3] A.B. (1613–42), 29 May 1620, 116ʳ.
[4] ibid.
[5] ibid., 19 June 1620, 116ᵛ.
[6] ibid., 4 Aug. 1620, 120ʳ.

sheriffs, and aldermen and was based on the theory that where there was no choice there could be no dispute. As in former times, the freemen were to assemble at the guild-hall on 1 May to nominate two aldermen for mayor. The elaborate formalities of the Composition of 1415 were retained, but the election was merely a ceremonious gathering. The electorate was ordered to nominate 'two of the ancientest aldermen in rank as have been sheriffs of the said city and have not before that time borne the office of mayoralty and have not been dispensed with all from bearing the same.'[1] In practice, the phrase 'two of the ancientest' was interpreted rigidly as the two aldermen under the chair with the greatest seniority, and hence it was known well in advance who would be nominated. If the freemen were deprived of their franchise, as was the case in London, so also were the magistrates. They were required, in the language of the by-law, 'by such scrutiny as is and hath been used [to] make choice of one of the most ancient in rank of the said two so nominated.' Careful scrutiny meant nothing more than consulting the Assembly Book to make sure which of the two men was first elected to the aldermanry.

The election of aldermen was also reduced to a *pro forma* occasion. Upon the death of an alderman, the mayor was permitted forty days to call the freemen of the ward together and to inform them that they must choose 'the most ancient in rank' of four ex-sheriffs who were 'the ancientest in rank'.[2] Once elected sheriff, nothing short of aldermanic displacement at the hands of his peers or his constituency, or the untimely intervention of God, could stop the man from eventually becoming mayor. No changes in the procedure for electing sheriffs are mentioned, but if a sheriff wanted to refuse office and agreed to pay a fine, 'a process known as 'compounding from office', he now had to do so before the election date. The Assembly was fully aware of the great importance of the shrievalty as the key to municipal preferment, and stressed that 'great care and circumspection' be used by both the magistrates and the commonalty 'seeing as from them are to come those that are afterward to be made aldermen and in their time to bear the place of mayoralty in this city'.[3]

Once the ordinance was passed, open opposition to seniority as the sole criterion for higher office passed quickly. For each of the

<hr />

[1] ibid., 119^r.   [2] ibid., 119^v.   [3] ibid., 120^r.

next twenty years, the commonalty nominated the two senior aldermen under the chair and the magistrates elevated the man with greatest tenure. The new scheme for electing aldermen was also scrupulously adhered to. In early 1621, for instance, the free-men of Conesford assembled to replace Alderman Alexander Thurston, deceased. The mayor, after reading aloud the 1619 letter of the King and the recent law for elections, proceeded to name in order the four ex-sheriffs who were 'the most ancient in rank': Robert Hornsey, William Bussey, Lionel Claxton, and Thomas Spendlove. The freemen dutifully chose Hornsey. Three days later the freemen of Over-the-Water gathered to replace Alderman Thomas Pettus, deceased. The mayor put forward Bussey, Claxton, Spendlove, and Matthew Peckover. Bussey was elected.[1] There were ex-sheriffs still resident in the city in 1621 of greater seniority than Hornsey, but they had compounded them-selves from office.[2]

An inherent weakness in the new election system shortly became evident: the 1620 ordinance did not prevent the hypothetical possibility of the freemen supporting a totally undesirable candi-date for the shrievalty. This became a reality in 1627 when John Kettle ran for sheriff. Certainly Kettle must rank high among the most persistently contumacious characters in the history of Norwich. He was granted his freedom in 1609 as a basket-maker,[3] but his speciality was making trouble. In 1617 the Mayor's Court ordered Kettle to remove the lattices before his glass windows; a second order was needed when Kettle ignored the first.[4] In 1618 he was told to remove an archway which obstructed the market-place, but he must have put up strong resistance because shortly afterwards the Assembly agreed 'that John Kettle for his abuse of the magistrates of this city shall stand from henceforth utterly disfranchised and hereafter be taken of the freedom of this city'.[5] Two years later he was again in trouble, this time for his refusal to

[1] ibid., 19 and 22 Mar. 1620/1, 119ᵛ, 121ʳ.

[2] Ex-sheriffs John Chapman and Michael Aldrich requested and were per-mitted to be spared the aldermanry shortly after the ordinance was passed, on account of advanced age and illness. Chapman had retired from the Council in 1619 after serving there for twenty-two years; Aldrich had been a councilman for twenty-one years until his retirement in 1616. ibid., 18 Aug. 1620, 121ʳ.

[3] Millican records: 'Johes. Kettle, non appr., 11 August, 7 Jac.' Millican, ed., *Freemen*, p. 14.

[4] M.C.B. (1615–24), 9 and 30 July 1617, 141ᵛ, 144ᵛ.

[5] A.B. (1613–42), 9 Nov. 1618, 97ʳ; M.C.B. (1615–24), 5 Sept. 1618, 208ʳ.

pay the poor rate and river tax. In this instance, Kettle's bene-
factor, Sir Charles Cornwallis, interceded on his behalf.[1]

Apparently Kettle was pacified for several years, but he reappeared in 1624 with a direct attack on the Court of Aldermen. In
May of that year, one George Fireby testified that Kettle had
accused the magistrates of extortion and had claimed that although
the revenues of the city were £3,000 per annum, the aldermen
taxed the citizens for every minor expense. Moreover, Kettle also
charged the alderman-justices with embezzlement to the extent of
£100 per year, for which they ought to be called to account by the
deputy-lieutenants for the county of Norfolk.[2] Two months later,
the intrepid Kettle reiterated his complaints direct to the Mayor's
Court, and he also took the opportunity to grumble about being
fined 16s. for leaving 'muck' in the streets. In September, ex-
sheriff John Lyng made further complaints about Kettle, and in
October he appeared before the Conesford sessions and made
outrageous speeches about the subsidies. When the magistrates
retaliated by arranging for Kettle to bear the burden of the next
Mayor's Feast, Kettle procrastinated and finally refused.[3] He also
refused to appear for the sheriffs' tourn when summoned in 1625,
and for yet another incident was imprisoned temporarily. Early in
1626 he was warned several times about burying his 'necessary' in
the castle dikes to the great annoyance of those that passed by.[4] In
the eyes of the magistrates there could not be found a more
contemptible and despicable man in Norwich. Kettle's candidacy
for the commons' sheriff in 1627 must have sent ripples of anxiety
through the magistrates' chambers.

The magistrates' version of the sheriffs' election is all that
remains, but apart from its bias against Kettle the narrative
appears reliable.[5] Before the election it was generally known 'that a
great multitude of mechanical men and other citizens of meanest
quality' had conspired that if the magistrates chose a person
objectionable to them, they would match him with John Kettle,

[1] ibid., 28 June 1620, 300ʳ. Cornwallis was a deputy-lieutenant of Norfolk and
his precise relationship with Kettle is unknown. For his activities in Norfolk
politics see Owens, 'Norfolk', pp. 50–1, 62–4.

[2] M.C.B. (1615–24), 26 May, 1624, 531ᵛ.

[3] ibid. (1624–34), 10 July, 29 Sept., 8 and 9 Oct. 1624, 6ᵛ, 14ʳ, 16ʳ.

[4] ibid., 2 Apr. and 14 May 1625, and 11 Mar. 1626, 38ʳ, 43ᵛ, 84ʳ.

[5] S.P. Dom., Chas. I, 78/53: Mayor and fourteen aldermen of Norwich to
Privy Council, 18 Sept. 1627.

a basketmaker, a man so unworthy of a place of magistracy [and] so rude and uncivil as he is not fit for common society, a man so addicted to railing and drunkenness as he hath been bound to his good behavior, and yet never reformed . . .

The aldermen, believing that the freemen would never seriously consider Kettle, spurned this political threat and elected Henry Lane. For some unknown reason Lane was totally unacceptable to many citizens, who reacted by placing Kettle's name in nomination for the commons' sheriff. In a poll of the voters taken by the steward, Thomas Atkin narrowly defeated Kettle by the slim margin of ten votes. Nevertheless, Kettle and his supporters claimed that the election was fixed and threatened to disrupt the swearing-in of new sheriffs. The 'great multitude of mechanical men' remains anonymous. Since the city had recently been struck by the plague and an unpopular loan for Charles was in the process of collection, discontent was prevalent. A large part of this discontent was naturally directed at the governing body, and thus John Kettle posed as an obvious rallying point for the opposition.[1] Indeed, Kettle's most recent act of defiance included another refusal to bear the Mayor's Feast and a claim, made the previous summer, that the mayor and aldermen intentionally made by-laws to oppress the poor and indigent freemen.[2]

Anticipating riots, the magistrates appealed to the Privy Council for support.[3] It responded decisively: Kettle was summoned to London, interrogated by the Privy Council, and committed to Fleet Prison. The Norwich magistrates were instructed to confirm the election of Atkin.[4] In late October they ordered Kettle to return to Norwich after his release from prison and, in a public assembly, to make a humble submission to the aldermen and promise to conform to the constitution and government of the city.[5] As a final humiliation, Kettle would pay a £40 fine for his refusal to contribute to the Mayor's Feast. On 12 December, Kettle

[1] It is interesting to note that both Henry Lane and Thomas Atkin were commissioners for the loan. ibid. Kettle's claim to represent the common man against a corrupt magistracy must have fallen on receptive ears.

[2] M.C.B. (1624–34), 23 June 1627, 148ʳ.

[3] S.P. Dom., Chas. I, 78/53: Mayor and others of Norwich to Privy Council, 18 Sept. 1627. See also 79/38: Mayor and others of Norwich to Privy Council, 27 Sept. 1627.

[4] *A.P.C.*, Chas. I, 1627–8, pp. 42, 62, 75, 77: 21 and 28 Sept. and 5 and 8 Oct. 1627.

[5] ibid., p. 114: 31 Oct. 1627.

appeared, accompanied by Sir Charles Cornwallis.[1] Kettle made his submission reluctantly, but not until he had first let loose an avalanche of insolent diatribe. After this parting barrage at authority, he was silent for many years, though his pugnacious spirit surfaced for a fleeting moment in 1636 when he charged the aldermen with overtaxing the townsmen and pocketing the profits.[2]

The prospect of John Kettle as sheriff may have startled many citizens of Norwich, but the thought of Kettle as alderman and eventually mayor must have shocked the magistrates profoundly. The election system urgently needed further amendment. Shortly after Kettle's abortive attempt at election, the magistrates sent letters to the Privy Council to secure authorization for the commons' sheriff to be chosen by the councilmen rather than the entire body of freemen, and for the aldermen to be chosen from the whole body of sheriffs, not solely the most ancient in rank.[3] The Privy Council, in complete sympathy, granted their permission and stated their willingness to punish severely anyone who would violate any future by-law for orderly elections.[4] With these blessings from Whitehall, the Assembly adopted an ordinance in March of 1627/8 which allowed for the election of any past or present sheriff to the Court of Aldermen, but the measure to restrict the electors of the commons' sheriff to the councilmen does not seem to have been accepted.[5]

The altercation of 1627 marked the end of conflict between the magistrates and the commons over the election of officeholders until the 1640s. The election by-law of 1627/8, however, cannot be credited with providing the antidote to refractory popular initiative in elections. As a result of the by-law the role of the freemen in the

---

[1] The episode is described in M.C.B. (1624–34), 12 Dec. 1627, 169r–170r. See R. W. Ketton-Cremer, *Norfolk in the Civil War* (Hamden, Conn., 1970), p. 52.

[2] M.C.B. (1634–46), 29 June 1636, 112v.

[3] ibid. (1624–34), 29 Sept. 1627, 162r.

[4] The Council wrote: 'And in case any person after the passing and enacting thereof shall refuse to submit and conform thereunto, that then you be hereby authorized and required to bind over every such person in good and sufficient bond . . . personally to answer the same before this board.' *A.P.C.*, Chas. I, 1627–8, pp. 140–1.

[5] A.B. (1613–42), 21 Mar. 1627/8, 239v. A change in election procedures would require an ordinance passed by the Assembly, as stipulated by charters and recognized by the Privy Council, yet the Assembly Book records no by-law governing the election of sheriffs. ibid.

election of magistrates was actually increased rather than impaired. The freemen continued to select one of the two sheriffs and after 1628 it was the ward electorates, and not the magistrates or seniority, which determined the selection of aldermen from among the pool of past and present sheriffs. Indeed, if the sole intent of the magistrates was to keep a Kettle out of their Court, the by-law provided no truly effective remedy. The freemen of the city could still elect a man like Kettle to the shrievalty; the freemen of one of the four wards could just as easily elect him to the aldermanry. The Kettle affair thus seems to have been the catalyst rather than the cause of the by-law, the purpose of which was to negate the undesired rigidity of the promotion system established by the 1620 ordinance. The difficulty was that once a man was elected sheriff neither the magistrates nor the commons could exercise any control over his elevation to the aldermanry and mayoralty. A promising citizen elected sheriff in one year might easily become undesirable as alderman a decade later for a variety of reasons, bankruptcy being the most obvious. This was already a very real danger early in 1627.[1] Upon the death of Alderman Edmund Cock in 1627/8, the sheriffs next in line were John Ramsey, John Lyng, and Nicholas Emms. As a consequence of the new by-law, none of them was ever elected alderman.

It is worth noting that no effort was made in 1620 or 1627 to make Norwich a closed corporation in which the magistrates handpicked their own successors. This alone would have eliminated the election controversies experienced in the city, would probably have received the endorsement of the Crown, and would have brought the government of Norwich into line with the oligarchical systems of other towns.[2] Limiting the electors of the commons' sheriff to the Common Council, as suggested in 1627, would have been a cautious first step in this direction, but even this was discarded. Possibly the fear of popular unrest or the predictable opposition of the Common Council and freemen served as a deterrent to sweeping change. Yet the magistrates, with the compelling support of Whitehall, could probably have enforced the implementation of

---

[1] In May 1627, four months before the disputed sheriffs' election, a motion was made in the Mayor's Court to repeal unspecified aspects of the 1620 ordinance concerning the election of aldermen. M.C.B. (1624–34), 16 May 1627, 138r.

[2] Certainly Norwich was not provided with the 'thoroughly oligarchic constitution' suggested by Hirst, *Representative of the People?*, p. 57.

oligarchical measures. Rather, the behaviour of the magistrates throughout the seventeenth century suggests that their mentality was tradition-oriented and they did not think in terms of innovation much less radical reconstruction, even if this would have benefited them. As long as problems did not arise there was no change. Only when there was a serious breakdown in the traditional structure or procedures did the magistrates recognize the necessity of alterations. Even under these circumstances, they limited their reaction to remedial measures which dealt narrowly with the concrete problem at hand while preserving tradition as much as possible.

In their efforts to correct one problem created by the 1620 ordinance, the corporation opened the door to another possibility of disputes in the election of aldermen, which the 1620 ordinance had been designed to prevent, and which was several years in becoming apparent. Thomas Carver and William Gostlyn were both willing to resort to dubious means to become alderman for Over-the-Water in 1632. After the election, which Carver won by five votes, both sides claimed the other had enlisted foreigners and non-residents to be voters. Requested by Gostlyn's supporters to examine the election, the Mayor's Court asked both parties to draw up a list of those voters objected to and, after careful examination, the Court decided in favour of Gostlyn.[1] The magistrates, however, thought the election so close that they preferred a second election in hopes of avoiding discontent. Carver would not consent to this. Efforts to persuade him in the Mayor's Court were equally ineffectual, and when the mayor finally threatened to take the matter before the Privy Council, Carver indignantly stalked out.[2] The next day a letter was sent to Whitehall and eleven days later a dispatch was received which demanded that Gostlyn be sworn an alderman immediately, which he was.[3] One positive result of the fracas did emerge: in future aldermanic contests the disputes were

---

[1] M.C.B. (1624–34), 22 Sept. 1632, 405^r; S.P. Dom., Chas. I, 225/46: Mayor and others of Norwich to Privy Council, 20 Nov. 1632; M.C.B. (1624–34), 14 Nov. 1632, 411^r.

[2] ibid., 16, 17, and 19 Nov. 1632, 411^v–412^r; S.P. Dom., Chas. I, 225/46: Mayor and others of Norwich to Privy Council, 20 Nov. 1632. One elector also claimed that Carver had threatened him for voting for Gostlyn.

[3] ibid.; M.C.B. (1624–34), 31 Nov. and 15 Dec. 1632, 414^r, 415^r. The response from Westminster may be found in *A.P.C.*, Chas. I, microcard series, 1632–3, 23 Nov. 1632, p. 292.

settled on the spot by a separation of voters, an examination of proper credentials, and a hand count.[1]

*   *   *

Since Whitehall and the magistrates usually shared the same political and social outlook on local affairs and since the latter relied on the paternal presence of the Crown as a deterrent against popular unrest and as a board of arbitration for local squabbles, a harmonious partnership between the two might be expected to have continued indefinitely. This was the case, for example, in London. Here almost all the magistrates consistently supported Crown policy during the eleven-year personal rule, despite persistent attacks on the chartered privileges of the city and incessant demands for loans and taxes.[2] As late as 1640 the Lord Mayor and aldermen of London made every effort to suppress anti-royalist riots and demonstrations, for which they received the sincere gratitude of the Privy Council.[3] Norwich, however, offers a contrast. During the 1630s and early 1640s relations with Whitehall broke down to such an extent that by the Civil War a considerable number of magistrates as well as a majority of Norwich citizens were prepared to oppose the King with money, petitions, even life. Moreover, the leadership of the growing opposition party was provided throughout by men within the Court of Aldermen. The loyalty of the London aldermen was no doubt due in some measure to the fact that the great majority of them were either directors of trading companies, holders of monopoly patents, customs farmers, or lenders to the Crown.[4] The personal fortunes of the Norwich aldermen, on the other hand, did not depend on the continuing goodwill of Whitehall. Nevertheless, only the strongest of grievances could have severed the traditional bonds of loyalty which had proved so useful to them in the recent past.

The extra-parliamentary and quasi-legal tax schemes contrived by a desperate monarchy in the 1630s have frequently been cited as

---

[1] See M.C.B. (1624–34), 5 June 1633, 435ʳ. This action was in accordance with a suggestion made by the Privy Council. *A.P.C.*, Chas. I, microcard series, 1632–3, 23 Nov. 1632, p. 292.

[2] Pearl, *London*, pp. 69–106 *passim*, esp. pp. 71, 105.

[3] Pearl has also suggested that the Crown's failure to secure a large loan from London in 1639 and 1640 was due to a genuine lack of security and credit, and not because of doubts concerning its political wisdom. ibid., pp. 71, 98–9, 104.

[4] ibid., pp. 91–4.

a primary cause of the Civil War. It is doubtful, however, that many Norwich citizens found this to be a major grievance. As elsewhere, the imposition of ship-money levies was greeted with bitterness in Norwich, but the seriousness of the complaints diminished as the decade wore on, and they must be viewed from the perspective of the city's long tradition of opposition to all forms of central taxation.

Although Norwich was known to be a wealthy city, when it came to paying taxes the citizens were rarely without some excuse for returning only a portion of the assessment. This pattern can be traced back at least to 1614. The Lords of the Council, reacting to the Addled Parliament, informed the city that many well-affected people had given plate and money as a sign of their affection for James, and that the King would be extremely pleased to receive a munificent donation from Norwich. The pleas of the Privy Council were in vain. Even the Earl of Suffolk reprimanded the mayor and aldermen for the meagreness of their gift, which he claimed unworthy of the second or third city of the kingdom and for which Norwich had offered no adequate excuse.[1] Reluctance to open their pockets for the royal treasury was not limited to the wealthier citizens. In 1622 Mayor Smallpiece informed the Privy Council that attempts to raise a contribution to the scale of a subsidy and a half were failing because of the poverty of some townsmen and 'the disaffection of others so numerous that their names can not be sent.'[2]

The plague of 1625 and 1626, which reportedly killed 1,431 people in Norwich, came at a time when Charles was making heavy financial demands on the city.[3] Late in 1625, after the magistrates had waged a losing battle against the plague and had doubled the poor rate, an appeal was registered with the Privy Council to be exempted from providing a loan.[4] The arrival of a ship-money writ in the spring of the following year came, thus, at a particularly inauspicious moment; the Assembly reacted by preparing a peti-

---

[1] Blomefield, *Norfolk*, III. 366. The wealthier citizens had contributed handsomely to a loan after the failure of the great contract, and apparently they did not desire to be so generous again.

[2] S.P. Dom., James I, 133/15: Mayor, etc. of Norwich to Privy Council, 13 Sept. 1622.

[3] Blomefield, *Norfolk*, III. 373, and A. D. Bayne, *A Comprehensive History of Norwich* (Norwich, 1869), pp. 214–15 provide good descriptions of the plague.

[4] M.C.B. (1624–34), 6 Aug. 1625, 63^r; Blomefield, *Norfolk*, III. 373.

tion to the Privy Council to have the tax eliminated or at least reduced.[1] In January of 1626/7 the city was confronted by the famous forced loan, which was added to the still unpaid ship-money.[2] Again the corporation lamented the impoverished condition of the city, which left them unable to supply even the 1625 assessment.[3] A final effort to escape taxation was made in the spring of 1627: the magistrates brashly suggested that the collection of ship-money was thwarting the collection of the loan, and if the former were removed the latter might be forthcoming.[4] Although ship-money went to Yarmouth whereas the loan went straight to the King's coffers, Charles would accept no excuses: two writs of *quo warranto* were brought against the mayor.[5] Pressed by the Privy Council to return the names of all defaulters, the magistrates did exert pressure on the townsmen to contribute to the loan. Nevertheless, in September almost one-third of the loan remained uncollected.[6]

When the first ship-money writ of the personal rule arrived in November 1634, the Assembly was deeply concerned about 'the weighty consequence of the business' and contemplated a petition.[7] For each of the next six years, in the autumn of each year, the citizens of Norwich were subjected to an additional ship tax. The Crown's request for ship-money, as a temporary levy within the sphere of the royal prerogative, had been transformed into a regular and annual assessment. Yet, loathsome though the tax was initially, the city complied with the levy with appreciably less resistance than in the 1620s.

The first writ generated considerable consternation. The city's

[1] S.P. Dom., Chas. I, 24/44: Deputy-lieutenant of Norfolk to Privy Council, 6 Apr. 1626 and 35/1: Mayor etc, of Norwich to Privy Council, 1 Sept. 1626; *A.P.C.*, Chas. I, 1625–6, pp. 150–1: 31 July 1626; A.B. (1613–42), 24 Aug. 1626, 225ᵛ.

[2] ibid., 2 Jan. 1626/7, 228ʳ; S.P. Dom., Chas. I, 51/1: Commissioners for Loan in Norfolk to Privy Council, 22 Jan. 1626/7. For the forced loan in Norfolk and Norwich see Owens, 'Norfolk', pp. 375–89.

[3] S.P. Dom., Chas. I, 52/3: Mayor and others of Norwich to Privy Council, 30 Jan. 1626/7.

[4] ibid., 61/83: Mayor and others of Norwich to Privy Council, [? Apr.] 1627.

[5] Blomefield, *Norfolk*, III. 374. In 1629 the Courts vindicated the mayor. See William Page, ed., *The Victoria History of the County of Norfolk* (London, 1906), II. 505–6.

[6] M.C.B. (1624–34), 26 May 1627, 139ʳ; S.P. Dom., Chas. I, 68/4: Commissioners for Loan in Norfolk to Privy Council, 14 June 1627; 75/52: same to same, 29 Aug. 1627. Of the total of £1,178, £375 was outstanding.

[7] A.B. (1613–42), 19 Nov. 1634, 310ʳ.

efforts to reduce the tax were not only unsuccessful but Charles actually increased the sum when he found the original assessment insufficient for the specific naval vessel he had in mind.[1] Nevertheless, by June 1635 almost the entire demand had been met and, while the remaining £30 was being gathered in, the second ship-money writ was received.[2] While the leading officials of five Norfolk boroughs co-operated in an effort to reduce the tax, the Norwich Assembly busily prepared its own petition to the Privy Council, complaining that they were forced to bear too high a proportion of the county tax.[3] This time the Privy Council consented to reduce the tax for the city by almost 30 per cent.[4] Even with this alleviation, Mayor Anguish informed Whitehall in February of 1635/6 that only £525 of the £744 had been returned and, owing to decay in trade and increases in the number of poor, he doubted that the citizens would come up with the remainder.[5] Indeed, exclaimed the mayor, 'the burden of this taxation lies so heavy upon this city as gives great occasion to the citizens to complain.' The Crown would not relent any further, and eventually the entire tax was paid.[6]

Despite this early commotion over ship-money, later assessments were calmly tolerated and paid in full in each of the four years following 1635. This is in sharp contrast to the county of Norfolk, where ship-money increasingly became the focus of political discontent between 1635 and 1640.[7] This is quite understandable.

[1] ibid., 19 Nov. and 22 Dec. 1634, 310[r], 311[v]; M.C.B. (1634–46), 20 and 22 Nov. 1634 and 21 Feb. 1634/5, 31[r–v], 32[r], 44[r].

[2] *A.P.C.*, Chas. I, microcard series, 1634–5, p. 463: Privy Council to High Sheriff of Norfolk, 9 Mar. 1634/5; M.C.B. (1634–46), 25 Apr., 24 June, 1 Sept., and 23 Nov. 1635, 52[v], 63[r], 73[v], 83[r]; S.P. Dom., Chas. I, 293/108: Sir John Wentworth, Sheriff of Norfolk, to Privy Council, 14 July 1635. Since ship-money in 1634–5 was required of the municipal corporations but not the county, one immediate problem with the collection was that some citizens left the city to escape the tax. *A.P.C.*, Chas. I, microcard series, 1634–5, pp. 553–4, 621–2: Privy Council to Mayor of Norwich, 5 May 1635; Privy Council to Dean and Chapter of Norwich, 18 June 1635.

[3] M.C.B. (1634–46), 1, 5, and 8 Sept. 1635, 73[v], 74[r], 75[r]; A.B. (1613–42), 3 Sept. 1635, 316[v]; S.P. Dom., Chas. I, 298/15: Memorial presented to Privy Council, 19 Sept. 1635.

[4] S.P. Dom., Chas. I, 301/78: Robert Mellinge to Privy Council, 31 Nov.1635.

[5] ibid., 313/94: Mayor Anguish and others of Norwich to Privy Council, 12 Feb. 1635/6.

[6] In February 1635/6, £525 was returned and the remaining £219 was returned in August 1636. ibid., 314/82: Ship-Money Receipt of 25 Feb. 1635/6 and 330/24: Ship-Money Receipt of 11 Aug. 1636.

[7] See Ketton-Cremer, *Norfolk*, pp. 90–103.

The expressed grievance of the corporation was never the constitutionality of the tax but its apportionment within the county. The city had been reluctant to provide one-third of the ship-money for the county in 1626, claiming that even in periods of prosperity they were incapable of one-twelfth,[1] and their complaints against ship-money in 1636 was that the sheriff of Norfolk had rated Norwich more than twice as high as customary.[2] After 1635 the tax ratio of Norwich to Norfolk was greatly reduced (Table 14). A

TABLE 14: *Ship-Money Assessments, 1634–1639**

		Norwich	Norfolk	% Norwich to Norfolk
1634	November	1,601 ⎫ 1,931	5,500 ⎫ 6,735	—
	February 1634/5	330 ⎭	1,235 ⎭	—
1635	August	1,100 ⎫ 774	8,000 ⎫ 8,000	13·7 ⎫ 9·7
	November	–326 ⎭	0 ⎭	— ⎭
1636	November	500	7,800	6·4
1637	November	400	7,800	5·1
1638	December	150	2,700	5·5
1639	December	400	n.a.	—

*The initial 1634 assessment included only certain corporations of Norfolk and Cambridgeshire and hence no percentage between Norwich and the county of Norfolk is possible for 1634, *H.M.C., 10th Report*, App. 2, Gawdy MSS., pp. 150–1: Mingay to Gawdy, 19 Dec. 1634. The figures for Norfolk are the totals for the entire county, including the corporations. M.C.B. (1634–46), 18 Dec. 1634, 21 Feb. 1634/5, 26 Dec. 1639, 35r-36r, 44r, 267r; S. P. Dom., Chas. I, 298/15: 19 Sept. 1635: 301/78: 13. Nov. 1635; 348/56: 20. Feb. 1636/7; 380/96: [?] Jan. 1637/8; 410/152: [Jan. 1638/9].

second reason given in the early complaints was the economically depressed condition of the city. Apparently the corporation was not merely offering its standard excuse of poverty, for poor harvests

[1] S.P. Dom., Chas. I, 535/158: Petition of Mayor and others of Norwich to Privy Council, n.d. Internal evidence suggests 1626 to be the date of this petition.
[2] ibid., 298/15: Memorial presented to Privy Council, 19 Sept. 1635, and 313/94: Mayor Anguish and others of Norwich to Privy Council, 12 Feb. 1635/6; M.C.B. (1634/46), 8 Sept. 1635, 75r. The Privy Council agreed that the assessment was disproportionate. *A.P.C.*, Chas. I, microcard series, 1635–6, pp. 111–12: Privy Council to High Sheriff of Norfolk, 21 Sept. 1635. Writing to Framlingham Gawdy, Anthony Mingay in Norwich complained: 'I am resolved, if you will take any boarders to come and live with you in the country to save charges, for here I am rated (and not worshipped) like a knight.' *H.M.C., 10th Report*, App. 2, Gawdy MSS., pp. 155–6: Mingay to Gawdy, 1 Dec. 1635.

and high prices in 1630 and 1631 coincided with a recession in the new drapery industry which lasted a full decade after the collapse in 1629.[1] Thirdly, the amount of the assessments was never really severe and each year Norwich paid less. The total assessment of £4,155 over six years was £445 less than the rate collected in 1642 for fortifying the city against Charles, and this was gathered only nine months after the magistrates had repeated the same tale of poverty to be found in the petition of 1635/6.[2] Lastly, the issue of ship-money after 1635 was replaced by a more urgent crisis which completely dominated the affairs of Norwich and split the city into factions. When the mayor suggested in November 1640 that if there were any grievances to be laid before Parliament they should be brought forth immediately, the citizens said nothing about arbitrary government or taxation, but responded with a vehement remonstrance against the 'tyranny and oppression' of Bishop Wren.[3]

*   *   *

Norwich, known to contemporaries as the city of churches, had always been an intensely religious community which for generations had been noted for its Puritan disposition.[4] Nonconformity in the city dates back to pre-Reformation days when Thomas Bilney first came to and then was arrested in Norwich, and it continued through Robert Browne and his sectarian followers.[5] When Archbishop Parker issued orders to punish Puritan ministers in 1574, Elizabeth privately instructed him to commence with Norwich.[6] The essence of Puritanism in Caroline Norwich was a

---

[1] S.P. Dom., Chas. I, 176/1: Mayor, etc. of Norwich to Privy Council, 1 Dec. 1630; 186/26: same to same, 4 Mar. 1630/1; 210/62: Justices of the peace in Norfolk to same, 24 Jan. 1631/2. Charles Wilson, *England's Apprenticeship, 1603–1763* (New York, 1965), pp. 74–5. See also Allen, 'Norwich Merchant Class', pp. 36, 38–9, 47–8.

[2] *C.J.* II. 869: 29 Nov. 1642; M.C.B. (1634–46), 12 Feb. 1641/2, 339ʳ.

[3] A.B. (1613–42), 30 Nov. 1640, 366ʳ; Bodleian Library, Oxford, Tanner MSS., 220, fos. 44, 116, 130, 147.

[4] There were thirty-four parishes, each with its own parish church, in Norwich during the sixteenth and seventeenth centuries. Newcastle, only slightly smaller in population, contained only four parish churches. Roger Howell, Jr., *Newcastle-upon-Tyne and the Puritan Revolution* (Oxford, 1967), p. 70.

[5] See John Browne, *History of Congregationalism and Memorials of the Churches in Norfolk and Suffolk* (London, 1877), pp. 10 ff; *V.C.H.*: *Norfolk*, II. 252–79. The best study of the Puritan movement in Norwich prior to 1640 is Kenneth Shipps, 'Lay Patronage of East Anglian Puritan Clerics in Pre-Revolutionary England' (unpublished Ph.D. thesis, Yale University, 1971), pp. 267–99.

[6] Bayne, *History of Norwich*, p. 243.

zealous religious attitude towards daily life and worship. The devout Puritan demanded strict observance of moral commandments by himself and the community, and he looked to the town magistrates, many of them Puritans like himself, to enforce discipline on errant sinners. The Mayor's Court functioned as a moral policeman: it punished the swearer and the drunkard, kept a vigilant eye on the alehouse, and chastised the gambler, bowler, and idle gamester.[1] Moreover, the aldermen exercised considerable patronage to advowsons and lectureships and, together with the councilmen, passed ordinances regulating religious affairs in the city.[2] In this capacity they passed Sabbatarian legislation in the Assembly and possessed complete authority for enforcing it in the Mayor's Court.[3]

Of all the Puritan concerns, perhaps the most vital was the presence of Puritan preachers.[4] The patronage of Puritan ministers and lecturers, a widespread phenomenon in Puritan-dominated corporations throughout England during the 1630s,[5] had long been a matter of crucial importance to and controversy within the Norwich corporation. In the years before 1620 the magistrates and councilmen possessed control over two lectureships at St. Andrew, one of the most famous nonconformist strongholds in East Anglia since the mid-Elizabethan period, and invariably they had sponsored Puritans.[6] In 1615, for example, an appointee to a lectureship at St. Andrew had been blocked by the bishop of Norwich on the grounds that the nominee 'refused to subscribe to the Articles of Religion and form of Church Government'.[7] Puritan lay patronage entailed not only the appointment but also the subsequent defence

---

[1] For a description of how the Mayor's Court could affect the social life of the community, see Sachse, ed., *Minutes*, pp. 24–9.

[2] A.B. (1613–42), 1615–1640 *passim.*

[3] For the importance of Sabbatarianism to the Puritans of East Anglia see Shipps, 'Lay Patronage', pp. 269–70. Municipal ordinances regarding Sabbatarianism were passed in 1615, 1623, 1629, 1631, and 1640, the most important being those of 1615 and 1629. A.B. (1613–42), 13 Dec. 1615; 26 Feb. 1615/16; 19 Dec. 1623; 12 May 1629; 20 Jan. 1631/2; 29 Sept. 1640; 41^r, 43^r, 185^{r-v}, 253^r, 276^v–278^r. For an example of enforcement see M.C.B. (1615–24), 7 Feb. 1615/16, 54^v.

[4] Paul S. Seaver, *The Puritan Lectureships: The Politics of Religious Dissent 1560–1642* (Stanford, 1970), pp. 4–5, 15–54.

[5] ibid., pp. 88–117.

[6] Shipps, 'Lay Patronage', pp. 267–70.

[7] *A.P.C.*, James I, 1615–16, pp. 147–8, 195–6: 10 May and 9 June 1615; M.C.B. (1615–24) 16 Oct. 1615, 38^r; A.B. (1613–42), 1 Dec. 1615, 40^v.

of Puritan preachers against episcopal interference. It was this issue more than any other which brought the Norwich corporation into conflict with successive bishops of Norwich from 1620 to 1640.

A major confrontation between the city and the Cathedral was occasioned by Bishop Harsnet's attempt to root out nonconformist preachers following his arrival in Norwich in 1619. In 1622 he forbade Sunday morning sermons and lectures in Norwich parishes and ordered parishioners to attend sermons given at the Cathedral. Late in 1623, more than 300 citizens presented a petition to the Mayor's Court against Harsnet lamenting the loss of sermons.[1] Had the mayor disapproved of the Puritan cause, the petition would probably have stopped there, but in 1623 Robert Craske, an ardent Puritan, presided over the Mayor's Court. The citizens' complaints were forwarded to London and ultimately reappeared in the House of Commons under the sponsorship of no less a figure than Sir Edward Coke.[2] Harsnet denied each of six accusations, including the charge that he discouraged preaching, in a meeting of committees for both houses, although his anti-Puritan enterprises earned him the praise of the King in the closing speech of Parliament.[3]

Few sermons were preached in Norwich following Harsnet's suppression of them, although Monday and Friday lectures continued at St. Andrew.[4] In 1627 the magistrates recommended in the Assembly that the corporation support the establishment of Sunday morning sermons in two city parishes at the same time as the Cathedral sermon was delivered; and the councilmen suggested that every preaching minister be encouraged to preach every Sunday in his parish church.[5] This did not result in more Sunday

---

[1] M.C.B. (1615–24), 31 Dec. 1623, 508ᵛ. The original petition with signatories has not survived.

[2] The grievances were enlarged in the Commons to six points: inhibition of preachers on Sunday morning, setting up and blessing of images, punishment of those who refused to pray to the East, punishment of a minister for catechizing his family and singing psalms, extortion, and refusal to register institutions. *C.J.* I, 7 May 1624, 699a–699b.

[3] The affair can be followed in ibid., 7–29 May 1624, 699–715 *passim*; L.J. III. 8–19 May 1624, 362–390 *passim*; *C.S.P.D.*, James I, 1623–5, pp. 238, 246, 249, 252, 265. See also Seaver, *Puritan Lectureships*, p. 115 and Shipp's, 'Lay Patronage', pp. 273–5.

[4] A.B. (1613–42), 14 Oct. 1625, 217ᵛ; M.C.B. (1624–34), 23 Oct. 1624, 18ʳ.

[5] A.B. (1613–42), 26 Nov. 1627, 236ʳ. The councilmen were convinced that many preachers would be more than willing to give sermons for no additional pay.

preaching because of the intransigence of Bishop Harsnet.[1] The
Puritans must have been relieved at the translation of Harsnet to
York and his replacement by Francis White in 1628/9. Supported
by Mayor Thomas Cory, the Puritans took advantage of this
opportunity to launch a Puritan campaign in the city. In May the
magistrates accepted a petition for freedom of preaching within the
city and agreed to present it to White upon his arrival.[2] Simultaneously, the Assembly passed a stiff Sabbatarian ordinance.[3] The
plea for more Sunday preaching fell on deaf ears; until 1636 only
one parish was permitted a morning sermon.[4]

The following year a group of twelve influential Norfolk men,
four of whom were Norwich aldermen, established a corporation
designed to purchase impropriations and advowsons in order to
enlarge the Puritan ministry in the county.[5] Patterned after and in
communication with a similar corporate enterprise in London,[6] the
Norwich feoffees purchased the advowson of St. Peter Hungate
and collected £200 which was sent to their 'prototrustees' in
London; in return, the London Puritans sent William Bridge to
preach at St. Peter Hungate.[7] Shortly after his arrival in Norwich,
Bridge endeavoured to convert the city into the outstanding centre
of Puritan preaching in East Anglia. His most notable success was
the establishment of a combination lectureship involving at least a
dozen county Puritan preachers at St. George Tombland, where
feoffee and alderman John Tooly was patron.[8] Richard Corbet, who
succeeded Bishop White in 1632, wrote sharp satires against the
Puritans but was less inclined to persecute them, and Puritan
preaching flourished in Norwich in the early 1630s.[9] Laud's

---

[1] Tanner MSS., 68, fo. 336.   [2] M.C.B. (1624–34), 23 May 1629, 242ʳ.
[3] A.B. (1613–42), 12 May 1629, 253ʳ.   [4] Tanner MSS., 68, fo. 336.
[5] The Norwich aldermen were Robert Craske, John Tooly, Augustine
Skottow, and Thomas Atkin. S.P. Dom., Chas. I, 531/134: n.d. For the other
eight trustees and their interrelationships see Shipps, 'Lay Patronage', pp. 281–4.
[6] The London feoffees, twelve in number consisting of four merchants, four
lawyers, and four clergymen, were organized in 1625/6 and suppressed by Laud
in 1633. Pearl, *London*, pp. 164 ff; Seaver, *Puritan Lectureships, Passim.*
[7] S.P. Dom., Chas. I, 531/134: n.d.
[8] Shipps, 'Lay Patronage', pp. 285–8. Laud had been informed that the
trustees had set down qualifications for conformity, 'but this only to the eye of
the world', and Bridge was referred to as 'an absurd and turbulent fellow'.
S.P. Dom., Chas. I, 531/134. For Bridge see *D.N.B.*, s.v. William Bridge.
[9] Browne, *Congregationalism*, pp. 81–4 and *D.N.B.*, s.b. Richard Corbett. For
biographical commentary on the bishops of Norwich from 1620 to 1640 see
Ketton-Cremer, *Norfolk*, pp. 51–88.

demand in 1633 for an examination into the state of religion in each diocese, however, did stir Corbet to suspend some lecturers, including Bridge's Friday lectures at St. George Tombland.[1] Four Norwich aldermen, including Tooly and fellow feoffee Augustine Skottow, were sent by the Mayor's Court to inform Corbet that it was the earnest desire of the mayor, recorder, steward, and entire Court of Aldermen that Bridge be restored. Bridge was shortly reinstated upon submission.[2]

Puritan preachers were certainly the biggest bone of contention between the Puritans and the bishops, but there were other issues which contributed in developing bad relations between city and Cathedral. Disputes between town officials and the Dean and Chapter are as old as city-bishoprics themselves, and haggling between the aldermanry and the Dean and Chapter under the episcopacies of Harsnet and Corbet was constant and heated.[3] A legal struggle over land outside the Cathedral walls commenced in 1632 which, owing to the complexity of the matter and the intransigence of both parties, required fourteen months to conclude.[4] Since the corporation rejected all arbitration that did not uphold it completely, ultimately it triumphed. It is interesting to note that the case was decided in favour of the city by Writ of Execution of the Great Seal in the month that Laud was named Archbishop of Canterbury. This issue did not in itself seriously imperil relations between city and Church, nor did the Norwich community in any way reveal open hostility towards Laud's collection for St. Paul's Cathedral,[5] but it must certainly have contributed to the friction.

Nonconformity was rampant in Norwich by 1635 and this was brought to the attention of Archbishop Laud following the metropolitan visitation made by his vicar general, Nathanial Brent.

---

[1] James Bliss and William Scott, eds., *The Works of William Laud* (Oxford, 1847–60), V. 328. Hereafter referred to as Laud, *Works*.

[2] M.C.B. (1634–46), 13 Sept. 1634, 21^r. See also Laud, *Works*, v. 328: The Archbishop's Account of his Province to the King for the year 1634.

[3] N.N.R.O., MSS. of Petition of Bishop Harsnet to the King Against the Encroachment of the Citizens, 1619–1628, n.d.

[4] N.N.R.O., MSS. on Differences between the Dean and Chapter and the City, 1630s. See also M.C.B. (1624–34), 1633 *passim* and A.B. (1613–42), 1632–3, *passim*.

[5] M.C.B. (1624–34), 30 Sept. 1633, and 19 Mar. 1633/4, 450^r, 472^r; (1634–46), 29 Nov. 1634, 32^v. A.B. (1613–42), 22 Sept. 1634, 305^r. Puritans in London could and did contribute to Laud's collection for St. Paul's in good conscience. Pearl, *London*, p. 161.

The mayor and his brethren did not bother to welcome the vicar general upon his arrival; indeed Brent believed they had deliberately snubbed him and he had to admonish a number of magistrates for walking indecently in the Cathedral during prayer time.[1] The entire diocese was becoming so delinquent that a strong bishop, a man Laud could fully trust, was urgently needed to enforce discipline.[2] The Archbishop seized the opportunity provided by Corbet's death to have Matthew Wren translated from Hereford to Norwich in November 1635. A better man to carry out Laud's ecclesiastical designs in the Norwich diocese could not have been found in all of England.[3]

Wren's attack on Puritanism in the city in 1636 was swift and decisive on three fronts. The first move was to crack down on the leading lay Puritans, especially those in the magistracy. Bishop Harsnet's attempts to limit drastically the number of Sunday morning sermons had resulted in the Puritans postponing sermons until Sunday afternoon. Wren's solution was to require all ministers to give sermons and homilies on Sunday morning so that the afternoon would be free for catechizing, and then to compel all the magistrates to attend the Cathedral service and sermon every Sunday morning.[4] King Charles expressed his approval of this scheme in a letter to the Norwich corporation in March: he ordered the magistrates to attend these Cathedral services, and even went so far as to command that his personally-signed letter be entered among the acts and ordinances of the city.[5] Later in the same month, Wren stormed down on the nonconformist clergy: eight Norwich ministers, including the notorious Bridge, were

[1] The metropolitical visitation was conducted in Norwich on 6, 7, 8 April 1635. Brent also suspected a number of ministers of nonconformity, but could prove nothing against them. S.P. Dom., Chas. I, 292/128: 16 July 1635.

[2] Laud had remarked in 1635/6 that 'the whole diocese is out of order'. Laud, *Works*, V. 334. On the necessity for a strong bishop, see S.P. Dom., Chas. I, 297/33: Archbishop Laud to Queen of Bohemia, 11 Sept. 1635. Corbet died on 28 July 1635, and Wren was appointed on 10 November 1635.

[3] For the close relationship between Laud and Wren, see Peter King, 'Bishop Wren and the Suppression of the Norwich Lecturers', *Historical Journal*, XI. 2 (1968), 239.

[4] Tanner MSS., 137, fo. 7: Wren to Clement Corbet, Chancellor of Norwich, 6 Mar. 1635/6. Laud states that sermons were given in only four churches on Sunday mornings. Laud, *Works*, V. 339–40. Wren later utilized this demand to defend himself from the accusation that he opposed sermons. Tanner MSS., 68, fo. 340.

[5] S.P. Dom., Chas. I, 316/18: King to Mayor, Sheriffs, Aldermen, etc. of Norwich, 14 Mar. 1635/6. M.C.B. (1634–46), 23 Mar. 1635/6, 97ᵛ–98ʳ.

suspended.[1] Lastly, Wren carried out a strict and detailed visitation in May 1636 designed to enforce uniformity and conformity of worship in the parish churches.[2]

Stunned by the effectiveness of Wren's vigorous assault, the Puritans of Norwich were slow in developing organized reaction. The traditional measure was first tried: as in 1623 and 1629, the Puritans resorted to the device of a formal petition. A first remonstrance to Bishop Wren, approved by the Assembly and presented by the mayor and aldermen in July, was apparently ignored, for in August the Puritans were busy formulating a strong petition against Wren to be delivered directly to either Laud or King Charles.[3] The Puritans needed to have their petition approved by the Assembly in order for it to be sent up in the name of the corporation of Norwich, but a majority in the Mayor's Court thought this action was too drastic. In the opinion of most aldermen, the more judicious approach would be a delegation of aldermen to Bishop Wren.[4] Two opposed groups were formed by the end of August: a minority of the magistrates, headed by Mayor Thomas Baker, strongly supported the Puritan petition, but a majority of aldermen adamantly opposed a petition addressed to the Crown. The result was a split within the ruling class of the city which prepared the way for the bitter party politics of the 1640s.

When it was clear to the Puritans early in September that Wren had no intention of relenting and that a majority of the aldermen were not sympathetic to their grievances, Mayor Baker, Town

---

[1] *H.M.C., 10th Report*, App. 2, Gawdy MSS., p. 158: Anthony Mingay to Framlingham Gawdy, 26 Mar. 1636, p. 158. See also Tanner MSS. 220, fo. 1 and 68, fo. 338. For lists of suspended clergy see Tanner MSS. 68, fo. 155 and 314, fo. 181; Brit. Lib., Pamphlets, E. 168 (24); Matthew Wren, *Parentalia* (1750), pp. 74–100. For secondary accounts consult D. W. Boorman, 'The Dioceses of Norwich and Ely Under Wren' (unpublished B. Litt. thesis, Oxford University, 1957); H. A. Lloyd Jukes, 'Bishop Matthew Wren and the nonconforming ministers of the Diocese of Norwich', *History Studies*, I. 2 (October, 1968), 13–2p; Shipps, 'Lay Patronage', pp. 289–93.

[2] Wren's visitation lasted from 2 May to 30 June. King, 'Bishop Wren', pp. 240–1. The injunctions, dated 1 May 1636, may be found in Tanner MSS., 137, fo. 9. See also *H.M.C., 10th Report*, App. 2, Gawdy MSS., p. 158: Mingay to Gawdy, 3 May 1636; Ketton-Cremer, *Norfolk*, pp. 63–5.

[3] A.B. (1613–42), 24 July 1636, 326^v; M.C.B. (1634–46), 15 Aug. 1636, 120^v.

[4] ibid.

Clerk King, and several aldermen met privately and plotted secret strategy.[1] The situation was rather desperate. Their only hope was to manage somehow to persuade the Assembly to approve the Puritan petition, and the next meeting on 21 September to swear in new sheriffs afforded the best opportunity. There was no way, however, of getting a majority of the aldermen, who determined privately the agenda of every Assembly meeting immediately before the Assembly was convened, to consent to such a procedure. Indeed, this had already been tried in August and the greater part of the aldermanry not only strongly opposed the presentation of a Puritan petition to the Assembly but also refused to believe the accusations against Wren contained in it.[2]

On 21 September the aldermen met as usual before the Assembly was convened and a routine agenda was approved. The non-Puritan aldermen, however, must have realized that something was amiss the moment they stepped from the Mayor's Court to the Assembly chamber. 'We had a very great assembly the like I never before saw', exclaimed Alderman Lane.[3] So many councilmen were present that many aldermen later suspected the Puritans of surreptitiously gathering them together for the occasion.[4] After all, was this not to be a routine meeting? Suddenly Mayor Baker pulled a petition similar to the earlier Puritan petition from his pocket and gave it to the town clerk to read.[5] Several aldermen objected strenuously and demanded their right to examine the petition and its signatories. Mayor Baker denied their request on the curious grounds that the petition was addressed to him personally and not to the aldermen. Furious debate followed, but in the end the Puritan-dominated Assembly passed a sweeping resolution:

[1] Tanner MSS., 68, fo. 159: William Allanson to Bishop Wren, [13–20] Sept. 1636. Allanson, curate at St. Mary, served as Wren's informer throughout the affair.

[2] ibid., 68, fos. 151, 152: Certain of the Aldermen of Norwich to Bishop Wren, 17 Oct. 1636. This petition, which was read before the magistrates, was reportedly signed by over 120 citizens and has since been lost.

[3] ibid., 68, fo. 149: Alderman Henry Lane to Wren, 14 Oct. 1636.

[4] ibid., 68, fos. 151, 152: Aldermen to Wren, 17 Oct. 1636. Fifty-three of the sixty councilmen were in attendance.

[5] The town clerk, Henry King, was deeply involved in the Puritan movement and had acted as agent for the twelve trustees of Norfolk. S.P. Dom., Chas. I, 531/134. See also Tanner MSS., 68, fos. 147, 159, 162.

It is agreed that a petition shall be exhibited to the King's Majesty and to the Lord Archbishop or to one or both of them to such purpose or effect as in the petition of the citizens and inhabitants made to Mr. Mayor and other magistrates of this city as mentioned.[1]

This was nothing less than a mandate for Puritan Mayor Baker and his associates of similar disposition to compose a petition to their own liking and forward it to the King in the name of the Norwich corporation.

The constitutional implications of this Assembly meeting involve two separate but closely related issues: the right of the councilmen to have their votes counted separately from the magistrates, and the right of the magistrates to cast a veto over Assembly transactions. Ancient charters required 'the assent of the said sixty of them [councilmen]' for approval of ordinances,[2] and in 1620 the councilmen had successfully prevented a mingling of votes on a proposed election ordinance. In 1628 the capacity of magistrates to vote on matters brought before the Assembly came up again.[3] Charters were produced, from which it was noted that the councilmen 'shall have such powers and authority as the councillors elected for the Common Council of London have there'.[4] The mayor then wrote a letter to London and the reply was that 'if the mayor, sheriffs, and aldermen can by their votes make the minor part the major, that then they may lawfully make an act, pass a lease, or constitute an officer . . .'[5] Consequently, the votes of councilmen and magistrates were mingled and the power of the magistrates was extended. Since all matters presented to the Assembly required the prior approval of the magistrates, the issue of aldermanic veto would appear moot. The unprecedented aspect of the September Assembly was that the Puritan petition had not and would not have received prior consent by the aldermen. Since the petition was improperly presented, the 1628 decision came into play and all that was needed for passage was the concurrence of a majority of councilmen and aldermen voting together. The ming-

---

[1] A.B. (1613–42), 21 Sept. 1636, 327ᵛ. Only six aldermen voted in favour of the petition. Tanner MSS., 70, fo. 104: Wren to Laud, 20 Nov. 1636. The number of aldermen present and how they voted is unknown.

[2] *C.C.R.* VI (1462–3), 147.

[3] N.N.R.O., Liber Albus, 20 May 1628, p. 145.

[4] *C.C.R.* VI (1462/3), 146.

[5] Cf. Pearl, *London*, p. 57. By this convoluted form of constitutional reasoning, if the London Common Council passed out of existence, then the Norwich Common Council would need to do likewise.

ling of votes deprived the aldermen of an independent veto. In effect, therefore, Mayor Baker stripped the aldermen of their legislative capacity altogether.

Tension in the aldermanry growing out of the 21 September meeting mounted, but Mayor Baker and the Puritan aldermen pressed forward with their plans. The precise content of the first two petitions is not known, but it is certain that the major grievance was Wren's treatment of ministers and lecturers.[1] At least Wren was so informed by William Allanson, his agent in Norwich who said: 'the silly Puritan mayor, and some others of that strain, are very earnest still to present their petition unto his Majesty in the behalf of some irregular ministers, who would be counted conformable'.[2] By October the opposition to the Puritans had lined up behind Alderman Henry Lane. When rumours spread through the city that John Carter, minister of St. Peter Mancroft, would present a petition to Charles in the name of the corporation,[3] Lane challenged the mayor openly in the Mayor's Court. If the petition were sent to the Crown in the name of the corporation, and if the aldermen were not permitted to see it before it was sent, Lane threatened that he would sponsor a counter-petition to the King disclaiming all knowledge of or participation in the Puritan petition.[4] It was a futile effort and Lane was treated roughly for his discourteousness to the mayor. On 13 October Aldermen Tooly and Shipdham left the city with the petition.[5] True to his word, Lane and nine other aldermen hastily penned a letter of support to Bishop Wren, in which they utterly disowned the petition.[6]

The petition itself is a curious document.[7] The central issue was that Wren had deprived the city of at least five or six conformable

[1] Tanner MSS., 68, fo. 159.

[2] ibid., 68, fo. 147: Allanson to Wren, 8 Oct. 1636. Allanson had been appointed vicar of South Walsham St. Mary by the Norwich Mayor's Court in 1630. M.C.B. (1624–34), 4 Aug. 1630, 196r; 26 Oct. 1632, 407r. Allanson resigned this post in 1632 and in 1636 was curate of St. Mary parish.

[3] ibid., Allanson suggested that Wren call Carter to account for the oath of canonical obedience.

[4] Tanner MSS., 68, fo. 149: Alderman Lane to Wren, 14 Oct. 1636; See also ibid., 68, fos. 151, 152.

[5] ibid.

[6] ibid., 68, fo. 153: Certain of the Aldermen of Norwich to Bishop Wren, 17 October 1636.

[7] The original petition with signatories is unfortunately non-existent. A copy of the grievances, in the hand of Matthew Wren, may be found in ibid., 68, fos. 160, 161.

preaching ministers and three weekly sermons, and that the sermons which remained were carefully restricted. In consequence, many wealthy citizens had left the city and others would depart in the future, leaving behind multitudes of poor people whom they had previously employed. Moreover, the number of indictments of popish recusants at the Quarter Sessions had jumped from three or four to some twenty per session, suggesting that popery had been on the increase since Wren's arrival in Norwich. The number of ministers actually forced out by Wren was and still is debatable, although the number of deprivations and departures was greater than at any time since Elizabeth's reign.[1] In response, Wren's supporters claimed that the persecution of refractory clergy was of great benefit to the city since they held dangerous doctrine; that the impoverishment of the poor was caused by plague in London resulting in economic hardship in Norwich and not by emigration from the city; and that it would have been better for the city if those who did leave had left sooner. Finally, the increase in Catholic indictments was attributed to Wren's diligence in tracking down recusants.[2]

Even after the petition had been sent, the Puritan magistrates continued to hold clandestine meetings. Bitter feeling persisted among the aldermen.[3] Throughout the entire affair the Puritan aldermen maintained contact with Ipswich Puritans, who were undergoing the same calamities and were preparing their own petition; and these dealings seemed dangerously conspiratorial to Wren's supporters. The bishop's informer observed that 'for our Norwich Puritans, though they be more civil, yet they are as malicious, and more crafty, than those of Ipswich'.[4] The fate of the Puritan petition was predictable. The King accepted it in Newmarket, whereupon he personally gave Wren his complete support

---

[1] Apparently eight Puritan ministers were driven from the city and four of the five regular weekday lecturers were silenced by 1637. Shipps, 'Lay Patronage', pp. 290–1.

[2] Tanner MSS., 68, fos. 147, 157, 159. For Wren's handling of recusancy in Norwich see K. J. Lindley, 'The Lay Catholics of England in the Reign of Charles I', *Journal of Ecclesiastical History*, xxii. 3 (July 1971), 209.

[3] Secret sessions were held at the homes of Town Clerk King and Alderman Craske, where they put strong pressure on moderates to join them. Tanner MSS., 68, fo. 162: Allanson to Wren, 24 Oct. 1636; *H.M.C., 10th Report*, App. 2, Gawdy MSS.: Mingay to Gawdy, 19 Oct. 1636.

[4] Tanner MSS., 68, fo. 162: Allanson to Wren, 24 Oct. 1636. For Wren's problems with Ipswich see Shipps, 'Lay Patronage', pp. 243–66.

for a continuation of the conformity campaign in Norfolk.[1] Indeed, upon learning from Laud that Bridge had left Norwich for Holland, Charles noted dryly, 'Let him go; we are well rid of him'.[2] By the end of the year Wren had also received the written support of fourteen Norwich ministers: a split in the clergy ran parallel to the split in the laity.[3]

Laud was overjoyed with Wren's success in 1636, although it took several more years to achieve even an outward appearance of conformity.[4] In several churches there were long delays before altar rails were erected,[5] and Puritan practices persisted in many parishes until detected and suppressed.[6] The Norwich corporation was successful in restoring John Carter, a popular minister with Puritan tendencies, to his cure at St. Peter Mancroft,[7] but they received a set-back in the protracted struggle over ministers' maintenance which was decided against them by the arbitration of the King.[8] Another discouraging note was the departure of Puritan Alderman Thomas Atkin in 1637 following his election as sheriff of London.[9] By the ordinance of 1620, Atkin was next in

[1] Tanner MSS., 68, fo. 104: Wren to Laud, 20 Nov. 1636.

[2] Laud, *Works*, V. 339.

[3] Tanner MSS., 68, fo. 164.

[4] Laud wrote to Charles: 'If this account [of Norwich diocese], given by my Lord of Norwich be true, as I believe it is, . . . he hath deserved very well of the Church of England, and hath been very ill rewarded for it.' Laud, *Works*, V. 341.

[5] Altar rails were constructed in St. Andrew only after considerable resistance, and rails were not installed in St. Peter Mancroft until after 1639. Tanner MSS., 68, fos. 8, 10: Corbet to Wren, 9 June and 17 Nov. 1637. See *East Anglian : Notes and Queries*, III (1866–8), 251–4. The importance of the location of the communion table and of altar rails as symbolic of the differences between Laud and the Puritans is discussed in John Campbell, 'The Quarrel over the Communion Table', *Historical Magazine of the Protestant Episcopal Church*, XL, no. 2 (June 1971), 173–183.

[6] Tanner MSS., 68, fo. 240.

[7] ibid., 68, fo. 1; *H.M.C., 10th Report*, App. 2, Gawdy MSS., pp. 158, 161–2, 163, 169; A.B. (1613–42), 13 Dec. 1639, 356ʳ.

[8] The ministers, supported by the bishop, desired tithes of 2s. 6d. in the £ according to rates and values of all houses, whereas the corporation preferred a system of voluntary contribution. A.B. (1613–42), 27 Nov. 1637, 2 and 31 Jan. 1637/8, 16 Mar. 1637/8, 336ᵛ, 337ᵛ, 338ʳ, 342ʳ; M.C.B. (1634–46), 22 Nov. 1637, 21 and 23 Dec. 1637, 26 Jan. 1637/8, 192ʳ, 194ᵛ, 196ʳ, 197ᵛ; *Privy Council Register, Facsimiles*, II (1637–8), 524–5: 21 Jan. 1637/8; III (1638), 61–4: 1 Apr. 1638; Humphrey Prideaux, *An Award of Charles I* (London, 1707).

[9] Atkin had been a leading promoter of the 1636 petition and he was described in 1637 as one of the two 'notorious undertakers for the schismatical faction', who encouraged parishioners not to approach the altar rails. Tanner MSS., 68, fos. 6, 8. Atkin later became Lord Mayor of London. See Pearl, *London*, pp. 311–13.

line to be mayor of Norwich in 1638 and the corporation challenged the legality of London's selection.[1] The corporation lost the
case, but Atkin expressed pleasure at leaving the city since, to his
mind, so many citizens of Norwich were being persecuted for
violating the bishop's orders and because there was so little good
preaching left in the city.[2] Possibly the same reasoning lay behind
Thomas Baker's decision to reside outside Norwich, until ordered
to return by the Mayor's Court.[3] The Puritan movement had
reached its nadir. On the basis of reports sent to him by Bishop
Montague, who replaced Wren in May 1638, Archbishop Laud
proudly informed Charles in 1639 that the diocese of Norwich was
'as quiet, uniform, and conformable as any in the kingdom, if not
more'.[4]

*   *   *

The Puritan movement in Norwich exhibited considerable political
strength in the 1620s and 1630s. This was most evident in the
ability of the Puritans to obtain the official intercession of the
Mayor's Court and Assembly in the defence of Puritan preachers.
In 1623, 1627, 1629, and 1634 the city government decisively
committed itself to the protection of the godly cause. Nevertheless,
the corporation was powerless if opposed by both Church and
Crown, as the episode with Bishop Harsnet demonstrates. When in
1636 the entreaties from the Mayor's Court to Bishop Wren were
ignored and the corporation's petition to King Charles proved a
futile last resort, the Puritans had little choice but to endure the
persecution as best they could. The movement was crippled but
not destroyed; it awaited an opportunity to take the offensive.
Unfortunately, it is not possible to determine with accuracy either
the number or the identity of the Puritans within the city, nor the
extent to which they operated as a political bloc in municipal
elections during the 1630s. Nor is there extant correspondence
among Puritan activists which might shed light on their organization, activities, and tactics. Given these limitations, observations

---

[1] A.B. (1613–42), 2 June 1637, 24 Feb. 1637/8, 18 June 1638, 335ʳ, 339ᵛ, 345ʳ;
M.C.B. (1634–46), 30 May and 6 June 1637, 162ʳ, 163ᵛ; *Privy Council Register:
Facsimilies*, I (1637), 77–8: 23 June 1637.

[2] *C.S.P.D.*, Chas I, 1637, pp. 218–19, 15 June 1637. Atkin also had a grievance against the lord lieutenant for Norfolk, who committed him for refusing to
appear at the Norwich musters in 1635. *A.P.C.*, Chas. I, microcard series,
1635–6, pp. 69–70: 29 July 1635; see also p. 101: King Charles to Privy Council,
24 Aug. 1635.

[3] M.C.B. (1634–46), 13 Mar. 1638/9, 239ᵛ.   [4] Laud, *Works* V. 364.

regarding the strength of the movement must necessarily be sketchy.

The leadership of the Puritan faction had clearly been provided by men within the Court of Aldermen. They supported efforts to bring Puritan preachers to the city and were prepared to use their office to defend them against episcopal intervention. The wealthy rulers of the city may well have been hard-headed, cautious, and conservative shopkeepers preoccupied with the economic prosperity of the community, but the Puritans among them were not willing to confine their religious proclivities to moral determinations delivered in cases brought before the Mayor's Court.[1] If the occasion required, as in 1636, the religious imperative was more important to them than the awareness that their actions would precipitate a conflict within the ruling class, destroy all hope of harmonious ties with the bishop of Norwich, and even imperil relations with Whitehall. Their weakness was that their numbers did not match their zeal. Although there were never fewer than half a dozen Puritans in the Court of Aldermen throughout the 1630s, they were always in the minority. Correspondence concerning the petition of 1636 identifies only eight active Puritan aldermen, whereas the two counter-petitions supporting Wren were signed by ten others.[2] The remaining six were either moderates or their religious preference is unknown, although some must have sided against the Puritans in withholding the petition from the Assembly. Moreover, in the years following 1636 the ranks of the known anti-Puritans increased at the expense of the unknown and moderate aldermen, whereas the number of known Puritans remained steady (Table 15).

The Puritan interest was more strongly represented in the Common Council. The vote on the Puritan petition in the Assembly session of 21 September 1636 is not known, but there must have been a Puritan majority in order for the measure to pass. Moreover, all but a few of the sixty councilmen were in attendance. Elections to the Council were held yearly, but the turnover during

[1] Sachse, ed., *Minutes*, p. 53. Sachse's interpretation is perhaps due to his total neglect of the 1636 petition controversy.

[2] This is according to the testimony of Bishop Wren, who examined the 1636 petition and observed the signatures of six aldermen on it. Tanner MSS., 70, fo. 104. On the basis of correspondence to Wren concerning the petition, the six aldermen were probably Thomas Atkin, John Tooly, Robert Craske, Thomas Baker, Thomas Shipdham, and Thomas Cory.

TABLE 15: *Religious Preference of Aldermen as of each September, 1633–1640**

	Anti-Puritan and future Royalist	Puritan and future Parliamentarian	Moderate or unknown
1633	8	8	8
1634	9	8	7
1635	9	8	7
1636	10	8	6
1637	11	8	5
1638	11	9	4
1639	12	8	4
1640	12	8	4

*Details concerning the religious stance of Norwich aldermen during the 1630s may be found in Evans, 'Political Elite of Norwich', pp. 109, 118–19, 484–515.

the 1630s was not significant and thus it is likely that there was a Puritan majority throughout the decade.[1] The collective will of the councilmen was not necessarily the same as that of the freemen of the city and the degree to which Puritanism had spread among townsmen prior to 1640 remains conjectural. Certainly there must have been many more Puritans in Norwich than the 120 to 140 people who reportedly put their names to the first petition against Wren.[2] A more impressive indication of Puritan strength in the city at large would come with the election of representatives for the Short Parliament and their success here suggests that in 1640 a majority of the politically-active citizens in Norwich were Puritans or at least willing to follow the Puritan lead.

The events of the 1620s and 1630s demonstrate that the promotion and protection of the Puritan movement in the city hinged on the diligent efforts of Puritan officeholders. Certainly this fact must have been more than evident to contemporaries. It thus follows that the election of Puritans to the Council and magistracy would be of paramount concern to the Puritans, and that some form of organized party machinery would be developed to achieve this end, which apparently occurred in Newcastle, for example.[3]

[1] Thirty-six of the councilmen of 1636 were councilmen in 1630 and thirty-four were councilmen in 1640. In no year during the 1630s were more than ten new councilmen elected and the average was 4·6 new councilmen per year.

[2] Tanner MSS., 68, fo. 159: Allanson to Wren, [13–19] Sept. 1636.

[3] Howell, *Newcastle*, pp. 107–8.

There is, however, no evidence that this was the case in Norwich. There is not even the slightest hint in any of the correspondence or records of an organized Puritan electoral strategy, or of contested elections in which religion played a role. Except in years of crisis, such as 1623 and 1636, Puritanism quite possibly did not seem to be a major issue in a town which passed Sabbatarian legislation with some regularity and which already maintained a stable of Puritan preachers. The absence of a political party structured to organize the nomination of predetermined candidates and mobilize electoral support, which itself cannot be proved, still allows for the possibility that Puritans voted consistently for Puritans before all other candidates whenever the opportunity arose. If religious considerations were a decisive factor in elections, then corresponding patterns should exist between the religious views of the various electorates and the men elected by them.

The annual election of sheriffs was the key to control of the corporation. The 1620 ordinance had established this office as the prerequisite for promotion to the Court of Aldermen, and the freemen and aldermen must have been aware that the vast majority of sheriffs would become aldermen within a decade after completing their one-year term of office.[1] Since the nomination and election of mayors was determined solely by seniority, the shrievalty elections were the only occasion upon which the entire body of freemen gathered to elect a magistrate and, similarly, the only opportunity the magistracy had to influence the future membership of their body. If religion was a factor in municipal elections during the 1630s, it should have been manifested here. The evidence suggests that it was not.

The sheriffs elected by the freemen provide no consistency in their religious and political behaviour. Puritans and future Parliament supporters Thomas Atkin, Adrian Parmenter, and Matthew Peckover as well as anti-Puritans and future Royalists John Daniel, William Gostlyn, Thomas Carver, and John Croshold were all elected to the shrievalty from 1627 to 1637. For their part, the magistrates selected two Puritans and future Roundheads, a

---

[1] Sixteen of the twenty-two sheriffs elected between 1626 and 1637 were elected aldermen before 1640. Sheriffs Robert Palgrave, Robert Thompson, and Richard Keepis never became aldermen, but Palgrave died the year after he had served as sheriff.

moderate, and a future Royalist.[1] Religion was clearly not the all-important factor in the minds of all electors, freemen and aldermen alike, in all of the elections. On the other hand, it may well have been the primary concern of some sectors of each of the two electorates. That is, if neither Puritans nor anti-Puritans possessed a majority, the final determination would be made by moderates, who might base their decision on criteria which were not religious in nature. This might explain why the magistrates as a body voted to prevent the presentation of the Puritan petition to the Assembly and yet could elect two Puritan sheriffs within the following three years.

The remaining electorates consisted of the freemen of the four wards voting separately for councilmen and aldermen. It is not possible to ascertain the geographical distribution of Puritan free-men within the city. However, in an account of parishes which conducted improper Sunday services in early 1636, eight of the ten listed were located in the wards of Wymer and Over-the-Water.[2] A year later Wren was notified of six parishes 'most out of order'; five were in Wymer and the sixth was in Over-the-Water.[3] The bulk of the Puritan leadership during the 1630s was also resident in these two wards. Moreover, it will be demonstrated in Chapter IV that when the Civil War polarized the city into rival parties, the inhabitants of these wards supported the Parliament side whereas the townsmen of Mancroft and Conesford were predominately moderate or Royalist. The religious viewpoint of the vast majority of councilmen in the 1630s remains unknown. However, most of the councilmen elected for Wymer and Over-the-Water during the 1630s later supported Parliament during the Civil War, whereas the councilmen elected for Mancroft and Conesford in the 1630s for the most part became moderates and Royalists.[4] Not all the

[1] They were Livewell Sherwood, Henry Watts, John Lombe, and John Osborne respectively. There is no correlation between the religious outlook of the mayor and the sheriffs elected by the magistrates. On the very day that Mayor Baker antagonized many of his brethren by presenting the Puritan petition to the Assembly, the magistrates swore in Sheriff John Freeman, who opposed the petition.

[2] Tanner MSS., 68, fo. 37: n.d., but clearly before Wren's purge.

[3] The parishes were St. Andrew, St. Helen, St. Benedict, St. Peter Hungate, St. Michael at Plea in Wymer and St. Clement in Over-the-Water. Tanner MSS., 68, fo. 120: R. Gamon, G. Cocke, and W. Allanson to Bishop Wren, 9 June 1637.

[4] See Chapter IV, Table 15.

adherents to the parliamentary cause in the Civil War were
Puritans; thus the conclusion that the wards of Wymer and Over-
the-Water were predominately Puritan during the 1630s and
elected to the Council men who were for the most part Puritan
must remain a conjecture with a high degree of probability. On the
other hand, since Puritans invariably supported Parliament during
the Civil War, only a minority of the freemen in Mancroft and
Conesford could have been Puritans and only a small fraction of
the councilmen elected by them could have been Puritan.

With the passage of the election by-law of 1627/8, the freeman
ward electorates were permitted to choose aldermen from among
the two existing sheriffs and all ex-sheriffs. Not once in the following twelve years was the senior ex-sheriff elected.[1] William
Allanson, Bishop Wren's informer in Norwich, was sensitive to the
important consequences of the election of Puritan aldermen and
instructed Wren to observe which ex-sheriffs as well as which
aldermen had joined the August petition of 1636.[2] It would
indeed be surprising if the townsmen were not similarly concerned.
If they were, however, it was only to a limited extent manifested at
the polls. The desire to choose a man of appropriate social stature
and a resident of their own ward was deemed a higher priority.[3] As
a consequence, the wards of Wymer and Over-the-Water did not
consistently elevate anti-Puritans and future Cavaliers.[4] The
freemen of Wymer elected either a resident Puritan or, none being
available, the resident ex-sheriff least inclined to take a hard line
against Puritanism. The Mancroft freemen on each of three
occasions selected the resident ex-sheriff who was least inclined to
support the Puritans. In 1637 the freemen of Over-the-Water
were presented with eligible ex-sheriffs of both religious factions
and chose a man who had strongly opposed the Puritan petition of

[1] A detailed examination of the twenty-one aldermanic elections from 1627
to 1640 may be found in Evans, 'Political Elite of Norwich', pp. 107–17.

[2] Tanner MSS., 68, fo. 159: Allanson to Wren, [13–19] Sept. 1636.

[3] After 1632 the freemen elected an ex-sheriff living in their own ward whenever possible with only one exception. The 1415 Composition prescribed that
freemen should confine their selection to men of their own ward unless 'there be
no so many sufficient in the same ward'. 'Composition of 1415', in Hudson and
Tingey, eds., *Records*, I. 97. This clause allows for subjective interpretation, but
apparently was honoured when possible.

[4] For example, of the five aldermen elected for Over-the-Water, two were
active anti-Puritans and a third was a moderate; and the Wymer freemen
elected two anti-Puritans and future Royalists in 1638.

the preceding year. And the freemen of Conesford exhibited a complete indifference to the religious persuasions of the eligible candidates.

*   *   *

In retrospect, the Puritans of Norwich did not constitute a socially, religiously, or politically radical movement and the breakdown of harmony between the customary authorities of Crown, Church, and corporation which occurred in the city between 1620 and 1640 was not precipitated by them. As a group of religiously motivated individuals, they were united in their concern for the establishment of and support for a Puritan ministry, their defiance of certain Anglican forms of worship, their desire to preserve the purity of the Sabbath, and their aspiration to construct the godly community. As early as the 1570s, ministers and magistrates in Norwich had managed to circumvent strict episcopal control and had created a local Puritan church responsive to their needs.[1] By the 1620s, Puritanism was a socially respectable movement with deep roots and its leaders were among the town's élite. The Puritan laity revealed no hostility towards either Whitehall or Canterbury and there is no evidence that they advocated the collapse of the ecclesiastical hierarchy prior to the Civil War. Indeed, it would seem that their only demand of the Church after 1620 was that it continue to permit them to pursue their goals in Norwich peacefully and without interference. From this perspective, the desire of the magistrates and corporation to preserve local religious autonomy was in keeping with their tradition-oriented mentality. On the other hand, in a broader sense such local autonomy might be construed as a subversive challenge to the existent Church structure, a viewpoint which Laud and Wren shared and perhaps rightfully so. In the final analysis, however, the roots of the political and religious unrest of the 1630s lay not so much in the innovations and agitations of militant Puritans as in an aggressive episcopal effort to extirpate an already entrenched Puritanism.[2]

---

[1] Patrick Collinson, *The Elizabethan Puritan Movement* (London, 1967), *passim*.

[2] This argument, which sees Charles, Laud, and Wren and not the Puritans as the true religious revolutionaries of the 1630s, consorts with a recent interpretation of Arminianism and Puritanism. See Nicholas Tyacke, 'Puritanism, Arminianism, and Counter-Revolution', in Conrad Russell, ed., *The Origins of the English Civil War* (London, 1973), pp. 119–43. See also Austin Woolrych, 'Puritanism, Politics, and Society', in E. W. Ives, ed., *The English Revolution 1600–1660* (London, 1968), pp. 87–92.

Prior to 1640, Puritanism was not a politically-oriented movement, yet its fortunes were linked to city government. During
years of episcopal tolerance—that is, within the context of local
autonomy—the presence of Puritan magistrates and a sympathetic
corporation was of great utility in sponsoring Puritan lectureships
and in enacting and enforcing local ordinances regulating the
desired moral and social behaviour. Although lacking a majority
in the Court of Aldermen, the Puritans apparently had no difficulty
in obtaining the endorsement of the corporation to peculiarly
Puritan initiatives before 1636, such as passing Sabbatarian legislation and bringing a fire-eater of the calibre of William Bridge to
Norwich. The connection between local Puritanism and the town
government was increased when Puritan practices became the
target of crusading bishops. Confronted with these assaults, the
Puritans appealed successfully to the magistrates and corporation
for protection as well as for sponsorship. First, a delegation of
magistrates would be sent to intercede with the bishop and then, if
this approach proved fruitless, the corporation would forward a
petition enumerating Puritan grievances to the national government. This policy was resorted to in 1615, 1623, and 1634; and the
same approach was adopted in 1636.

The uncompromising severity of Wren's persecution and the
subsequent petition against the bishop resulted in a crisis within
the corporation. The cohesion of the magistracy buckled. The non-
Puritan magistrates who had previously acquiesced to Puritan
measures were left to choose between local custom and established
ecclesiastical authority in the person of Wren; either they retired
temporarily to the sidelines, or they joined Wren's camp. The
Puritans were left with only a determined hard-core minority in the
Court of Aldermen supported by an overwhelming number in the
Common Council. Nevertheless, the extent to which Puritanism
became politicized was limited in the years immediately following
1636. Apparently no concerted effort was made to develop a
political party apparatus to facilitate the election of Puritan
magistrates, alter electoral procedures to allow greater advantage
for Puritan candidates, or force their opposition from office. The
most plausible explanation for this is that the thrust of local Puritan
animosity was directed against Wren and not against non-Puritan
magistrates who in less intimidating circumstances had demonstrated a willingness to accept Puritan measures. Moreover, there

was nothing a fully Puritan magistracy could have done to halt or even mitigate Wren's persecution given the intransigence of the Crown and the absence of Parliament.

By 1640 the plight of the Puritans was urgent. The unprecedented thoroughness of Bishop Wren's campaign, which threatened the very survival of Puritanism in the city, led to a willingness on the part of Norwich Puritans after 1640 to take bolder steps in order to safeguard the movement. The indifference, if not outright hostility, of the King in 1636 made the Puritans realize that they could never trust the Crown and would have to find their champion in Parliament. On the local level, they came to recognize the imperative of a purely Puritan magistracy. In order to achieve this end, the Puritan religious faction of the 1630s was transformed into the parliamentary-Puritan political party of the 1640s and ideology entered electoral politics on a grand scale. In the ensuing struggle for control of the city government from 1641 to 1643, the parliamentary-Puritan activists arising from the religious confrontations of the 1620s and 1630s were forced to come to grips with electoral procedures and regulations resulting from the constitutional crises of the 1610s and 1620s.

IV

Norwich and the English Civil War, 1640-1645

By 1640 the Puritans of Norwich formed a majority among the politically-active freemen and within the Assembly chamber. They were also strongly represented in the magistracy. Nevertheless, they were still suffering from the onslaughts of Bishop Wren and they lacked control over the Court of Aldermen. When Charles I summoned the first Parliament in eleven years in early 1640, the Puritans were stirred to action. Their first steps were neither extreme nor new: petitions containing their grievances against Bishop Wren were sent to both the Short and Long Parliaments. As friction between the Crown and Parliament steadily increased, the Puritans were joined by men supporting Parliament and thus the term 'parliamentary-Puritan' is used to describe this larger group. By mid-1641 their strategy focused on an effort to gain the upper hand in the corporation but to avoid a direct confrontation with the Court of Aldermen. Accordingly, they utilized successfully their electoral strength among the freemen to elect parliamentary-Puritans to the magistracy while maintaining restraint in other political activities. On the eve of the Civil War they held a dominant position in the Court of Aldermen and the corporation immediately committed itself to the Parliament camp. The parliamentary-Puritan electoral strategy continued to operate, but a pocket of Royalists still remained in the magistracy when a Royalist uprising threatened Norfolk in 1642/3. Thus the Royalist aldermen, many of whom had supported Wren in 1636, were purged from office. The influence of the Crown, the bishops, and the Royalist segment of the corporation had disintegrated completely by 1643 and the triumphant parliamentary-Puritan corporation then carried out a devastating destruction of the Anglican Church in the city.

Events in Norwich throughout the 1640s did not noticeably affect the national political struggle, but events in Westminster and London did have profound repercussions in Norwich. In this concern for and response to national affairs, Norwich was similar to London but seems to have differed from many other cities. The very provincialism of provincial townsmen prior to 1640 has already received attention,[1] and the insularity of local communities in general and towns in particular has recently been suggested as a central ingredient of life in the provinces during the Civil War.[2] The common denominator to be found in London and Norwich was the presence of a large and active Puritan community which had shared a similar experience and encountered a similar predicament. In the 1630s the Puritans of the two cities had adopted the same solution in an attempt to establish a Puritan ministry and had undergone a similar fate at the hands of the Anglican bishops.[3] As in Norwich, the London Puritans in 1640 commanded a majority among the politically-active townsmen and in the Common Hall, although not in the Common Council; the London Puritans were also a minority in the magistracy.[4] Given the close economic and social contact between merchants of the two cities as well as the similarity in political institutions,[5] the endeavours of the London Puritans to take advantage of their voting strength and wrestle control of the corporation from their opponents could trigger similar tactics by the Puritans of Norwich. The Civil War period in

[1] For example, see MacCaffrey, *Exeter*, pp. 1–2.

[2] Everitt points out: 'Most towns and counties were far more interested in living a life of their own, in which politics played merely an intermittent part, than in supporting either roundheads or cavaliers.' Alan Everitt, 'The County Community', in E. W. Ives, ed., *The English Revolution, 1600–1660* (London, 1968), p. 49. Everitt stresses the same theme in *Change in the Provinces: The Seventeenth Century* (Leicester, 1969), pp. 8–12. Recently Hirst has offered a partial corrective. He suggests that the issues of primary importance in municipal politics were local rather than national, yet by 1640 there was a growing interest (especially in the larger towns) in national affairs to the extent that 'even those boroughs which had shown themselves entirely localist in the 1620s were now extending their interests outside the town walls . . .'. Hirst, *Representative of the People?*, pp. 45, 54–9, 110, 136, 145–53, 182–3.

[3] Pearl, *London*, pp. 160–96; Seaver, *Puritan Lectureships*, pp. 240–66.

[4] Pearl, *London*, pp. 3, 79, 91, 94–106, 113–16, 160, 276. Apparently this political division between an agitated and discontented citizenry and a conservative magistracy extended to other towns, including Bristol and Newcastle. See Zagorin, *Court and Country*, p. 147.

[5] One contemporary noted in the 1630s that Norwich trade 'doth consist almost wholly in commerce with Londoners, from whom they used weekly to receive many thousand pounds'. Bodleian, Tanner MSS., 68, fo. 147: William Allanson to Samuel Wright, secretary to Bishop Wren, 8 Oct. 1636. The chief market for the Norwich textile industry was London. The important economic and ideological ties between Norwich (and other East Anglian cities) and London is stressed in Clive Holmes, *The Eastern Association in the English Civil War* (Cambridge, 1974), pp. 7–10.

Norwich, therefore, must be viewed within the context of the larger national conflict.

Circumstances in London and Norwich were not precisely analogous. London's size, wealth, strategic importance, and proximity to Whitehall and the Houses of Parliament is the most obvious difference. The parliamentary-Puritans of London were successful in dominating elections to the Court of Aldermen in 1641,[1] but the rate of turnover was not quick enough to keep up with the rapidly changing national scene. The political crisis between the Crown and Parliament in late 1641 and early 1642 forced the London parliamentary-Puritans to take bolder steps in an effort to capture city government. As a consequence, the struggle for supremacy in London led, after December 1641, to a serious constitutional confrontation between the Common Council and the Court of Aldermen. This did not occur in Norwich where the parliamentary-Puritans were not required to make a commitment to national affairs until the outbreak of war; and by this time they were already the dominant party in the magistracy, so a revolutionary programme was an undesirable risk and unnecessary. With the abandonment of the seniority system in the election of mayors and the removal of aldermen from office in accordance with procedures set down in the Composition of 1415 (but not used since the sixteenth century), the constitutional history of Norwich from 1640 to 1645 was more one of restoration than revolution. A second difference between Norwich and London involves the personnel of the opposed parties. The parliamentary-Puritans and Royalists of London represented different social and economic interests, whereas in Norwich the religious and ideological rhetoric did not correspond with a deeper clash of conflicting socio-economic groups. The parliamentary-Puritan victory in Norwich did not bring to power a group of men whose wealth, occupations, and social backgrounds differed markedly from previous magistrates.

* * *

Puritans throughout England were prepared to seize the political initiative and launch a counter-offensive against Anglican persecution when King Charles sent out writs in 1639/40 authorizing elections for Parliament. Parliamentary elections in Norwich were distinctive in two respects. First, whereas many boroughs had succumbed to the pressure of outside patrons, at least one and

---

[1] Pearl, *London*, pp. 114, 158-9.

usually both of the representatives of Norwich were resident citizens.[1] Second, election in many towns was the exclusive privilege of the governing élite, but in Norwich the electorate had consisted of the entire freeman citizenry since 1415.[2] The only restriction limiting the selection of citizen members of Parliament was that freemen had previously confined their choice to the aldermen.[3] The magistrates of both Norwich and London were powerless to prevent the Puritan-dominated freemen of the former, and the Common Hall of the latter from returning well-known Puritans to Westminster.[4] Alderman John Tooly, perhaps the most prominent Puritan magistrate in Norwich, and Thomas Atkin, the controversial ex-alderman of Norwich and an alderman of London in 1640, were elected to represent the city.[5] They could be counted

---

[1] See J. E. Neale, *The Elizabethan House of Commons* (London, 1949, rev. 1963), pp. 139 ff; J. H. Plumb, 'The Growth of the Electorate in England from 1600 to 1715', *Past and Present* ,45 (Nov. 1969), 96, 98–100; Hirst, *Representative of the People?*, Chap. 5. For Elizabethan Norwich see Pound, 'Elizabethan Corporation of Norwich', pp. 334–40. In each of the eight parliamentary elections between 1600 and 1629 at least one of the elected burgesses was a Norwich citizen. The non-citizen members of Parliament were Sir Henry Hobart, Kt. (1603/4), William Denny, Esq. (1620, 1623/4, 1625), and Sir John Suckling (1625/6). Hamon le Strange, *Norfolk Official Lists* (Norwich, 1890), p. 141.

[2] The 'Composition of 1415', in Hudson and Tingey, eds. *Records*, I. 107. Plumb lists Lincoln, Exeter, Reading, Oxford, Cambridge, Leicester, Northampton, and King's Lynn as boroughs which did not recognize the right of freemen to vote. Plumb, 'Growth of Electorate', pp. 100–1. Hirst, however, has calculated that freeman franchises were far more numerous than governing body franchises by 1641. Hirst, *Representative of the People?*, p. 90.

[3] There are neither election returns nor detailed descriptions of member of Parliament elections until the last years of Charles II. Pound, 'Elizabethan Corporation of Norwich', pp. 334–40 suggests that the magistrates controlled these elections during the Elizabethan period, but there are no extant records which clarify the manner in which the nominees were determined during the period under discussion here.

[4] Pearl, *London*, pp. 101–2, 176–93. National issues, and religious grievances in particular, were frequently the primary consideration in the Short Parliament elections. For the example of Salisbury, see P. A. Slack, 'An Election to the Short Parliament', *Bulletin of the Institute for Historical Research*, 46 (1973), 108–114. In London and some other towns the reformers in opposition to the Crown were strongly backed by the propaganda of an involved Puritan ministry, who urged citizens to vote for the appropriate candidates. John K. Gruenfelder, 'The Election to the Short Parliament, 1640', in Howard S. Reinmuth, Jr., ed., *Essays in Honor of David Harris Willson* (Minneapolis, 1970), pp. 180–230. It is not known whether Puritan ministers were similarly active in Norwich.

[5] The election of Atkin is especially interesting in that he was no longer an alderman of Norwich. In 1638 he had requested a discharge from the Court of Aldermen and the Assembly had consented. N.N.R.O., A.B. (1613–42), 18 June 1638, 345ʳ.

on to air the Puritan grievances against Wren in the House of Commons. Despite the stormy brevity of the Short Parliament, they did so. On 18 April a petition from the city of Norwich, which claimed that the visitation articles devised by Wren led many honest men to sell their estates and leave the country, was presented in the Commons.[1]

The seniority of aldermen under the chair brought Henry Lane, the architect of the anti-Puritan petition of 1636, to the mayoralty in mid-1640. Perhaps he was instrumental in the selection of John Osborne, no friend to the Puritan cause, as the magistrates' sheriff in September.[2] The freemen, for their part, were determined to have as their sheriff a man more to their own tastes. Casting a wide net, they chose John Dethick of London. A one-time apprentice of Thomas Atkin and a wealthy merchant, Dethick joined the London subcommittee to raise funds for a parliamentary army in 1641 and later became an alderman and a political Independent.[3] The unprecedented aspect of Dethick's election was that he had settled permanently in London and had requested a discharge from holding any public office in Norwich. The magistrates consented to the discharge, but the Assembly refused and Dethick was elected by the freemen.[4] The freemen may also have been angered by the first of two Catholic scares which the city endured prior to the Civil War. On 4 September Mayor Lane wrote to the Privy Council that he had received information that the city would be attacked and burned by 12,000 men. Catholic alarms were common occurrences in the larger cities in September 1640. They coincided with and perhaps resulted from the political crisis arising from the presence of the Scottish army in Newcastle and cries for a new Parliament.[5]

[1] *C.J.* II. 6. The original petition with the signatures of many citizens has not survived, but a copy of the text of the petition may be found in the library of the House of Lords. See also *H.M.C., 4th Report*, p. 24.

[2] Parliament declared Osborne a delinquent in 1642 for his refusal to provide proposition money and in 1642/3 he was ejected from the Court of Aldermen.

[3] Millican, ed., *Freemen*, p. 105; Shipps, 'Lay Patronage', pp. 282–3; Pearl, *London*, p. 253n.

[4] N.N.R.O., M.C.B. (1634–46), 26 Aug. 1640, 293^r: A.B. (1613–42), 3 Oct. 1640, 364^v.

[5] Details may be found in *C.S.P.D.*, Chas I, 1640–1, p. 51: Privy Council to Sir W. Denny and Henry Lane, 12 Sept. 1640; pp. 99–100: Sir W. Denny and Henry Lane to Privy Council, [25 Sept.] 1640. See also *Privy Council Register, Facsimilies*, Chas I, 1640, p. 263: Mayor Henry Lane and Sir W. Denny to Privy Council, 11 Sept. 1640. For Catholic scares see Robin Clifton, 'The Popular

When the King's writ proclaiming a second meeting of Parliament arrived in October, almost all of Norfolk was prepared to support the parliamentary opposition.[1] Paradoxically, the members of Parliament returned by Norwich were more moderate than the extremists of the preceding spring, but the election was disputed and presiding sheriff John Osborne, unwilling to offend either side, returned two indentures to the House of Commons.[2] Both indentures listed Richard Harman, who had recently completed his term as mayor. Harman had apparently declined to take sides in the petition controversy of 1636; he later proved to be inactive in the Commons, and in 1643 he refused to contribute to a voluntary collection for the parliamentary army. At best he was never more than a lukewarm supporter of Parliament during the Civil War.[3] The dispute centred on the second member. One indenture named Puritan Alderman Tooly; the other listed moderate Richard Catelyn, who was neither a freeman nor a resident of the city, yet had far outpolled Tooly.[4] Although Catelyn's politics in late 1640 remain obscure, from then on he carefully kept his distance from the parliamentary opposition. By late 1642 he was drifting towards the Royalist standard, in 1643 his estate was sequestered, and ultimately he was dismissed from the Commons.[5] However, after a review

[1] Only two of the twelve members of Parliament returned by Norfolk to the Long Parliament were Royalists. M. F. Keeler, *The Long Parliament 1640–1641, A Biographical Study* (Philadelphia, 1954), p. 56. See also Alfred Kingston, *East Anglia and the Great Civil War* (London, 1897), pp. 2–3. Of the Eastern Association counties, however, Norfolk was apparently one of the slowest to respond to national issues and Puritanism in the county was largely an urban phenomenon. Holmes, *Eastern Association*, pp. 17–18, 24–5.

[2] *C.J.* II. 22: 7 Nov. 1640. See also Keeler, *Long Parliament*, pp. 56–7 and D. Brunton and D. H. Pennington, *Members of the Long Parliament* (Cambridge, Mass., 1954), p. 81. The partially damaged indentures may be found in P.R.O., Returns into Chancery of members of Parliament, C 219/43.

[3] Brunton and Pennington, *Members*, p. 233; Keeler, *Long Parliament*, pp. 203–4 and App. I. See also Brit. Lib., Add. MSS., 22619, fos. 146, 149; Evans, 'Political Elite of Norwich', p. 499.

[4] Harman received 1,089 votes, Catelyn 906, and Tooly 275. Keeler, *Long Parliament*, pp. 56, 57n. Catelyn did have a residence in Lakenham, a suburb of Norwich lying outside the walls. N.N.R.O., Poor Rate Returns for 1633–4.

[5] Keeler, *Long Parliament*, p. 57; *C.J.* II. 763a, 845b: 12 Sept. and 12 Nov. 1642; *East Anglian: Notes and Queries*, new ser. V (1892–4), 223; Catelyn was disabled from sitting on 30 September 1645. *C.J.* IV. 295b.

Fear of Catholics during the English Revolution', *Past and Present*, 52 (August 1971), 23–55; K. J. Lindley, 'The Lay Catholics of England in the Reign of Charles I', *Journal of Ecclesiastical History*, XXII. 3 (July 1971), 215–19.

of the indentures and the election, the House of Commons approved Catelyn and warned Sheriff Osborne that they took a dim view of the 'great misdemeanor in him' for returning two indentures.[1]

Surviving evidence is too scanty to determine the issues in the disputed election. Possibly it involved a defeat of the Puritans at the hands of moderates. Yet it is also possible that the religious factor and national politics were subordinated to purely local considerations and in particular to the reluctance of townsmen to have a county candidate forced upon them.[2] Subscriptions to the rival indentures show that some known Puritans supported Catelyn, whereas a number of prominent non-Puritans backed Tooly. Mayor Henry Lane, for example, favoured Tooly. Moreover, Catelyn was hardly an anti-Puritan. He, as well as Tooly, had been a trustee for the advancement of religion in the 1630s and no less a figure than John Pym spoke in favour of Catelyn's election when the controversy was heard in the House of Commons.

Whatever the issues may have been, the Norwich Assembly reacted quickly. The election of a foreigner was declared a departure from ancient charter and a breach of city liberties, and Catelyn's supporters were condemned. An ordinance was then passed which set a stiff £5 fine on any freeman who voted for a foreigner in the future and prescribed imprisonment for failure to pay.[3] Even if the election did not centre on religious issues, the result was that the city Puritans and later parliamentary-Puritans were deprived of active spokesmen in Westminster during the critical years which followed. Catelyn and Harman were in sharp contrast to the vocal and radical Puritan members of Parliament for London, who frequently ignored the conservative Court of Aldermen and forged a vital and direct link with the parliamentary-Puritan party in the capital.[4]

---

[1] ibid., II. 22: 7 Nov. 1640. Also, Wallace Notestein, ed., *The Journal of Sir Simonds D'Ewes* (New Haven, 1923), p. 5. Hereafter referred to as D'Ewes, *Journal*.

[2] These interpretations are provided by Holmes, *Eastern Association*, p. 24 and Hirst, *Representative of the People?*, pp. 124, 138, respectively.

[3] A.B. (1613–42), 28 Oct. 1640, 365ʳ. Catelyn later took the freeman's oath on 3 April 1641. The ordinance was repealed on 23 September 1641, for some unknown reason. ibid., 3 Apr. 1641, 367ᵛ; 23 Sept. 1641, 375ᵛ. Earlier in October the Assembly criticized the High Sheriff of Norfolk for not permitting qualified Norwich citizens to vote in the election of knights of the shire. ibid., 16 Oct. 1640, 364ᵛ. See also Hirst, *Representative of the People?*, p. 40.

[4] Pearl, *London*, pp. 112–14, 197–236.

In the first days of the Long Parliament in early November, the parliamentary-Puritans of London and their members of Parliament energetically presented lengthy petitions covering a wide range of complaints,[1] but it was not until 30 November that Mayor Lane requested in the Norwich Assembly that grievances to be laid before Parliament should be brought forward.[2] The Puritans quickly resumed the attack on Bishop Wren. On 23 December a petition from Norwich was presented to the House of Commons complaining about Wren's taxation schemes in the city.[3] The imprisonment of Wren in the Tower on 30 December was an invitation for far stronger action and the Norwich Assembly reacted accordingly. A second and much more comprehensive petition, which incorporated the contents of the petition to the Short Parliament, was approved on 11 January and sent up to Parliament. Wren was charged with introducing popish superstitions, rites, and ceremonies as well as disrupting the religious life of the community; the local conformist clergy were also strongly condemned.[4] The change in the religious climate since the days of 1636 may be measured by the open disavowal of the Assembly petition by only two of the aldermen present.[5] Another

[1] ibid., pp. 174–5, 210–11. The London petitions were circulated without the approval of the Court of Aldermen and were presented to the House of Commons even though they were officially disowned by the Lord Mayor and aldermen.

[2] A.B. (1613–42), 30 Nov. 1640, 366ʳ.

[3] *C.J.* II. 57: 23 Dec. 1640. This may be the petition in Tanner MSS., 220, fo. 130 pertaining to Wren's tax for the maintenance of the clergy. Wren had also obtained a royal order requiring all disputes on tithes to be heard in Chancery or in his own episcopal court. Zagorin, *Court and Country*, p. 154. The impeachment of Wren was on 19 December, the day after Laud was impeached.

[4] Tanner MSS., 220, fo. 44: Petition of the Inhabitants of Norwich; fo. 116: Articles of Grievances preferred by the inhabitants of Norwich Against Dr. Wren. In a letter dated the day the petition was approved, a sympathizer of Wren wrote: 'This morning our citizens are very busy at an Assembly . . . to determine the case against Wren in the worst possible light. Some aldermen are seeking out all innovations in doctrines at the request of the burgesses.' ibid., 68, fo. 336: [?] to Edmund Dey, 11 Jan, 1640/1. The petition was referred by the House of Commons to the Committee on Bishop Wren. D'Ewes, *Journal*, p. 284n. On 27 January it was reported to the House of Commons that fifty-two families of Norwich had departed for New England owing, according to Rushworth, to 'Bishop Wren's pressing their conscience with illegal oaths, ceremonies, observations, and many strange innovations'. John Rushworth, *Historical Collections* (London, 1721), IV. 158.

[5] A.B. (1613–42), 11 Jan. 1640/1, 356ᵛ. The two aldermen were William Gostlyn and John Freeman, both of whom paid the price for their Royalist proclivities in 1643.

petition in February supported Minister John Carter against persecution by Bishop Montague.[1] The Puritans were also resolved to reassert their insistence upon proper religious worship. Travelling through Norwich in January, Thomas Knyvett wrote to his wife: 'Conventicles every night in Norwich, as publicly known as sermons in the daytime, and they say much more frequented.'[2]

At some time during the ensuing spring the magistrates filed their own grievances against the ignominious treatment they had received at the hands of the Cathedral clergy during Sunday morning services.[3] It had been Wren's idea in 1636 to coerce the mayor, sheriffs, and aldermen to attend the Cathedral every Sunday without fail, and the magistrates had reluctantly complied.[4] Not only were the élite of the city seated in uncomfortable chairs and exposed to chilling draughts, but they were also situated directly underneath an overhead gallery. At one time a Bible was dropped on the mayor and broke his spectacles and on other occasions there were other enormities, such as cutting and mangling the magistrates' gowns as they knelt in prayer. These forms of humiliation reached a peak in 1640:

That at the time of the present mayor that now is, upon that Sunday the day before the Knights of the Shire were chosen in October last, Alderman Shipdham [a leading Puritan], Justice of the Peace and sitting next the mayor, somebody most beastly did conspurcate and shit upon his gown from the galleries above; and the Sunday immediately after some from the galleries let fall a stool which narrowly missed the mayor's head, and at another time one from the said gallery did spit upon Alderman Baret's head.

This was too much. Even the aldermen who had supported Wren in 1636 set their hands to this petition. Wren may not have instructed the Cathedral clergy to humiliate the magistrates in the

[1] D'Ewes comments that this petition was presented on 23 February 1640/1 by some citizens of St. Peter Mancroft parish. The Commons voted that Montague's suspension of Carter from preaching was void. D'Ewes, *Journal*, p. 389.

[2] Bertram Schofield, transcriber and ed., *The Knyvett Letters, 1620–1644* [Norfolk Record Society Publications, xx] (Norwich, 1949), pp. 98–9.

[3] Tanner MSS., 220, fo. 147: The Humble Petition of the Mayor, Sheriffs, and Aldermen of the City of Norwich, n.d. The petition is known to have been sent up before 29 May, when one of the signatories died.

[4] See Chapter III and Wren's report on his diocese in Laud's account to the King in 1637, cited in Laud, *Works*, V. 348.

above manner, but he was responsible for the magistrates' presence in the Cathedral and not effective in preventing their humiliation.

The petitions forwarded to Westminster are as illuminating in what they did not deal with as in what they did. First, they were limited to religious grievances. Unlike their counterparts in London, Norwich citizens did not register their concern over ship-money, monopolies, the Scottish War, or, early in 1641, the trial of Strafford. Moreover, the petitions dealt only with local religious abuses involving Bishops Wren and Montague. The Puritans did not venture into the national arena with their own ideas of what should be done concerning Church reform. In particular, the corporation did not officially respond to either the Root and Branch petition delivered to the House of Commons in December or the April petition calling for ecclesiastical reform, both of which originated in London and had agitated its citizenry.[1] Up to mid-1641, therefore, the Norwich Puritans did not follow the lead of London and their petitions against Wren followed the same approach as and were no more radical than the 1623 petition against Bishop Harsnet.

By one of those twists of fate which not infrequently influence historical change, the Puritans were denied leadership in the mayoralty in 1640, and their prospects for the future were little better. The seniority system which had elevated Henry Lane in 1640 dictated that he would be followed by William Gostlyn, who had denounced the petitions of 1636 and 1640/1 and would later be imprisoned as a Royalist.[2] Gostlyn, in turn, would be succeeded first by the inactive, octogenarian John Loveland and then by Thomas Carver, both of whom had also objected to the 1636 petition.[3] The Puritans needed no reminder of 1623, 1629, and 1636 to realize the importance of a Puritan mayor in times of stress. When the ailing Mayor Lane requested to be relieved from office late in February 1640/1, none other than John Tooly was chosen deputy-mayor to fill his place.[4] The election of a new mayor on 1 May should have numbered the days of the brief Puritan mayoralty

<hr>

[1] The Root and Branch petition was signed by between 10,000 and 20,000 London townsmen; the April petition possessed some 8,000 signatures and was delivered to the House of Commons by some 10,000 citizens. Pearl, *London*, pp. 214, 216.

[2] See Evans, 'Political Elite of Norwich', pp. 497–8.

[3] A.B. (1613–42), 11 Jan. 1640/1, 356^v; 28 Apr. 1642, 382^r.

[4] M.C.B. (1634–46), 26 Feb. 1640/1, 305^r.

for years to come, but the freemen abandoned seniority and nominated Carver and Adrian Parmenter, third and fourth in seniority. The magistrates chose Carver to be the mayor-elect. Neither the Mayor's Court Book nor the Assembly Book offers any clue to explain this first departure from the 1620 ordinance. Nevertheless, the event has the hallmarks of a carefully conceived Puritan manoeuvre even though Carver was hardly a Puritan.

The September 1640 election of a Lord Mayor in London was probably the catalyst for the Norwich mayor's election.[1] The Common Hall of London was not required by law to nominate the senior alderman under the chair, but by tradition their two nominees included the senior alderman, who was then chosen by the magistrates. Confronted with a senior alderman who was a known adherent of the royal Court, the Puritan-dominated Common Hall, in an unprecedented affront to tradition, nominated two anti-Court aldermen far down the seniority list. An inevitable dispute flared up and the Privy Council ordered a new election. In a compromise tactic, the Common Hall again refused to nominate the senior alderman, but did name the alderman second in seniority even though he was linked to the Crown. The Privy Council accepted the compromise despite the irregularity. The similarity between this election and the Norwich mayor's election six months later is obvious. The nomination of Carver and Parmenter was not a radical departure from the seniority principle, as had occurred before 1620, and the Puritan majority of freemen did not attempt to force two Puritans on the Court of Aldermen. The magistrates had the power to declare the nominations void, but the Puritans had reason to believe they would accept them and elect Carver, in order to prevent turmoil. After all, deputy-mayor Tooly might well obstruct any opposition, and the Privy Council could hardly be expected to rush to the magistrates' support after the precedent established in London.

There is an additional element in the mayoral election which deserves attention. The freemen had passed over not only Gostlyn but Loveland as well. Carver's candidacy was not much of an improvement on Gostlyn's and surely less desirable to the Puritans than the more moderate, deaf, and eighty-five-year-old Loveland. In short, why did the Puritan freemen not nominate Loveland? Carver was desperately ill late in May, and his condition may well

[1] The following is taken from Pearl, *London*, pp. 110–12.

have been known at the beginning of the month.[1] If he were to become too ill to perform his mayoral duties, precedent from the previous February stipulated that a previous mayor be chosen to carry on, and this could have resulted in a Puritan mayoralty again. On the other hand, if mayor-elect Carver were to die before assuming office, constitutional confusion would arise because the 1620 ordinance made no provision for the death of a mayor-elect, although it did make arrangements for the death of a mayor. In these circumstances the Puritans, with a majority in the Common Council, could work the situation to their advantage. Moreover, this is precisely what occurred. Therefore, by nominating Carver the Puritans could reasonably expect that one of their faction would occupy the mayor's seat without the necessity of a show-down with the aldermanry. Even if Carver survived his year of office, the Norwich Puritans would have set a very useful precedent.

To label the 1641 mayor's election a calculated triumph of the Puritans is conjectural. Yet the violation of a city ordinance, which had been observed without exception for twenty years, requires some explanation. In any case, subsequent events played directly into the hands of the Puritans. Thomas Carver died on 29 May. Even before his death the Common Council insisted upon greater freedom in the nomination of his replacement.[2] A decision on 4 June that the election procedure should be determined by the Assembly rather than the Court of Aldermen suggests that the Puritans had the upper hand.[3] The 1620 ordinance required that upon the death of a mayor one of the two ex-mayors with greatest seniority should serve for the remainder of the term.[4] In 1641 this would have been either Richard Rosse or Alexander Anguish, both of whom were destined to be removed from the aldermanry for their Royalist leanings. On 11 June the Assembly avoided this dilemma by claiming that the death of a mayor-elect was not the same as the death of a mayor.[5] They argued further that the citizens

---

[1] A.B. (1613–42), 26 May 1641, 371ʳ.

[2] ibid.

[3] This is not unusual, since in constitutional issues as well as legislation the charters were clear that no decisions were to be made without the consent of the Common Council.

[4] A.B. (1613–42), 11 Aug. 1620, 119ᵛ. The election of John Tooly as deputy-mayor the previous February was, technically, a violation of the 1620 ordinance and suggests that the Puritans were prepared to ignore the seniority clauses of the ordinance before the 1 May mayor's election.

[5] ibid., 11 June 1641, 371ʳ⁻ᵛ.

should proceed to a new election in which all aldermen except those who had been mayors during the past three years were eligible for nomination. This was a reversion to the original charter of Henry IV. At the same Assembly meeting a number of councilmen asserted that the 1620 ordinance was 'in some sort repugnant to the charters of the city' and urged for its abolition; but the ordinance was not taken off the books. On 16 June another election was held. The freemen nominated Adrian Parmenter and Richard Ward and the magistrates chose the senior of the two, Parmenter, to be mayor.[1] The Puritans thus had one of their own to preside over a Puritan Mayor's Court.[2]

By June there were almost as many Puritans and future supporters of Parliament as anti-Puritans and future Royalists in the Court of Aldermen, and the balance rested with the moderates.[3] Certainly these moderate magistrates were aware of the strong Puritan feelings of the citizenry. They must also have been alert to the rise of Pym in the House of Commons. Nor was there a united Royalist front. Since the Crown was definitely out of favour in both town and county, some faint-hearted, anti-Puritan aldermen on occasion preferred co-operation to opposition.[4] Enough aldermen must have been willing to permit the anti-episcopal mood of the freemen and councilmen to be voiced, for otherwise the 1640/1 petition against Wren could never have reached a vote in the Assembly. Here the Norwich magistracy acted differently from the London magistrates, who steadfastly refused to give their official support to similar petitions.[5] However, a reversal of the fortunes of Pym's party in the Commons might well have strengthened the

[1] ibid., 16 June 1641, 371^v.
[2] The election of Parmenter as mayor gave the Puritans a 5:4 edge in the Mayor's court (mayor plus alderman-justices of the peace). A tenth member, Richard Harman, was serving in the House of Commons. The Puritans were Parmenter, Shipdham, C. Baret, Baker, and Tooly; the Royalists were Rosse, A. Anguish, J. Anguish, and Lane. If Gostlyn had been mayor the Royalists would have had control over the Mayor's Court, which may have been a factor in the election controversy.
[3] Of the aldermen who had not been mayor, six were clearly Royalists (Gostlyn, Ward, Freeman, Daniel, Croshold, and Osborne), four were Parliament men (Thacker, Burman, Peckover, and Sotherton) and four were moderates (Loveland, Barber, Utting, and Lombe). Omitting Harman, this adds up to ten Royalists, nine Puritans, and four moderates on the aldermanic bench.
[4] The activity of Royalist aldermen between 1640 and 1645 is discussed below.
[5] Pearl, *London*, p. 116. Pearl identifies only five parliamentary-Puritans compared to thirteen Royalists in the London Court of Aldermen.

Royalist resolve and swayed the moderates to the Royalist side, thus bringing the magistracy into alignment with their brethren in London. Consequently, the Norwich Puritans could not count on implementing their plans for religious reform unless they either transferred power from the magistracy to the Assembly or got rid of the Royalist aldermen. In 1641 they commenced cautiously with the former approach, and in 1643 they resorted to the latter as well.

Two days after the second mayoral election of 1641, the Council raised the question of what powers the mayor and aldermen had on their own account and what matters required the consent of the Common Council.[1] A committee consisting of eight aldermen and eight councilmen was appointed by the Assembly to consider the issue. Three of the eight aldermen were anti-Puritans, but the Council guaranteed a parliamentary-Puritan majority on the committee by naming men of this party to six of the eight positions.[2] Another committee was formed in October to consider desired changes in the charter and report to the Assembly,[3] but there is no record of a report having been made and the charter was not amended. The first committee continued to meet, but only one concrete result emerged from their deliberations before January. In December the Puritans scored a gain when it was resolved that the presentation and settling of advowsons in which the patron was the corporation should be the prerogative of the entire Assembly and not the magistrates alone, as it often had been in the past.[4]

The following April the old matter of voting rights in the Assembly was revived. The impetus for this reconsideration probably came from the constitutional struggle being waged in London rather than from the committee appointed by the Norwich Assembly. The London Common Council and Court of Aldermen were hotly divided on precisely the same issues which had disturbed Norwich in 1620, 1628, and 1636.[5] In February the Crown-

---

[1] A.B. (1613–42), 18 June 1641, 372[r].

[2] The five Puritan aldermen on the committee were Parmenter, Tooly, Shipdham, C. Baret, and Thacker; the three Royalists were Lane, A. Anguish, and Gostlyn. The Puritan councilmen named to the committee were Puckle, Sherwood, Watts, T. Baret, Ashwell, and Skottow. All these men would later become magistrates. The political affiliation of councilmen Steven Leverington and Francis Norris is not known. So at least eleven of the sixteen committeemen were parliamentary-Puritans.

[3] A.B. (1613–42), 25 Oct. 1641, 376[v].

[4] ibid., 21 Dec. 1641, 377[v].

[5] Pearl, *London*, pp. 151–4.

oriented London aldermen, faced with a revolt by the Common Council, insisted upon their right to vote separately on measures generated within the Council and thus their privilege of casting an aldermanic veto. This was connected to their additional claim to determine the agenda of Council sessions whereby they could prevent a proposal from being presented to the Council unless they had voted on and approved the matter in advance. The Common Council, which had been captured by the parliamentary-Puritans in the elections of the preceding December, contested both claims. In March a committee of the House of Commons arbitrated the controversy in favour of the Council. The decision of the Norwich Assembly in April was that a matter 'which belongs to the Assembly to pass upon' needed the consent of both a majority of the magistrates and a majority of the councilmen present.[1] This was a reversal of the 1628 decision calling for a mingling of votes, and guaranteed that the parliamentary-Puritan majority in the Council, never very great, would not be upset by the votes of Royalist and moderate magistrates. On the other hand, the magistrates retained a veto power, which was tantamount to acknowledging the illegality of the passage of the 1636 petition.

The initiatives of the Norwich Puritans had been very cautious and conciliatory compared to the radical actions of the parliamentary-Puritans of London. In the struggle for power in London, there was a noticeable decline in respect for constituted authority and at times the city tottered on the brink of revolution. The Norwich Puritans apparently wished to avoid this and seemed to adopt a wait-and-see policy. They had the political muscle in the city and the Assembly to challenge established election procedures and attack the traditional authority of the Court of Aldermen, but they preferred not to take measures which would unravel the political and constitutional fabric. It is true that the seniority principle was abandoned in the mayor's election of 1641, but the Puritans in the Common Council were not willing to abolish the 1620 ordinance altogether. The London magistrates successfully reimposed seniority in the mayoral elections of September 1641,[2] and the Norwich citizens also honoured seniority the following

---

[1] A.B. (1613–42), 23 Apr. 1642, 381ᵛ. The ordinance did not clarify whether the Common Council could participate in determining the Assembly agenda.

[2] Pearl, *London*, pp. 124–5.

May, even though it meant the election of Gostlyn. Apparently the Norwich freemen did not make a bid to elect both sheriffs in September 1641 as the Common Hall had the previous June,[1] nor did they attempt to increase their numbers in the Common Council in 1642 following the example provided by the London elections of the previous December.[2] The Norwich Assembly, in June 1641, established the committee machinery which could have usurped power from the magistrates, but very little transference of authority resulted. Whereas the London Common Council destroyed the dominance of the Court of Aldermen and assumed control during the first half of 1642, nothing similar occurred in Norwich and the only change (voting procedure in the Assembly) was more moderate than the solution reached in London. Hence from 1641 to mid-1642, the only occasions on which the Norwich Puritans made constitutional alterations were not only in response to events in London but also correspond to only those changes made in London which had received the official approval of the Privy Council or Parliament.

If the Norwich parliamentary-Puritans were less forceful and daring than their London counterparts in realigning city government prior to mid-1642, they were also much less aggressive in voicing their opinions on national politics and influencing affairs in Parliament. The London Common Council sent a number of highly inflammatory petitions to the House of Commons in the seven months before the outbreak of war, but Norwich was content to respond to rather than to precipitate events. To be sure, the crisis brought on by Charles's abortive attempt to seize the Five Members in January 1641/2 spurred many East Anglian constituencies to petition Parliament and demonstrate their support, and Norwich was no exception. When their M.P.s suggested weakening the petition, the Mayor's Court refused to make alterations and,

---

[1] ibid., pp. 120–2. A committee of the House of Lords in August had mediated in favour of the Common Hall, on the grounds that the election had not been performed on the appointed day. There is no evidence to prove that the freemen of Norwich used this as justification to usurp the magistrates' choice of one sheriff. Nevertheless, it is curious to note that the entry of the 8 September sheriffs' election is out of place in the Assembly Book and comes after the entry of a 23 September Assembly meeting. Moreover, the sheriff supposedly elected by the magistrates, Matthew Lindsey, became one of the most active Parliament men and was elected mayor in 1650.

[2] Pearl, *London*, pp. 132–9. The number of new Norwich councilmen elected in 1640, 1641, and 1642 were 7, 3, and 6 respectively.

asserting that 'the city will at no hand be cast into the country', informed the M.P.s that if they refused to present the petition in the Commons then the city's agents should not be prevented from doing so. Apart from this, the only known petitions to come from Norwich during this period expressed complaints concerning parliamentary taxes.[1] The reluctance of Norwich to assume a more involved role was typical of other towns and boroughs; only London had real impact on events. The oft-repeated assertions of Royalist apologists during the Restoration that the true instigators of the revolution were municipal corporations are fallacious.[2] Many towns, such as Norwich, were deeply concerned with the issues which divided the Crown and the House of Commons and were influenced profoundly by the unfolding drama of national politics, but they were the followers and not the leaders in the national confrontation. Why this was so is not entirely clear. The major factor may well have been the traditional social and political subordination of merchants and other townsmen to the landed class of gentry and nobility.[3]

All hopes for a peaceful settlement between King Charles and the House of Commons had disappeared by July 1642. It was only a matter of time before military conflict replaced accusations and recriminations. The portent of war was as clear in Norwich as elsewhere in the country. As the Assembly contemplated preparations for the defence of the town, both the parliamentary-Puritans and their opponents became more active.[4] While supporters of the Crown gathered to toast the King's health and ridicule the leaders at Westminster, supporters of Parliament formed a volunteer company and broke their silence on national affairs. According to a published version of their petition to the House of Lords, 'many thousands of the inhabitants of Norwich' lamented 'the dayly growing evils and almost desperate diseases which have overspread

[1] M.C.B. (1634–46), 12 Feb. 1641/2, 339^r and 16 Apr. 1642, 345^r; A.B. (1613–42), 11 Mar. 1641/2, 379^r; Holmes, *Eastern Association*, pp. 25–8.

[2] See Zagorin, *Court and Country*, pp. 119–31, 155.

[3] Zagorin suggests that many corporations harboured hostility to the Crown, but refrained from expressing their grievances because of their social inferiority, their distaste of creating dissension within their midst, their traditional pre-occupation with local matters combined with the absence of a national bourgeois consciousness, and their fear of jeopardizing civic interests by risking royal disfavour. ibid.

[4] On 21 July, for example, the Assembly placed an order for six barrels of gunpowder. A.B. (1642–68), 21 July 1641, 1^r.

the whole body of this kingdom, both in Church and State'.[1] Not surprisingly, their first condemnations were reserved for 'the multitude of frivolous, ridiculous, and unwarranted [religious] ceremonies, pressed with the vehemence of suspension, excommunication, and deprivation' of many godly ministers. Citing monopolies, illegal taxations and imprisonment, and impartial justice 'as if government had been set free from restraint of laws' the townsmen decried the subversion of liberty as well as religion. In their minds the chief culprits were evil councillors, courtiers, Jesuits, and bishops, but they were also critical of the reluctance of Parliament to rectify the situation. Their own recommendations including the return of the King and the removal of the popish lords from the upper House, but their central concern was that the country be armed and ready for war.

Although the Norwich corporation had provided no public protestations or demonstrations of their loyalty to Parliament since the preceding February, the parliamentary-Puritans had secured an ascendant position in the magistracy as well as in the Common Council. The opportunity to demonstrate their allegiance to Parliament came on 28 July. On that day Captain Moses Treswell, bearing a commission signed by the Earl of Lindsey to collect 100 volunteers for the king, entered the city.[2] The magistrates called an urgent meeting the next day and the seventeen aldermen present agreed unanimously to prevent Treswell from beating his drums. When he ignored the order and attempted to collect soldiers, the city sheriffs arrested and committed him.[3] Within days the hapless Treswell was turned over to the House of Commons, which in turn expressed its gratitude for the city's fidelity. Although M.P.s Catelyn and Harman were decidedly cool in their support of Parliament now that the critical moment had come, the magistrates

---

[1] Brit. Lib., Thomason Collection, 669. f. 6. (54): *To the Lords. The Petition of Many Thousands of the Inhabitants of Norwich*, London, 16 July 1642, printed for George Tomlinson and R. C. Also republished on 27 August as *A True and Exact Relation of the Present estate of the City of Norwich*, for D. Bradley, Th. E. 114. (27). The petition is not mentioned in either corporation book and the published version makes no mention of the corporation. The mobilizing force behind the petition is unknown. I am thankful to Holmes, *Eastern Association*, p. 56 for the activities of city Royalists at this time.

[2] M.C.B. (1634–46), 29 July 1642, 355^v.

[3] ibid. The magistrates deemed it prudent, however, to inform the King of their actions.

were committed.[1] When a proclamation from the King requesting the aid of his subjects in suppressing the rebels arrived in Norwich in late August, the Court of Aldermen ignored it.[2]

From the outset of the war, the first concern of the corporation was the defence of the city in anticipation of a Royalist attack that never materialized. On the day Treswell was apprehended, the magistrates ordered that in the future the gates were to be locked and a double watch set up.[3] On 5 August the House of Lords placed responsibility for the trained bands and other military affairs in the hands of deputy-lieutenants for the city.[4] The latter were also instructed to confine recusants to their homes, arrest anyone who tried to raise forces against Parliament, and defend the future proceedings of Parliament from aspersions. According to one account, Cavaliers to the number of 150 horse and 300 foot soldiers were roaming the outskirts of Norwich in mid-August, but the same writer added that more than 2,000 armed men in the city were ready to 'live and die in the defence of Parliament'.[5] For the remainder of the year the deputy-lieutenants drilled the trained bands, formed a volunteer company, fully stocked and secured the magazine, and maintained close contact with Parliament.[6] Special care was taken in arranging city watches for the dual purpose of protecting the city from enemies outside the walls and preventing 'fanatics' from destroying the city from within.[7] The financing of

[1] Add. MSS., 22619, fo. 34: 30 July 1642; *C.J.* II. 698, 701: 1 Aug. and 3 Aug. 1642. See also Th. E. 112. (16): *Joyfull Newes from Norwich wherein is declared how the Earle of Lindsey endeavored to raise a party against the Parliament*, London, 17 August 1642, printed for T. Rider. The Treswell affair and its immediate aftermath were the decisive events in establishing the loyalties of Norfolk as well as Norwich M.P.s. See Holmes, *Eastern Association*, pp. 56–7.

[2] M.C.B. (1634–46), 27 Aug. 1642, 359ᵛ.

[3] ibid., 29 July 1642, 355ᵛ.

[4] *L.J.* V. 265–7: 5 Aug. 1642. Before the Civil War the city did not have its own deputy-lieutenants. See Owens, 'Norfolk'.

[5] Th. E. 114. (15): *Newes from the Citie of Norwich*, London, 26 August 1642, printed for Th. Clapham.

[6] *C.J.* II. 701, 704: 3 and 5 Aug. 1642; *L.J.* V. 266–7, 468, 574: 5 Aug. and 29 Nov. 1642 and 26 Jan. 1642/3; A.B. (1642–68), 3 and 15 Aug. and 1 Dec. 1642, 1ᵛ, 4ᵛ; M.C.B. (1634–46), 22 Oct. and 29 Nov. 1642, 365ᵛ, 367ᵛ.

[7] In November 1641 an attempt had been made by two Catholics, one at each end of the city, to burn Norwich down by setting fires simultaneously. Th. E. 179. (10): *Bloody Newes from Norwich : or, a True relation of a bloody attempt of the Papists in Norwich to consume the whole city by fire*, London, [27 November] 1641, printed for John Greensmith. Th. E. 147. (1): *Foure Wonderfull, Bloudy, and Dangerous Plots discovered : from Norwich, where a Train of Papists had conspired the firing of the Citie*, London, [May] 1642, printed for John Gilbert.

these military preparations was taken out of the proposition money, which was collected and distributed by John Tooly.[1]

With the collapse of the Royalist party in London and with almost all parts of East Anglia lining up behind Parliament by late 1642, the Royalist aldermen were in a precarious position.[2] As was the case with the Royalist aldermen of London, they either quietly acquiesced to the parliamentary-Puritans or retreated from politics altogether once war became a reality. There was little these London or Norwich magistrates could do other than to refuse to pay proposition money, for which they suffered imprisonment. At least two Norwich aldermen, John Daniel and John Osborne, went to gaol rather than pay this tax.[3] None of the Royalist aldermen were willing to go as far as future magistrate Robert Holmes, who walked around his ward with a companion late at night claiming he was the King's watch.[4] As long as the Royalist aldermen offered no political opposition, however, the parliamentary-Puritans in London and Norwich were content not to interfere with their lives, property, or offices.

Peaceful coexistence between the parliamentary-Puritan and Royalist magistrates in Norwich could not survive the formation of the Eastern Association. The parliamentary ordinance forming the Association, passed in December 1642, called for a military union of Norfolk, Suffolk, Essex, Cambridge, and Hertfordshire and required local officials to raise the requisite money for local fortifications and munitions by a compulsory levy. Moreover, men who had formerly refused to pay proposition money or obstructed

---

[1] *C.J.* II. 837, 868–9: 7 and 29 Nov. 1642. A total of £600 of the proposition money was used for the defence of the city. Alderman Tooly's accounts for the expenditure of these funds may be found in N.N.R.O., Various Accounts and Correspondence, 1642–50, n.p.

[2] Walter Rye has commented: 'When the storm broke, probably no county was warmer in favor of the Commonwealth than Norfolk.' Rye, *A History of Norfolk* (London, 1885), p. 86. On the other hand, Holmes has concluded that the local M.P.s and deputy-lieutenants 'whilst nominally securing Parliamentary control of the shire, consistently pursued policies designed to avoid pushing those whose sympathies were not behind Westminster into revolt'. Holmes, *Eastern Association*, p. 60. Livewell Sherwood and Hamond Craske were appointed captains of the volunteers. *C.J.* II. 868–9: 29 Nov. 1642. Sherwood was an ex-sheriff and councilman in 1642; he and Craske were later elected aldermen.

[3] ibid., II. 896: 19 Dec. 1642.

[4] Add. MSS., 22619, fo. 40: 3 Dec. 1642. Holmes's companion was William Hardingham, who refused also to pay the proposition money. See Ketton-Cremer, *Norfolk*, pp. 157–9.

Parliament or who now refused to pay the new tax were to have their weapons and horses confiscated and put to the service of the Association. On the last day of January 1642/3, Parliament took steps to implement the ordinance: the two captains or either of the sheriffs of Norwich were instructed to enter the homes of recusants, refusers to contribute to proposition money, or others who had as much as spoken out against Parliament, and authorized these officials to seize all arms, horses, and ammunition.[1] This was more than Mayor Gostlyn could endure. Abetted by Recorder Francis Cory, Gostlyn attempted to obstruct the order and by mid-February both were under investigation by the Eastern Association Committee.[2] In late February Lord Grey of Warke, the newly-appointed Major-General of the Association, concluded that a special visit to Norwich was necessary. On 1 March, the Mayor's Court agreed that 100 men, complete with arms and horses, should be collected and dispatched to Cambridge.[3] In order to get the necessary horses, a number of aldermen and councilmen were appointed to seize those of known Royalists. Gostlyn, who conveniently absented himself from this meeting, was adamantly opposed to such confiscation and refused to approve the orders. For his defiance he was arrested and quickly removed to Cambridge by Lord Grey.[4] With the mayor out of the city for an indefinite period, the dependable Adrian Parmenter was once again named deputy-mayor.

The reaction against Gostlyn marked the beginning of a purge which forced all non-co-operative Royalist aldermen from office by the end of March. Gostlyn's recalcitrance was not the sole factor which incited the Parliament men to clean the magisterial chambers. Early in March a Royalist resurgence spread throughout Norfolk and some of the Norwich aldermen may have been involved in an abortive conspiracy led by Augustine Holl to take over the city on 5 March.[5] Under the circumstances, the presence of Royalists in positions of authority constituted a threat which could

[1] *L.J.* V. 583: 31 Jan. 1642/3. For the formation of the Eastern Association and Norfolk reaction to it, see Holmes, *Eastern Association*, pp. 64–9.
[2] *C.J.* II. 967: 16 Feb. 1642/3.
[3] M.C.B. (1634–46), 1 Mar. 1642/3, 379ʳ.
[4] ibid., 4 Mar. 1642/3, 380ʳ; Blomefield, *Norfolk*, III. 383–4.
[5] Blomefield states that a number of magistrates were implicated, but he provides neither names nor a reference source. ibid., p. 384. See also Ketton-Cremer, *Norfolk*, pp. 176–7. Holl was a resident of Heigham, a suburb of Norwich.

no longer be tolerated. On 13 March the Assembly, after sending off another contingent of men and horses to Cambridge, ordered that letters be sent to Aldermen Lane, Daniel, and Osborne commanding them either to return to their homes and explain their absence from the Court of Aldermen, or be removed from office.[1] With municipal elections coming up in only a few days, the Mayor's Court was hastily convened on 18 March and, with fifteen members present, Lane, Daniel, and Osborne were ejected from office.[2] The parliamentary resolve may well have been bolstered by the presence of Oliver Cromwell, who stopped over in Norwich on 17 March and then rushed to Lowestoft to quash a Royalist uprising there.[3] His return to Norwich with prisoners on 20 March, the first day of the city's elections, could not have been purely coincidental. The elections resulted in eighteen new councilmen and five new aldermen.[4]

The moderates who trimmed their sails to the prevailing wind and the vacillating Royalists who prudently went along with the Roundheads were left unmolested, but the core of the Royalist party in the magistracy was obliterated within the space of a month. Table 16 lists all aldermen who were absent from at least one of three critical meetings in 1642 and 1642/3. The extent of the purge may be gauged by the fates of the first seven aldermen. Lane, Osborne, and Daniel were removed on 18 March 1642/3. Rosse was removed at the same time, although the immediate cause is unknown.[5] Gostlyn languished in a Cambridge gaol throughout March and April. There was no need to force John Anguish from office since his days were numbered by his failing health; he was

---

[1] A.B. (1642–68), 13 Mar. 1642/3, 6^{r-v}.

[2] M.C.B. (1634–46), 18 Mar. 1642/3, 381^v.

[3] A. D. Bayne, *Royal Illustrated History of Norfolk* (Great Yarmouth, n.d.), II. 174–5. For the Royalist failure in Lowestoft see Ketton-Cremer, *Norfolk*, pp. 179–84; W. C. Abbott, ed., *The Writings and Speeches of Oliver Cromwell* (Cambridge, 1934–47), I. 218–20.

[4] A.B. (1642–68), 20–24 Mar. 1642/3. Livewell Sherwood, Matthew Lindsey, and Robert Baron replaced Daniel, Lane, and Osborne. William Symond replaced Thomas Shipdham, who had died, and Samuel Puckle took the seat of Richard Rosse. All were well-known Parliament men and were sworn into office on 26 March 1643. M.C.B. (1634–46), 26 Mar. 1643, 381^v.

[5] There is no mention in the Assembly Book or the Mayor's Court Book that Rosse was forced out of office, but Blomefield asserts that he was removed for favouring the King. Blomefield, *Norfolk*, III. 385. Rosse may also have been in failing health, for his will is dated 10 July 1643, and was proved in April 1645. N.N.R.O., N.C.C., 4 Burlye (1645).

buried on 24 April 1643. John Freeman was impeached by his
ward on 3 May.[1] The penalty for drifting into the Royalist camp
was now clear, and in case the moderates had not learned the lesson
they were reminded by the ejection of Alexander Anguish in April
1644, on the trumped-up charge of fraud, deception, and corrup-
tion in the execution of justice.[2]

TABLE 16: *Aldermanic Absenteeism, 1642–1643**

	29 July 1642	1 March 1642/3	18 March 1642/3
Henry Lane	absent	absent	absent
John Osborne		absent	absent
John Daniel		absent	absent
Richard Rosse	absent	absent	absent
William Gostlyn		absent	absent
John Anguish	absent	absent	absent
John Freeman		absent	
John Loveland	absent	absent	
Thomas Baker	absent		
John Croshold	absent		
John Utting			absent
	17 present	15 present	16 present
	6 absent	8 absent	7 absent

*Alderman Harman, member of Parliament, was in London, leaving twenty-
three aldermen in Norwich. The absence of John Loveland may be explained by
his great age. Attendance is taken from the Assembly and Mayor's Court Books.

The events of March 1643 confirmed the supremacy of the
parliamentary-Puritans in all levels of government. The trouble-
some seniority ordinance, however, was still in force. In 1643
Thomas Barber, who had opposed the 1636 petition and had done
very little to aid the Puritan movement, was next in line to be
mayor.[3] Having just stomached the mayoralty of Gostlyn, the
parliamentary party had no desire to repeat the experience and the

[1] M.C.B. (1634–46),3 May 1643, 384ʳ. Freeman managed to maintain his
status as alderman.
[2] A.B. (1642–68), 4 Apr. 1644, 16ʳ⁻ᵛ. The Assembly was willing to drop the
charges against Anguish if he would relinquish office. On 7 January 1661/2 the
Assembly renounced this order.
[3] John Loveland had greatest seniority, but had recently compounded out of
the mayoralty. ibid. (1613–42), 28 Apr. 1642, 382ʳ. Barber was followed in
seniority by John Thacker and John Freeman.

Assembly ordered the 1620 law to be inoperative for the forthcoming election.[1] The commons then passed over Barber and nominated two staunch Parliament men, John Thacker and Matthew Peckover; and Thacker was chosen mayor-elect by the magistrates.[2] The next year the Assembly settled the issue once and for all, this time at the expense of John Freeman, the senior alderman in rank. Declaring the 1620 ordinance to be very 'inconvenient', they declared void its provisions relating to the election of mayors.[3] Aldermen were still to be chosen from among the ex-sheriffs as set down in 1620 and 1627/8, but the freemen would no longer have to nominate a mayor they did not want. With their old freedoms restored, the freemen proceeded to the polls and elected John Tooly to a second term.

Shortly after the elections of March and 1 May 1643, the parliamentary-Puritan party turned to the problem of religious reconstruction. Since the petitions against Wren two years before, the corporation's involvement in the religious life of Norwich had been very limited. In 1643, however, they resumed the lead both in dismantling the Anglican Church in Norwich and in bringing well-known Puritan preachers to the city. The House of Commons had passed an order in September 1641 disavowing the practice of bowing at the name of Jesus, permitting the removal of rails from the communion table, and calling for the abolition of images. Soon afterwards the altar rails were removed from many parish churches in Norwich, and where they were not taken down by the parishioners the mobs did the work for them.[4] The following February the Puritan apprentices threatened to storm the Cathedral, rip out the altar rails, and pull down the organ.[5] The Dean and Chapter quickly decided to remove the altar rails themselves in the hope that the apprentices would be appeased and the organ preserved. The expected riot never took place, but the Puritans claimed a victory. A Parliament ordinance of August 1643, which called for the destruction of all monuments of superstition and idolatry,

[1] ibid. (1642–68), 3 Apr. 1643, 6ᵛ. The previous September the Common Hall of London had also ignored seniority in its mayoral nominations.

[2] ibid., 1 May 1643, 9ᵛ.

[3] ibid., 4 Apr. 1644, 16ʳ⁻ᵛ.

[4] *East Anglian: Notes and Queries*, III (1866–8), 253.

[5] Th. E. 140. (17): T. L., *True Newes from Norwich. Being a certaine relation how that the Cathedrall Blades of Norwich . . . did put themselves into a posture of defence, because that the Apprentices of Norwich would have pulled down their Organs*, London, [February] 1641, printed for Benjamin Allen and I. B.

provided official sanction for sterner measures.[1] This time the corporation and the magistrates were in the forefront of the assault. In November the Court of Aldermen ordered the sequestration of Bishop Hall's property, and in January they decided that the £100 originally sequestered was only half of what Hall should have paid.[2] Within days a group of iconoclasts, led by two aldermen and one of the sheriffs, forced their way into the Cathedral and deanery, smashed the stained glass windows, beat down walls, tore up monuments, demolished the altar, and publicly burned surplices, hymn-books, and relics.[3] The magistrates heartily applauded this activity: less than two weeks later they named a committee to search parish churches and destroy scandalous pictures, crucifixes, and images and gather incriminating information on 'scandalous' ministers.[4] Later, early in March, some religious paintings, which somehow survived the first iconoclastic onslaught, were discovered in St. Swithin and St. Peter Mancroft; the Mayor's Court promptly ordered them to be burned in the open market.[5]

Preaching by Puritan lecturers and ministers, with the support and protection of the corporation, had been a feature of religious life before Wren's purge. By 1640, however, the ranks of Puritan preachers had been decimated. One visitor to the city in 1640/1 noted that 'there is but two preaching ministers that goes for currant amongst them in the whole city, vidz. Carter and Hall'.[6] In December 1641 the Common Council had gained the right to join

[1] C. H. Firth and R. S. Rait, eds., *Acts and Ordinances of the Interregnum 1642–1660* (London, 1911), I. 265–6. Another parliamentary ordinance dealing with the same matter was passed in May 1644. ibid., pp. 425–6.

[2] M.C.B. (1634–46), 22 Nov. 1643, and 10 Jan. 1643/4, 400^r, 410^r. The committee for sequestration had been operative since the preceding March and had already sequestered the Duke of Norfolk's palace in July. ibid., 20 May and 10 July 1643, 385^r, 394^v.

[3] Bishop Joseph Hall, *Hard Measure* (1647) in Blomefield, *Norfolk*, III. 389–90, 579. The best narrative of Hall's affairs during the Civil War is in Ketton-Cremer, *Norfolk*, pp. 224–37. The aldermen were John Greenwood and Matthew Lindsey and the sheriff was Thomas Toft, who was soon to be elected alderman. A year later the aldermen ordered the Dean and Prebend to destroy any pictures or crucifixes which escaped the first demolition. M.C.B. (1634–46), 1 Mar. 1644/5, 445^v.

[4] ibid., 23 Jan. 1643/4, 411^r. For similar iconoclastic activities in Norfolk see Ketton-Cremer, *Norfolk*, pp. 252–7.

[5] M.C.B. (1634–46), 9 Mar. 1643/4, 415^r.

[6] Schofield, ed., *Knyvett Letters*, pp. 98–100: Thomas Knyvett to his wife, 17 Jan. 1640/1. Henry Hall was parish chaplain at St. Andrew and in 1640 was a member of the Divines' assembly in London.

the magistrates in appointing lecturers sponsored by the corporation, but they took no action until after the purge of 1643. This delay may well have resulted from a hesitation to take action until the national government had provided the lead.[1] Two days after the mayoral election of Thacker, the Assembly invited the notorious William Bridge to return to Norwich and deliver Friday morning sermons at St. Andrew.[2] Bridge had just founded the first Independent church in Yarmouth and within a year he organized an Independent church in Norwich.[3] In August the Assembly induced Edward Reyner, who had been evicted from the county of Lincoln by the Earl of Newcastle's forces, to preach at St. Andrew on Monday mornings.[4] Three months later Timothy Armitage was hired to give Wednesday lectures at St. Michael Coslany.[5] Armitage was later to become pastor of the Independent church and, with Bridge, was superintendent of numerous non-conformist congregations in Norfolk and Suffolk.[6] The corporation also obtained permission from the House of Commons in November 1643 to nominate and appoint ministers to preach in the Cathedral on Sunday mornings.[7]

In 1644 and 1645 the military, political, and religious policies commenced in 1642 and 1643 were brought to a successful conclusion. The city continued to supply the parliamentary war machine with money and, when necessary, additional troops.[8]

[1] The House of Commons had promised religious reform in the Grand Remonstrance of 22 November 1641. A decision was reached in April 1642 to convene a national assembly, but the Westminster Assembly did not actually meet until July 1643.

[2] A.B. (1642–68), 3 May 1643, 10ʳ. Bridge had fled to Holland in the midst of Wren's persecution, and returned to England in 1641 to preach before the House of Commons.

[3] *D.N.B.*, s.v. William Bridge. See also Bayne, *History of Norwich* (Norwich, 1869), pp. 245–9.

[4] A.B. (1642–68), 25 Aug. 1643, 11ᵛ. Reyner returned to Lincoln in October 1645 to preach for the corporation there and in 1662 he was ejected from his benefice. *D.N.B.*, s.v. Edward Reyner.

[5] A.B. (1642–68), 16 Nov. 1643, 13ʳ.

[6] *D.N.B.*, s.v. Timothy Armitage. Armitage died in 1655.

[7] *C.J.* III. 298: 1 Nov. 1643. The complete letter may be found in Various Accounts and Correspondence, 1642–50, n.p. The magistrates also moved their seats to the east end of the Cathedral. After 1643/4 seats were also reserved in the Cathedral for the councilmen by order of the Assembly. A.B. (1642–68), 20 Feb. 1643/4, 14ʳ.

[8] On 26 March 1644, for example, the Mayor's Court ordered two companies together with as many horses as could be gathered to report to Cambridge. M.C.B. (1634–46), 26 Mar. 1644, 417ʳ. For the gathering of money and troops see Holmes, *Eastern Association*, pp. 87, 139, 166–70.

When the Roundheads triumphed at Marston Moor outside York, the magistrates proclaimed a day of thanksgiving on which they paraded through the city in their resplendent robes to the roar of cannon and the ringing of bells.[1] For those citizens whose conscience was torn between duty to Commonwealth and obedience to Crown, the pulpits thundered out advice on the best course of action. In a sermon delivered at the swearing-in of Mayor Tooly in 1644, John Carter assured his listeners that to support Parliament was to oppose an evil Court circle but not the King. Hence the good Christian must defend both true religion and the Crown as defended by Parliament and be willing to sacrifice life and property in the process.[2] The eviction of Alderman Anguish and the replacement of Recorder Cory by Samuel Smith in the spring of 1644 brought to an end the political purges begun the preceding year.[3] In religious affairs, the Assembly set up a committee to examine scandalous ministers in early 1645 and later in the year the old church services were discontinued and the celebration of Christmas was forbidden.[4]

*   *   *

The triumph of the parliamentary-Puritans in capturing the Norwich corporation had been gradual, peaceful, legal, and

[1] M.C.B. (1634–46), 17 July 1644, 430ᵛ. Other days of thanksgiving were held on 15 Mar. 1644/5, 21 June, 25 July, and 6 Dec. 1645.

[2] The sermon concluded: 'You must endeavor the public good before your own. You must be content to bear any load of pains, or charge, to procure the wealth and prosperity of the Kingdom, that the Reformation may be perfected, true religion established, popes, superstition, and the proved tyrannical hierarchy may be utterly extirpated, the rights and privileges of Parliament and the liberties of the Kingdom preserved; that the King's person and authority in the preserva tion of true religion may be defended . . .' Th. E. 411. (6): John Carter, *The Nail hit on the head*, 17 June 1644 in Carter, *The Nail and the Wheel. Both described in two sermons in the Greenyard at Norwich*, London, 1647, printed by T. Macock for M. Spark. The argument that Parliament forces were not marching against the King but against a corrupt and papistical court was the official line adopted by Parliament and was used by invading Scottish forces in January 1643/4. Indeed, the Solemn League and Covenant required men to swear 'to preserve and defend the King's Majesty's person and authority'.

[3] A.B. (1642–68), 3 May 1644, 20ʳ. The fidelity of Recorder Cory to the Parliament side had been suspect as early as February 1642/3. C.J. II. 967: 16 Feb. 1642/3. Samuel Smith had been a deputy-lieutanant for the city and had served on the committee for sequestration. ibid., p. 884. When Cory threatened to contest his ouster, the Assembly sent a petition against him to Parliament. A. B. (1642–68), 5 and 13 June 1644, 20ᵛ. The orders to remove Anguish and Cory were both renounced by the Assembly on 6 January 1661/2.

[4] ibid., 3 May 1645, 31ᵛ; M.C.B. (1634–46), 24 Dec. 1645, 465ᵛ.

non-provocative. The aldermanic purge and the overhaul of the Council in 1642/3 did not alter dramatically the balance of power between the rival parties; it merely continued a trend which had been developing since 1640. A consistency in voting patterns from 1640 to 1645 suggests that Norwich freemen went to the polls with political and religious considerations in mind. This permitted the parliamentary-Puritans not only to have members of their own party elected to the magistracy but also to prevent magisterial recruitment by their opposition. Quite possibly it was this rise to power by means of electoral strategy which allowed Norwich to escape the revolutionary excesses of London.

Although the political affiliation of the magistrates can be determined by their reactions to unfolding events, the lists of voluntary subscribers for the regaining of Newcastle by the forces of Parliament in 1643 must be used to ascertain the political stance of councilmen and ward electorates.[1] The Norwich magistrates are not known to have exerted any pressure for contributions; at least seven aldermen refused to volunteer money, and a majority of Norwich citizens chose not to. Refusal to donate may well have been based on reasons neither political nor religious, such as temporary lack of funds or disapproval of voluntary contributions as a method of taxation. Therefore, it would seem as though those who refused to contribute would include all Royalists, most moderates, and even some parliamentary sympathizers. On the other hand, those who did contribute freely, with the knowledge that their generosity and loyalty in no way exempted them from other heavy taxes, would seem to be ardent Parliament men.

These assumptions concerning the Newcastle Collection are supported by an examination of the behaviour of magistrates whose political positions before 1645 can be determined by their actions on other matters. Of the 229 contributors, twenty-two were members of the political élite and twenty-one of these are known to have been strong parliamentary-Puritans.[2] Some held commissions in the parliamentary army, served on sequestration committees, assisted in the confiscation of Royalist horses and ammunition, or in other ways publicly committed themselves against the

---

[1] N.N.R.O., Subscriptions for Regaining Newcastle, 1643.
[2] A full discussion of the subscription and a breakdown of contributors and non-contributors by parish may be found in Evans, 'Political Elite of Norwich', pp. 516–33.

interests of the Crown.[1] Among those who refused to donate, some are known to have been Royalists, some moderates, and some active Roundheads. None of the aldermen impeached and removed from office made a contribution. Of the 274 non-contributors listed, sixteen were members of the political élite whose political position before 1645 can be established firmly. Ten of these were Royalists like William Gostlyn and Robert Holmes. Four of the sixteen were moderates with inclinations in one direction or the other but without commitment. Of the remaining two, one was Edmund Burman, who had been a member of numerous parliamentary-Puritan committees, including the Committee for Associated Counties by appointment of the House of Commons. The other, William Davy, also participated in important committees, two of which were the committee to investigate scandalous ministers and the committee to demolish paintings and images in churches. Since it is reasonable to assume that the behaviour of the political élite was not different from that of other citizens listed in the Collection, it may therefore be concluded that a contribution almost invariably designates the donor a parliamentary-Puritan. Refusal to donate does not necessarily indicate a Royalist, although it is highly improbable that a non-contributor would be a strong parliamentary-Puritan.

On the basis of the Newcastle Collection, there was no significant change in the political composition of the Common Council at any time between 1640 and 1645. As Table 17 shows, 24 of the 50 councilmen of 1640, still alive in 1643 and known to be residing in the city, contributed to the Newcastle Collection; and 27 of the 60 councilmen of 1645 were contributors. Since a sizeable number, perhaps 30 per cent, of the non-contributors were moderates and a few may well have been Parliament men, these figures agree with the known parliamentary-Puritan bias of the Council throughout this period. There was no significant change in the political views of the councilmen of the different wards, but the distribution of contributors among the four wards is striking. Whereas only 5 of the 28 councilmen for Conesford and Mancroft in 1643 were contributors, 22 of the 32 councilmen for Wymer and Over-the-Water donated. This difference between wards was already in evidence in 1640. In the following five years, the freemen of Wymer and Over-the-Water quite clearly preferred men who ultimately supported

[1] The sole exception was the venerable John Loveland.

TABLE 17: *Political Division of the Common Council, 1640–1645**

		1640	1641	1642	1643	1644	1645
Conesford	A	3	3	4	4	4	4
	B	4	4	4	5	5	4
	C	3	3	3	3	3	4
Mancroft	A	2	2	1	1	1	1
	B	5	4	4	5	7	7
	C	7	9	10	10	8	8
Wymer	A	11	13	13	12	12	13
	B	5	6	7	7	7	6
	C	0	0	0	1	1	1
Over-the-Water	A	8	7	7	10	10	9
	B	0	1	2	1	2	2
	C	2	2	2	1	0	1
Total	A	24	25	25	27	27	27
	B	14	15	17	17	17	15
	C	12	14	15	16	16	18

A: listed as contributor to Newcastle Collection, 1643
B: listed as having refused to contribute
C: not listed as having refused to contribute, but was not a contributor and known to be residing in the city in 1645

*The councilmen known to have died before 1644 or believed to be dead or to have left the city before 1644 have been omitted.

Parliament, whereas the freemen of Mancroft and Conesford elected men who would not voluntarily contribute to the parliamentary army. Of the 22 Wymer and Over-the-Water men who were elected to the Council for the first time from 1640 to 1645, 16 were contributors, but only 4 of the 16 new councilmen for Mancroft and Conesford contributed. The election of councilmen implies that the freemen of the wards of Wymer and Over-the-Water were much more strongly supportive of the parliamentary-Puritan party than the freemen of Mancroft and Conesford. An analysis of all subscribers to the Newcastle Collection and the signatories to the Solemn League and Covenant confirms this to be the case.[1]

Although the freemen of Mancroft and Conesford resisted whatever pressure may have existed to elect solely Parliament men to the Council, every alderman elected from 1642 to 1647 was without exception a Roundhead. An examination of elections to the Court of Aldermen reveals that intimidation, if resorted to, was neither decisive nor necessary. There were never more than eleven eligible candidates for the aldermanry during these years and at one point in 1643 there were only three ex-sheriffs available. After the election of Royalist John Osborne by the freemen of Mancroft in June 1641, there was only one non-parliamentarian ex-sheriff, Robert Thompson, in the city during the Civil War.[2] Moreover, every indication of Thompson's financial status suggests that he was not the stuff of which aldermen were made.[3] Since the eligible candidates for the aldermanry were all supporters of Parliament, the freemen of the various wards had no choice but to elect Roundheads in each of the eleven elections from 1642 to 1647, whether they wanted to or not.[4]

The key to the parliamentary-Puritan electoral strategy, and consequently to their success in legally and peacefully capturing and assuring control of the magistracy, lay therefore in the election of sheriffs. Although the parliamentary-Puritans were outnumbered in two of the four wards, their clear majority in the freeman electorate and, by the outbreak of war in 1642, in the magistracy guaranteed them the last word in these elections. If the freemen of

[1] This will be discussed in further detail below.

[2] It is not even known for certain that Thompson was a Royalist, although he refused to contribute to the Newcastle Collection. Since he was taxed for the river and streets in 1649, we know that he was still alive and resident in St. Peter Mancroft parish during these years. The one ex-sheriff in 1642/3 who neither contributed nor refused to contribute was parliamentarian William Symond.

[3] On the tax on personal estate in the 1645 assessment for Fairfax's troops, Thompson was rated at 6*s*. This compares with an average in excess of 13*s*. per alderman on the same tax. There were more than thirty inhabitants in St. Peter Mancroft alone who were taxed more than Thompson.

[4] On the eve of the purge in 1642/3, for example, seven of the nine past and present sheriffs later contributed to the Newcastle Collection; the exceptions were Thompson and Symond.

Mancroft and Conesford had not been required to limit their choice to present and past sheriffs, they could have precipitated a constitutional crisis by electing Royalists. This may well explain why the Assembly never repealed the clauses of the 1620 ordinance regulating the election of aldermen, but twice dispensed with and finally repealed the provisions touching the election of mayors.[1] There were more wealthy citizens in the city who refused to contribute than did contribute to the Newcastle Collection, yet nine of the ten sheriffs elected from 1641 to 1645 were contributors. The exception, Richard Bateman, was certainly no Royalist. As Table 18 shows, nine of these same ten sheriffs were residents of

TABLE 18: *Sheriffs Elected, 1640–1645*

	Behaviour on Newcastle Collection	Residence*
1640: John Osborne	refused	St. Peter Mancroft (M)
John Dethick	(not listed)	(London)
1641: Matthew Lindsey	contributed	St. Peter Mancroft (M)
Robert Baron	contributed	St. Andrew (W)
1642: John Greenwood	contributed	St. Andrew (W)
John Rayley	contributed	St. Andrew (W)
1643: Thomas Toft	contributed	St. Clement (OW)
Richard Bateman	(not listed)	St. Clement (OW)
1644: Thomas Baret	contributed	St. John Maddermarket (W)
Bernard Church	contributed	St. George Colegate (OW)
1645: John Cory	contributed	St. Saviour (OW)
William Rye	contributed	St. Saviour (OW)

* M: Mancroft
   W: Wymer
OW: Over-the-Water

Wymer and Over-the-Water wards. The only resident of Mancroft to be chosen sheriff, Matthew Lindsey in 1641, was the most influential of the few wealthy parliamentarians in his ward. Obviously this pattern is not coincidental. Political affiliation was a paramount criterion in selection and no man not a Roundhead was

[1] The laws governing elections were read to the voters before each aldermanic election. In January 1642/3 the Mayor's Court refused to accept the election of an alderman who had not been sheriff and ordered new elections. M.C.B. (1634–46), 26 Jan. 1642/3, 374ᵛ–375ʳ.

elected or had a chance of being elected sheriff during the Civil War.

The parliamentary-Puritan dominance of the shrievalty and thus recruitment to the aldermanry had a telling effect on the political composition of the magistracy. The Court of Aldermen, which had opposed the Puritans in 1636, was still potentially hostile to them in 1640 (Table 19). By August 1641, however,

TABLE 19: *Politics and the Aldermanry, 1640–1643**

	1 August 1640	1 August 1641	1 August 1642	1 August 1643
Royalists	11	10	9	4
Parliamentary-Puritans	8	9	10	15
Moderates	5	5	5	5

*The parliamentary-Puritans are easily identifiable, but it is often difficult to distinguish between the moderate and the Royalist since the Royalists offered no active resistance. Since no litmus test can be used, the political careers of moderates and Royalists prior to and shortly after 1643, provided in Evans, 'Political Elite of Norwich', pp. 484–515 have been used.

there were almost as many parliamentary-Puritan as Royalist aldermen and the normal processes of attrition and replacement totally favoured the former. The events of 1642 left the Royalist magistrates in the minority and with little will to oppose the alliance of the corporation with Parliament. The purge of 1642/3 brought to a dramatic end any possibility of Royalist obstruction or interference from within the aldermanry. Yet it did not constitute a grave crisis: it merely accelerated what would otherwise have occurred more slowly. With the parliamentary-Puritan supremacy in the Court assured for the future and the Royalist uprisings in Norfolk quashed by Cromwell, the purge may even have been welcomed by the Royalist aldermen. They had already ceased to have any influence in corporation affairs and they wanted no association with the politics of their fellow magistrates.

The manner in which the Norwich parliamentary-Puritans successfully manipulated electoral politics sheds light on a possible explanation for their reluctance to take more radical actions in 1641 and 1642. The parliamentary-Puritans of London were compelled to adopt revolutionary measures which were not necessary in Norwich. In 1640 there were only five parliamentary-Puritans on the twenty-six-member aldermanic Bench of London. From this point until December 1641 five vacancies arose; and four of these were filled by parliamentary-Puritans, who joined a Court which continued to side officially with the King. The celebrated flight of the five M.P.s into the heart of London followed by the confrontation over the militia bill imposed an immediate political imperative on the London Common Council to challenge and overthrow the traditional power of the Court of Aldermen. The Norwich parliamentary-Puritans could afford to wait and time was on their side. The parliamentary-Puritans of neither city were interested in altering the constitution in order to permit more popular participation in government. They changed the constitution only when they needed to and only because they wanted their party in power.[1] Apart from the election of mayors, it is extremely doubtful that the parliamentary-Puritan magistrates of Norwich ever contemplated significant constitutional change. First, the existing constitution protected the ascendancy and supremacy of their own party. And, second, they were members of the same socio-economic élite as the men they replaced.

* * *

Many towns experienced changes in governmental personnel during the Civil War and Interregnum. Often these changes were a resolution of local squabbles which antedated the Civil War and not a consequence of bitter strife between Parliament men and Royalists over national issues.[2] Howell has pointed out, for example, that in Newcastle a correspondence exists between a protracted economic and social conflict in the decades before 1640 and the division into Parliament and Crown supporters during the war. The real contest here was not over national affairs; it was a struggle of the lesser hostmen and other trades against the mercers' and hostmen's domination of the town's economic and political life. The purges which took place in Newcastle after 1644 thus involved little more than the replacement of one socio-economic clique by

[1] Pearl, *London*, p. 249.

[2] Barnstaple, Bristol, Durham, Exeter, Leicester, and Rye are examples of towns in which one clique of politicians replaced another. Clark and Slack, eds., *Crisis and Order*, p. 25. For the desired neutrality of many towns during the war see William A. Hayden Shilling, 'The Central Government and the Municipal Corporations in England, 1642–1663' (unpublished Ph.D. thesis, Vanderbilt University, 1970), Chap. 2.

another.[1] Chester is another example. Johnson has stressed that the split here between parliamentarian and Royalist in 1642 was 'the expression and outgrowth under national labels of the political struggle in which they had been engaged throughout the early seventeenth century'.[2] Unlike Newcastle and Chester, London was deeply immersed in the national struggle, but the contest for control of the corporation also had socio-economic overtones. Brenner has shown that the Royalist magistrates not only favoured the Crown and the Church but also represented the socio-economic interests and political hegemony of the Levant and East India Company merchants and, to a lesser degree, the Company of Merchant Adventurers. The leadership of the parliamentary-Puritans, on the other hand, included men representing the politically-excluded traders who concentrated on colonial commerce, the 'colonial-interloping complex'. The victory of the parliamentary-Puritans in London, therefore, was both the triumph of a political and religious ideology and the overthrow of one social and economic group by another.[3] Norwich was an exception. An analysis of the citizenry and the leadership of the rival parties which follows suggests that there were no economic or social grievances underlying the religious and political rift and the ascendancy of the parliamentary-Puritans did not bring a new socio-economic group to power.

The magistrates who espoused the parliamentary cause in Norwich were members of politically-established trades and, in consequence, their elevation to office did not transform the occupational composition of the Court of Aldermen from what it had been in previous decades. Of the thirty-seven magistrates who held office from 1642 to 1645, twenty can be clearly identified as parliamentary-Puritans and eight as Royalists.[4] Far from being

---

[1] Howell, *Newcastle*, pp. 162–4, 177, 343. Howell states that the split in towns in 1643 was 'merely an older struggle now disguised by new names and fought out in terms of a national struggle with which it had little positive identification'.

[2] A. M. Johnson, 'Politics in Chester during the Civil Wars and Interregnum, 1640–1662', in Clark and Slack, eds., *Crisis and Order*, p. 204.

[3] Robert Brenner, 'The Civil War Politics of London's Merchant Community', *Past and Present*, 58 (Feb. 1973), 53–107. The 'colonial interloping complex' helped to engineer the downfall of the older merchant companies, but they themselves did not come to the fore until the army captured the city in 1647.

[4] The parliamentary-Puritans were Baker, C. Baret, T. Baret, Baron, Burman, Cory, Greenwood, Lindsey, Parmenter, Peckover, Puckle, Rayley, Rye, Sherwood, Shipdham, Symond, Thacker, Toft, Tooly, and Watts. The Royalists

'new men' of politically-excluded trades, eleven of the parliament-ary-Puritans were grocers and four others were merchants. These two trades had dominated officeholding during the Elizabethan period and they continued to account for more than half the aldermanic Bench in 1620 and 1630.[1] The influx of Parliament men to the magistracy did result in four more grocers and merchants on the Court in 1645 than in 1640, but the trade structure of the Court of Aldermen in 1645 was not appreciably different from what it had been in 1630.[2] Although the leadership of the parlia-mentary-Puritan party was drawn primarily from the grocers and merchants, not all of the prominent members of these trades supported Parliament. One of the known Royalist magistrates was a grocer and two others were merchants; and two of them were ejected from office in the purge. The other trades which had traditionally provided officeholders were also divided. Table 20 lists the trades and reaction to the Newcastle Collection of the eighty-four aldermen and councilmen of 1645. Not all men who refused to contribute were Royalists, but it would seem very likely that none of the prominent trades overwhelmingly favoured one side or the other.

The parliamentary-Puritan officeholders were also wealthy men, but neither more nor less so than their predecessors or their opponents. Eighteen of the twenty parliamentary-Puritan magis-trates identified above were taxed for personal estate in an assess-

[1] Pound, 'Elizabethan Corporation of Norwich', pp. 140–8. The correlation between cloth, Puritanism, and parliamentarianism in towns during the Civil War has frequently been assumed and has been recently documented for the county of Somerset. David Underdown, *Somerset in the Civil War and Interreg-num* (Newton Abbot, 1973). It is interesting to note that the worsted weavers of Norwich were split in their loyalties and did not provide the backbone of the Puritan leadership.

[2] A detailed, statistical examination of the relationship between trades and officeholding may be found in Evans, 'Decline of Oligarchy', pp. 67–75. See also Evans, 'Political Elite of Norwich', pp. 469–82, 551–66. In 1630 the Court of Aldermen consisted of 8 grocers, 5 merchants, 2 drapers, 2 mercers, 2 scriveners, 2 ironmongers, a hosier, a baker, and an apothecary. In 1645 the Court con-tained 9 grocers, 4 merchants, 4 hosiers, 2 drapers, 2 worsted weavers, a mercer, a brewer, and a vintner.

were A. Anguish, J. Anguish, Daniel, Freeman, Gostlyn, Lane, Osborne, and Rosse. The remaining nine magistrates were Barber, Bateman, Church, Cros-hold, Harman, Lombe, Loveland, Sotherton, and Utting. These party affiliations are based on the political biographies of the magistrates found in Evans, 'Political Elite of Norwich', pp. 484–515.

TABLE 20: *Trades and Political Affiliation of Aldermen and Councilmen, 1645*

Trade	Aldermen		Councilmen		Total	
	A	B	A	B	A	B
Worsted Weavers	1	1	10	9	11	10
Grocers	6	3	3	6	9	9
Hosiers	3	1	2	2	5	3
Merchants	3	1	1	1	4	2
Mercers	–	1	2	3	2	4
Drapers	1	1	–	2	1	3
Bakers	–	–	3	1	3	1
Apothecaries	–	–	1	2	1	2
Brewers	1	–	–	1	1	1
Scriveners	–	–	1	1	1	1
Ironmongers	–	–	–	2	–	2
Goldsmiths	–	–	–	2	–	2
Others	–	1	4	1	4	2
Totals	15	9	27	33	42	42

A: contributed to Newcastle Collection
B: did not contribute

ment for Sir Thomas Fairfax's troops in 1645.[1] Fifteen of these eighteen were rated 10s. or more for personal estate, which placed them among the wealthiest eighty-four (upper 5 per cent) of the freemen. Nine of the twenty-seven councilmen of 1645 who donated to the Newcastle Collection were also taxed 10s. or more for personal estate. The sheriffs' elections were pivotal in determining the future personnel of the Court of Aldermen and assuring that it would be parliamentary-Puritan in character. Of the ten sheriffs elected from 1641 to 1645 (all of whom were parliamentary-Puritans), eight were among the eighty-four wealthiest citizens and all were among the wealthiest 7 per cent of the freemen. For purposes of comparison, in 1576 the aldermen and one-third of the councilmen were among the 100 wealthiest townsmen.[2] The magistrates of the Restoration were similarly chosen from the 100

[1] For the parliamentary act authorizing the tax see *A. & O.* I. 614–26: An Ordinance for Raising and Maintaining of Forces for the Defence of the Kingdom, under the Command of Sir Thomas Fairfax, Knight, 17 Feb. 1644/5.
[2] Pound, 'Social and Trade Structure', pp. 53–4.

most affluent citizens. In summary, the requirement of wealth in the recruitment of magistrates was neither relaxed nor made more restrictive for parliamentary-Puritan officeholders during the Civil War. As the issues which had separated the parliamentary-Puritans from their opponents had divided the more prominent trades, so also they divided the wealthy élite of the city. Of the twenty-two wealthiest councilmen in 1645, nine contributed to the Newcastle Collection whereas thirteen did not. The median assessment of the councilmen who contributed was 7s. 6d. and for the councilmen who refused it was 8s.[1] Of the wealthiest 203 citizens in 1645, seventy contributed to the Collection and 133 did not. If perhaps one-fourth of the non-contributors were moderates and one-eighth even were Parliament men, then there would be a near parity between parliamentary-Puritans and Royalists among the 200 wealthiest citizens in Norwich.

The leadership of the conflicting parties cannot be distinguished on the basis of social background, family connection, or age. Both sides attracted men who were foreign-born as well as the sons of long-established Norwich families. Three parliamentary-Puritan magistrates and four Royalist magistrates were the sons of previous aldermen.[2] The median date of obtaining freedom for the Royalists was 1610 and for the parliamentary-Puritans it was 1613. Clearly, the leaders of the Roundhead party were not young men and most were probably over fifty years old.[3] For the councilmen who contributed to the Collection in 1645, the median date for becoming a freeman was 1623 whereas for the non-contributing councilmen it was 1622. There is no evidence that the political life of Norwich prior to 1640 involved a conflict between prominent and rival families, and the nucleus of the two sides during the Civil War cannot be defined in this manner. City politics had already ceased to be determined by a limited number of ruling families by the 1620s and 1630s.[4] Moreover, there is abundant evidence that

---

[1] Of the eight Royalist magistrates, only four were taxed for personal estate in the collection for Fairfax's troops and their median assessment was 11s. 6d. The median assessment for the parliamentary-Puritan magistrates was 12s.

[2] They were T. Baret, Peckover, Tooly, A. Anguish, J. Anguish, Gostlyn, and Lane.

[3] Only seven of the twenty parliamentary-Puritan magistrates became freemen after 1620 and none after 1630. If the average age of becoming a freeman is accepted to be twenty-five then the median age of the parliamentary-Puritan magistrates in 1643 was fifty-five.

[4] Evans, 'Decline of Oligarchy', pp. 58–9.

members of prominent families were themselves divided in their
loyalties when the Civil War broke out.[1]

Although social and economic factors do not account for the
separation of Parliament men and Royalists, two clear patterns
underlying political affiliation do emerge. The first involves the
concentration of parliamentary-Puritans in the wards of Wymer
and Over-the-Water, and of Royalists in Mancroft and Conesford.
It has already been pointed out that 69 per cent of the councilmen
for Wymer and Over-the-Water contributed in 1645 to the
Collection, whereas only 18 per cent of the councilmen for
Mancroft and Conesford were contributors. All but one of the ten
parliamentary-Puritan sheriffs from 1641 to 1645 were residents of
the first two wards. Of the twenty parliamentary-Puritan magistrates, fifteen were residents of Wymer and Over-the-Water and
five lived in the Puritan stronghold of St. Andrew. Six of the eight
Royalist magistrates lived either in Conesford, Mancroft, or the
parishes of St. Gregory and St. John Maddermarket, which lie in
Wymer but are adjacent to the parish of St. Peter Mancroft; and
none of the Royalist magistrates resided in either Over-the-Water
or St. Andrew. Of the 203 wealthiest citizens in 1645, 48 per cent
of those who resided in Wymer and Over-the-Water contributed
to the Newcastle Collection, but only 8 per cent of those who
resided in Mancroft and Conesford were contributors. An examination of all contributors to the Collection supplemented by tax
assessments of 1644–5 and fragmentary evidence from signatories
to the Solemn League and Covenant shows that the geographical
distribution of parliamentary-Puritans and Royalists among the
town's élite was also true for the rest of the townsmen.

A parochial analysis of the Newcastle Collection in conjunction
with a Two Month Assessment of 1644 and the Assessment for
Fairfax's troops of 1645 reveals which parishes were most and
which were least parliamentary-Puritan.[2] Although all townsmen
who gave to the Newcastle Collection are named, the list of those
who withheld contributions is incomplete, and more so in some

[1] See Allen, 'Norwich Merchant Class', pp. 248–53.
[2] What follows is a summary of a parochial survey of the Newcastle Collection
and the surviving Covenant lists, found in Evans, 'Political Elite of Norwich',
pp. 516–33. The Two Month Assessment, dated 7 August 1644, is located in
Brit. Lib., Add. MSS., 22619, fo. 204 and includes totals for parishes but not
rates for individuals.

parishes than others.[1] One method of determining parliamentary strength in a parish is to measure the ratio of Newcastle Collection contributors to the total number of townsmen assessed in 1645; the higher the ratio the more parliamentary-Puritan the parish. A second method involves a comparison of the amount of money contributed by parishioners to the Collection with what they were accustomed to paying on regular subsidies. The percentage of the Collection contributed by each parish compared with the percentage of the Two Month Assessment exhibits which parishes donated generously and which gave only a small part of their real wealth. The results show that the most parliamentary-Puritan parishes established by the first method correspond to the most parliamentary-Puritan parishes established by the second. Conversely, those parishes in which the percentage of contributors was low also gave considerably less than would have been required had the Newcastle Collection been a mandatory tax. In the parish of St. Michael Coslany, for example, there were twenty-five contributors to the Collection and thirty-one parishioners taxed for personal estate in 1645; and the parish contributed 9·3 per cent of the Newcastle Collection compared with 3 per cent of the 1644 Two Month Assessment. This is in sharp contrast with St. Peter Mancroft, where only nine of the 121 potential contributors actually donated to the Collection; and the parish contributed only 4·1 per cent of the Collection whereas it paid 15·8 per cent of the Two Month Assessment. Lastly, the parishes in which the list of non-contributors was most complete are the same parishes indicated to be most parliamentary-Puritan in sympathy. That is, in the more Parliament-oriented areas the Collection was pressed more rigorously and a high percentage of those who could but did not contribute were recorded, whereas in the least parliamentary-Puritan sections of Norwich many well-to-do townsmen were simply omitted from the list of non-contributors.

The partial parish returns of signatories to the Solemn League and Covenant support these findings.[2] Willingness to sign one's

---

[1] Many prosperous citizens taxed in the assessment for Fairfax's troops are not listed as either contributors or non-contributors in the Newcastle Collection. Since there were no contributors whose names were omitted from the lists (the individual contributions equal the known total contribution), these citizens did not contribute but their names were not included among the non-contributors.

[2] Parliament passed an act on 5 February 1643/4 requiring all men in England over the age of eighteen to subscribe to the Solemn League and Covenant; lists

name to the Covenant does not present a true test of religious and political affiliation. In early 1644, when the Covenant was passed through the city, the corporation had already evicted known Royalists from the aldermanry and was firmly committed financially and militarily to the parliamentary cause.[1] Further, the Committee for Sequestration for the city had been organized and was functioning, and the Norwich Assembly had restored the Puritan ministers and ordered the destruction of scandalous pictures and images in churches. Moreover, twenty of the twenty-four aldermen signed the Covenant, and the remaining four may well have signed, but were residents of parishes for which the Covenant returns have not survived. For these reasons, it would appear probable that all moderates and even some fair-weather Anglicans would agree to subscribe to the Covenant, even though King Charles had publicly condemned it and ordered his subjects to refuse to sign.[2] This is confirmed by the consenting signatures of well-known Norwich Royalists. On the other hand, refusal to sign is an indication of strong anti-parliamentarian feeling, and none of those who denied their signatures are known to have aided the parliamentary-Puritan effort in any way other than mandatory taxation. Of the parishes for which lists are still extant, those with a high percentage of refusers to sign are among those shown to be least parliamentary-

[1] In September 1643, for example, the Mayor's Court decided that additional money should be raised, as requested by the House of Commons. In order to achieve the desired result, the aldermen of every great ward were instructed to meet in one of the churches in the great ward and collect whatever money they could. The ministers were told to incite the people to contribute freely; and the aldermen were to write down the names of those persons who neglected to attend, send for them, and 'persuade' them to give freely. M.C.B. (1634–46), 11 Sept. 1643, 399v.

[2] C. V. Wedgwood, *The King's War, 1641–1647* (Manchester, 1958), p. 234. The Covenant was drawn up in August 1643 and signed by the members of Parliament on 25 September. Many men supported the Covenant for military and political reasons; Cromwell, Pym, and Vane, who certainly were not Presbyterians, endorsed the Covenant.

of both subscribers and non-subscribers were to be kept. *A. & O.* I. 376–8. Lists of signatories to the Covenant in Norwich were compiled for each parish, but lists for only sixteen of the thirty-four parishes are still extant in the N.N.R.O. Only some of the lists are dated. Presumably most were compiled after early March 1643/4, when orders were sent to Norwich to put the parliamentary ordinance into effect. *H.M.C., 10th Report,* IV. 220: Hobart, Potts, *et al.* to Erasmus Earle, 29 Feb. 1643/4. Assuming that 100 per cent subscription was not obtained for any parish, only eight of these sixteen lists include names of those who refused to sign. The parishes of St. Michael Coslany and St. Swithin, which list only one refuser to subscribe, are also suspect.

Puritan on the basis of the Newcastle Collection; and parishes
with a small minority who refused to sign correspond to strong
parliamentary-Puritan parishes as indicated by the Collection,[1]
Since all adult males over the age of eighteen were required to
respond to the Covenant, it appears that the politico-religious
position of the taxable townsmen of each parish is representative of
the remainder of inhabitants in that parish.

Ten of the eleven most parliamentary-Puritan parishes were in
the wards of Wymer and Over-the-Water and seven of the ten
parishes least parliamentary-Puritan were in Mancroft and
Conesford.[2] If the parishes are grouped into wards, as shown
in Table 21, the extent to which Wymer and Over-the-Water
were more parliamentary-Puritan than Mancroft and Conesford
may be measured. The ward with the largest number of contributors was Over-the-Water. This ward and the sub ward of
Mid Wymer account for more than two-thirds of the total number
of contributors. Almost half of the Over-the-Water residents
assessed for personal estate in 1645 donated to the Collection.
Moreover, Over-the-Water contributed almost half the Collection,
yet paid only one-fourth of a regular subsidy. In each of these
categories Wymer is second, with Mancroft and Conesford showing
very limited support in comparison. Evidently ideological commitment to the parliamentary side was an important consideration in
the election of councilmen in Wymer and Over-the-Water. In both
wards the percentage of councilmen who contributed to the relief of
Newcastle far exceeded the percentage of taxpayers who contributed to the same cause (Table 22). There seems little doubt that the
parliamentary-Puritans were actively mobilizing their strength at

---

[1] For example, the parliamentary-Puritan parish of St. Peter Permountergate
contributed 3·1 per cent of the Newcastle Collection and paid 2·0 per cent of the
1644 assessment; 80 per cent of the taxable townsmen of this parish contributed
to the Collection, and 3·2 per cent of the names returned on the Covenant refused
to sign. In contrast, St. Peter Mancroft contributed 4·1 per cent of the Newcastle
Collection and paid 15·8 per cent of the 1644 assessment; fully 33·8 per cent of
the names returned on the Covenant had refused to sign.

[2] The most parliamentary-Puritan parishes were St. Margaret, St. John
Maddermarket, St. Andrew, St. Helen (Wymer), St. Martin at Oak, St. Mary
Coslany, St. Miahel Coslany, St. George Colegate, St. Saviour, St. Clement
(Over-the-Water), and St. Peter Permountergate (Conesford). The least parlia-
mentary-Puritan were St. Peter Mancroft, St. Giles (Mancroft), St. Peter
Southgate, St. Etheldred, St. Julian, All Saints, St. John Timberhill (Cones-
ford), and St. Benedict, St. Peter Hungate, St. Martin at Palace (Wymer).

TABLE 21: *Ward Totals for Newcastle Collection, Two Month Assessment, and 1645 Assessment*

Ward	Newcastle Collection*			Number Assessed 1645	Newcastle Collection		Two Month Assessment 1644	
	A	B	C		£	%	£	%
CONESFORD	14	17	31	53	24.10.0	4·7	63. 9.8	13·6
MANCROFT	15	36	51	185	73.15.0	14·3	113. 6.8	24·6
WYMER	91	136	227	292	170. 0.0	32·9	174.16.4	38·0
OVER-THE-WATER	109	85	194	231	248.10.0	48·1	109.12.0	23·8
Totals	229	274	503	761	516.15.0	100·0	461. 4.8	100·0

* A: number of contributors to Newcastle Collection
B: number of listed non-contributors to Newcastle Collection
C: total of A and B

the elections in Wymer and Over-the-Water, but were unable to add to their strength in Mancroft and Conesford.

TABLE 22: *Councilman and Taxpayer Contributors to Newcastle Collection, 1645*

	Over-the-Water	Wymer	Mancroft	Conesford
Councilmen of 1645 who contributed	9 of 12 (75%)	13 of 20 (65%)	1 of 15 (7%)	4 of 12 (33%)
Taxpayers of 1645 who contributed	109 of 231 (47%)	91 of 292 (31%)	15 of 185 (8%)	14 of 53 (26%)

The second pattern underlying political affiliation involves the religious factor. The leadership of the Royalist party was composed of men who had objected to the Puritan petition of 1636 and included Aldermen Gostlyn, Freeman, Lane, and John and Alexander Anguish. The remaining signatories to the letter of support to Bishop Wren either refused to abet the parliamentary effort or had died before the Civil War started. There is no known case of a magistrate who was a Puritan Royalist. Not all of the adherents to Parliament were Puritans, but the backbone of the party in the Civil War consisted of men who were animated by religious issues and strongly opposed the Church establishment. Their leader was evidently Alderman John Tooly, who had been so instrumental in bringing Puritan preachers to Norwich and defending them against Anglican bishops during the 1630s. The parliamentary-Puritan party of the Civil War seems to have been an outgrowth of the Puritan faction of the preceding decade. The geographical concentration of parliamentary-Puritans in Wymer and Over-the-Water tends to confirm this. All six of the Puritan aldermen who had managed the Puritan petition were residents of these wards. Eight of the ten parishes which Wren learned were conducting improper Sunday services early in 1636 were located here and likewise all six of the parishes 'most out of order' in 1637. The parochial neighbourhood and the local parish may have been the most decisive factor in determining political alignment.

*   *   *

Two basic themes have been stressed concerning Norwich during the Civil War. The first concerns the impact of national affairs on local politics. There has not been a thorough investigation of the reaction of provincial urban governments to the breakdown in national government and the subsequent Civil War. Nevertheless, recent research has tended to discredit the older generalization that towns were at the forefront of the revolution. Howell has argued that provincial towns are too frequently portrayed as if they were small-scale replicas of London; this approach, he suggests, has obscured the local character of urban politics.[1] In support of this interpretation, Clark and Slack have pointed out that London, Gloucester, Coventry, and Birmingham are isolated cases of political involvement in national issues and that they shared in common a vigorous Puritan leadership.[2] Norwich clearly conforms to this second group. To be sure, the citizens of Norwich were concerned first and foremost with overthrowing the Laudian practices imposed by Wren and restoring Puritan ministers and worship in the city; not with advising Westminster on how to reorient national religious and ecclesiastical policy. To this extent Norwich continued an earlier preoccupation with local affairs. The grievances of the Puritans were particularist in origin and stemmed from Wren's persecution of the 1630s, but they were not peculiar to Norwich. Within the first months of the Long Parliament it must have been clear to all Englishmen that the resolution of local religious conflict between Puritan communities and Laudian bishops would, in the end, be settled in Whitehall and Westminster, not on the local level. Thus they became intensely interested in the developing hostility between Parliament and the Crown and they exerted their energies once war became a reality to encourage their towns to support Parliament. If Parliament lost, their hopes were destroyed. This, at least, was the case in Norwich and London. Additional studies are needed to test whether those towns which emerged from provincial isolation and engaged in partisan politics during the Civil War did so as a consequence of local Puritan activism in reaction to Anglican persecution.[3]

A second and closely related theme is the ideological nature of

---

[1] Howell, *Newcastle*, pp. 336–9. Howell cites Bristol as well as Newcastle as conforming to this model. See also David Underdown, 'A Case Concerning Bishops' Lands: Cornelius Burges and the Corporation of Wells', *English Historical Review*, 78 (1963), 21–3.

[2] Clark and Slack, eds., *Crisis and Order*, p. 25. See also Hirst, *Representative of the People?*, pp. 151–3.

[3] See Seaver, *Puritan Lectureships*, pp. 89–90.

politics during this period. If there were social and economic issues involved, they were omitted completely from the surviving documents. The leadership of the rival parties exhibits no significant differences in its occupations, wealth, or social background. The triumph of the parliamentary-Puritans did not appreciably alter the socio-economic composition of the magistracy or change traditional socio-economic criteria for political recruitment. Once they were undisputedly in power after 1643, they did not pass ordinances which benefited particular trades and they revealed no desire to reshape the political, social or economic structure. This is understandable since the new magistrates and their Royalist opponents were similarly members of the same urban élite and shared a concern for preserving the traditional order. Their opposition had nothing to do with economic privilege or social conflict. Voting patterns, petitions to Parliament, political purges—every indication points to religious beliefs or adherence to Crown or Parliament as the basis of partisanship. The parliamentary-Puritan programme was exclusively politico-religious in nature: they wanted to remove the Royalists from civic power, to support Parliament in the war with the King, to destroy the hatred prelatical Church which had almost destroyed them, and to construct a godly community on new foundations. They were successful in each of the first three goals, but only preliminary steps had been taken in achieving the last.

V

Presbyterians, Independents, and the Commonwealth, 1645-1653

The defeat of the Royalist armies in 1645 brought a much-needed respite from military conflict to England. The guns of war were silenced, but the political and religious settlement sought by the victorious parliamentary-Puritans was as elusive as ever. From the Short Parliament to the end of the Civil War, the Puritans of Norwich had maintained cohesion within their own ranks. This was not because the fiery and militant Puritans who formed the backbone of the parliamentary-Puritan party were in agreement on all matters. They were not. From the outset of the Long Parliament, and before, they were united in what they despised and feared—episcopal tyranny and the imposition of Laudian ceremony —but their agreement did not extend to considerations of the form of a new Church which would replace the hated Laudian prelacy. Confronted with a common enemy and the imperative to win the war, the local Puritans, regardless of their sectarian preference, were cemented into a single alliance which did not need and did not have a constructive religious programme to hold it together.[1] They knew what they wanted to destroy and, once Parliament had provided its sanction, they dismantled the established Church and 'popish innovations' with a vengeance. Fortunately, the question of what they wanted to create in its place did not arise and their potential differences lay dormant.[2] Actually, there was little incentive for them to confront a problem which they did not

[1] This assessment of the Puritans in Norwich corresponds with recent interpretations of the religious attitudes and behaviour of the Puritans in London and the House of Commons. See J. H. Hexter, *The Reign of King Pym* [Harvard Historical Series, 48] (Cambridge, Mass., 1941) and Hexter, 'The Problem of the Presbyterian Independents', *American Historical Review*, 44 (1938–9), 29–49, reprinted in Hexter, *Reappraisals in History* (London, 1961), pp. 163–84. Until late 1644, the Puritans of London had been united for ecclesiastical reform and the prosecution of the war. Valerie Pearl, 'London's Counter-Revolution', in Aylmer, ed., *Interregnum*, p. 30.

[2] There is no evidence that the Norwich corporation, or any of the citizens or ministers, disputed the issue of church structure until 1645.

believe was theirs to resolve. In the years leading up to and during the Civil War, the Puritan citizens and corporation had demonstrated a consistent reluctance to take unprecedented actions lying outside the city's traditional jurisdiction unless these steps had previously been adopted by London or approved by Parliament. The frustrated desire of the corporation to unite parishes in the city illustrates this.[1] Thus, in the matter of ecclesiastical reconstruction the Norwich magistrates awaited guidance from higher authority, and this guidance was not forthcoming until late 1645.

During the war, the Long Parliament had carried out its design to destroy the organization of the old Church and its leaders with zeal. In comparison, its pledge to provide a new structure was not so earnestly or unanimously pursued and thus proceeded at a snail's pace.[2] In June 1643 Parliament delegated the responsibility of devising a new scheme of church government to the Westminster Assembly of Divines, which would then report its recommendations to Parliament. The Westminster Assembly convened in July 1643 and from the start its deliberations floundered on the shoals of overriding political and military considerations. The House of Commons, led by John Pym, concluded in mid-1643 that Scottish arms were needed in the war effort and negotiations were opened in the hope of inducing covenanter armies to cross the border into England. As a precondition to intervention, the Scots insisted that the English Church be brought into conformity with the Presbyterian Church in Scotland. Pym and many of his Puritan followers were certainly not Presbyterians, but the exigency for Scottish military aid led them to accept the Solemn League and Covenant in September 1643 and to invite Scottish participation

---

[1] On 16 July 1644, the Assembly first considered a petition to Parliament for uniting parishes and a month later a petition was accordingly sent up to M. P. Harman. N.N.R.O., A.B. (1642–68), 16 July 1644, 22; N.N.R.O., M.C.B. (1634–46), 17 Aug. 1644, 432ᵛ. Five months later Harman wrote to Mayor Peckover that he had done his best, but there was great difficulty in getting the bill for uniting parishes past the committee stage. Brit. Lib., Add. MSS., 22619, fo. 146: 22 Jan. 1644/5. The Assembly was still agitating for some action in December 1645. A.B. (1642–68), 18 Aug. and 19 Dec. 1645, 33ᵛ, 37ʳ.

[2] For an outline of church affairs during this period see Lawrence Kaplan, 'English Civil War Politics and the Religious Settlement', *Church History*, 41 (1972), 307–25; Claire Cross, 'The Church in England, 1646–1660', in Aylmer, ed., *Interregnum*, pp. 99–120. See also W. A. Shaw, *A History of the English Church during the Civil Wars and Under the Commonwealth 1640–1662* (1900).

in the Westminster Assembly. The Assembly, therefore, was serving two masters, linked by temporary expedience and not common religious goals. With the need to satisfy not only Parliament but the Presbyterian Scots as well, the Divines' discussion dragged on throughout 1644. Thus, up until 1645, Parliament did not even debate much less advocate a national religious formula. Finally, when the Anglican Church had been destroyed, Laud executed, and the Royalist armies scattered in total defeat, the issue of ecclesiastical reform could no longer be postponed. In July 1645, only weeks after Cromwell's victory at Naseby, the Assembly presented the House of Commons with their completed plan, which was very close to Scottish Presbyterianism. Acrimonious dispute in London and Westminster followed, which lasted for the remainder of the decade. In Norwich this took the form of a bitter struggle between the Independents, the Presbyterians, and the political allies attracted to them.

The terms 'Presbyterian' and 'Independent' must be used with caution. The old view that these groups were mutually exclusive politico-religious parties has been successfully attacked and most historians today would deny that national politics from 1645 to 1650 can be understood in the simplistic terms of a conflict between them.[1] The temptation to refrain from using these labels altogether in the following discussion has been resisted because the vocal and antagonistic factions in Norwich referred to each other as 'Presbyterians' and 'Independents' and each possessed a nucleus animated by common religious aspirations. The two groups can be defined on the basis of what the local participants revealed their objectives to be. The primary goal of the Norwich Presbyterians was to divide the city into classical presbyteries headed by carefully examined non-sectarian ministers. They also wanted the city corporation to petition the House of Commons for the establishment of a national Presbyterian Church and the removal from offices of responsibility of those men who refused to belong to

---

[1] In 1938 Hexter fired the first shot in this ongoing debate. Hexter, 'Presbyterian Independents'. For current viewpoints on the controversy see 'Debate: Presbyterians, Independents, and Puritans', *Past and Present*, 47 (May 1970), 116–46 with contributions by Blair Worden, Valerie Pearl, David Underdown, George Yule, Hexter, and Stephen Foster. A strong support for Hexter's main theme may be found in David Underdown, *Pride's Purge : Politics in the Puritan Revolution* (Oxford, 1971), *passim*.

it.[1] The Norwich Independents, who insisted on the independence of the individual congregation rather than a hierarchy of congregational, classical, and synodical assemblies, and who had already set up their own church in the city, opposed both the local and national goals of the city Presbyterians.[2] In particular, the Independents advocated religious toleration.

The strife between Presbyterians and Independents dominated Norwich affairs from 1646 to 1649 and was the decisive factor in reshaping political alliances. The efforts of the local Presbyterians to establish a Presbyterian church system in the city met the resistance of equally resolute and resourceful Independents and their supporters. This does not mean that all citizens and magistrates were adherents of one faction or the other. Indeed, it does not appear as though either faction could claim a majority in the corporation or the town at large. The balance was thus held by moderates, many of them 'Erastian Puritans' who on different occasions could support either Presbyterians or Independents.[3] Lurking in the background were many Anglican-Royalists who still carried some influence. Nor did the city live in religious and political isolation. As in the first half of the decade, so after the Civil War the citizens of Norwich were influenced by the partisan polemics generated in London and Westminster. The same shifting

[1] The Norwich Presbyterians shared the basic view of their counterparts in the capital. The London Presbyterians of this period were men who sought neither to restore the pre-war political structure nor push revolution further. Opposed to a restoration of Royalist government in church and state, they wanted the implementation of religious Presbyterianism and a consolidation of their own political power in the city. Fearful of religious and political radicalism, they desired a restored monarchy which would ideally support both them and a Presbyterian system. Therefore, they wanted to establish Presbyterianism, prevent toleration, destroy the sectaries, get rid of the army, and restore the King. Brenner, 'London's Merchant Community', pp. 86–7.

[2] William Bridge, the organizer of the Congregational Church in Norwich, was one of the leaders of the Independent minority within the Westminster Assembly As early as 1643, when the Assembly was clearly inclined towards some sort of Presbyterian solution, Bridge and other ministers appealed directly to the nation for a limited toleration for independent congregations outside the state system. T. Goodwin, *et al.*, *An Apologeticall Narration* (1643); Anthony Wood, *Athenae Oxonienses* (London, 1691), II. 250.

[3] Hexter has defined 'Erastian Puritans' as men favouring a sharp reduction of clerical power in general and of the power of bishops in particular, and who wanted part of the King's ecclesiastical prerogative transferred to Parliament. Hexter, 'Presbyterian Independents', p. 178. The Norwich Erastians would oppose the creation of an unbridled ministry free from the control of secular government.

political tides which led to the formation of a conservative coalition elsewhere in England in late 1647 and early 1648 similarly resulted in a conservative offensive in Norwich. The climactic result was a bloody holocaust in April 1648. The conservative party had previously exhibited considerable electoral strength, but their failure in this April riot coupled with the triumph of the Independents and the army on the national scene meant their downfall. Independents were in control of the city from this point on and the corporation officially welcomed the execution of Charles I and the proclamation of the Commonwealth in 1649. They may not have possessed a broad base of electoral strength, but with the aid of ordinances which disqualified their opponents from voting or holding office, they were unchallenged politically and were able to force their remaining opponents from the magistracy.

*   *   *

As the Civil War drew to a close, the Westminster Assembly, with the influential backing of the Scottish party, the London government, and many ministers in London, favoured immediate adoption by Parliament of the Presbyterian form of worship and church government. In January 1644/5 Parliament approved the elimination of the Book of Common Prayer and its replacement by the Directory of Worship.[1] Eight months later Parliament took another step towards Presbyterianism by confirming its support of the Directory and passing an ordinance which regulated the election of church elders, and divided London into twelve classical elderships.[2] At this point, Speaker Lenthall, the controversial target of John Lilburne's poisoned pen, sent instructions to Norwich.[3] The settlement of the Presbyterian church government, he wrote, was conducive to the establishment of truth and righteousness in the kingdom. The Norwich magistrates were ordered to consider and implement a division of the city into classical presbyteries and select godly ministers to administrate them. When this had been accomplished, they were to report to the House of Commons 'with all expedition'. No reply from Norwich was ever sent.

Speaker Lenthall's enthusiasm for Presbyterianism was not matched by a majority of the members of Parliament. They had no

---

[1] Firth and Rait, eds., *Acts and Ordinances*, I. 582–607.
[2] ibid., pp. 749–54, 754–7.
[3] N.N.R.O., Various Accounts and Correspondence, 1642–50: W. Lenthall to Mayor and Aldermen of Norwich, 25 Sept. 1645.

intention of acceding to the demands of the Westminster Assembly and the London corporation for a 'high' or 'rigid' Presbyterian system in which the new Church, free from state control, exercised jurisdiction throughout the nation in its own ecclesiastical courts. Petitions from London repudiating religious toleration and calling for acceptance of the Westminster proposals were registered in November of 1645 and January and March of 1645/6.[1] The House of Commons continued to balk. By April the religious Presbyterians in London had strengthened their alliance with the conservative-peace party in the House of Commons headed by Denzil Holles. The fruit of their co-operation was the 'Humble Remonstrance and Petition', which was approved by the London government and passed on to Parliament in late May. The petition opened with a defence of Presbyterian church government, and then went on to demand that no man should be allowed to hold public office who was disaffected to the new Church. Moreover, a speedy settlement with the King should be concluded and a close union with Scotland effected. Immediately the Independents and other enemies of the Presbyterian-peace party coalition prepared their own counter-manifesto. Pamphlet warfare broke out. The House of Commons resented outside interference and pressure, but in late June it agreed to implement the Presbyterian religious system and the Directory of Worship with the important proviso that appeals from the hierarchy of church courts could be filed with a committee of Parliament.[2] From the summer of 1646 until Pride's Purge in late 1648, this modified 'parliamentary' or 'Erastian' Presbyterianism enjoyed the official support of central government. Unlike its Scottish counterpart, it was a voluntary system dependent upon the energy and initiative of local clergy and laity.[3]

The reaction of Norwich citizens to unfolding events in London during the winter of 1645/6 and the early spring of 1646 is not known. The official corporation books give no indication whatsoever that either the Mayor's Court or the Assembly were aware of,

---

[1] The following description of events in London is drawn from Pearl, 'London's Counter-Revolution', pp. 35–7 and Brenner, 'London's Merchant Community', pp. 87–8.

[2] This led the Scot, Robert Baillie, to label the new arrangement 'but a lame Erastrian Presbytery'. For the Erastian character of the settlement, see Kaplan, 'Religious Settlement', pp. 313–25.

[3] Cross, 'Church in England', pp. 110–11.

much less troubled by, larger national developments until September 1646. Three polemical pamphlets published during the summer and autumn, however, present the entirely different picture of a city sharply divided into rival religious factions.[1] *Vox Populi*, an inflammatory Independent attack on the Presbyterians in Norwich, disagrees with *Hue and Cry* and *Vox Norwici*, which were printed in rebuttal of *Vox Populi*, on some important details of what transpired in the city. There is enough agreement, however, to piece together a sufficiently accurate narrative of the conflict. The pamphlets are important not only for providing insight into the intense hatred of the two sides for each other, but also for establishing that Norwich politics in many respects ran parallel to and indeed were associated with those of London.

Early in June 1646 the London Remonstrance was before the House of Commons and pressure was mounting for its acceptance. Aware that the fate of church government in England was hanging in the balance, the Norwich Presbyterians were eager for the city corporation to send Parliament a petition endorsing the London Remonstrance. The magistrates and other citizens customarily gathered on the guild day, the ceremonious occasion on which the new mayor was sworn in, to hear a sermon. On 16 June the Presbyterian minister Thornbeck preached to the assembled throng the need to act in the cause of religious reform, and condemned the Independents for their obstruction.[2] It is not clear whether Thornbeck exhorted the citizens to prepare a petition for the magistrates, but this was undoubtedly what he and other Presbyterian ministers in the city had in mind. The following day Thornbeck and seven other ministers appeared at the Mayor's Court and requested the new mayor, Henry Watts, to call a special meeting of the Assembly to approve their remonstrance.[3] Some

[1] Brit. Lib., Thomason Collection, E. 351. (7): *Vox Populi, or the people's cry against the clergy*, London, 1646, printed by Tho. Paine for John Pounset; Th. E. 355. (13): *An Hue and Cry after Vox Populi*, London, 25 September 1646, printed for Edward Martin in Norwich; Th. E. 358. (4): *Vox Norwici, or the cry of Norwich vindicating their Ministers from the lying Libell intitled Vox Populi*, London, [19 October] 1646, printed for William Frankling and sold by Richard Tomlins.

[2] According to *Vox Norwici*, Thornbeck lived in Steeple-Bumsted in Essex before coming to Norwich. He had been excommunicated for his refusal, despite warnings from the ecclesiastical courts, to read the Service Book on Wednesdays and Fridays.

[3] The other ministers were Carter, Stinnet, Fletcher, Bond, Stukely, Toft, and Mitchell. Brief biographical comments on them may be found in *Vox Norwici*.

aldermen asked to see the petition, but the ministers refused, with the comment that the magistrates could discover its contents in the Assembly. Despite this irregular procedure, which has interesting parallels with the 1636 Puritan petition controversy, the Mayor's Court consented to the ministers' request.

On 19 June the magistrates and councilmen met in the Assembly chamber and the ministers read their petition. No copies of the petition were provided and no notes were allowed to be taken. The original petition has been lost, but one of the Independent councilmen wrote down the major headings and they later appeared in *Vox Populi*.[1] *Hue and Cry* vigorously defended the clauses of the petition against the criticism voiced in *Vox Populi*, but it did not deny that the latter provided a more or less accurate synopsis of the petition.[2] The first and central grievance was that the House of Commons had not yet given satisfaction to the London Remonstrance. The Norwich petition insisted that men who refused to join the Church should be ejected from offices in the Church, the Commonwealth, and the army. Further delay would prolong spiritual hardship, it continued, since three-quarters of the parishes in the city were without ministers, there were no church officers to look after the poor, and children were not being baptized. The petition also contained a clause declaring the April declaration of the House of Commons against the Westminster Assembly to be 'a grieving of the hearts of God's people'.[3] The petition did not stop with religious Presbyterianism; like the London Remonstrance, it also supported the peace party in the Commons with the plea that negotiations with King Charles be concluded successfully on the basis of the propositions for peace drafted over a year before. After listening to the petition, the Assembly expressed a desire to have a copy of it and a week to think things over, but the ministers

[1] *Vox Populi* mentioned that the list of points contained in the petition was reproduced from memory because the original copy was unobtainable. *Hue and Cry* claimed that Thomas Ashwell was discovered taking notes and that the account of the petition printed in *Vox Populi* came from this course.

[2] The tenth article of the petition, according to *Vox Populi*, was that traitors to the King were not being executed. *Hue and Cry* denied that such a clause was in the petition.

[3] On 17 April the House of Commons issued a declaration covering both political and religious matters. In particular, the Commons proclaimed that it had no intention whatsoever of relinquishing ultimate control over the state church and allowed that it would protect 'tender consciences' from rigid uniformity. The Westminster Assembly was also chastised for interfering with Parliament.

refused and demanded immediate passage. Debate then broke out in the Assembly, in the midst of which Minister John Carter acknowledged that his party was being advised by some 'great persons' in London.[1] As passions rose, the fruitless Assembly session was brought to an end.

The Independents were not sitting idly by while all this was taking place. As in London, they rushed to circulate their own counter-petition for the corporation and Parliament as soon as they learned of the Presbyterian petition. The thrust of their message was revealed by *Vox Populi* to be unqualified praise for the good work of Parliament in bringing peace and prosperity to England. *Hue and Cry*, which refers to this counter-petition in the most despicable terms and obviously sought to discredit it, claimed that the Independents would have failed in their designs had they not been willing to practise deception. Apparently the Independents took their petition to the local Committee of Accounts, where it received several signatures, and then passed it around the city in the name of 'the Committee'. Many people subsequently signed under the mistaken impression that it had been approved by the Committee for the County. Moreover, according to *Hue and Cry*, those who subscribed were either durnk or the worst malignants in Norfolk and the mayor and aldermen rejected it with indignation. In the meantime, a third petition was drawn up which accepted the Covenant and the Presbyterian form of government. The mayor and an unknown number of aldermen signed this more moderate petition and prepared to send it up to London. The Independents, however, bargained that they would give up their petition if the Presbyterians would put aside both of theirs. The telling blow may have been the advice of the Committee for the County, which told both factions to desist, on the grounds that Parliament had enough to do, and the upshot of the whole affair was that none of the petitions were forwarded to Parliament.

The decision by the House of Commons to sanction a modified Presbyterianism did not end the feuding in either Norwich or London. On 10 August a pamphlet was published in London whose title, *Truth Vindicated from the unjust accusations of the Independent*

---

[1] The author of *Vox Populi* wanted to know the identity of these 'great persons' as well as their connections; this information was not discovered then and is not known now.

Society in the City of Norwich, speaks for itself.[1] In a forwarding preface, the author confessed that he had once wished to join with the Norwich Independents, but gradually saw the errors of their ways. The schisms, factions, and divisions which existed in England were blamed on Independents who have led others into darkness, which caused the author to hope that 'my life and conversion shall be a real refutation of my traducers, and proclaim them liars'. The main points of *Truth Vindicated* are that the Presbyterian Church of England is a true church of Christ and that it is a sin to separate from the true church; that the Independent Society of Norwich is not a true church of Christ, and therefore it is a sin to join it. Although scriptural citations abound, the tract hardly represented a serious challenge to the theological foundations of Independency.[2] What the author lacked in penetrating theological argument he more than made up for in slander. In his conclusion he observed that men who join the Independents are easily recognized: many of them are remiss in their family duties, reject and spurn their former friends, spread malicious rumours against 'our brethren the Scots', and in general are noted for their inclination towards immorality, prevarication, egotism, and public disobedience.

The Independents retaliated with an even more scurrilous pamphlet. In late August *Vox Populi* was printed in London and shortly appeared in Norwich. Its condemnation of the Presbyterians went far beyond a mere denunciation of the Presbyterian remonstrance and the schemes to have it accepted by the corporation. Echoing the themes of Independent literature already current in London the unknown author claimed that the Presbyterian system amounted to a clerical tyranny no less oppressive than its Anglican predecessor. The activities of the ministers in Norwich were proof of this. First, they infuriated the people by impassioned rhetoric and, striking when the iron was hot, used them to threaten and get their way with the magistrates. Then, acting as though they

---

[1] Th. E. 351. (4): S. T. [Sampson Townsend], *Truth Vindicated from the unjust accusations of the Independent Society in Norwich*, London, 10 August 1646, printed by Th. Harper for Gifford Galton.

[2] S. T.'s major proof that the Church of England is the true Church of Christ ran as follows: that Church in which salvation is obtained and God worshipped according to the Word is the true Church of Christ. In the Presbyterian Church of England, salvation is obtained and God worshipped according to His Word. Therefore, this Church is the true Church of Christ.

were the oracles of God and with no other authority for their high-handed tactics, they attempted to force their petition past the magistrates and coerce the Assembly into consenting to it. In short, the Presbyterian reformation was nothing other than 'the establishment of power, authority, and estate in the hands of the clergy, [and] we hear nothing almost in every pulpit, but church discipline, uniformity . . .'. This accusation was clearly intended to play on the fears of Erastian-minded Englishmen that Presbyterianism would usher in an unbridled clericalism which secular government would be powerless to control. In a perfect statement of the Independent position that new presbyter is but old priest written large, *Vox Populi* vituperated:

Is this all the quarrel and cause of our wasting wars? What, to pull down the prelate and set up the Presbyter? To change only the name and not the nature of a tyrannizing state? To take away the miter from the head of the prelate and fasten it upon the head of the Presbyter?

The second major assertion against the Presbyterians put forward by *Vox Populi* was that they were leading England into another Civil War. Instead of campaigning against the drunkard, swearer, idolator, and adulterer, they spent their time composing petitions against those who disagreed with them ideologically. In the process they created dissension within the country and, even more dangerous, sowed discord between the people and Parliament. Although they claimed they were the peace party, in truth they were the chief disrupters in the kingdom. If they really had the best interests of England at heart, they would realize that peace and toleration were more important than uniformity. The author of *Vox Populi* made his meaning perfectly clear: 'rigid episcopacy brought about the wars before, [and] rigid Presbytery will do the like the second time'.

Vox Populi predictably evoked an enraged Presbyterian reaction in Norwich. On 25 September *An Hue and Cry after Vox Populi* was printed there and within a month a second pamphlet *Vox Norwici, or the cry of Norwich vindicating their ministers from the lying Libell intitled Vox Populi* made its appearance in London. *Hue and Cry* opened by labelling the Independents schismatics, sectarians, and heretics and ridiculed their 'intolerable toleration'. The Independent charge that the Norwich ministers were improperly interfering in politics and intimidating the magistrates must have struck a sensitive area, for both pamphlets rigorously and repeatedly denied that this was the case. Whereas *Vox Populi* stated that Thornbeck explicitly instructed his listeners to circulate a petition, *Vox Norwici* and *Hue and Cry* insisted that he merely pleaded for the citizens to strive for religious reform, but not necessarily to proceed by way of petition. As for the refusal of the ministers to read their petition to the magistrates or leave it for them to examine, the Presbyterian pamphlets defended the ministers on the grounds that it was only a rough draft and difficult to read. To leave it with the Mayor's Court would have risked unacceptable delay and might have led to the Court amending it beyond recognition. Moreover, the petition, if handed over, would have been placed in the custody of the town clerk, whose wife was a known Independent. The ministers never tried to force the petition down the throats of the reluctant magistrates or dictate to them what to do. *Hue and Cry* allowed that Minister Thornbeck called the Independents 'incendiaries' between the two kingdoms, but denied that Presbyterian preaching was divisive or caused disturbance. Actually, according to *Hue and Cry*, Thornbeck had only spoken the truth because the Independents were doing their utmost to foment war between England and Scotland.

None of the four pamphlets provide a clear picture of the relative strength of the Presbyterian and Independent factions among the citizens and within the corporation. The difficulty in making this determination is compounded by the loss of all three of the petitions. As each side claimed the support of the majority of townsmen, there probably were many of both persuasions in the city. The mayoral election of early May suggests, however, that the Independents were in the minority among the freeman electorate: the Presbyterian Henry Watts and the ageing, incapacitated John Loveland were nominated, leaving the magistrates with little choice but to elect Watts. The alliance of the Presbyterians of London with the peace party in the House of Commons introduced an additional dimension into the political equation. As in London, the success of the Norwich remonstrance depended not only on the strength which the religious Presbyterians and Independents could muster within their own ranks, but also on the support given them by their political 'fellow travellers', the Royalists and Erastians. Undoubtedly, these latter groups played a key and perhaps decisive role in city politics, but as with the Presbyterians and Independents, it is impossible to gauge their numerical strength. Their politico-religious behaviour was unpredictable in the constantly changing national and local scene from 1645 to 1649.

The Royalists of Norwich had been living in quiet obscurity for several years, but the coalescing Presbyterian-peace party movement gave them a new lease on political life. Connections between these fundamentally conservative groups were already evident in London in early 1646 and their co-operation was even more marked after June 1646.[1] What the Royalists in England wanted was a speedy and peaceful agreement between King Charles and Parliament on terms favourable to the Crown. Their conviction was that this and nothing less could restore national unity and stability. The great majority of Royalists believed in the necessity of a state church, but their first preference would not have been a 'rigid' Presbyterianism. Nevertheless, if the King could reach an accommodation with Presbyterianism, so could they. In July 1646 Parliament framed a new set of propositions and presented them to Charles. The central religious provisions were that Charles would subscribe to the Covenant and that religion would be settled according to the Covenant and with the advice of the Westminster Assembly. These terms were clearly intended to satisfy the Scots, whose covenanter armies were entrenched in the north of England and in whose custody Charles was held. Charles had utterly disavowed the Covenant several years before, but he had shown some willingness to reconsider in his dealings with the Scots. His response to Parliament on 1 August was not negative and the door was left open for negotiation and reconciliation. At this point the conservative tide was running strong in the city of London. In late September Sir John Gayre, whose sympathies had never really been with Parliament during the Civil War, was elected Lord Mayor.[2] The same current was flowing in Norwich. In the shrievalty elections of 8 September, the freemen named Robert Holmes, who had been an unabashed Royalist during the Civil War and had attained some notoriety by strolling the Norwich streets at night claiming he was the king's watch.[3]

The overwhelming majority of the London Common Council,

[1] Pearl, 'London's Counter-Revolution', pp. 35–8.
[2] ibid., p. 38. Gayre had deliberately been passed over by the Common Hall in previous elections because of his political views. A recent writer has referred to him as 'notoriously Royalist'. Wedgwood, *The King's War*, p. 560.
[3] Add. MSS., 22619, fo. 40: 3 Dec. 1643.

Court of Aldermen, and ministry in 1646 and 1647 was Presbyterian. This was also true of the ministers of Norwich, but not of the magistrates and councilmen. The corporation seems to have been either incapable or undesirous of anything other than vacillation and drift in late 1645 and 1646. Speaker Lenthall's directions of the previous autumn for the formation of a Presbyterian system had been shelved. The Court of Aldermen permitted the ministers to present their remonstrance to the Assembly, and Mayor Watts and 'well-affected' aldermen signed the third, moderate Presbyterian petition. On the other hand, if more than half the aldermen had put their names to any Presbyterian enterprise, *Hue and Cry* would surely have trumpeted this fact triumphantly. The more adamant Royalists had been purged from office in 1643 and 1644, but there remained a number of aldermen who were political and religious moderates. Indeed, for their sheriff in September 1646, the magistrates chose Richard Wenman, who made a lifelong career of religious and political moderation.[1] To the extent that these moderate magistrates were Erastians, they would have been very reluctant to support the organization of a local religious power which could compete for authority with the magistrates themselves.[2] For their part, the common councilmen refused to pass the June remonstrance, but certainly this was not because their body, any more than the magistracy, was dominated by Independents. Less than a week after *Vox Populi* appeared in Norwich, the magistrates and councilmen issued an official declaration against this 'scandalous' pamphlet in the Assembly.[3] They stressed that

---

[1] As a councilman, Wenman had been named to the committee to maintain volunteers on 3 April 1643, yet he did not contribute to the Newcastle Collection. He was appointed by the Assembly to the committee to investigate scandalous ministers in 1645 and he was elected alderman in 1648. He served on the Court throughout the Commonwealth, but was quick to pledge support for Charles II in 1660 and voluntarily took the oath of allegiance and supremacy. In 1660 he was even named to a committee charged to investigate all acts passed by the Assembly from 1642 to 1660 and determine which of these should be renounced. He was finally removed from office in 1677/8 for his nonconformist leanings. See Evans, 'Political Elite of Norwich', p. 514.

[2] It seems logical that the Independent *Vox Populi* would not have stressed the fear of clerical tyranny if there had been no Erastian-minded men who might be moved by such an argument. Nor would *Hue and Cry* and *Vox Norwici* have so vociferously rebutted this accusation. More than the Independents, it was the Erastians in the House of Commons who thwarted the hopes of Presbyterianism, entertained by the Westminster Assembly and the London corporation.

[3] A.B. (1642–68), 2 Sept. 1646, 45ʳ.

none of them had in any way contributed to *Vox Populi* and did not know of the pamphlet until it had been published. Moreover, they 'utterly' condemned it, especially those parts which attacked the ministers, and they wanted the unknown author punished.

The prospect for the establishment of Presbyterianism in Norwich was bright in the last months of 1646. In October and November the Assembly finally managed to unite some of the parishes.[1] On 5 December the preliminary step towards Presbyterianism was made when the Assembly appointed a committee to determine who should have the power to nominate elders and who should appoint classes, and to report at the next session of the Assembly.[2] This was the high-water mark for Presbyterianism in Norwich. Although neighbouring Suffolk was successfully divided into classical presbyteries at this time,[3] the Norwich Assembly did not meet again until late February and the Assembly Book leaves no indication that church matters were even discussed. A second letter from Speaker Lenthall directed to Mayor Watts and other city dignataries, which reiterated the contents of his earlier letter, arrived in mid-January and received the same treatment as the first.[4] Attempts to control non-ordained ministers, who were most probably sectarians, were also doomed to failure. The magistrates asked M. P. Thomas Atkin what policy should be followed with regard to them. Atkin replied that debates were going on into the early morning on this issue and advised the magistrates to postpone action until the Commons had reached a decision.[5] The hopes of the Presbyterian party had turned so gloomy in the winter of 1646/7 that rumour reached Atkin that Minister John Carter was planning to leave the city owing to the lack of respect accorded him and the refusal of many of his parishioners to pay him what had been promised.[6] All that Atkin could do was to express his hope

[1] ibid., 5 Oct. and 19 Nov. 1646, 46r-v. The united parishes were St. Martin at Oak and St. Mary Coslany, St. Julian and St. Peter Permountergate and St. Peter Hungate, St. George Tombland and Sts. Simon and Jude, and St. Saviour and St. Augustine. Blomefield, *Norfolk*, III. 392.

[2] A.B. (1642–68), 5 Dec. 1646, 47r.

[3] Alan Everitt, *Suffolk and the Great Rebellion, 1640–1660* [Suffolk Record Society, 3] (Ipswich, 1961), p. 35.

[4] N.N.R.O., Various Accounts and Correspondence, 1642–50: W. Lenthall to Mayor, *et al.* of Norwich, 19 Jan. 1646/7.

[5] Add. MSS. 22620, fo. 45: Thomas Atkin to Mayor and others of Norwich, 25 Jan. 1646/7. See also fo. 105: Copy of ordinance against non-ordained ministers, 31 Dec. 1646.

[6] ibid., fo. 48: Atkin to Mayor Watts, 28 Jan. 1646/7.

that Carter would not depart and to lament the divisions among the magistrates.

Information about the inability of the Presbyterians in Norwich to implement their programme between December 1646 and June 1647 and the impact on the city of national affairs leading up to the London counter-revolution in July 1647 is obscure. There are no extant pamphlets, proposed petitions, or correspondence which clarify either of these matters. Moreover, the Assembly Book adds no information and the volume of the Mayor's Court Book covering the period from September 1646 to 1654, which would surely have provided some clues, has been lost. In the city at large, the Presbyterian and Royalist conservative coalition which had brought Robert Holmes to the shrievalty in 1646 was still operating. In May the freemen nominated for the mayoralty John Utting, a political conservative and friend of John Carter, and John Croshold, who was forced out of office in 1648/9 and restored in 1660/1 'for his loyalty to your Majesty's late royal father'.[1] The Royalist townsmen may have been eager to support the Presbyterians politically and thus keep Independents out of office, but after December 1646 they may well have been hesitant to aid the Presbyterians in their religious designs for the city. The frantic and futile efforts of the Scots to convert Charles to Presbyterianism before handing him over to Parliament and departing from England in December and January could have had a telling impact on local Royalists.[2] In the final analysis, however, the fate of Presbyterianism in Norwich was decided in the guild-hall and not on the streets.

If the Norwich corporation had been predominately Presbyterian, Lenthall's letters would have been put into effect and the June remonstrance would have been adopted. If the corporation had been dominated by Independents, the Court of Aldermen and the Assembly would never have so strongly condemned *Vox Populi* or taken the preliminary first measure towards Presbyterianism in naming the committee of late 1646. The inescapable conclusion is

---

[1] Bodleian, Tanner MSS., 311, fo. 60.

[2] In this context it is noteworthy that John Carter was minister of St. Peter Mancroft, which was the wealthiest parish in the city and clearly the most Royalist parish during the Civil War. For Carter to contemplate leaving the city in January because his parishioners refused to provide an adequate living suggests that although many Royalists were eager to back the conservative political movement they were less than willing to support the Presbyterian religious programme.

that neither religious extreme commanded a majority and the balance hung with the moderates. They, or most of them, must have sided with the Independents in blocking the establishment of Presbyterianism from the autumn of 1645 to the summer of 1646. Then, when Charles and Parliament appeared to be on the verge of reaching an agreement accepting religious Presbyterianism, they must have begun to reconsider their position on church government. After December 1646, they reverted to what may have been Erastian predilections when Charles had been turned over to Parliament and the immediate possibility of a national Presbyterian settlement had diminished. They must also have been aware of the House of Commons' hostile reception of a London petition favouring 'high' Presbyterianism and a conservative political policy.[1] Their motivations are conjectural, but they steadfastly continued to thwart Presbyterian hopes throughout the spring of 1647. This analysis is further substantiated by John Carter's censure of the moderate and trimming magistrates in June.

Mayor-elect John Utting invited Carter to give the guild day sermon in late June 1647, as Thornbeck had done the year before. Carter's long association with the Puritan movement dated back to the halcyon years before Wren's arrival. He had helped to manage the Puritan petition against Wren and had suffered episcopal suspension; his credentials as a religious reformer and Presbyterian preacher were unmatched in the city. In 1644 he had delivered a stirring guild day exhortation in support of Parliament and the parliamentary-Puritan magistracy on the occasion of John Tooly's inauguration. In mid-1647, however, his former optimism and enthusiasm had gone: he lashed out at the magistrates with such embittered and astonishingly frank criticism that many an alderman must have winced. The text of the lecture was Galatians 4:16 'Am I therefore your enemy, because I tell you the truth?'[2] And

---

[1] Apart from its political demands, the London petition called for a stricter church, the outlawing of separatist congregations, punishment for heresy, and exclusion of non-Covenanters from office. The petition was organized in December, before the departure of the Scots, and the House of Commons arrested three prominent citizens responsible for distributing printed copies. Slightly modified petitions were sent from the London government to Parliament the following January and March. Pearl, 'London's Counter-Revolution', pp. 41–2.

[2] Th. E. 411. (6): John Carter, *The Wheel Turned by a voice from the throne of Glory*, 22 June 1647, in Carter, *The Nail and the Wheel. Both described in two several sermons in the Greenyard at Norwich*, London, 1647, printed by J. Macock for M. Spark.

the truth from Carter's point of view was that the aldermen deserved censure for their betrayal of the godly cause. It was bad enough that the magistrates allowed the Sabbath to be profaned by boys playing in the streets and venders selling fish in the market. More serious was that they had accomplished little for the advancement of reformation and religion and seemed much more inclined to indulge in lavish feasts. Their past record was appalling: they had done nothing but accommodate themselves and flatter the prevailing power. With a new piper playing a different tune, the magistrates danced a different jig. This was true in the days of 'popish innovation and prelatical tyranny', and it was no less true now:

Separatism is now grown into great request, and they that but the other day were driving on towards Rome as fast as they could, have now altered their course and are hurrying towards Amsterdam; they are gotten out of the Church of England already, and the superstitious malignant hath given the right hand of fellowship to the separatist.

The religious reform which had appeared so promising during the Civil War, had not been continued. The vacillating magistrates were partly to blame for this; the rest of the blame lay with the sectarians. This led Carter to launch a tirade against the Independents for opposing uniformity in church government, worship, confession of faith, and catechism.

Having excoriated the magistrates for their lack of religious zeal in general, Carter then took them to task for their failure to implement Presbyterianism during the past year. He pointed out that magistrates and ministers must stand or fall together, yet the spiritual advice and guidance of the ministers had been ignored. They had petitioned the Court of Aldermen for the removal of scandalous ministers, the union of parishes, and the invitation of more godly preachers, but they had precious little to show for it. For two years the letter from the Speaker of the House of Commons had been allowed to gather dust. Only recently the mayor had gathered together all those concerned with the problem of church government and it appeared as though the whole issue could be settled in one night. Yet once again matters had come to a standstill and there was no settlement.[1] Aware that the plight of

---

[1] Carter did not provide a date for the near success of Mayor Watt's attempt to establish Presbyterianism, nor did he specify when the Mayor's effort had proved

Presbyterianism in Norwich was also true of England as a whole, Carter thundered out an apocalyptic prophecy of doom: as the chariot wheels of the kingdom continue to move forward in strange and dreadful ways 'truly we can see nothing by the wheeling of things, but the ruin of all: of religion, and laws, and utter desolation of the whole land'. The only hope was to pray to God, who was leaving England and laughing at its destruction, to return among them.

The antipathy of Presbyterians towards Independents contained in Carter's sermon was mutual. At some point in 1647 Michael King, Independent minister of St. Michael Coslany, was removed from office on the testimony of one John Blancher, a shoemaker, who swore that he saw King drunk on the very day he had delivered the sacraments.[1] When news of this reached Samuel Richardson, a one-time resident of Norwich presently dwelling in London, he published the episode and concluded:

[this] demonstrates the crimes of an unconscionable fellow, and our arch enemy, because a violent Presbyterian; although at the first we joined with them in fellowship, communication, and association, yet since their Covenant which is most destructive to our Christian Liberty, though we were forced to make use of them, we hate them as ill as the Cavaliers.

Nevertheless, with the overthrow of the London Presbyterian-peace party counter-revolution in late July and early August and the subsequent rise of Cromwell, the army, and the sectarians, the Independents of Norwich were clearly in a favoured position. Carter appears to have been correct about the vacillating proclivities of the magistrates. Whereas in 1646 they had elected Wenman to the shrievalty, in 1647 they sponsored Thomas Ashwell.

---

[1] *Newes from Norwich; or, an Exact Relation* . . . , London, 1647, printed by Sam. Richardson. The pamphlet does not provide a date for King's removal nor the authority which removed him.

---

unproductive. It is possible that the trimming magistrates so detested by Carter were responding to erratic events in London and Westminster. During the first two weeks of June the Presbyterian-peace party in London and in the House of Commons commenced preparations for war with the army and were very close to triumph. When the army leaders started to march their troops slowly on London, put forward a moderate proposal of their own, and presented charges of impeachment against eleven of the most prominent Presbyterian leaders in the Commons (June 16), the Presbyterian Common Council of London started to waver. Carter's sermon was delivered on 22 June.

Ashwell had been a captain in the army in 1642 and in December 1645 he was promoted to major.[1] His religious affiliation with the Independents was widely known: it was Ashwell, *Hue and Cry* had claimed, who had secretly and improperly taken notes of the Presbyterian petition in the Assembly of 19 June 1646, and passed them on to the author of *Vox Populi*.[2]

The Presbyterians were not the only discontented group in Norwich in 1646 and 1647. For several years an excise tax had irritated the lesser tradesmen, especially the butchers and brewers. This regressive and unpopular tax, first imposed in 1643, covered a wide variety of goods, including the essential commodities of meat and ale; and the burden of it fell most heavily on the poor.[3] There were repeated demonstrations against it in many parts of England, but apparently they took a more violent turn in Norwich than elsewhere.[4] Administered from the home of Alderman Adrian Parmenter since November 1643,[5] the tax engendered resistance which reached a peak in November 1646. When news of the disturbances reached the House of Commons, it ordered the Norwich magistrates to assist in collecting the tariff and to arrest the leading agitators.[6] The magistrates made a token effort, but clearly their hearts were not in it. Parmenter described their attempts to the excise commissioners in a letter of 17 December.[7] The two sheriffs had attempted to take into custody James Sheringham, one of the agitators, but when the butchers learned of it, they rushed to the market-place and violently rescued him. A battle followed and several officials were beaten, disarmed, and stripped. Two days later a mob armed with clubs gathered near the guild-hall, yet the magistrates were able to disperse them with threats. Nevertheless, Parmenter concluded, the situation was

[1] Blomefield, *Norfolk*, III. 382–3; M.C.B. (1634–46), 23 Dec. 1645, 465ʳ.

[2] *Hue and Cry* stated that Ashwell was 'one at whose house their tribe [the Independents] meets notwithstanding his faithful engagement among the rest'. Under the control of the army, London elected an Independent to be Lord Mayor.

[3] For the enforcement of the excise tax in London and the popular discontent it gave rise to, see Pearl, 'London's Counter-Revolution', pp. 39–40, 43.

[4] Underdown, *Pride's Purge*, pp. 40–1.

[5] Blomefield, *Norfolk*, III. 388. The parliamentary act authorizing the excise tax was passed in July 1643 and enlarged the following September. *A. & O.* I. 202–14, 274–83.

[6] Add. MSS., 22620, fo. 96: 26 Nov. 1646.

[7] Tanner MSS., 59, fo. 610: Adrian Parmenter and others to Commissioners for Excise, 17 Dec. 1646.

desperate and the magistrates were afraid they would be chopped in pieces by the butchers.

On 28 December Parmenter again took up his pen to inform the commissioners that the butchers were as abusive as ever and adamantly refused to pay the tax. Efforts to force them to do so were again met with violence, and the magistrates were no longer able to cope with the matter.[1] Early in January the butchers gained confidence and allies as the tax rebellion spread to Norfolk. Joined now by the brewers, the butchers boasted that they would sacrifice their lives before they would forfeit a single penny. Parmenter, completely hamstrung, sent an urgent appeal to the commissioners for assistance.[2] Discussion of the Norwich tax riots reached the floor of the House of Commons in mid-January.[3] The House continued to discuss the matter throughout March, and a number of M.P.s claimed that the trouble arose from the magistrates' failures to perform their duties.[4] The excise unrest was still serious enough in June for the Commons to send additional instructions to the city.[5] The riots in Norwich and elsewhere did lead Parliament to reform the administration of the tariff, but nothing short of its complete abolition would have satisfied the lesser tradesmen in Norwich. London also experienced a series of excise tax riots in February and these tended to strengthen the counter-revolutionary movement.[6] There is no evidence, however, that the Norwich mobs were in any way connected with the Presbyterian clique in a 'Kirk and King' alliance as in London; nor is it clear what impact, if any, these popular disturbances had on the magistrates' deliberations concerning a religious settlement in the city.

To the list of discontented townsmen of late 1647 must be added the Royalists. The election of Sheriff Holmes in 1646 and the nomination of Alderman Croshold for the mayoralty in 1647 attest to their resurgence in popularity. Their local hopes, however, were

---

[1] ibid., 59. fo. 623: same to same, 28 Dec. 1646.

[2] ibid., 59. fo. 649: same to same, 8 Jan. 1646/7. Parmenter added that the butchers had not paid the excise tax since the preceding June.

[3] *C.J.* V. 58a: 20 Jan. 1646/7.

[4] Add. MSS. 22620, fo. 45: Thomas Atkin to Mayor and others of Norwich, 25 Jan. 1646/7; fo. 56: Atkin to Henry Watts, Mayor, 4 Mar. 1646/7.

[5] *C.J.* V. 249b: 19 June 1647. The riots did result in a softening of some of the provisions of the excise tax regulations in February 1646/7 and August 1647, but the tax continued to be a source of grievance. *A. & O.* I. 916–20, 1004–7.

[6] Pearl, 'London's Counter-Revolution', pp. 38, 43.

too dependent on events elsewhere in England over which they had no control. With the capture of the King by the army early in June, the failure of the conservative counter-revolution of London in July and early August, and the subsequent dominance of the House of Commons by the political Independents, their future was bleak. The Commons, while it negotiated with the King on the basis of the Heads of Proposals drawn up by the army leaders, was determined to prevent Royalists from capturing public offices. An act was passed in September which prohibited the election to municipal office of any man who had been in the armies against Parliament, had assisted the Royalist forces, or had been sequestered from office in any city or corporation.[1] A month later another ordinance was approved which prevented these men from voting as well as being elected, and the Committee for Indemnity was empowered to remove any officeholders and call for new elections.[2] London deserved special consideration: yet another act was passed against disaffected persons just before the Common Council elections in December.[3] Similarly, early in March 1647/8, the House of Commons prepared and hastily approved an ordinance for Norwich to take effect before the annual municipal elections.[4] All persons who had been imprisoned or sequestered, had refused to obey the ordinances of Parliament, or had aided the Crown at any time during the Civil War were ineligible to run for mayor, recorder, steward, alderman, sheriff, or councilman for one year beginning 12 March 1647/8. Further, these same persons were not allowed to vote in the election of any of the above offices and under no circumstances should present officeholders faithful to Parliament be displaced.[5]

An explosive situation had developed in Norwich by the spring of 1648. The Presbyterians, who counted Mayor Utting among their members, were frustrated and disillusioned; the Royalists were barred from voting and attaining office; and the lesser trades-

---

[1] *A. & O.* I. 1009: 9 Sept. 1647.

[2] ibid., 1023–5: 4 Oct. 1647. The ordinance of 9 September had proved defective because it dealt solely with future elections and thus excluded the Royalists already in office. Also, the first act did not provide for punishment and effective enforcement. For a further discussion of these acts and their impact on urban government, see Shilling, 'Municipal Corporations', pp. 52–66.

[3] *A. & O.*, 1045–6: 17 Dec. 1647; Brenner, 'London's Merchant Community', pp. 93–4.

[4] *C.J.* V. 489, 493: 10 and 13 Mar. 1647/8.

[5] *L.J.* X. 113–14: 14 Mar. 1647/8.

men chafed at the excise tax. All three groups could point to the central government and the army which now upheld it as the source of their grievances. Moreover, whatever ties had previously existed among them were further cemented by events on the national level in late 1647 and 1647/8. The army's treatment of the London corporation in 1647 was ominous for conservative groups in other towns. The army remodelled important London committees in favour of Independents, instigated the impeachment of five aldermen (including Royalist John Gayre) who had been involved in the Presbyterian offensive of the previous summer, and dispatched soldiers to the Common Hall to ensure the election of an Independent to the mayoralty.[1] The flight of Charles from the army to the Isle of Wight in November and his decision to reopen negotiations with the Scots brought added determination to the conservative coalition throughout England. Their resolve was given greater urgency by the army's growing implacability against the King, and the espousal of socially revolutionary designs by levellers and republicans in its midst. To this must be added the social unrest which always follows in the wake of a succession of bad harvests and extremely high prices for essential commodities. As is invariably the case, the lower levels of society were hardest hit and government, both central and local, frequently became the target of their complaints against shortages, high prices, and high taxes. A dangerous level of alienation and discontent spread across England during the winter.[2] In the spring and summer of 1648, a series of Royalist rebellions and anti-government, anti-army riots sprang up in East Anglia.[3] Each had its origins in local grievances, but many would probably not have surfaced had it not been for the frenzied atmosphere of uprising, violence, and disorder which, like a brush fire, swept across the region.

Within this larger context, the inflammable situation in Norwich needed only a spark to set it off. This was provided by an election controversy in early spring and led to a violent and deadly riot in late April. As the single most dramatic occurrence in Norwich during the seventeenth century, the events are well

[1] Brenner, 'London's Merchant Community', p. 93.
[2] See Underdown, *Pride's Purge*, pp. 90–7.
[3] Uprisings in East Anglia were staged in Bury, Linton, Newmarket, Colchester, Thetford, Stowmarket, and Cambridge in addition to Norwich. Everitt, *Suffolk*, p. 14.

documented.[1] The parliamentary ordinance against disaffected persons had resulted in the displacement of fully two-thirds of the London common councilmen and their replacement by Independents in December.[2] The ordinance for Norwich, however, failed to produce even the slightest Independent victory at the polls in mid-March;[3] on the contrary, it was the conservative group which took the initiative. On 21 March the freemen of Mancroft gathered for their first aldermanic election since 1644 to replace John Lombe, deceased.[4] Roger Mingay and Richard Wenman, both residents of the ward, were nominated and the freemen elected Mingay by a substantial majority.[5] But Mingay was a Royalist and had never been sheriff; consequently he was ineligible for office by both the 1620 ordinance and the ordinance passed by Parliament earlier in March. Apparently the Mancroft freemen, the most Royalist in sympathy during the Civil War and encouraged by the Royalist revival of 1647/8, deliberately challenged the two laws which had denied Royalists the power and influence of public office. Mayor Utting, also a Mancroft resident, could have declared the election void, but chose not to. Six days later, on the anniversary of King Charles's accession, Utting permitted bonfires and feasts.

The anti-Royalists were alarmed. In mid-April an alderman, one of the sheriffs, and several other citizens rode to London and

---

[1] Th. E. 438. (6): *A True Relation of the Late Mutiny in Norwich, 24 April*, London, April 1648, printed for George Whittington; *A Perfect Diurnal of some passages in Parliament and the Daily Proceedings of the Army under his Excellency the Lord Fairfax from Monday the 24th April till Monday the 1 of May 1648*, London, 1648, reprinted in John L'Estrange, ed., *East Counties Collectanae* (Norwich, 1872–3), pp. 182–3; Tanner MSS., 57, fo. 35: Christopher Baret to Speaker Lenthall, 4 May 1648, reprinted in Henry Cary, ed., *Memorials of the Great Civil War in England, 1642–52* (London, 1842), I. 399–403; account of the riot compiled by the Committee of Complaints presented to the House of Commons on 12 Sept. 1649, *C.J.* VI. 294–5. Blomefield also had access to an important source which cannot be located. Since his narrative is especially insightful on the activities of the magistrates, he possibly had access to the now missing Mayor's Court Book. Blomefield, *Norfolk*, III. 393–6. The best secondary account may be found in Ketton-Cremer, *Norfolk*, pp. 334 ff.

[2] J. E. Farnell, 'The Usurpation of Honest London Householders: Barebone's Parliament', *English Historical Review*, 82 (1967), 24–30.

[3] Only five of the sixty councilmen of 1647 were not returned to the Council in 1648. Two who were not, Thomas Ashwell and William Davy, were ineligible owing to their election to the shrievalty the previous September.

[4] The will for John Lombe was proved in December 1647. N.N.R.O., N.C.C., Wills Proved, 137 Barker.

[5] A.B. (1642–68), 20 June 1659, 201ᵛ.

personally presented a petition to the House of Commons.[1] Utting was accused of being in league with 'malignants' to elect some aldermen contrary to the recent ordinance of Parliament. The Commons hastily ordered the magistrates to put the March election ordinance into effect and passed the citizens' petition to the Committee of Complaints. The latter immediately sent a messenger to Norwich to escort Utting to London in safe custody and appointed Alderman Christopher Baret to act as temporary mayor during his absence.[2]

The messenger received an unexpected reception upon his entrance into Norwich on Friday, 21 April. When he informed Utting of the summons to appear before Parliament and answer for his actions, the mayor called a special meeting of the Court of Aldermen for Saturday.[3] According to *A True Relation*, only six aldermen came to it, one of whom was Roger Mingay, recently sworn into office by the mayor. The purpose of the meeting was to draw up a petition testifying to Utting's good behaviour and to give reasons why he should remain in Norwich despite the orders of the House of Commons. This was accomplished. A petition was subsequently passed around the city on Saturday and Sunday and supposedly was signed by hundreds of citizens.[4] Townsmen remembered well the fate of William Gostlyn, the mayor who had been spirited away and gaoled in 1642/3, and a large number of them assembled on Sunday to pledge their loyalty to Utting and their determination to prevent his removal. That night the mob locked the city gates and set up an armed watch outside Utting's house despite the protests of the mayor himself.[5]

The next morning the mob, numbering in excess of 1,000, reassembled in the market-place.[6] The Court of Aldermen was called to an emergency session. Pleas were heard from some aldermen to raise the city forces, but other aldermen who supported

[1] *C.J.* V. 535: 18 Apr. 1648; VI. 294–5: 12 Sept. 1649. The petition, entitled 'The Humble Petition of Divers of the Justices, Sheriffs, and Citizens of the City of Norwich', has since been lost.

[2] ibid., Various Accounts and Correspondenc*p*, 1642–50: H. Elsing, Clerk of Parliament, to Norwich, 18 Apr. 1648 and William Lenthall to Christopher Baret, 20 Apr. 1648.

[3] *A True Relation*, 1648, n.p.

[4] Blomefield, *Norfolk*, III. 394.

[5] ibid.

[6] ibid.; N.N.R.O., Mayor's Book MSS., 37^r, numbered the mob to be between 500 and 600.

Utting prevented this move.[1] A request to send letters to troops quartered in the county was also blocked. In the meantime, the mob was whipped up into an ugly mood and, hearing rumours that the mayor was about to leave for London, they took off in pursuit of the messenger of the House of Commons. The messenger fled as quickly as he could, without the mayor and lucky to get out of town with his life.[2] The mob was now completely out of control: shortly before noon they stormed Sheriff Ashwell's house and secured arms.[3] By two o'clock in the afternoon they were roaming the city at will, plundering and ransacking the homes of known Parliament supporters. All pretence of order had vanished completely. In the confusion, a number of citizens escaped from the city and contacted Colonel Fleetwood's regiment, which by good fortune happened to be mustering twelve miles outside Norwich on that day.[4] At about four o'clock the regiment arrived in the city and immediately opened fire on the rioters. With blood flowing freely on both sides, the troops eventually cornered the rioters in the Committee House, a building which also served as the central ammunition depot for the entire county and was stocked with almost 100 barrels of gunpowder. In the fury that followed, the magazine exploded with a tremendous roar. Windows were shattered, the whole city shook, and so many bodies were dismembered and scattered that it was impossible to count them.[5] The catastrophe effectively ended the riot and by nightfall Colonel Fleetwood's troops were in control of the city.

The complicity of Mayor Utting and other magistrates in the riot is not altogether clear. A Royalist friend of the mayor, in a letter dated 24 April, complimented Utting on his efforts to protect the messenger from harm, assuage the fury of the mob, and co-operate with other magistrates in preserving order.[6] The Norwich

---

[1] *A True Relation*, 1648, n.p. The aldermen supporting Utting are not named.

[2] Tanner MSS., 57, fo. 35: Baret to Lenthall, 4 May 1648.

[3] *A True Relation*, 1648, n.p., and Blomefield, *Norfolk*, III. 395.

[4] *A Perfect Diurnal*, 1648, n.p.; John Rushworth, *Historical Collections* (London, 1721), VIII. 1071–2.

[5] *A True Relation*, 1648, n.p. estimated that 200 rioters were killed in the explosion; *A Perfect Diurnal* put the figure at 120; and the Committee of Complaints approximated the damage at £20,000. For additional details, based on depositions taken by the magistrates following the blast, see Ketton-Cremer, *Norfolk*, pp. 334–41.

[6] Tanner MSS., 311, fo. 6: Joseph Paine to Richard Bensley, 24 Apr. 1648. In 1643 Paine had refused to collect proposition money and the following the

Assembly and the House of Commons viewed matters differently. In May a petition from Norwich requested the House of Commons to investigate the riots and the House responded by appointing a committee to look into it.[1] In the extended proceedings which followed, the Norwich Assembly refused to pay Utting's expenses and even offered to bear the costs of prosecution against him.[2] Hearings dragged on until September 1649 when the Committee of Complaints concluded that Utting had agitated the citizens with his petition, made no effort to stop the riot once it had started, and tried to shut the city gates to keep the troopers out.[3] Throughout the whole affair he was abetted by alderman and ex-mayor John Tooly, who was alleged to have openly encouraged the rioters. Both men were declared 'Grand Delinquents' by the House of Commons, who then fined Utting and Tooly £500 and £1,000 respectively, disabled both from holding any office, and committed them to Fleet Prison.[4] The rioters suffered a worse fate at the hands of a commission of oyer and terminer in December 1648.[5] Eight were executed and numerous others were fined, imprisoned, or both.[6]

The riot involved much more than just the Utting affair. In a letter early in May, Christopher Baret acknowledged that the immediate cause of the riot had been the petition in defence of Utting, but added that 'I doubt not time will evince there was a greater plot in it and a design further of than we are yet aware of.'[7] According to one witness, the central issue was national politics:

[1] *C.J.* V. 553, 559–60: 8 and 16 May 1648.

[2] A.B. (1642–68), 23 June and 26 Aug. 1648, 65^v, 69^v.

[3] *C.J.* VI. 294: 12 Sept. 1649. The investigation had been turned over to the Committee for Complaints in April. ibid., 188: 17 Apr. 1649.

[4] Utting was imprisoned for six months and Tooly for three months. ibid. 304: 9 Oct. 1649. The fines were to be paid to the Norwich Assembly, and in 1650 they agreed to reduce Utting's fine to £200 and Tooly's to £400. A.B. (1642–68), 5 July and 3 Sept. 1650, 99^r, 100^v.

[5] See ibid., 26 Oct. and 8 Nov. 1648, 69^v, 71^r; *C.J.* VI. 92, 94: 1 and 7 Dec. 1648.

[6] ibid., 294: 12 Sept. 1649; *A Complete History of the famous City of Norwich* (Norwich, 1728), p. 49; A.B. (1642–68), 8 Jan. 1648/9, 71^v.

[7] Tanner MSS., 57, fo. 35: Baret to Lenthall, 4 May 1648.

corporation refused to bail him out of a Cambridge gaol. M.C.B. (1634–46), 18 Nov. 1643, 400^r and 24 July 1644, 431^r. He later became mayor in 1660 and was knighted by Charles II.

I believe that you have heard that this town, as well as other places, was much divided, some against the Parliament and Army, and others for them, which caused a difference betwixt not only the meaner sort of people, but even amongst those which were in chiefest place in the city, and the disaffected party do so increase, that the rest were often times openly scorned and derided by them.[1]

Apart from championing the mayor, the mob had been driven by pro-Royalist and anti-excise passions. By Sunday night the movement to protect Utting was rapidly being converted into a Royalist rebellion; and on Monday the insurrectionists openly claimed they were acting for the King and would purge the Common Council and the Court of Aldermen by plucking the Roundheads out.[2] *A True Relation* adds that at the height of the rebellion cries of 'for God, King Charles, and the Mayor' could be heard and the rioters anticipated armed support from the countryside.[3] The lesser tradesmen and apprentices, who formed the great majority of rioters,[4] also ravaged the excise office in Parmenter's home.[5]

There was a religious aspect to the events leading up to and including the riot. In his quest for a conservative movement in the city, Mayor Utting had been willing to accommodate the religious inclinations of the Royalists, as well as to aid them in gaining office. Indeed, he had gone too far in permitting a revival of Anglicanism to satisfy many Presbyterians. A petition expressing their grievances was circulated early in April and presented to the mayor.[6] The petition complained that faithful ministers were slighted and discouraged whereas ejected ministers were encouraged, and that the old service and Prayer Book were being used instead of the Directory of Worship. These Presbyterians called for a thorough reformation, the execution of ordinances dealing with the demolition of pictures and other objects of superstition and

---

[1] Th. E. 437. (12): T. S., *A Letter from Norwich of the Blowing up of the Magazine there*, London, 25 April 1648. See also Cary, ed., *Memorials*, pp. 399–403.

[2] Blomefield, *Norfolk*, III. 394–5.

[3] *A True Relation*, 1648, n.p.

[4] This is the conclusion reached by Ketton-Cremer following a thorough analysis of the depositions taken from the participants. He adds that they 'had blundered into an ill-conceived demonstration against the dominant power'. Ketton-Cremer, *Norfolk*, p. 348.

[5] Blomefield, *Norfolk*, III. 395.

[6] ibid., p. 393. According to Blomefield the petition, which has not been located, was signed by 150 townsmen.

idolatry in churches, and, above all, a prohibition against preaching by ejected ministers. This petition made no mention of the mayor's political dealings with the Royalists, but the petition presented to the House of Commons on 18 April did. The difference was one of authorship. Since the delegation which appeared before the House of Commons was headed by Sheriff Thomas Ashwell and Alderman Thomas Baret, another Independent and son of Alderman Christopher Baret, we may assume that it was the Independents, not the Presbyterians, who appealed to Parliament for assistance.[1] In addition to his political indiscretions in favouring Royalists, Utting was accused of countenancing malignant and sequestered ministers preaching publicly in the city.[2] The Independents certainly wanted no part of the Directory of Worship or a Presbyterian Church settlement, but they would have wholeheartedly agreed with the Presbyterian petition that these practices of Utting must be stopped, and their petition expressed their concern.

When the rebellion had gathered steam, the Royalists could be expected to support it and the Independents to oppose it vigorously. The Presbyterians were caught in the middle and left with a difficult decision. It appears that the riot split this group. On the one hand, the riot was anti-Parliament, anti-army, and anti-Independent. It also came in the midst of rumours in England that an army was being raised in Scotland for the establishment of Presbyterianism, the disbandment of Fairfax's army of sectaries, and for immediate negotiations with Charles.[3] Utting was a Presbyterian and Tooly was certainly neither a Royalist nor an Anglican,[4] but they were eager to join in a common cause with the Royalists to swing Norwich into the camp against Parliament and its Independent-army leadership. Other magistrates in Norwich may have been reluctant to go as far as Utting and Tooly in

---

[1] The House of Commons ordered on 18 April that the petitioners merited the gratitude of Parliament. *C.J.* V. 535b.

[2] Blomefield, *Norfolk*, III. 393; *C.J.* VI. 294 a-b: 12 Sept. 1649.

[3] Reginald R. Sharpe, *London and the Kingdom* (London, 1894), II. 270–3.

[4] The dedication of Carter's sermon of June 1647 read: 'To the Right Worshipful Mr. John Utting, Mayor of the City of Norwich, John Carter dedicates this poor and unworthy piece; and as he preached the sermon at his request, so now he presents it to him for his use, with appreciation of all grace, honor, happiness, and good success in his government.' Carter, *Wheel Turned*. Tooly was the leading Puritan in the city during the 1630s and the Civil War and had been more closely associated with the parliamentary effort during the war than any other magistrate.

committing themselves to support of the riot, yet enough of them were willing to back Utting and the rebellion to the extent of successfully voting down motions to raise city forces or call in troops on the morning of 24 April.[1] That Royalists and Presbyterians, so well noted for their political and social conservatism, could become associated with mob activity might seem surprising. It had been precisely this phenomenon, however, which had characterized the Presbyterian-peace party–Royalist counter-revolution in London the preceding July.[2]

On the other hand, the riot was pro-Royalist. It was one thing to utilize the aid of Royalists in establishing Presbyterianism; it was quite another to risk the elevation of Royalists and Anglicans into power. Insurrection was dangerous business, especially when it involved a violent and potentially uncontrollable and unpredictable mob which chanted Royalist slogans and was anti-Puritan in mood. *A True Relation* claimed that if troops had not arrived when they did, 'it is thought they would scarce have found a godly man alive, either of Presbyterian or Independent in this city'. These considerations may have led some Presbyterians, already anxious about the revival of Anglicanism early in the month, to refrain from joining with Utting and Tooly. Only two days after the riot, the Assembly agreed that a day of thanksgiving should be celebrated for deliverance from the rebellion, and none other than John Carter consented to preach the principal sermon.[3]

The riot, at least as far as the mob is concerned, appears to have been a spontaneous outburst in response to national and local developments. There is no evidence of a conspiracy involving Royalist or anti-Parliament parties outside the city.[4] Nevertheless, what occurred in Norwich bears striking similarities to the riot of 9 and 10 April in London. As in Norwich, the conservative faction in London had been gaining ground in the winter of 1647/8

---

[1] The identity of these magistrates is not known. Since the ardent Royalists had already been evicted in 1643 and 1644, they were either moderates or Presbyterians.

[2] Pearl, 'London's Counter-Revolution', pp. 29–30, 33, 42–3, 50–1.

[3] A.B. (1642–68), 26 Apr. 1648, 62r.

[4] Conspiracy aspects of the riot were still under investigation in June 1650. Mayor Rayley wanted subpoenas to interrogate some of Utting's friends. His agent in London, John Balderston, offered the names of several men who were 'the most likely men I could think of to give the truest information of Mr. Utting's effort both in the county and the city . . .'. Add. MSS., 22620, fo. 169: John Balderston to Mayor Rayley, 12 June 1650.

amidst widespread discontent with the army and Independents. Again, as in Norwich, deprived ministers were occupying pulpits and using the Book of Common Prayer.[1] It is difficult to believe that the London uprising did not influence Norwich townsmen even though the documents make no mention of any connections. In both insurrections the major participants were the apprentices and lesser tradesmen, and in each case the mob was exhorted by Royalist slogans.[2] Certainly the Norwich community must have been familiar with what had happened in London and the riot there most probably was an inspiration for many townsmen of Norwich to take to the streets.

Two days after the riot, and one day after Mayor Utting had voluntarily left for London, the Norwich Assembly met to confirm Christopher Baret as deputy-mayor, approve a £200 gift of gratitude to the soldiers, and reconsider the election of Mingay. By a vote of forty to twelve, it declared that Mingay's election and swearing-in was void and illegal by both election laws, and Wenman was authorized to occupy Mingay's seat on the Court.[3] The politico-geographical division of the city during the Civil War was still in evidence: seven of the eight councilmen who did vote for Mingay were from Conesford and Mancroft, whereas nineteen of the twenty-eight councilmen who opposed Mingay represented Wymer and Over-the-Water.

The next bit hurdle for the parliamentary forces to cross was the mayor's election on 1 May. Despite the abortive riot, there was ample reason to expect another commotion. The House of Commons acted quickly. On 27 April it ordered the temporary disenfranchisement of all those who had assisted or taken part in the riot and the ineligibility of all aldermen who in any way were connected with the tumult.[4] The Commons added that the magistrates would be held responsible for the execution of these orders. They were also aware that something more than a parliamentary declaration was called for. To make sure that their will was

[1] Sharpe, *London*, II. 270–3.

[2] ibid. The Royalist cause had been gaining ground among both apprentices and merchants in London during the winter of 1647/8. The cry of the mob in London, which numbered three or four thousand, was 'now for King Charles'. It is also interesting to note that in both cities the apprentices had been angered by the parliamentary decree of 1647 against the celebration of Christmas. Blomefield, *Norfolk*, III. 392.

[3] A.B. (1642–68), 26 Apr. 1648, 63v.

[4] *C.J.* V. 546: 27 Apr. 1648.

enforced, the Committee of Both Houses dashed off a letter to Colonel Fleetwood, which thanked him for the good service of his regiment on the previous Monday and commanded him to position as many troops around the city as he thought necessary to protect the peace on the next Monday.[1] The soldiers were instructed not to interfere with free elections, and, from deputy-mayor Baret's description, they performed admirably.[2] In a poll that was carried out, in Baret's words 'with that quietness and peaceableness as was wonderful', the freemen properly nominated Edmund Burman and Robert Baron. Burman was then chosen mayor-elect by the magistrates.

There were no other major incidents in 1648. The city government was unwaveringly obedient to Parliament during the second Civil War. In June the Assembly voted overwhelmingly to make Ralph Wollmer, the lieutenant of the horse troops guarding the city, an honorary freeman.[3] On the same date the Assembly informed Lord General Fairfax by letter that Norwich would defend itself against any force raised without the authority of Parliament. True to its word, the corporation rushed a company of troops to Yarmouth in July when that city was endangered by Royalist ships.[4] The freemen and magistrates complied with the ordinance of Parliament in the election of sheriffs in September and then made elaborate preparations for Lord General Fairfax to visit the city and stay at the home of Adrian Parmenter.[5] The loyalty of the city government to Parliament even extended to a congratulatory letter to Oliver Cromwell in the critical days of the King's trial and execution of late January 1648/9.[6]

*   *   *

Charles I was convicted and beheaded in January 1648/9. Shortly afterwards the House of Lords was abolished and the Commonwealth proclaimed. A king had been toppled, the Lords had been eliminated, and the House of Commons had been purged. A militant minority, whose power was based on the sword and not the

---

[1] *C.S.P.D.*, Chas I, 1648–9, p. 52.

[2] Tanner MSS., 57, fo. 35: Baret to Lenthall, 4 May 1648.

[3] A.B. (1642–68), 23 June 1648, 65r.

[4] *C.S.P.D.*, Chas. I, 1647–8, pp. 170, 205: 7 and 20 July 1648.

[5] A.B. (1642–68), 8 and 25 Sept. 1648, 68r–v. The House of Commons sent a special order to Norwich in early September to prevent delinquents from voting or being elected to office. Various Accounts and Correspondence, 1642–50: H. Elsynge, Clerk of Parliament, to Norwich, 1648.

[6] A.B. (1642–68), 26 Jan. 1648/9, 74r. The letter itself is no longer existent.

ballot, held power. This undoubtedly constituted a revolution in national government. A corresponding revolution in local politics and society might have been expected, but never took place. The explanation for this is that the Rump, that remnant of the Long Parliament which continued to sit in Westminster following Pride's Purge, was more concerned with establishing a stable and respected government acceptable to the country at large than in extending the revolution to the provinces. Their policy with regard to county establishments and corporations, to the extent that they had one, was to stifle whatever opposition challenged their legitimacy and not to throw out local magistrates and install radicals in their places. During 1649 the Rump thus moved against some corporations, such as London, Exeter, and Winchester, which were noted for their opposition.[1] In its campaign for public recognition, the Rump passed an ordinance on 2 January 1649/50 which required all Englishmen to take the Engagement acknowledging loyalty to the Commonwealth.[2] The intent of the House of Commons was to secure the publicly declared allegiance of magistrates in counties and towns, and otherwise not to interfere except where need arose. Local magistrates not committed ideologically to the Commonwealth but willing to take the Engagement were left unmolested. Moreover, enforcement of the Engagement was not quickly pursued and, in some areas, haphazardly enforced. Far from sponsoring a drift to the 'Left', the Rump carefully avoided steps which would encourage the lower orders to grasp for power.

In such circumstances, the impact of the first years of the Interregnum on provincial urban governments was by no means uniform.[3] The extent to which local officeholders were purged and towns radicalized depended upon the strength of local radical groups and the willingness or unwillingness of magistrates to take the Engagement. Apart from compliance with the Engagement, the Rump was content to let the localities work out their own accommodations. Some cities, including Newcastle, Bristol, and

---

[1] Underdown, *Pride's Purge*, p. 304. Underdown's chapter on 'The Revolution and the Communities' is indispensable in understanding the relationship between central and local government from 1649 to 1652.

[2] The Engagement stated: 'I do declare and promise, that I will be true and faithful to the Commonwealth of England as it is now established, without a King or a House of Lords.' *A. & O.* II. 325–9. Refusal to subscribe could result in a forfeiture of legal rights.

[3] The following is drawn from Underdown, *Pride's Purge*, pp. 297–324 and Howell, pp. 338–42.

York, had already been remodelled during and after the first Civil War by the ejection of Royalists. They remained largely untouched, 'sub-political' to use Professor Howell's term, by the national confrontation of political Presbyterians and Independents. Here there was no second revolution and political life continued without major interruption. In a number of towns new men came to office solely because sitting magistrates refused the Engagement; Exeter and Orford are examples. The ripples emanating from London did have revolutionary vibrations in some other corporations, but frequently this amounted to little more than a change of personnel at the top. Only a few towns, such as Bedford and High Wycombe, actually experimented with democracy. In the absence of leadership and intervention from Westminster, the hopes of extended political participation and religious reformation entertained by local revolutionary minorities were, with but few exceptions, not realized. Even more than in the counties, local governments in the towns generally endured the Commonwealth with reluctant acquiescence and went on in the old way.

Of the major provincial capitals, only Norwich is known to have been strongly affected by the political and religious crises which split Parliament and London from 1645 to 1649.[1] The Norwich supporters of Parliament and the army, who had so narrowly averted a disaster in April 1648 and had then repeatedly demonstrated their loyalty to national government, needed only a propitious moment to commence their own purge of the corporation. This came in late January 1648/9. On the same day that the congratulatory letter was sent to Cromwell for his many favours to the city, the Assembly decreed that the parliamentary ordinance concerning city elections of the preceding March would remain in effect for the forthcoming elections.[2] An additional proviso stipulated that all men who had helped spread the petition defending Utting or had participated in the riot were ineligible to vote or be

[1] Howell suggests that the lack of significant movement to the Left and the absence of conflict between the various branches of government in Newcastle, Exeter, York, and Bristol implies that the attitude of drifting, or neutralism, with respect to national affairs was more widespread than has been suspected. Howell, *Newcastle*, p. 342. If true, this new generalization would not apply to Norwich.

[2] A.B. (1642–68), 26 Jan. 1648/9, 74ʳ. Parliament had passed an act in December regulating London Common Council elections. *A. & O.* I. 1252–3. The Norwich Assembly, however, took the initiative in formulating its own election ordinance and was not reacting to pressure from Parliament.

elected to office, and all officeholders guilty of complicity in the riot were to be displaced. This marked the end of political life for Aldermen Utting, Tooly, Croshold, Sotherton, Gostlyn, and Thacker, and a turnover of more than one-third of the Common Council.

The purge and natural attrition had taken its toll of a group of moderate aldermen who had cautiously steered a middle course since the first days of the struggle between King and Parliament. Six in number, they had constituted a sizeable bloc in the Court of Aldermen from 1642 to 1648: John Croshold, John Freeman, William Gostlyn, John Lombe, John Loveland, and Matthew Sotherton. From the beginning, most of them had neither put up resistance nor retreated from office, as was the case with the ejected Royalists of 1642/3, and yet they had been excluded from the most important committees which determined policy on vital issues prior to 1648.[1] None of them, for example, had voted for Samuel Smith to replace Recorder Cory in 1644.[2] The conservative movement headed by Utting in 1648 brought a number of these reluctant moderates out of the woodwork. The documents describing the riot do not mention their involvement on Utting's behalf, yet none of them voted for Wenman to occupy Mingay's seat,[3] and only one

---

[1] These were the committees to collect arms and horses for Cambridge in March 1642/3 (M.C.B., 1 Mar. 1642/3, 379ʳ), to gather additional arms for Cambridge later the same month (M.C.B., 26 Mar. 1643, 381ᵛ), to maintain watches and two bands of volunteers in April 1643 (A.B., 3 Apr. 1643, 6ᵛ), to sequester delinquents (*C.J.* III. 49: 17 Apr. 1643; M.C.B., 20 May 1643, 385ʳ), to look after the disaffected, to order and dispose of forces, and to oversee collection of funds in August 1643 (Mason, *Norfolk*, I. 291), to eliminate scandalous pictures, crucifixes, and images in churches (M.C.B., 23 Jan. 1643/4, 411ʳ), to prepare charges against Recorder Cory and Alderman Anguish (A.B., 20 Feb. 1643/4, 14ᵛ), to examine scandalous ministers (A.B., 3 May 1645, 31ᵛ), to act as commissioners of excise (Tanner MSS., 59, fo. 610), and to determine who had the power to nominate elders and appoint classes (A.B., 5 Dec. 1646, 47ʳ). John Lombe served on the committee to maintain watches and volunteers in 1643, but none of the other committees.

[2] Gostlyn, Lombe, and Loveland voted for Recorder Cory to remain in office; Croshold, Freeman, and Sotherton were absent. A.B. (1642–68), 3 May 1644, 20. It is interesting to note that Tooly and Thacker, both strong Parliament men in the early 1640s, as well as Utting voted for Cory to retain office.

[3] Croshold and Sotherton voted for Mingay to stay in office, Freeman abstained, and Loveland and Gostlyn were absent. Lombe had died in late 1647. Tooly and Thacker were the only other aldermen to vote for Mingay. Utting, of course, was in London. A.B. (1642–68), 26 Apr. 1648, 62ᵛ. When Sotherton was restored to office in 1660, the Assembly Book states that he had been ejected because he signed the petition supporting Utting. Ibid., 30 Nov. 1660, 136ᵛ.

of the five, Freeman, joined fifteen other aldermen in June in voting for Lieutenant Wollmer to be an honorary freeman.[1] Apparently it was owing to their connection with Utting's group in 1648 that Croshold, Gostlyn, and Sotherton were ousted by the Assembly's decree of 1648/9. Loveland, ninety-three years of age at the time of the purge, died later in 1649 and fence-straddler Freeman managed to retain his seat until he, too, left office in 1650.

Since the corporation had already proved its loyalty and had taken steps to clean its own political chambers even before the Commonwealth was declared, there was no need for the Rump to intervene in Norwich as it did in London. In September 1649 Parliament passed an ordinance requiring all civic officials to take an oath of loyalty to the Commonwealth.[2] A little more than two months later M.P. Thomas Atkin wrote to Mayor John Rayley that the aldermen and councilmen of London were taking the pledge and the magistrates of Norwich would do well to follow suit.[3] The corporation was in no hurry to follow his advice. The famous act of 2 January, which few towns welcomed enthusiastically,[4] required the Engagement to be subscribed by all adult men before 20 February. On 10 January Atkin informed Mayor Rayley of the latest news on national politics and included a copy of the act for subscribing the Engagement.[5] Again the corporation stalled. Parliament pushed the deadline for compliance back to 20 March, but it is doubtful that the Norwich corporation would have met this deadline had not Atkin threatened the magistrates.[6] In early March, with municipal elections only a week away, Atkin wrote to the mayor and expressed his regret that 'any of your aldermen scruple at the signing the Engagement; if they refuse to act in their places they must be otherwise supplied'.[7] He then ominously drew attention to two London aldermen who had been sent to

[1] ibid., 23 June 1648, 65ʳ.
[2] *A. & O.* II. 241–2: 5 Sept. 1649.
[3] Add. MSS. 22620, fo. 139: Thomas Atkin to Mayor John Rayley, 29 Nov. 1649.
[4] Underdown, *Pride's Purge*, pp. 304–5.
[5] Robert Bell, ed., *Memorials of the Civil War* (London, 1849), II. 115–16.
[6] Atkin was perhaps the staunchest and most tireless supporter of the Commonwealth in London. Underdown, *Pride's Purge*, pp. 304–5.
[7] Add. MSS. 22620, fo. 133: Atkin to Rayley, 21 Mar. 1649/50. In some towns, such as Nottingham, Presbyterian ministers successfully urged opposition to the Engagement on the grounds that it was incompatible with the Solemn League and Covenant. It is not known whether the Presbyterian ministers of Norwich attempted to obstruct the Engagement.

Newgate Prison for their refusal to subscribe and who would not
be released until they took the oath. 'And then if they desire to
sign,' Atkin continued, 'we will consider of it.'

According to Blomefield, enforcement of the Engagement
resulted in the displacement of many aldermen.[1] This is an exag-
geration. Nine aldermen left the Court between April 1649 and
April 1650, but not more than four of the vacancies could have been
caused by ejections from office.[2] Twenty new men joined the
Common Council for the first time in 1650, but half of the vacancies
they filled resulted from the elevation of councilmen to the
shrievalty and aldermanry. Moreover, it would be surprising if
Norwich officeholders in large numbers had refused to take the
Engagement when Englishmen of almost all political parties did
not trouble their consciences over it and complied.[3]

The decision of the Assembly to extend the parliamentary
ordinance of 1647/8, with additions, to 1649, and the Engagement
of 1649/50 served to guarantee that these magisterial vacancies
would not be filled by political conservatives. Each of the seven
sheriffs elected in 1647, 1648, and 1649 opposed the election of
Mingay as alderman and was associated with the pro-parliamentary
activity of the Assembly.[4] Owing to the deaths of mayors in 1649
and 1650, five men held the mayoralty from 1648 to 1651 and every
one of them was associated with the Independent-Parliamentarian
faction.[5] An unprecedented phenomenon arose in the election of
aldermen during this period. After the election of Richard Wenman
and Robert Cory to the Court of Aldermen in April 1648, there
were only seven ex-sheriffs remaining in the city.[6] By the elections

[1] Blomefield, *Norfolk*, III. 399.
[2] At least five aldermen died during 1649: Alexander Peckover, Christopher
Baret, Robert Baron, Matthew Peckover, and John Greenwood. The will for
John Freeman was proved on 20 November 1651, so it is possible that he also
died and was not removed. Aldermen William Barnham and Thomas Toft are
omitted from the list of aldermen for 1650, but both returned to the Court by
April 1651; cause for their exclusion in 1650 is unknown.
[3] See Christopher Hill, *Society and Puritanism in Pre-Revolutionary England*
(New York, 1967), pp. 409–12.
[4] They were Thomas Ashwell, William Davy, William Barnham, Robert
Allen, John Man, Alexander Peckover, and Samuel Brewster. Peckover died in
office and was replaced by Brewster.
[5] They were Edmund Burman, Robert Baron, Thomas Toft, Matthew
Lindsey, and Thomas Baret.
[6] Robert Thompson, John Grey, Richard Bateman, William Rye, Robert
Holmes, Thomas Ashwell, and William Davy.

of 1649 three additional sheriffs joined this list.[1] The dismissal of six aldermen and the death of another meant that seven of these ten candidates were elevated early in 1649. Of the remaining three ex-sheriffs, only one, Robert Holmes, was qualified to be an alderman and he was a Royalist.[2] When it became necessary to elect four new aldermen in the summer of 1649 before the next election of sheriffs, Holmes was passed over each time in favour of Samuel Brewster, Alexander Peckover, Hamond Craske, and Thomas Johnson, none of whom had been sheriff.[3] In permitting the election of four non-sheriffs, the magistrates were departing from the same 1620 ordinance which had been cited against Mingay's election in 1648. On the other hand, there was no alternative, especially since Holmes was probably declared ineligible by the election regulations of 1648 and 1649. The problem was exacerbated in the spring of 1650, when deaths and dismissals from the Engagement created five more vacancies. One of the slots was filled by Sheriff John Man, but the other four new aldermen had never been sheriff.[4]

The political deck was almost completely stacked against the conservatives in the election of aldermen in 1649 and 1650. With the freeman electorate reduced by the election ordinances, the Independent-Parliamentarians controlled the choice of sheriffs. These sheriffs formed the pool of eligible candidates for aldermanic elections and, with the heavy turnover of aldermen, they were guaranteed almost immediate promotion to the Court. When

[1] Sheriffs William Barnham and Robert Allen, and John Salter, sheriff in 1639, who had compounded out of the aldermanry for seven years in 1642.

[2] The unacceptability of Robert Thompson is discussed in Chapter IV. John Grey appears to have left the city for Suffolk by 1649. He is listed as a ratepayer in 1645 in St. Michael at Plea but is not listed in the rates for the river and streets in 1649. His will, dated in 1651, suggests that he was living in Suffolk. London, Somerset House, P.C.C., Wills Proved, 44 Berkeley.

[3] Brewster replaced Matthew Peckover, whose will was proved in 1649. N.N.R.O., Norfolk Archdeaconry Court, Wills Proved, 1649, 139ᵛ–141ᵛ. There is an entry in the Assembly Book for 3 September 1649, which excuses Hamond Craske from the shrievalty for three years since he has already been chosen alderman. A.B. (1642–68), 84ʳ. Since Alexander Peckover was elected alderman after the 1649 elections and died before the 1650 elections, he is not listed as an alderman in the yearly lists of officeholders in the Assembly Book, but his will, dated 22 July 1649, identifies him as 'citizen and alderman of Norwich'. N.A.C., Wills Proved, 1649, 257ᵛ–259ʳ. Johnson replaced Mayor Robert Baron, who died on 1 August and was replaced on 3 August. A.B. (1642–68), 83ʳ.

[4] The four non-sheriff aldermen were Nicholas Pointer, Giles Woods, John Reade, and John Andrews.

the supply of sheriffs had run out, the ward electorates, reduced by the election ordinances, were free to consider any citizen so long as he had not aided the Crown in the Civil War, or Utting and the rioters in 1648. A total of sixteen aldermen were elected in 1649 and 1650 and thirteen of these new magistrates had voted for Wenman to replace Mingay in 1648. How can the election of the three anomalies be explained? One of them was John Salter, a sheriff in 1639 who had compounded out of the aldermanry for seven years in 1642: he undoubtedly owed his election in 1649 to the shortage of sheriffs. The other two, Thomas Johnson and John Reade, were both elected by the freemen of Mancroft at times when there were no past or present sheriffs available and the freemen of this conservative ward were thus able to opt for more moderate men.[1]

Through death and dismissal, a considerable turnover in political personnel from the end of the Civil War to the beginning of the Protectorate had taken place. Only seventeen of the councilmen of mid-1652 were members of the Common Council in mid-1648, and only thirteen had been in the Assembly in 1645. Eleven of the aldermen of mid-1652 were members of the Court in mid-1648 and only seven had been on the Court in 1645. The corporation had been almost completely remodelled, yet the occupational composition of both chambers remained remarkably stable. Men of seventeen different trades sat in the Council in both 1645 and 1652.[2] The number of grocers and worsted weavers, who continued to dominate, remained constant, although there were three more worsted weavers and three fewer grocers in 1652.[3] The Court of Aldermen contained men of nine trades in 1652 compared with eight in 1645. As in the Council, there was a slight increase in the number of worsted-weaver aldermen from two to five and a marginal decline in grocers from nine to eight.[4] A consequence of long-term economic transformations, the gradual rise of worsted,

[1] Salter, Reade, and Johnson were all councilmen in April 1648.

[2] The trades of the 1652 councilmen have been gathered from Millican, ed., *Freeman*. The trades of five councilmen cannot be determined beyond doubt and are omitted from this analysis. See Chapter IV, Table 20 for 1645.

[3] The most heavily represented trades in the Council in 1652 were worsted weavers, grocers, bakers, scriveners, and mercers with 22, 6, 5, 4, and 3 members respectively.

[4] The most heavily represented trades in the Court of Aldermen in 1652 were grocers, worsted weavers, merchants, hosiers, and drapers with 8, 5, 3, 2, and 2 members respectively. In 1645 these same trades had accounted for 9, 2, 4, 4, and 2 aldermen respectively.

weavers to public office, had set in before 1645 and continued after 1660.[1] As Table 23 shows, there was a sharp drop in the wealth of councilmen in all four wards as measured by tax on personal estate in 1645. This was not the case, however, with the Court of Aldermen. Whereas the mean tax on personal estate of the aldermen of 1645 was 14s. 5d., the mean of the aldermen of 1652 on the same assessment rose to 15s. 8d.[2]

TABLE 23: *Wealth of Councilmen by Ward, 1645 and 1652**

	Conesford	Mancroft	Wymer	Over-the-Water
1645: mean	5s. 8d.	10s. 9d.	9s. 11d.	9s. 1d.
median	4s. 0d.	6s. 0d.	10s. 0d.	9s. 0d.
1652: mean	5s. 9d.	5s. 6d.	5s. 5d.	5s. 9d.
median	2s. 0d.	5s. 0d.	4s. 0d.	5s. 0d.

*Figures given are tax on personal estate in the 1645 Assessment for Fairfax's Forces. Six of the 1645 councilmen were not taxed for personal estate in that year. Eleven of the 1652 councilmen were not included in the 1645 tax for personal estate.

That the Commonwealth did not bring to power a new social and economic group of men is especially apparent if the sixteen aldermen elevated in 1649 and 1650 are considered separately. In terms of wealth, occupation, and age they are almost indistinguishable from the parliamentary-Puritan magistrates of the first Civil War period on the one hand, and the twelve new aldermen elected from 1660 to 1663 on the other.[3] The wealth of the new aldermen of 1649–50, again as measured by tax on personal estate

[1] See Chapter II.
[2] The median tax of the aldermen fell from 10s. 6d. to 10s. Thomas Johnson, alderman in 1652, cannot be located in the 1645 assessment.
[3] The new aldermen of 1649–50 were Allen, Andrews, Ashwell, Barnham, Bateman, Brewster, H. Craske, Davy, Johnson, Man, Peckover, Pointer, Reade, Rye, Salter, and G. Woods. Before the politically-motivated ejection of aldermen commenced in 1660, six of these men had died and two were discharged from office upon their own request. Of the remaining eight, six were removed from office between 1660 and 1663. John Man, the wealthiest man in the city, and John Salter, who owed his election to the Court in 1649 to the fact that he was one of the very few ex-sheriffs in the city who was not really a Commonwealth man, retained their seats. There were twelve new aldermen appointed between 1660 and 1663, not including the aldermen who were returned to their seats in late 1660. They were Bendish, Briggs, Coldham, Herne, Heyward, Lawrence, Long, Manser, Markham, Norris, H. Watts, jr., and H. Woods. The four aldermen appointed by the royal commissioners in July 1662, are included.

in 1645, was comparable to the wealth of the parliamentary-Puritan magistrates of 1642/5.[1] Three of the new aldermen—John Man, John Reade, and John Andrews—were among the ten wealthiest citizens in Norwich. Moreover, eleven of the sixteen new aldermen were among the eighty-four citizens taxed 10*s.* or more for personal estate in 1645; and of the nine Restoration aldermen taxed in 1660, seven were among the eighty highest ratepayers.[2] Nor was there a marked change in occupations between the Commonwealth aldermen and their Restoration replacements. Four of the former were worsted weavers, four were grocers and merchants, two were hosiers, and two were mercers. In contrast five of the new aldermen of 1660–3 were worsted weavers, three were grocers, one was a merchant, and another was a hosier. With rapid magisterial turnover during the 1640s, the Commonwealth aldermen would be expected to be younger than the Restoration aldermen. They were, but only because the Restoration aldermen were older than average.[3] The most striking difference between the parliamentary-Puritans and Royalists in the first Civil War concerned their residence. The same applies to the Commonwealth and Restoration recruits. The Roundhead ward of Over-the-Water provided six of the sixteen new aldermen whereas only one of the twelve new aldermen of 1660–3 lived in this ward.

The new magistrates of the Interregnum were not men of politically obscure trades and they were not social upstarts. They had espoused no schemes for social or economic reform before 1649 and they introduced no radical programmes in these areas once they had gained power. The corporation did successfully lobby the House of Commons for legislation favouring the depressed worsted-weaving industry in 1650.[4] Since the economic prosperity of the whole city depended so heavily on textile production, the magistrates' efforts in this regard cannot be construed as benefiting a narrow economic interest in which a few of them were personally involved. London offers an interesting contrast. Here

[1] The median tax on personal estate for the 1649–50 aldermen was 10*s.*

[2] Aldermen Hayward, Long, and Markham were not included in the 1660 tax.

[3] The median date of becoming freemen for the new aldermen of 1649–50 was 1626 (twenty-three years prior to 1649) whereas for the new aldermen of 1660–3 it was 1632 (twenty-eight years prior to 1660).

[4] M. P. Atkin pressured strongly for the weaving ordinance. Bell, ed., *Memorials*, II. 114–16. *A. & O.* II. 451–5. The act was renewed in 1653 for an additional year. ibid., 775–80. See also *C.S.P.D.*, Interregnum, 1655–6, p. 201: Petition from worsted weavers of Norwich and Norfolk, 3 Oct. 1655.

the gradual eclipse of the Presbyterians by the Independents after mid-1647 had definite socio-economic implications. The trades of the Presbyterian leaders who held sway from 1645 to 1647 reveal, according to Professor Pearl, that they were members of a single roughly-defined socio-economic group; for the most part they were engaged in domestic trades and were not part of the élite merchant circle which dominated the magistracy before the Civil War.[1] The Independent triumph permitted the 'colonial-interloping complex' merchants, but not other overseas merchants, to come to office. Only one group in a larger Independent coalition, composed mostly of non-merchants, they nevertheless secured a strategic place in the Commonwealth government. The militant and expansionist commercial policy of the Commonwealth was really their policy: they had a key role in its formation and they personally profited from it.[2]

The new Commonwealth magistrates of both Norwich and London were advanced Puritans but not social or political radicals. Neither group wished to revolutionize the governmental structure of their cities. In particular, neither group wanted to increase citizen participation in the election process or to bring lower social groups into the ruling élite. The difference between the two cities is that the London magistrates had to cope with incessant radical demands for political change whereas the Norwich magistrates did not. Cries for further reform beyond the moderate constitutional adjustments of the first Civil War, primarily from levellers and republicans, were heard constantly in London after 1643. They increased in intensity after 1647.[3] The veto powers of the Lord Mayor and aldermen were abolished in 1649, but few of the radicals' demands for greater constitutional democracy were met. With the blessings of the Rump, the London magistrates refused to alter election procedures, eliminate the monopoly rights of the Great Companies, or permit democratization of the Great Companies themselves.[4] There was no known agitation for increased popular control over the government of Norwich from 1645 to 1653. Nor is there evidence of a political conflict between the

[1] Pearl, 'London's Counter-Revolution', p. 34.
[2] Brenner, 'London's Merchant Community', pp. 92–105.
[3] Sharpe, *London*, II. 289–300; Margaret James, *Social Problems and Policy During the Puritan Revolution, 1640–1660* (London, 1930, 1966), pp. 223–40; Farnell, 'Barebone's Parliament'; Howell, *Newcastle*, pp. 340–1.
[4] Underdown, *Pride's Purge*, pp. 325–7.

magistrates and the Common Council or, as in London and some other cities, between either of these bodies and the freeman citizenry. Consequently, there were no changes in the political structure during this period. The reasons why this was so seem obvious. First, officeholders were cashiered readily to keep up with changing events. Second, the democratic reforms designed to enlarge freeman participation, which stirred leftist groups in London, Bedford, and some other towns, were already a reality in Norwich. The citizens and councilmen of Norwich, in short, had long possessed the involvement in political affairs that citizens of some towns, confronted with closed oligarchies, now aspired to.[1]

The Norwich Independents and their allies who triumphed in 1648, 1649, and 1650 had neither a constructive constitutional, social, nor economic programme. What, then, did they stand for? More accurately, what were they opposed to? Before 1649 their activities were limited to a reaction against moves made by their opponents. They were against both the establishment of a Presbyterian church system and a possible revival of Anglicanism in the city. They were against the corporation giving its official support, by way of petition, to the religious and political goals of the conservative Presbyterian-peace party in London and the House of Commons. They were against the Royalists and others who sought to capture the town and convert it into a conservative stronghold in defiance of Parliament and the army. Firmly in the saddle after the 1648 riot, they supported the Commonwealth in lieu of other alternatives, although some of them may have been hesitant to commit themselves publicly to an approval of the revolution in national government as entailed in the Engagement. Much of their energy was consumed in consolidating their position, prosecuting the rioters of 1648, taking steps to prevent the outbreak of another rebellion, and offering tokens of loyalty to the army and Common-

---

[1] In London, for example, the major goal of the radicals in the Common Council in 1650 and 1651 was to enlarge the representation of Common Hall from the liverymen to all householders. Farnell, 'Barebone's Parliament', pp. 36 ff. If this had been successful, the London political system would have come closer to that which had long been in existence in Norwich. The best documented case of the advance of democracy concerns Bedford, where the freemen agitated for participation in the election of major officials and for the establishment of an annual elective common council. See C. E. Parsloe, 'The Corporation of Bedford, 1647–64', *Transactions of the Royal Historical Society*, 4th Scr. 29 (1947), 151–65.

wealth.[1] This included the adoption of a new freeman's oath substituting fidelity to the Commonwealth for loyalty to the monarchy.[2] They were successful in keeping a lid on reactionary activities. The major threat was a Royalist plot intended for Norfolk which was discovered in the autumn of 1650. At least twenty-four conspirators were condemned and executed in Norwich, yet the townsmen do not seem to have been involved.[3] Apart from protecting the interests of the Rump, maintaining themselves in power, and handling routine matters in a routine way, the only discernible objective of the Independents and their allies after 1648 was to advance the religious reformation in an Independent direction.

The Independents were eager to strike down 'scandalous' ministers. Precisely which men they had in mind is not known and

[1] Many of these activities have already been alluded to. In 1648 and 1650 the Assembly named committees to settle the city militia and provide for watches; in the tense days of January 1648/9, the Assembly ordered a special band of foot soldiers 'in regard of the present dangers of the time'. Various committees were named to prevent citizens from paying Utting's costs in London and to collect the fines assessed him by Parliament, to make arrangements for a commission of oyer and terminer for the rioters, and to collect fines from persons convicted in the Quarter Sessions. Another committee was charged with defending Recorder Smith against Cory's writs of restitution and a committee was named to investigate the riot in connection with the election ordinance of January 1648/9. Still another committee oversaw the expense of soldiers and made sure these debts were promptly paid. The Assembly did not forget to provide M. P. Atkin with a £50 gratuity for his favours in 1648/9, and in April 1649 it declared a public day of thanksgiving to commemorate the overthrow of the riot. A.B. (1642–68), 1648–51, *passim*.

[2] The new freeman's oath read: 'Ye shall swear that you shall be true and faithful to the Commonwealth of England, and in order thereunto you shall be obedient to the just and good government of this city of Norwich: you shall to the best of your power maintain and preserve the peace, and all the due franchises thereof and according to your knowledge and ability do and perform all other such acts and things as do belong to a freeman of the said city.' Millican, ed., *Freemen*, p. xii. The adoption of a new oath was in response to a parliamentary ordinance passed in February 1648/9. *A. & O.* II. 2. Parliament also prescribed a fidelity oath for mayors and other officials the following September, which was a portent of the coming Engagement. ibid. II. 241–2. The corporation also purchased the fee farm rent for £650 following a parliamentary act for selling fee farm rents belonging to the state. ibid. II. 358–62; A.B. (1642–68), 1 May 1650, 97r.

[3] The plot was uncovered on 7 October 1650 and the trial took place between 30 December and 10 January. A full list of those condemned may be found in *A Complete History of the famous City of Norwich* (Norwich, 1728), p. 50. See also Blomefield, *Norfolk*, III. 399–400. The plotted insurrection and the discovery of it does not seem to have disturbed Norwich and there is no mention of it in the Assembly Book.

their success or failure in forcing them out is also obscure, but the Assembly Book testifies to their determination. When the Assembly learned in June 1648 that Richard With, curate of Cossey, had been imprisoned by the County Committee for his disaffection to Parliament, it promptly discharged him from officiating at his cure.[1] In August the Assembly named a committee to decide what ought to be done with scandalous ministers and in January the Assembly contemplated an ordinance permitting it to receive information concerning scandalous ministers and remove those found unworthy.[2] Apparently nothing came of this, for in April the Assembly took a different tack and inquired of Parliament whether the act regulating the election and dismissal of officeholders extended to scandalous and sequestered ministers.[3] When the Assembly learned that the act did cover ministers, it appointed a committee to prepare charges against them.[4] On 25 May 1649, the committee made its report and yet another committee was named to interview the suspected ministers and take the appropriate action.[5]

The Assembly was also resolved to make arrangements for its own religious needs and set an example for the community. Its predilections reveal its Independent inclinations. In 1650 the magistrates agreed that sermons should be given before the mayor and aldermen each Sunday morning in the Dutch Chapel.[6] Additional seats were added for the councilmen and the Assembly commenced a search for a proper minister to provide sermons.[7] The search reached all the way to New England, and preparations were made to bring Independent minister Thomas Allen to Norwich.[8] By the winter of 1651/2 Allen had arrived in England and was soon giving the Sunday sermon in the Dutch Chapel.[9] When Timothy Armitage, the pastor of the Independent congregation in Norwich, died in 1657, Allen was selected to take his place. The Assembly was left with the task of finding a replacement to

[1] A.B. (1642–68), 23 June 1648, 65ʳ.
[2] ibid., 4 Aug. 1648, 67ᵛ; 26 Jan. 1648/9, 74ʳ.   [3] ibid., 6 Apr. 1649, 77ᵛ.
[4] ibid., 13 Apr. 1649, 78ʳ; May 1649, 81ᵛ.   [5] ibid., 25 May 1649, 82ʳ.
[6] ibid., 8 Sept. 1650, 102ʳ.   [7] ibid., 31 Jan. and 14 Feb. 1650/1, 106ᵛ, 108ʳ.
[8] ibid., 17 Oct. 1651, 120ʳ. Thomas Allen was born in Norwich, educated at Caius College, appointed to St. Edmund parish in Norwich. He was silenced by Wren in 1636 and went to New England in 1638. *D.N.B.*, s.v. Thomas Allen.
[9] On 25 February 1651/2 Allen received a £10 gratuity from the Norwich Assembly, and on 2 April it was agreed that he should receive a stipend of £20 per quarter. A.B. (1642–68), 25 Feb. 1651/2, 123ʳ; 2 Apr. 1652, 124ʳ; 2 Nov. 1652, 132ᵛ.

preach before the magistrates and councilmen.[1] A special committee named by the Assembly in April 1657 concluded that a revolving lectureship utilizing the talents of a combination of Norfolk and Suffolk ministers should be set up for this purpose.[2] The Assembly's satisfaction with Allen's work in Norwich is manifested in an increase in his salary at St. George Tombland and an invitation in 1657/8 to preach Wednesday sermons.[3]

The corporation was not so successful in two other projects initiated in 1648 and 1649. One was to provide proper maintenance for a godly ministry, which involved a further union of parishes. The other was to obtain jurisdiction over the Cathedral and its environs. Since both required the consent of Parliament, they were destined to be dragged out for a long time with nothing but frustration and disillusionment as an end product. With so many parishes in the city, there were bound to be problems in locating, appointing, and paying such a large number of ministers. In August 1648 the Assembly named a committee to examine the problem of ministerial salaries.[4] Another committee was appointed the following January with the additional task of uniting parishes.[5] By November 1649 the Assembly decided that money raised in different parts of the city would be placed in a common stock rather than the older arrangement which gave all the money collected in each area to the minister of that area.[6] The committee's considerations on uniting parishes resulted in the preparation of a petition to Parliament.[7] The House of Commons managed to get through two readings of a bill to satisfy Norwich in February 1649/50, but it was

[1] Timothy Armitage was chosen pastor of the Norwich Independent Church on 26 July 1647. B. Cozens-Hardy, ed., *Old Meeting House, Norwich, and Great Yarmouth Independent Church*, [Norfolk Record Society Publication, 22] (Norwich, 1951), p. 4. Despite his duties as rector of St. George Tombland and pastor of the Independent Church, Allen continued to give his weekly sermon until the summer of 1657. A.B. (1642–68), 6 Mar. 1656/7, 179ᵛ. Allen was evicted during the Restoration. Browne, *Congregationalism*, p. 593.

[2] A.B. (1642–68), 8 Apr. and 4 May 1657, 182ʳ, 183ᵛ. The remuneration was set at 20s. per sermon. A year later a new committee to nominate ministers was appointed. ibid., 1 Apr. 1658, 190ʳ.

[3] Armitage's salary of £58. 4s. 4d. was considerably less than the £20 per quarter which Allen had received from the Assembly since 1652. When Allen moved to St. George Tombland he was given £21. 15s. 8d. in addition to Armitage's salary so that his pay would not be diminished. C.S.P.D., Interregnum, 1657–8, p. 92: 9 Sept. 1657.

[4] A.B. (1642–68), 4 Aug. 1648, 67ᵛ.   [5] ibid., 26 Jan. 1648/9, 74ʳ.
[6] ibid., 11 and 25 May and 14 Nov. 1649, 81ᵛ, 82ʳ, 88ʳ.
[7] C.J. VI. 336: 20 Nov. 1649.

then allowed to languish in committee with similar bills for other towns.[1] The Assembly revived its own committee in September 1650, added extra members to it five months later, and heard reports from it throughout 1651 without any real progress.[2] Petitions were forwarded to Westminster in 1651, 1652, and 1654 and a revised committee was still working on the problem in 1656, all to no effect.[3]

The design to bring the Cathedral and its precincts under the jurisdiction of the Norwich corporation, for the expressed purpose of providing a stock for the poor, was more fruitful but never entirely successful. After several attempts to persuade the House of Commons to pass an act turning the Cathedral over to the city, Parliament finally obliged in March 1650 by giving the corporation jurisdiction over the Cathedral close and the Bishop's Palace.[4] By May of the same year the Assembly directed a committee to draw up a petition for the biggest prize, the Cathedral itself.[5] It was to no avail. Similar petitions were sent up in 1651/2 and 1652/3.[6] For a fleeting moment in 1654 it appeared that the corporation would gain additional concessions. A parliamentary ordinance which would have enlarged the jurisdiction of the city, however, was laid aside by an order in Council when the landowners and inhabitants within the precinct of the Cathedral close petitioned the Committee of the Council to maintain their peculiar jurisdiction distinct from the city.[7] The Assembly, undaunted by past failure, sent petitions directly to Cromwell in 1656 and 1657 for control over the Cathedral and the livings of the Dean and Chapter; but these petitions were no more successful than their predecessors.[8]

[1] ibid., 354, 370: 1 and 22 Feb. 1649/50.

[2] A.B. (1642–68), 8 Sept. 1650, 101ᵛ; 14 Feb. 1650/1, 108ʳ; 3, 22, and 30 May 1651, 113ᵛ, 114ʳ⁻ᵛ.

[3] ibid., 20 Apr. and 8 June 1652, 127ʳ, 129ʳ; 21 Aug. and 6 Nov. 1654, 153ʳ, 154ᵛ; 7, 16, and 30 Jan. 1656/7, 177ᵛ, 178ʳ⁻ᵛ; M.C.B. (1654–66), 27 Oct. 1656, 44ʳ. This is the last mention in the corporation Books of efforts to unite parishes.

[4] A.B. (1642–68), 26 Oct. 1648, 70; 20 Mar. 1648/9, 77ʳ; 19 Mar. 1649/50, 93ʳ; *C.J.* VI. 387: 26 Mar. 1650.

[5] A.B. (1642–68), 13 May 1650, 98ʳ.

[6] ibid., 16 Jan. and 25 Feb. 1651/2, 122ʳ⁻ᵛ; 5 Jan. 1652/3, 134ᵛ.

[7] The inhabitants of the close claimed that they received high prices for the lands of the Dean and Chapter. Turning the land over to the city would lower land values and impoverish many purchasers. The Council advised Cromwell to appoint four men from Norwich and its suburbs to be justices of the peace for the Cathedral precinct. *C.S.P.D.*, Interregnum, 1654, p. 97: 14 Apr. 1654.

[8] A.B. (1642–68), 8 Oct. 1656, 176ʳ; 4 Aug. 1657, 184ᵛ. Disputes over control of ecclesiastical lands occurred elsewhere. See, for example, Underdown, 'A Case Concerning Bishops' Land', pp. 18–48.

*   *   *

The period from 1645 to 1653 in Norwich was in many respects a continuation of the early 1640s. The factional strife which characterized both periods was similar in nature and in its impact on local politics. In both periods the city was strongly influenced by but had little influence on national affairs. The city did not recede into provincial isolation after 1645, as did many other towns. National political issues were hotly disputed in Norwich and, translated in terms applicable to the city, provided the ideological basis of factional partisanship. Politically-active citizens kept one eye riveted on the guild-hall and the other on London and Parliament. The central concern, as in the years leading up to and during the Civil War, was religious differences and not local social or economic issues. Political and religious affiliation continued to be of paramount significance in recruitment to civic office, and magistrates were displaced solely to serve partisan interests. In both periods the factions vied for control of the corporation in order to protect and advance their political and religious goals. In neither period was there a shift to the Left or fundamental alterations in the structure of government.

As national affairs played such an important role in defining local politics in Norwich, so also the rise, fall, and realignment of political and religious groups in London and Westminster had a telling effect on the vicissitudes of Norwich factions. This was as true of the Independents, Presbyterians, and Royalists after 1645 as it had been of the parliamentary-Puritans during the Civil War. One new element, however, was introduced into the political equation. The national government was no longer willing merely to appeal to and hope for local support. The Laudian Church had attempted to impose its national religious programme on local communities, but the royal government of the 1630s had devised no consistent or comprehensive policy towards municipal corporations other than strong support for corporations in maintaining order.[1] In the 1620s and 1630s the Crown was viewed by corporations such as Norwich as a convenience to be appealed to in times of local crisis. In neither theory nor practice was it conceived to be

---

[1] Shilling, 'Municipal Corporations', Chapter I. Cf. J. H. Sacret, 'The Restoration Government and Municipal Corporations', *English Historical Review*, 45 (Apr. 1930), 235–6. Hirst has suggested recently that Crown support for oligarchical corporations prior to 1640 was motivated by little more than 'considerations of internal security'. Hirst, *Representative of the People?*, pp. 47–50, 69.

a power which unilaterally dispensed with long-established local political processes in order to secure the local ascendancy of adherents to its own ideology. Even in the midst of the Civil War, Parliament made no concerted effort to remodel corporations or restructure borough politics. After 1645, however, the state increasingly intervened in municipal corporations to ensure that local government was staffed by men loyal to the prevailing power in Parliament.

State intervention took two forms. The first was the device of the religious or political oath. The Solemn League and Covenant, required by act of Parliament of all Englishmen, established the precedent. Non-compliance, however, did not entail political repercussions. In this regard the Engagement of 1650 was a much more ominous precedent and a harbinger of the political and religious oaths required of officeholders during the Restoration. Nevertheless, as a means of regulating the recruitment of local magistrates, oaths demanded both before and after 1660 were of dubious value. The second device, the direct remodelling of corporations by the state, was much more immediate and effective. Parliament engaged intermittently in this activity as the need arose in 1645 and 1646.[1] but the legislation of September and October 1647 ushered in a new era in the relationship between central and local government. The Independent- and army-dominated Parliament, which passed ordinances restricting electorates and the eligibility of candidates for office, and empowered the Committee of Indemnity to purge corporations, was reacting in the aftermath of a counter-revolutionary crisis. Their action was viewed as a temporary and necessary expedient; it was not a preconceived plan or policy to reduce permanently the municipalities to central control. Without this state intervention, however, the Independent-army-Rump faction in Norwich would not have been able to consolidate its position.

---

[1] As boroughs were recaptured from the Royalists at the end of the Civil War, Parliament moved to purge Royalist magistrates from some of these key cities. This occurred in York, Bristol, Chester, and Exeter between September of 1644 and April of 1646. Shilling, 'Municipal Corporations', pp. 49–52.

VI

The Conservative Restoration, 1653—1678

From 1653 to 1678 the Norwich corporation exhibited paradoxical shifts in attitude towards the national government. The Assembly had welcomed the execution of Charles I in 1649 with a congratulatory letter to Cromwell; nine years later, during the last months of the Protectorate, the Assembly sent another letter to Cromwell effusively praising his benevolent rule. Yet, within two years, the corporation enthusiastically celebrated the return of the Stuarts with ringing bells, a huge voluntary gift, speeches, and other demonstrations of loyalty.[1] And although the Royalist sentiments displayed in 1660 by a majority of officeholders and citizens alike were genuine, by the late 1670s the city and the magistracy were definitely drifting into opposition to the Crown and the state Church.

At the outset of the Interregnum, political conditions in Norwich and London were analogous: in both cities the events of 1649 and 1650 had brought to power a politico-religious group lacking widespread citizen support.[2] With the collapse of the Commonwealth, the citizens of moderate and conservative political views reasserted their once dominant power in local affairs. Whereas the conservative reaction in London dates from the dissolution of the Nominated Parliament and the establishment of the Protectorate in December 1653, in Norwich it goes back to mid-1653 and perhaps earlier. The moderate-conservative bloc in Norwich was strong enough to prevail in local civic elections and to triumph in hotly contested parliamentary elections in 1654 and 1656, but it had only a minimal impact on the composition of the Court of Aldermen because of an uncommonly low level of magisterial attrition. Up to the last year of the Interregnum, the political and religious

[1] According to one account, when the Restoration came 'probably few cities were more glad to welcome back the Stuarts than Norwich'. Page, ed., *Victoria History of Norfolk* II. 514.
[2] Farnell, 'Barebone's Parliament', pp. 45–6; Brenner, 'London's Merchant Community', pp. 91, 106–7.

views of a majority of the magistrates continued to be at variance with popular opinion in the city. Following the dismissal of the Protectorate in 1659, however, the ranks of the moderate-conservative magistrates were increased by moderate-Commonwealth aldermen who could not tolerate the rule of the army or the restored Rump. Thus a majority of the citizens and half of the magistrates supported General Monck and the King's return in 1660.

The impact of the Restoration on Norwich went through two stages. In the first phase the corporation was almost unaffected until the core of the Commonwealth party was purged from office in 1660/1. The second phase, which commenced in the spring of 1661 and lasted until mid-1663, was dominated by two issues. One was the ultimately unsuccessful attempt of the Crown to impose direct control over the corporation by remodelling the city charter. The other was a rift within the moderate-conservative coalition of old Royalists and Presbyterians whose co-operation had been so influential since the late 1640s. By a series of legislative enactments, the Anglican-dominated Cavalier Parliament attempted to drive Presbyterians from municipal office and deny them freedom of religious worship. As a consequence, a fundamental politico-religious realignment and a basic shift in electoral power took place in Norwich. Discriminated against politically and religiously, Presbyterians suddenly found themselves in the same non-conformist camp as the Independents. After 1663 the task of ensuring that the city and corporation remained Anglican and Royalist was left with the remodelled magistracy. They were not successful. The nonconformists were too numerous and determined, the safeguards against their resumption of political office were too inadequate, and the magistrates were too negligent in rigorously enforcing the laws which did exist. By the late 1670s conventicles were heavily attended and nonconformists had made significant inroads into the magistracy. Local Anglicans, in turn, were determined to renew the persecution and purge the corporation. The stage was thus set for the Whig–Tory controversy which rent Norwich during the next decade.

*　　*　　*

On the eve of the Protectorate, the Norwich corporation was still firmly in the grip of the local Independent–army–Rump coalition. Although the men of this group may have held a variety of

viewpoints on fundamental issues, they were linked by a basic politico-religious concern and a common historical experience.[1] Their
initial rise to power had been due to the overthrow of the April
riot of 1648 and had been confirmed by the defeat of the King's
forces during the second Civil War. The political hegemony which
they subsequently established came as a consequence of the purge
of 1649, the application of the Engagement, and the enforcement
of the parliamentary and local ordinances which imposed political
qualifications on both the electorate and candidates. Their control
of the corporation thus rested not on their own political base in the
city, but rather on the continuance of the Rump and army in
national power. Their triumph had come at the expense of a rival
coalition of Royalists, moderates, and Presbyterians with conservative views.[2] This group, which had demonstrated impressively
its predominant voting strength within the freeman electorate
prior to 1648, was temporarily eclipsed but by no means
extinguished during the Commonwealth. Indeed, the moderate-
conservative bloc was prepared to reassert its latent electoral
muscle as soon as circumstances would permit it to do so without
impunity.

The first signs that the moderate-conservative freemen were
stirring again came in 1651, but they did not seize the initiative in
civic elections until 1653. When the freemen gathered at the guild-
hall in May 1651 to nominate two men for the mayoralty, they

[1] The surviving documents do not allow for a further breakdown of this coalition into its component factions. Presumably some of its members were republicans whereas others were Cromwellians, swordsmen, Fifth Monarchy Men, and
other sectaries. They may well have been joined by some Presbyterians who
maintained strong support for Parliament. As described in the previous chapter,
they were united in their opposition to monarchy and (excluding the Presbyterians
in their midst) to a strong central church. They wanted to continue local religious
reform and supported the Commonwealth. As a group, they had supported
Parliament in both Civil Wars, opposed the Norwich rioters and the election of
Roger Mingay to the magistracy in 1648, accepted the Engagement, and participated in the committees appointed by the Assembly to continue religious reform.
Much of their unity may have been due to the aggressive activities of their
opposition.

[2] These men may be identified as those who were Royalists during the Civil
War, supported Utting's party in 1648, or were purged from office in 1649 and
1650. Of these men who survived the Interregnum, almost all either maintained
their tenure or were restored to office. The term 'moderate-conservative' is
preferred to 'Presbyterian-Royalist' because the Presbyterians during the 1650s
were not united. See George R. Abernathy, Jr., *The English Presbyterians and the
Stuart Restoration, 1648–1663* [American Philosophical Society, new ser. 55,
pt. 2] (Philadelphia, 1965), pp. 17–25.

opted for Bernard Church and John Salter. The former had refused to vote against the seating of Mingay on the aldermanic
Bench in 1648 and the latter had refused both to pay proposition
money and to contribute to the Newcastle Collection during the
Civil War.[1] What makes the freemen's choice especially striking is
that of fourteen eligible aldermen, Church and Salter alone had
not voted against Mingay in 1648. The freemen exhibited no further defiance until two and a half years later.[2] The election of
Sheriffs Christopher Jay and Roger Mingay in September 1653,
two months before the Protectorate was formed, raises questions
that cannot be answered. It is curious, for example, that the
magistracy, heavily weighted against the moderate conservatives,
should choose Jay: he had absented himself from the 1648 Mingay
vote, had been dropped from the Common Council in the purge
elections of 1649, and would advance the moderate-conservative
cause in the future.[3] Even more problematical is the selection of
Mingay by the freemen. The Assembly Book entry for 26 April
1648 states explicitly that a case against Mingay involving the
presentation of evidence and the testimony of witnesses had clearly
established his ineligibility for office by the recent parliamentary
ordinance.[4] Presumably this parliamentary ordinance for munici-

[1] Church contributed £4 to the Collection for the Recapture of Newcastle, was
elected sheriff in 1644, and became an alderman in late 1646. Nevertheless, there
is no evidence to prove that he was the 'zealous Parliamentarian' suggested by
Basil Cozens-Hardy and Ernest A. Kent, *The Mayors of Norwich, 1403–1835*
(Norwich, 1938), p. 86. When the Restoration came, Church maintained his
office and continued to serve as alderman until 1682. See Evans, 'Political Elite
of Norwich', pp. 493–4.

[2] In 1652 William Barnham and William Tooke were the mayoral nominees; in
1653 Tooke and John Man were nominated. Little is known about Tooke. As a
councilman in 1648, he was absent from the Assembly on the day Mingay's
election was voted on; he would later be nominated for the mayoralty in 1661.
Barnham and Man, on the other hand, had both voted against Mingay and they
were the magistrates' choice for mayor-elect. The election of John Knights and
Roger Whistler as the commons' sheriff in 1651 and 1652 would not seem to have
been controversial.

[3] Twenty-three of the twenty-four aldermen of 1653 had been members of the
Assembly in April 1648: eighteen had voted against Mingay, two had abstained,
and three had been absent. Those who opposed Mingay were: Allen, Andrews,
Ashwell, Baret, Barnham, Bateman, Burman, Cory, Davy, Man, Parmenter,
Pointer, Puckle, Rayley, Rye, Symond, Toft, and Woods. The two aldermen
who had abstained were Church and Johnson, and the absentees were Salter,
Tooke, and Watts. Jay later became a member of Parliament in 1661 and was
included in a list of proposed Knights of the Royal Oak prepared by Charles I.
Cozens-Hardy and Kent, *Mayors*, p. 89.

[4] N.N.R.O., A.B. (1642–68), 26 Apr. 1648, 62ᵛ.

pal elections, which the Rump had extended for three years in late 1652, would have prevented the candidacy of Mingay in 1653 as it had in 1648.[1] Whether the freeman electorate was still restricted in this election or why they chose to challenge the election laws in 1653 and not earlier remains a mystery.[2] Nor is it known why the magistrates did not challenge the election and declare it void. Lastly, nothing is known of the circumstances in which Jay and Mingay were elevated to the Court of Aldermen within months of their election to the shrievalty.[3]

Such was the state of affairs in Norwich when Oliver Cromwell was installed as Lord Protector on 12 December 1653. For the next five years the political life of the community would be influenced by changing developments on the national level. The Cromwellian Protectorate has received widely conflicting interpretations; one recent revision has even suggested that it was not basically Cromwellian.[4] Viewed in terms of its treatment of rural and urban communities, the Protectorate should be seen neither as a reformist military dictatorship nor as a constitutional conservative regime. Rather, it vacillated, and at different points was each in turn.[5] From December 1653, when the Protectorate was established in accordance with the Instrument of Government, until the spring of 1655, the central government pursued policies designed to bring about reconciliation, settlement, and stability. Cromwell personally favoured moderation towards the Royalist enemies of the Commonwealth and took steps to win over those sections of the traditional governing class which had supported Parliament during the first Civil War but had been alienated by the excesses

---

[1] Firth and Rait, eds., *Acts and Ordinances*, II. 620–1 : 8 Oct. 1652.

[2] One possibility is that the citizens may have believed that the increasingly weak and ineffective Nominated Parliament would be too absorbed in its own affairs and internal dissension to enforce the ordinance.

[3] Jay and Mingay are listed as aldermen in the 1654 listing of officeholders in the Assembly Book. The date of their election may have been either before or after their election to the shrievalty.

[4] George Heath has argued that Lambert and the generals controlled central government by dominating the Council of State; the Lord Protector had few powers independent of the Council and Cromwell was little more than a figurehead. George D. Heath, 'Cromwell and Lambert, 1653–1657', in Ivan Roots, ed., *Cromwell: A Profile* (London, 1973), pp. 72–90.

[5] The following description of the Protectorate and the stages through which it passed is drawn from David Underdown, 'Settlement in the Counties, 1653–1658' and Austin Woolrych, 'Last Quests for a Settlement, 1657–1660', in Aylmer, ed., *Interregnum*, pp. 165–82, 182–204.

of the Rump and the Nominated Parliament.[1] This stage came to an end when the first Protectorate Parliament proved a failure and Royalist rebellion broke out. The second stage, which lasted from mid-1655 until the end of 1656, is associated with the Council's division of the country into military districts ruled over by the notorious major-generals. During this period the state abandoned its earlier non-intervention and accommodation in local affairs in favour of direct controls and repression. Finally, from early 1657 to Cromwell's death in September 1658, the Lord Protector and the state reverted to the earlier policy of moderation. Here the turning point is marked by the overthrow of the major-generals by the second Protectorate Parliament and the subsequent adoption of a conservative revision of the constitution, the Humble Petition and Advice. Provincial society and government was once more returned to traditional groups and procedures.

The immediate reaction of the corporation and citizens of Norwich to the dissolution of the Nominated Parliament and the formation of the Protectorate is not known. The official books of the corporation are of little help.[2] Indeed, a reading of the Assembly Book, in which there is no reference to local political faction and no mention of national affairs for the year 1654, leaves the impression that the city was quiet and the citizens were either undisturbed by or indifferent to what was going on in the capital. The chance survival of a petition sent to Cromwell by citizens complaining about the town's election for the first Protectorate Parliament, however, reveals that the divisive political passions of 1648 were still alive.[3] Obviously, the petition presents only one side of the

---

[1] Paul H, Hardacre, *The Royalists During the Puritan Revolution* (The Hague, 1956), pp. 106–31; Ivan Roots, 'Cromwell's Ordinances: The Early Legislation of the Protectorate', in Aylmer, ed., *Interregnum*, p. 147.

[2] The Assembly Book records only two meetings between 25 November 1653 and 3 May 1654. No mention of national affairs during this period is made. The Mayor's Court Book covering this period is missing and the next volume begins with 10 February 1654/5. In March a petition from the mayor, twenty-two aldermen, and over 700 citizens of Norwich was sent up. Concerned with the prospect of a mail delivery monopoly, the petition concluded: 'having bought our liberties at vast expense of blood and treasure, we hope not again to be troubled with distasteful monopolies, but to have liberty to convey our letters freely'. *C.S.P.D.*, Interregnum, 1654, pp. 25–6.

[3] P.R.O., S.P. Dom, Interregnum, 73/89: The Humble Petition of Divers Well Affected Citizens of the City of Norwich, [1653]. Local historians must constantly treat official corporation books with caution: the mere fact that these books provide no clue of the existence of faction or controversy does not mean that faction and controversy did not exist.

dispute and presumably it is biased. Nevertheless, it provides the only remaining account of the election and thus a narrative of what transpired must be taken entirely from it.

In mid-July, on the date and at the time and place designated by Sheriffs Jay and Mingay, the eligible voters assembled. The Instrument of Government specified that men who had acted against Parliament at any time since 1641 would be excluded from voting or standing; the mayor and aldermen had declared in advance that this clause must be honoured. The first nominee of the freemen was Colonel Charles George Cocke. Although there were a large number of people present, no one was nominated to stand against him. After some time had passed, Cocke was conceded to have won the first slot without an actual poll being taken. The electors then proceeded to nominate Thomas Baret and Bernard Church for the second seat and Church won the election. At this point many of the voters assumed that the election was over and went home. Sheriffs Jay and Mingay, however, had other ideas. They suddenly proclaimed that a second election would be held immediately at a different location and, despite the provisions of the Instrument of Government and the instructions of the mayor and aldermen, announced that *all* freemen would be allowed to vote. When a sizeable crowd had gathered at the new site, the sheriffs took another poll. This time the nomination of Cocke was contested and he was defeated by John Hobart. The final outcome was that Jay and Mingay returned the names of Hobart and Church as the borough representatives to Parliament.

An examination of the petition against the election of Hobart and the 101 signatories to it brings the controversy into sharper focus. The petitioners did not associate themselves with any political or religious label other than the vague reference to themselves as 'well-affected citizens'. Nevertheless, their identity and the men they supported for Parliament leaves little doubt that they represented the core of the Independent–army–Rump coalition. None of the petitioners had been present at the Assembly meeting which decided Mingay's status as alderman in 1648; every one of them had voted against Mingay. In addition, the petition also carried the names of four men who had founded the Independent Church of Norwich in 1644.[1] Six of the petitioners were aldermen and eight were councilmen. All of these officeholders, some of

[1] Cozens-Hardy, *Old Meeting House*, p. 4.

whom are known to have been Independents, had either opposed vigorously the 1648 riot, were active as deputy-lieutenants during the Commonwealth, or were members of the more important Assembly committees between 1648 and 1652.[1] Lastly, all but one of these aldermen and one of these councilmen would later be ejected from office during the Restoration.[2]

The petitioners stated clearly that they went to the election with the intention of nominating Colonel Charles George Cocke and Alderman Thomas Baret. In 1648 Cocke had been appointed by the House of Commons to a committee charged to investigate the April riot and the violation of the parliamentary election ordinance. Shortly afterwards he was named a deputy-lieutenant for Norwich and in 1650 he was elected steward for the city.[3] Thomas Baret was even more closely identified with the Independent–army–Rump coalition. The eldest son of the deputy-mayor chosen by the House of Commons to replace Utting in 1648, Baret had been a member of the delegation which had presented the petition against Utting to Parliament and he voted against Mingay becoming an alderman.[4] Like Cocke, he was also appointed by the House of Commons in 1648 to be a deputy-lieutenant for the city and he was very active in the politico-religious committees named by the Assembly.[5] Moreover, Baret also had a military background. During the first Civil War he had been a captain of a company of foot and in 1649/50 he was promoted to the rank of lieutenant-colonel.[6] Cromwell and the Protectorate Council evidently had great confidence in his military capacity and his loyalty to the regime: faced with the threat of Royalist insurrection in 1655, Cromwell personally entrusted Baret with command over the military defences of the city.[7]

---

[1] The aldermen were Ashwell, Baret, Davy, Pointer, Puckle, and Rayley.
[2] Alderman Rayley was not ejected. Only one of the councilmen had died before 1660; of the remaining seven, six were removed from office.
[3] *C.J.* V. 559–60, 578: 16 and 30 May 1648; *L.J.* X. 261: 16 May 1648; A.B. (1642–68), 13 Apr. 1650, 95ᵛ.
[4] Blomefield, *Norfolk*, III. 385; A.B. (1642–68), 26 Apr. 1648, 62ᵛ.
[5] *C.J.* V. 578: 30 May 1648. Baret served on the committees for paying troops and settling the militia, sequestration, uniting parishes, securing town control over the Cathedral, arranging Sunday church services for the magistrates, and ejecting scandalous and ignorant ministers. A.B. (1642–68), 3 May 1648, 64ᵛ; 4 Aug. 1648, 66ᵛ; 26 Oct. 1648, 70ʳ; 25 May 1649, 82ᵛ; 14 Nov. 1649, 88ʳ; 31 Jan. 1650/1, 106ᵛ; 8 June 1652, 129ʳ; 5 Jan. 1652/3, 134ᵛ; 21 Aug. 1654, 153ʳ.
[6] Blomefield, *Norfolk*, III. 387; *C.S.P.D.*, Interregnum, 1650, p. 504: 27 Feb. 1649/50.
[7] N.N.R.O., M.C.B. (1654–66), 23 June 1655, 9ᵛ.

The petitioners did not describe the faction which opposed them as either Royalist or Presbyterian, but they did condemn them as 'the old spirit which so long in so many choices they had opposed, now wrought again'. The culprits, in their minds, were Sheriffs Jay and Mingay. Of Church and Hobart, the former was less controversial since the petitioners acknowledged that he had fairly defeated Baret in the election. Traditionally at least one of the two M.P.s was an alderman. Although none of the aldermen of 1654 had voted for Mingay in 1648, two had abstained; Church was one of the abstainers. In a technical sense, John Hobart was, as the petitioners claimed, a 'stranger' to Norwich in that he was not a freeman of the city. Yet he had been a resident of St. Giles's parish since at least 1649 and he had close contacts with prominent Norwich citizens.[1] There are dangers in characterizing a man on the basis of the company he keeps, but Hobart was definitely travelling with moderate and anti-Independent companions during 1648.[2] Nothing concrete, however, is known about his political leanings until after his election in 1654, when he quickly established himself as a staunch critic of the Protectorate.

The significance of the Norwich parliamentary election lies not only in the election of Church and Hobart but also in the Protectorate's failure to respond favourably to the petition and disallow the election. The framers of the Instrument of Government had clearly given the Council of State the power to do so. Clause XIV of the Instrument disfranchised voters and disabled candidates who had been in opposition to Parliament; and clause XVI specified heavy penalties to be imposed on disqualified men who did vote.[3] As a further safety precaution, clauses XVII and XXI stipulated that the Council of State would be the final judge in review-

[1] There were two John Hobarts living in Norwich during the Civil War and Interregnum. The Mr. John Hobart elected to Parliament should not be confused with Sir John Hobart, a resident of St. Stephens parish and the largest contributor in the city to the Collection for Regaining Newcastle. Mr. John Hobart appears in the 1649 rate for the river and streets as a resident of St. Giles and is shown as still residing in this parish in the 1660 tax for disbanding forces.

[2] See, for example, Bodleian Tanner MSS., 311, fo. 36: Joseph Paine to Richard Bensly, 24 Apr. 1648 and fo. 38: Justinian Lewyen to [John Hobart], 27 Apr. 1648.

[3] The 'Instrument of Government', in J. P. Kenyon, ed., *The Stuart Constitution* (Cambridge, 1966), pp. 342–8. A discussion of the Instrument and the 1654 elections may be found in Ivan Roots, *The Great Rebellion, 1642–1660* (London, 1966), pp. 82–4.

ing the returns and ensuring that all candidates 'shall be such (and no other than such) as are persons of known integrity, fearing God, and of good conversation . . .'. No person was authorized to sit in Parliament without the prior approval of the Council. Thus the case presented by the Norwich petitioners would seem to have had a good chance of success. If their narrative was accurate, the behaviour of the sheriffs was highly irregular by any standards and called for investigation. Moreover, the sheriffs had permitted men to vote who should have been disfranchised and thus, as the petitioners reminded the Council, 'the Instrument of the Government was slighted as an affirmative law'.[1] Lastly, the Council of State would not be likely to conclude that Hobart and Church had sufficient integrity, adequately feared God, and had decent conversation if it was intent on a strict enforcement of the Instrument and packing the Parliament in the process.

For whatever reasons, the Council did not overturn the Norwich election. There is no evidence that the sheriffs were warned, much less punished. Nor did the Council push its constitutional right to reverse many of the other county and borough election disputes, which were more numerous than usual.[2] Presumably the government, which had been courting the traditional governing class with lenient policies for nine months, valued highly the importance of establishing the legitimacy of the state and the new constitution. A purge of the House of Commons before it had even convened would have rekindled memories of Pride's Purge and the unpopular Rump and would thus have jeopardized the hopes for settlement.[3] As a result, when Hobart and Church made their way to Westminster for the opening of Parliament on 3 September, they found themselves surrounded by many like-minded moderates and

[1] The supporters of Hobart were described as men of 'imprisonments or noted disaffections, together with the crew of hostlers, tapsters, barrowmen, some whereof were no freemen, together with abundance of inferior or indigent people, some of them taking alms, and some mutineers'. The petitioners also complained that 'the considerate restriction of elections to matter of estate was wholly excluded'.

[2] Roots, 'Cromwell's Ordinances', p. 157.

[3] The early Stuart House of Commons had clearly established its right to resolve election disputes without interference from Whitehall. During the first week of the 1654 Parliament, the Committee of Privilege pointedly reasserted the Commons' privilege to judge its own election returns and boldly overruled the Council of State on at least two cases. Roots, *Great Rebellion*, p. 185. The Humble Petition and Advice would also insist on this privilege of the House of Commons.

conservatives and even a number of crypto-Royalists.[1] Before leaving Norwich, Hobart delivered a conciliatory speech to the citizens and magistrates of the city. He even praised Charles George Cocke in an attempt to mend his local political fences.[2] After all, his major grievances were not against the petitioners but against the national government.

The major political problem confronting the new Parliament, and one that made itself apparent during its first sessions, was that many of the moderate and conservative M.P.s agreed with the republican members that the Instrument of Government would have to be amended. Even though the constitution prohibited parliamentary attacks on the constitution, the Commons agitated for change.[3] In an effort to stave off further assaults on the Instrument, Cromwell demanded that the M.P.s subscribe to an Engagement by which they would swear to refuse to support efforts to alter the constitution. This threw the M.P.s representing the county and boroughs of Norfolk into a quandary.[4] Only one of them signed Cromwell's 'Recognition' immediately. The rest scurried off to dine and consult together. Ultimately the majority agreed to put aside their complaints against the Instrument in order to prevent an open confrontation, and one which they did not believe they could win, with Cromwell. There were, however, three die-hard Norfolk opponents to the Instrument who refused to join the majority, and two of these were John Hobart and Bernard Church.

---

[1] Professor Roots's preference for the terms 'moderate' and 'conservative' rather than 'Presbyterian' and 'Royalist' has been followed. As for the majority of M.P.s returned in the 1654 election, Roots adds that 'the usefully vague epithet" Presbyterian" fits most of them'. ibid., p. 184. See also H. R. Trevor-Roper, 'Oliver Cromwell and His Parliaments', in Roots, ed., *Cromwell*, pp. 120 ff.

[2] Tanner MSS., 52, fo. 114. Hobart lamented the petition against his election and expressed his desire for greater peace and less faction in the city. As for Cocke, Hobart added that he was a man 'whose abilities as they are far above whatever I can in any way pretend to, so his personal obligations upon me are so many . . .'. Apparently the speech had some effect; the Assembly made Hobart a freeman on 21 August. A.B. (1642–68), 21 Aug. 1654, 153^{r-v}.

[3] The twelfth clause of the Instrument stipulated that the sheriff or other presiding officials over M.P. elections must present an acknowledgement 'that the persons elected shall not have power to alter the government as it is hereby settled in one person and a Parliament'. 'Instrument of Government', in Kenyon, ed., *Stuart Constitution*, p. 344. Certificates from the sheriffs of Norwich have not been located.

[4] This account is taken from Goddard's Journal in J. T. Rutt, ed., *Diary of Thomas Burton, Esquire* (London, 1828), I. xxxv–vi.

They were not alone in the Commons in their persistent opposition: continued attacks on the Instrument led to Cromwell's dissolution of the first Protectorate Parliament in late January 1654/5.

The prospect for a national settlement, damaged by the failure of Parliament, was dealt another serious blow by the abortive Royalist uprising which fizzled out in March 1654/5. The Norwich magistrates, eager to prevent a repetition of the 1648 riot, put the entire city on alert and set up night watches.[1] Whether the magistrates really feared another riot is not known, but they certainly had plenty to worry about. By the spring of 1655, as in the spring of 1648, the moderate and conservative freemen had dominated city elections for eighteen months. Their most recent triumph had taken place the previous September, less than two months after the controversial parliamentary elections. Joseph Paine was chosen to succeed Mingay as the commons' sheriff. Thus, in the space of one year, the freemen had elected Church and Hobart to Parliament, Mingay to the shrievalty and aldermanry, and now Paine to the shrievalty; and all four of these men were not only known moderate conservatives but were also close friends.[2] Undeterred by the unhappy fate of the Royalist insurrections in March 1655, the wards of Wymer and Over-the-Water then elected Paine and Robert Holmes respectively to the Court of Aldermen in April. It was Holmes who had pretentiously advertized his Royalist sentiments during the first Civil War, who had marked the return of the Royalists to electoral politics in 1646 with his election to the shrievalty, and who had been conspicuously passed over for pro-

[1] M.C.B., 14 and 19 Mar. 1654/5, 4^{r-v}.

[2] In 1643 Paine was fined £10 for his refusal to collect proposition money. The following year he was temporarily gaoled in Cambridge; the Norwich magistrates considered providing bail but decided to leave him in gaol. In 1648 he supported Mayor Utting's actions. In 1660 Paine was elected mayor and was knighted by Charles II. One of his closest friends in Norwich was Hobart. In 1648, for example, Paine wrote of 'my noble friend Mr. John Hobart'. Hobart was out of town during the 1648 riot, at which time Paine sheltered his family and boarded up the shattered windows of his house. The friendship continued at least until 1659, when Hobart addressed Paine in a personal letter as his 'very worthy friend'. In the same letter Hobart refers to his other close friend Bernard Church. In a will drawn up in 1651, Roger Mingay made provision for his daughter Susan, who was married to Joseph Paine's eldest son Robert. In the same will, Mingay left £2 for his friends Paine and Bernard Church to purchase rings in memory of him. M.C.B. (1634–46), 18 Nov. 1643 and 24 July 1644, 400^r, 431^r; Tanner MSS., 311, fos. 36, 38, 58; N.N.R.O., N.C.C., Wills Proved, 233 Tennant.

motion to the Court of Aldermen during the Commonwealth. And then, barely two weeks after he was sworn an alderman, Holmes was nominated by the freemen for the mayoralty, together with John Salter. Left with little choice, the magistrates settled on Salter to be mayor-elect.

The Royalist uprisings were far more important for the response they evoked from the state than for the threat they posed to it. During the summer of 1655, Cromwell and the Council devised a new method for extending centralized control over the countryside. Henceforth the nation would be divided into military provinces and each province would be presided over by a major-general. At first the duties of these new arbiters of local society were vague; they were more carefully defined in October when a detailed list of instructions was issued.[1] The full scope of their responsibilities was intimidating to local communities, which resented centralization. Equally significant was that there were no stated limitations to what the major-generals could do on their own. The principal function of the new system was to secure the loyalty of the provinces to the central government, yet in order to obtain this the major-generals were unrestricted in their authority to intervene in local affairs as they saw fit.[2] One project which attracted the personal attention of a number of major-generals was the remodelling of municipal corporations. The legal justification for their intervention was another extension of the parliamentary statute of 4 October 1647. Designed to regulate local elections, the original statute was extended by the Rump on 8 October 1652 for three years, and then again by Cromwell on 21 September 1655, this time for an indefinite period.[3] Subsequently, during late 1655 and early 1656, major-generals carried out purges in Bristol, Lincoln, Gloucester, Bedford, Tewkesbury, and other corporations.[4]

[1] See Kenyon, ed., *Stuart Constitution*, pp. 348–50.

[2] For the activities of the major-generals as a group, see Underdown, 'Settlement', pp. 174–6; Christopher Hill, *God's Englishman: Oliver Cromwell and the English Revolution* (London, 1970), pp. 175–9; Ivan Roots, 'Swordsmen and Decimators – Cromwell's Major-Generals', in R. H. Parry, ed., *The English Civil War and After, 1642–1658* (London, 1970), pp. 78–92. A full examination of the activities of the major-generals in towns is needed. The impression that they intervened on a grand scale has led Professor Roots to conclude: 'Charles II and James II learned a lot about the possibilities of increasing royal influence over the towns from the example of the Protectorate.' Roots, *Great Rebellion*, p. 182.

[3] *A. & O.* II. 620–1; Abbott, ed., *Writings and Speeches*, III. 828–9.

[4] Shilling, 'Municipal Corporations', pp. 94 ff.

Some of the major-generals proved to be lackadaisical and had little impact on local affairs in their province; others were strict, rigorous, and controversial. Among the latter was Hezekiah Haynes, whose domain included Norfolk and Norwich. He had a special concern for towns. He once reported: 'if corporations be not soon considered, the work now upon the wheel will certainly receive a stand'.[1] Moreover, his bite could be as vicious as his bark. In December 1655, for example, he descended on Colchester and thoroughly reduced the corporation to submission.[2] Haynes must have been aware of the gains scored by the moderate conservatives in Norwich soon after his arrival in East Anglia, yet there is no evidence that he made an effort to purge the city corporation. The most plausible explanation for this is that it was not the corporation which needed to be purged, but the charter which needed to be amended.

The moderate-conservative bloc had triumphed in each of the four aldermanic elections held during the conciliatory first phase of the Protectorate, yet the Independent–army–Rump group still possessed a clear majority.[3] They could and did use this majority to continue their partisan projects, to elect one of the two sheriffs, and to pick the mayor from the freemen's nominees.[4] Two weeks before the mayoral election of 1656, for example, the magistrates ordered that the following 23 April would be a day of thanksgiving to celebrate the city's 'deliverance from the mutiny' of 1648.[5] The mayoral election of 1656 may also have been influenced by a possible threat of major-general intervention if the municipal election ordinance extended by Cromwell the previous autumn was not observed. In either event, on 1 May the moderate-conservative bloc was dealt its first electoral set-back since before

[1] Thomas Birch, ed., *A Collection of State Papers of John Thurloe* (London, 1742), IV. 257.

[2] J. H. Round, 'Colchester During the Commonwealth', *English Historical Review*, 15 (1900), 648–58.

[3] Fourteen of the aldermen of early 1656 had voted against Mingay's election in 1648; six of these aldermen had also signed the petition against Hobart. In addition to Jay, Mingay, Paine, and Holmes, the moderate-conservatives could also count on Church and Salter. The remaining four aldermen (Tooke, Wenman, Johnson, and Watts) cannot be associated clearly with either group.

[4] In the shrievalty elections of 1654, for example, the magistrates chose John Andrews as their sheriff. Andrews had opposed Mingay's election in 1648, served on numerous Assembly committees from 1648 to 1650, and would be removed from office during the Restoration.

[5] M.C.B. (1654–66), 16 Apr. 1656, 29ʳ.

the Protectorate.[1] The problem which Haynes and the Independent–army–Rump magistrates confronted was how they could continue to prevent the moderate-conservative faction, with their previously demonstrated ability to dominate freeman elections, from winning future contests and eventually gaining control over the corporation. What was needed, in short, was a basic change in electoral procedures and regulations. In the first Assembly meeting to follow the mayor's election, the desirability of revising the charter was brought up for discussion.[2]

Norwich was one of many corporations which contemplated a surrender of its charter to the state during the summer of 1656. In the spring of 1656 the Council of State, for reasons which are not clear, had established a Committee for Municipal Charters. The subsequent activity of this Committee has convinced some historians that it was devised in order to ensure that corporations would be controlled by local Cromwellians, who in turn would exercise their influence to guarantee that supporters of the regime would be elected to Parliament. The role played by the major-generals was to pressure and coerce the corporations into surrendering their charters to the Committee for appropriate revision.[3] On the other hand, it has been argued that the surrender of the charters which occurred at this time stemmed, with few exceptions, from local initiative.[4] Too little is known about the attempt to obtain a revised charter in Norwich to add much to this controversy; and because the proposed revisions were later either destroyed or lost, it cannot be ascertained whether the proposed charter was designed to restructure the corporation to the advan-

[1] The mayoral nominees, Samuel Puckle and Bernard Church, suggest that the circumstances surrounding the election were peculiar. Puckle had voted against Mingay in 1648 and had joined in the petition against Hobart in 1654. Church was associated with the other political camp. Moreover, Church had already served as mayor. Because the 1620 election ordinance prohibited second mayoral terms and had been observed with only one exception since then, the nomination of Church for a second term seems strange. The magistrates' selection of Puckle over M. P. Church also demonstrates that the Court of Aldermen as a body still preferred the Independent–army–Rump faction.

[2] A.B. (1642–68), 3 May 1656, 172^r.

[3] J. H. Round, 'Cromwell and the Electorate', *The Nineteenth Century*, 46 (1899), 947–56 and Round, 'Colchester During the Commonwealth', pp. 641–64. See also Shilling, 'Municipal Corporations', p. 107.

[4] S. R. Gardiner, *History of the Commonwealth and Protectorate (1649–1656)* (London, 1901), III. 291–4.

tage of the Independent–army–Rump faction.[1] Even if this was the intent (and all citations in the Assembly Book referring to a revision of the charter were subsequently renounced during the Restoration), it is not known whether Major-General Haynes or the Council of State was involved. Several points, however, are clear. The first is that there was a prolonged and ultimately unsuccessful attempt to obtain a new charter which antedated the Protectorate and continued after the reign of the major-generals. The second is that the corporation clearly favoured a revised charter and the only response it received from the central government was obstruction and delay.[2]

The first mention of a possible revision of the city charter dates from the last months of the Rump Parliament. The Rump had shown no interest in revising town charters until late 1652, when it set up a Committee for Corporations.[3] A number of towns were subsequently ordered to surrender their charters. Although several corporations, including Great Yarmouth, resisted strenuously, the Norwich Assembly does not appear to have been against a new charter. A committee headed by the mayor and seven aldermen was appointed to consider possible alterations, but no action seems to have been taken before Cromwell abruptly dissolved the Rump in April 1653.[4] The Assembly Book records no further consideration of charter revision until 1656, when the Protectorate established its own Committee. This would imply that although the Norwich corporation may have welcomed an opportunity to revise the charter, the initial impulse came from the

---

[1] The case of Colchester, which also lay in Haynes's district, is suggestive. In both towns a minority group which had come to power during the Commonwealth was confronted in 1656 by a more conservative electorate intent on electing additional conservatives. The magistrates of Colchester complained that their old charter gave 'too great a power . . . to the people to slight the magistracy of the place' and requested a new charter to create a more closed corporation. Round, 'Colchester During the Commonwealth'; Underdown, *Pride's Purge*, p. 325. Colchester was the only town to receive a new charter before the parliamentary elections of 1656.

[2] The case of Norwich makes it difficult to accept the claim that throughout the Interregnum there was a continuing effort by the state to dominate municipal elections through a remodelling of charters. See B. L. K. Henderson, 'The Commonwealth Charters', *Transactions of the Royal Historical Society*, 3rd. ser., VI (1912), 129–62.

[3] Shilling, 'Municipal Corporations', pp. 78–81.

[4] A.B. (1642–68), 28 Jan. 1652/3, 135ʳ. There is no evidence that the city received any prodding from Westminster, but it should be noted that M.P. Thomas Atkin was one of the more active members of the Rump's Committee.

national government. Whether external nudging was or was not involved, later events would suggest that the corporation was much more interested in altering the charter than the state. The committee appointed by the Norwich Assembly in May 1656 continued its deliberations throughout the summer and in late September the draft for a new charter was approved by the corporation.[1] In order to expedite matters and improve chances of a favourable outcome, Mayor Puckle and the town clerk were ordered to deliver the charter to Cromwell personally.[2]

By the summer of 1657 the rule of the major-generals had been swept away and the Protectorate was once again sailing in a more moderate and conservative direction. Nevertheless, the Norwich Assembly continued to press the state into approving its desired charter. In August the mayor and town clerk were dispatched to London to see whether they could clear the log-jam.[3] More fruitless months passed. In late October the Assembly lamented that more than a year had passed with no result, but there was little they could do other than send the mayor, recorder, and steward to London with fresh instructions.[4] This did stir up some activity, but it was not long before the proposed charter was enmeshed in bureaucratic red tape.[5] In the early summer of 1658 the town clerk was twice dispatched to London for further consultation on the charter.[6] The death of Oliver Cromwell in the autumn of 1658 did not deter the corporation. Over two years had now expired. In February 1658/9 the Norwich Assembly wrote a letter to Richard Cromwell in which it tried to convince him that his father had approved of the new charter.[7] As soon as Oliver understood the proposed alterations, the letter read, he 'readily was so pleased' and forwarded it to the Council, which in turn passed it on to the Committee for Charters, which in turn referred it to the Council at Law, which was working on it when Oliver died. This is the last

[1] ibid., 11 June and 30 Sept. 1656, 176ʳ. The contents of this proposed charter are not known. However, this and all other acts of the Assembly concerning the revision of the charter were officially renounced after the Restoration.

[2] ibid., 8 Oct. and 11 Dec. 1656, 176ʳ, 177ʳ.

[3] ibid., 24 Aug. 1657, 184ᵛ.   [4] ibid., 30 Oct. 1657, 187ʳ.

[5] On 17 November a petition for a Norwich charter was referred to committee for report; the following 9 February the charter was placed on the agenda, but there is no record that action was taken. *C.S.P.D..*, Interregnum, 1657–8, pp. 169, 182.

[6] A.B. (1642–68), 18 May and 21 June 1658, 192ᵛ, 193ᵛ.

[7] ibid., 24 Feb. 1658/9, 197ʳ.

recorded reference to the corporations project to procure a new charter during the Interregnum. Certainly Oliver Cromwell cannot be accused of trying to force a new municipal charter on a reluctant Norwich.

The assault of the major-generals on the municipal corporations had a third dimension: direct intervention in the parliamentary election held during the late summer of 1656. Quite possibly the Council of State would have been more hesitant in summoning a second Protectorate Parliament had it not been for the assurances offered by the major-generals that they could effectively exercise their local influence to provide a more agreeable House of Commons. Thus, as the August election approached, the major-generals stepped up their activities across the country.[1] Norwich had been spared a purge of the corporation and apparently it had not been coerced into surrendering its charter, but the city did experience the full impact of Haynes's determination to thwart the re-election of Hobart and Church.

On 10 August Major-General Haynes wrote to the Council of State that in Norwich 'the movement afoot is to make a worse choice in this election than in the last'.[2] Rumours had reached him that some of the opposition party considered Hobart too moderate and wanted to drop him in favour of a different candidate. Haynes knew, however, that the real threat was still posed by Hobart, 'a person as closely maligning the government and good men as any other in Norfolk'. The Major-General was especially exasperated by a Mr. Boatman, a popular local preacher who supported Hobart and 'who is as captain of all the more ordinary sort of people who have votes in the election'. Boatman had previously managed to circumvent Haynes's persecution: 'for though I have denied him his liberty to preach in Norwich, he hath got, since his coming down, to preach in a church about two miles of the city, and draws multitudes after him.'[3] Five days later Haynes informed the Council that he was continuing his attempts to block Hobart's

[1] A discussion of the major-generals and the election of 1656 may be found in Paul J. Pinckney, 'A Cromwellian Parliament: The Elections and Personnel of 1656' (unpublished Ph.D. thesis, Vanderbilt University, 1962).

[2] The following account of the election is drawn from Birch, ed., *Thurloe Papers*, V. 296–7, 311–13, 328. These are four letters from Haynes to Thurloe and Cromwell written from 10 to 20 August.

[3] Haynes's actions against Boatman were apparently exceptional. There are very few allusions to restrictions on ministers in the reports from the major-generals to Thurloe. Hardacre, *Royalists*, p. 115.

election and was still trying to work out how to deal with Boatman; but on the same day he wrote to Cromwell that supporters of the godly party were so discouraged by the strength of the opposition that many were convinced that it would be a waste of time even to turn up for the election. The Major-General's worst fears came true for Norfolk as well as Norwich. In a letter of 20 August to the Council, he described the disaster:

there was such a clear combination, as never was known before, to bring in persons of apparent contrary principles to the government, and but few of them such as contained to own the Parliament interest, by which choice the profane, malignant, and disaffected party and scandalous ministry are only gratified.

In Norwich, John Hobart and Bernard Church once again saddled their horses for Westminster.

If Hezekiah Haynes was upset by Hobart's triumph, so also was the Norwich corporation. Only a week after the Parliament had opened, Hobart wrote a defiant letter to Mayor Samuel Puckle, one of the petitioners against his first election in 1654.[1] The corporation had made some now unknown request of their member of Parliament, who retorted that 'I am at present, and perhaps forever, disabled to serve you in employment of this kind.' He further lectured his constituents that although he was elected by Norwich he was not elected for Norwich:

That I am not suffered to represent you in Parliament. If those things which shall there be done, prove to the glory of God and the peace and freedom of this our nation, I shall exceedingly rejoice by what instruments soever they be affected.

This lofty independence may not have endeared Hobart to the corporation, but it did not prevent him from success in the parliamentary elections of 1658/9. On this occasion he delivered a speech to his constituents in which he denied the accusation that he was an ungodly man of no conscience.[2] In a vague insight into his personal political leanings on the eve of the Restoration, Hobart denied that the great sacrifices made in the Civil Wars had led to nothing but chaos in the government and country. He opposed a complete Restoration, but he was uncertain what should be done and

[1] Tanner MSS., 52, fo. 168: Hobart to Puckle, 23 Sept. 1656.
[2] ibid., 51, fos. 16, 17, 18.

humbly admitted his own limitations in extricating England from its present difficulties.[1]

The parliamentary election of 1656 demonstrates that the reign of the major-generals did not reverse the moderate-conservative tide which had been flowing since before the Protectorate. Three weeks after this election, the freemen went to the guild-hall and chose another moderate-conservative sheriff.[2] By early 1657 their period of trial had come to an end: the major-general system was dismantled and the state adopted a non-interventionist policy towards local government. The mayoral nominees of 1657 and 1658 leave little doubt as to where the sentiments of the freemen lay. In 1657 there were twelve aldermen who had not served as mayor; eight of these men had been elevated during the Commonwealth and four during the Protectorate. The freemen confined their nominees to the latter: Jay and Holmes were nominated in 1657 and Mingay and Paine were nominated in 1658. The freemen were thus controlling the election of mayors by a process strikingly similar to that used in the decade prior to the seniority ordinance of 1620. The moderate-conservative coalition did not, however, make any advances in the Court of Aldermen during this period. There is a simple explanation for this: no aldermanic deaths or resignations occurred between 1654/5 and the summer of 1660.

The parliamentary and municipal elections reveal clearly that political concerns associated with national affairs continued to play a dominant role in Norwich politics during the 1650s. Successful in the elections to both of Oliver Cromwell's Parliaments, the moderate-conservative coalition had triumphed also in the election of the five commons' sheriffs from 1653 to Cromwell's death, the four aldermen elected during this period, and both mayoral nominees in 1655, 1657, and 1658.[3] Presumably they would also have gained the upper hand in the magistracy had not the rate of attrition been

[1] The text of Hobart's speech suggests that although he had always favoured the moderate-conservative opposition to the Protectorate, he was not a Royalist. At one point he told his listeners: 'It is not, it seems, a work of repairing the good old fabric of this nation's government upon its just foundations, but a new creation; alas, how unable and in every way unfit am I for such a work.' ibid.

[2] This was James Long. In 1648 Long had been one of only eight councilmen to vote for Mingay. In 1649 he lost the Common Council seat which he had held for the preceding three years.

[3] A complete list of sheriffs elected from 1647 to 1660, their connections with the Independent-army-Rump faction, and their fate as officeholders after 1660 may be found in Evans, 'Political Elite of Norwich', pp. 229–30.

so low. As a consequence, the majority of Norwich magistrates were politically out of step with the more conservative citizenry during the Protectorate and up to the Restoration. This explains why the magistrates consistently chose the less conservative of the mayoral nominees in every election from 1651 to 1659. After 1657 they could continue to pursue their partisan projects: sponsorship of Independent preacher Thomas Allen was continued and the negotiations with the state for a revised charter and for municipal control over the Cathedral were pushed forward.

The attitude of most magistrates and citizens towards Cromwell and the Protectorate in 1657 and 1658 must have been ambivalent. Men of almost all political shades between staunch Royalist and ardent republican could find some things in the Protectorate to applaud, and many things to condemn; and they could all agree that Cromwell was unpredictable.[1] At least officially, the Norwich corporation expressed strong support for both Cromwell and the Protectorate. In April of 1658 the Assembly approved and sent to London a remonstrance which praised Cromwell in strong terms:

We the mayor, sheriffs, aldermen, and common council of your Highness' city of Norwich taking notice of the great and wonderful providence of almighty God in bringing you to this place of magistracy in these three nations. . . .

We therefore, everyone of us for himself, and as the representatives of the whole body of this city, in the name of the rest of the same city, do humbly desire your Highness to accept of a free and voluntary submission to your Highness' power and authority and willing subjection to your just and good government, who will always study and endeavor, as much as in us lieth, the peace, safety, and welfare of these nations, which will much strengthen the hands of your authority; and will always to the utmost of our power assist your Highness in the defence of the true reformed religion, the preservation of your Highness' person, and in maintaining the just rights and privileges of the people. . . .[2]

It is curious to note that the Assembly appointed Independent–army–Rump aldermen Puckle and Parmenter, rather than Mayor

[1] The Protectorate's limited success in satisfying the moderate-conservative groups in England after 1656 is discussed in Underdown, 'Settlement', pp. 178–82; Hardacre, *Royalists*, pp. 122 ff.; Abernathy, *Presbyterians*, pp. 17, 21–2.

[2] A.B. (1642–68), 16 Apr. 1658, 191ʳ. The petition does not provide a clue as to why the corporation decided to express their support for Cromwell at this time. The corporation may have hoped to flatter Cromwell into supporting the Cathedral and charter projects. On the other hand, the petition may have been carefully timed to have some impact on the mayoral election two weeks away.

Jay, to take the petition up to Cromwell. On 3 May the Assembly was prepared to punish those of its members who were absent from the 16 April meeting unless they immediately consented to the petition. Two of these absentees were Independent–army–Rump aldermen Toft and Rye, both of whom were evicted from office during the Restoration.[1] Within four days of the death of Oliver Cromwell on 3 September, the Mayor's Court declared his eldest son Richard as the new Lord Protector.[2] Less than a month later the Assembly forwarded an address to Richard stressing their support for the new regime and expressing their belief that Oliver had been an instrument of God's will.[3] But in the minds of some magistrates and townsmen there must have been a question as to whether this instrument was sent by God to punish or reward them.

Only fragmentary insights remain into the attitude of the citizens of Norwich to the rapid pace of events between the death of Oliver Cromwell and the famous march of General Monck to London in January 1659/60. Surely the calling of Richard Cromwell's Parliament in 1658/9, the dissolution of Parliament and the demise of the Protectorate the following April, the recall of the Rump in May, the Royalist uprisings in August, the dissolution of the Rump by the army grandees in October, and the restoration of the Rump in late December 1659 must have had some impact on them. From the little that is known, neither the freemen nor the corporation were entirely consistent in their behaviour. John Hobart was returned to Parliament for a third time in January 1658/9 and a moderate conservative was chosen as the commons' sheriff the following September.[4] Yet the nominees for mayor in May, when the army was in control and the recall of the Rump and its 'Good Old Cause' was imminent, included a ringleader of the Independent–army–Rump faction.[5] The corporation, for its part, pursued its desired charter with Richard in February and, as

[1] ibid., 3 May 1658, 192ᵛ.

[2] M.C.B. (1654–66), 7 Sept. 1658, 84ʳ. Petitions of support and loyalty to Richard Cromwell in mid-September were common; they do not necessarily reflect confidence in the new Lord Protector.

[3] A.B. (1642–68), 19 Oct. 1658, 195ᵛ–196ʳ.

[4] The commons' sheriff for 1659, John Lawrence, joined the Council in 1654, was elected to the Court of Aldermen in 1661, and became mayor in 1669.

[5] William Davy, the mayor elected in 1659, was a strong Independent who had voted against Mingay in 1648, signed the petition against Hobart in 1645, and was forced from the Court of Aldermen in 1660/1. The only other petitioner against Hobart to be nominated for mayor from 1654 to 1660 was Samuel Puckle in 1656, the year of the major-generals.

it had done on two previous occasions, prepared the city defences against possible Royalist uprising in August.[1] On the other hand, there is one sign that reconciliation was taking place within the Assembly. In 1658 Roger Mingay had been elected mayor. At the conclusion of his tenure, in June 1659, the Assembly passed a resolution testifying to Mingay's good government and defending his good name.[2] This resolution blamed the refusal of the Assembly to accept Mingay's election in 1648 wholly on the technicality that he had not previously served as sheriff; no reference was made to his ineligibility owing to his politics and the parliamentary election ordinance.

*　　*　　*

Discontent was widespread and growing in England as the winter of 1659 set in. The government, ruled by the sword of the army leaders, was increasingly unpopular. Demands for a Parliament were ever more frequently and loudly voiced. Even the army grandees recognized their diminishing hold on power and consented in December to restore once again the already discredited Rump. But it was not just a Parliament which many Englishmen wanted; they demanded a 'free Parliament' and it was clearly understood that by this they did not mean the Rump. The centre of disaffection was London. Early in December the apprentices rioted against the army and in support of a free Parliament. On 21 December the elections for the London Common Council witnessed a marked growth in the number of moderates and conservatives, many of whom were thought to be Royalists and some of whom boldly let their preference for monarchy be known. Recent elections for new aldermen had also returned some pro-Royalists.[3] Conservative political opinion, so active in the capital, was also quickening elsewhere in the country. As the Rump members prepared to take their familiar seats in Westminster, this moderate and conservative sentiment focused on General George Monck and his army in Scotland. Viewed as the only person who could save England from military despotism and social anarchy, Monck was especially appealing to Presbyterians who hoped he

---

[1] M.C.B. (1654–66), 15 Aug. 1659, 105ʳ. On 1 July the corporation sent a petition of unknown content to the Rump, which thanked the city through Alderman Atkin. A.B. (1642–68), 1 July 1659, 202ʳ; *C.J.* VII. 723: 19 July 1659.

[2] A.B. (1642–68), 20 June 1659, 201ᵛ.

[3] Godfrey Davies, *The Restoration of Charles II, 1558–1660* (Oxford, 1955), pp. 256–7.

would restore a Presbyterian monarchy. Royalists, a little more cautious and suspicious, also cast their eyes to the north. On 30 December Monck and his army crossed the border into England and commenced a glacial but triumphant progress towards London. His intentions were vague; he stated only that he wished to protect Parliament, not to restore the King. But everywhere he went he was showered with speeches and petitions of support from moderates and conservatives who correctly saw in Monck an enemy of the Rump and the army leaders.

The moderates and conservatives in Norwich, who had been waiting for a possible hour of deliverance since 1648, seized this opportunity to voice their opinions. When Monck had approached within thirty miles of the gates of London in late January, he was presented with a Declaration from the gentry of Norfolk and the city of Norwich.[1] The document contains the signatures of so many officeholders and private citizens of Norwich that it might almost be considered an address from the city. Of all the petitions received by Monck as he marched south, this Declaration was the boldest and the most defiant.[2] First were listed the grievances and laments; the distractions and divisions in state and Church, 'the miseries of an unnatural war, the too frequent interruptions of government, the impositions of several heavy taxes, and the loud outcries of undone and almost famished people, occasioned by the general decay in trade . . .'. Norwich appears to have been severely depressed by an economic slump and the complaint on this score was not mere rhetoric.[3] But there were many counties and towns in England which had stated similar grievances. What makes the Norfolk and Norwich Declaration unique is the proposed remedy: the excluded members of Parliament should be returned to their rightful seats without the obligation of taking the Engagement or any other oath and until this was accomplished 'the people of England cannot be obliged to pay any taxes'. In a particularly

[1] N.N.R.O., A Letter and Declaration of the Gentry of the County of Norfolk and the County and City of Norwich to his excellency Lord General Monck. This is reproduced in Hamon Le Strange and Walter Rye, eds., *An Address from the Gentry of Norfolk and Norwich to General Monck in 1660* (Norwich, 1913).

[2] Davies, *Restoration*, p. 272.

[3] In mid-December the magistrates were hard pressed to deal with the social impact of the economic decline: 'Forasmuch as the necessities of the poor are exceedingly increased for want of work by reason of the deadness of trade, and by sickness and disease which have befallen many . . .'. M.C.B. (1654–66), 13 Dec. 1659, 110ᵛ.

audacious move, the address was presented first to the Rump, where it created quite a storm, before it was delivered to Monck at St. Albans.[1]

The Declaration must be interpreted as thinly-veiled support for the restoration of the Stuarts, as well as a strong and blatant attack against the Rump and the swordsmen. The Declaration, which itself did not overtly call for the return of Charles, cannot be construed as Royalist simply because it was addressed to Monck. If the General personally favoured a restoration of the Crown, he proved to be a master at keeping his political preferences to himself. Not until 19 March did he openly declare for Charles. On the other hand, the demand for a restored Parliament was widely understood as tantamount to support for the Stuarts.[2] Therefore, the contents of the Declaration leads to the surmise that it represented the point of view of old Royalists and 'new Royalist' Presbyterians who had constituted the moderate-conservative bloc in the city since 1646. They would also have been joined in 1658/9 by some disillusioned Commonwealthmen and the remainder of Presbyterians who had supported the Protectorate when it stood between them and sectarianism, but turned against the Rump when the Protectorate was abolished in May 1658.[3]

A close look at the 794 signatories to the Declaration reveals that the 'Good Old Cause' had lost much of its earlier support within the corporation.[4] Fourteen aldermen and twenty-five councilmen

---

[1] Lord Richardson, Sir John Hobart, and Sir Horatio Townshend presented the address personally to the speaker of the House on 28 January; the Rump responded by threatening the three men with the Tower. That the address was more a statement of political criticism directed against the Rump than a petition of personal support for Monck is suggested by the General's cool reception of it. Monck was given a copy of the address 'lest any person in our absence misrepresent us or our intentions'. Davies, *Restoration*, p. 272.

[2] Certainly this was the attitude of the Commonwealthmen; on 9 Febuary the Rumpers listened to a petition from Praise God Barebones which condemned 'a general boldness [that] hath been taken to plead a necessity of returning to the government of king and lords. . . , or, which is all one, for a return of the justly secluded members, or a free Parliament, without due qualifications'. Cited in ibid., p. 279.

[3] ibid., p. 23; Douglas R. Lacey, *Dissent and Parliamentary Politics in England, 1661–1689* (New Brunswick, 1969), pp. 3–4; Abernathy, *Presbyterians*, pp. 25–38.

[4] Because of the similarity of Norfolk names, the illegibility of some signatures, and the presence of both Norwich citizens and county men on each of the eight pages of signatories, it is impossible to compute how many of this total were Norwich citizens. Given the unusual pagination, there is also the possibility that some sheets or names have been lost. Lastly, there are some citizens

signed the address. Of the ten aldermen who did not sign the Declaration, two are known to have been affiliated with the moderate-conservative group.[1] This leads to the cautionary observation that although the Declaration would not include the name of any ardent supporter of the Rump, not all the members of the conservative faction signed. The other eight aldermen who do not appear have several features in common: each had voted against Mingay in 1648, six had been elevated to the aldermanry between 1648 and 1651, five of the eight were petitioners against Hobart in 1654, and none was still in office in 1663.[2] Among the aldermen who did sign the Declaration were men long associated with the moderate-conservative bloc, such as John Salter, Robert Holmes, Christopher Jay, and Bernard Church. Of particular interest is the inclusion of six aldermen who had supported the Independent–army–Rump party a decade before.[3] The signatures of these magistrates testify to the disillusionment and dissatisfaction of many members of the old 1648 party with army-republican Rump government of 1659. Their switch of affiliation meant that the adherents to the Commonwealth were now in the minority in the Court of Aldermen. Therefore, in the last months and days of the Commonwealth in England, the majority of magistrates in Norwich looked forward to the restoration of the Stuarts.

In mid-February the secluded members returned to Parliament and the rule of the Rump was over. With the government now dominated by Presbyterians well disposed towards monarchy, arrangements were made for a Convention Parliament, which everyone assumed would make the necessary preparations for

---

[1] Roger Mingay and Richard Wenman did not join in the Declaration. It is also noteworthy that Robert Holmes did not sign the original Declaration but is included in the printed broadsheets; this suggests that he wanted to be associated with the Declaration only upon second thoughts. It is altogether possible that the Declaration was not strong enough for the tastes of these men. Wenman, for example, was Charles's personal nomination for mayor in 1661.

[2] They were Allen, Ashwell, Baret, Davy, Pointer, Puckle, Rye, and Toft. Only two of the one hundred petitioners against Hobart's election in 1654 signed the Declaration. They were Alderman John Rayley and his son William.

[3] They were Andrews, Barnham, Man, Parmenter, and Rayley. They had all voted against Mingay in 1648.

---

whose names are not on the address, but who appear on a broadside printed slightly later in London. Hence the percentage of the freemen to subscribe cannot be determined. The signatures of the subscribing aldermen have been compared with other signatures by these magistrates to guarantee authenticity and correct identity, but this has not been done for councilmen.

Charles's return. After 16 March, when the Long Parliament finally dissolved itself, the restoration of the Stuarts became more imminent with each passing day. Finally, on 1 May, the Convention Parliament declared that 'the government was and ought to be by King, Lords, and Commons', and seven days later it proclaimed Charles Stuart to be King of England. During this period of three months, many corporations looked on silently attempted no internal adjustments, and waited for further events to unfold. In other towns, like Oxford, conservatives and Royalists were elected to local office.[1] In Norwich the pattern of conservative triumphs in municipal elections, which had continued with only slight interruption for six years, persisted. In the second week of April the freemen followed the lead set by London the previous December: sixteen new councilmen were elected in what has every hallmark of being a purge of the extremists. Fourteen of the fifteen displaced councilmen had not signed the Declaration to Monck.[2] Seven of the nine councilmen who had petitioned against Hobart's election in 1654 were among those not returned. The M.P. election for the Convention Parliament also reflects the changing times. Ex-mayor and Presbyterian William Barnham was coupled with Thomas Rant, both of whom were signatories to the Declaration.[3] The mayor's election, which fell on the same day that the Convention Parliament proclaimed the necessity for a government of King, Lords, and Commons, witnessed the nomination of Joseph Paine and Robert Holmes and the former was selected mayor-elect by the magistrates.

As soon as it was clear that the Convention would restore the monarchy, the corporation of Norwich commenced a public display of loyalty which lasted for the duration of the year. Three days before Charles was officially declared King, the Mayor's Court ordered the old arms of state to be removed from its chamber.[4] On 10 May the city received the order from Parliament proclaiming Charles as King and the magistrates immediately made preparations for a solemn parade through the city the following day.[5]

---

[1] Shilling, 'Municipal Corporations', pp. 141–4.

[2] Only one of the twenty-five councilmen who signed the Declaration was not returned to the Council.

[3] Rant was not a Norwich citizen, but was sworn in as a freeman on 13 April by the Assembly. A.B. (1642–68), 13 Apr. 1660, 207ʳ. Rant was later named deputy-lieutenant for Norwich and served on the commission appointed to execute the Corporation Act in 1662.

[4] M.C.B. (1654–66), 5 May 1660, 119ᵛ.

[5] ibid., 10 May 1660, 119ᵛ.

Several days later the crowds were still burning bonfires and revelling to such an extent that public order was endangered and the magistrates had to step in to curtail the festivities.[1] Soon after Charles arrived in England, the aldermen and councilmen rushed to make supplication to the Declaration of Breda and took a statement of loyalty and obedience which acknowledged that 'his Majesty [is] the rightful and undoubted heir to the Crowns of these kingdoms of England . . .'.[2] During the summer the fee farm rent, which the city had purchased in 1650, was voluntarily restored.[3] The magistrates knew that the restitution of this ancient payment to the Crown merely attempted to make a virtue out of what would otherwise become a necessity. Something more lavish was called for. A large voluntary contribution to Charles was decided upon and the citizens responded with a free gift in the amount of £1,000.[4] In August the aldermen and councilmen voluntarily took the oaths of allegiance and supremacy.[5] Then, in September, the Assembly named a committee to go over the Assembly Book and report back which acts and orders passed during the Civil War and Interregnum should be disavowed and repealed.[6] The following January the magistrates were given an additional opportunity to demonstrate their allegiance. When they learned that an anti-Royalist uprising in London had been suppressed, the aldermen

---

[1] ibid., 12 May 1660, 120r.

[2] ibid., 30 May, 4, 6, and 8 June 1660, 121r, 122r-v. Aldermen Tooke, Puckle, Rye, and Holmes are omitted from the subscribers in the Mayor's Court Book, but on 8 June, which was two days within the forty-day limit set down in the Declaration itself, the Assembly passed a resolution adopting the Declaration and pledge of obedience and loyalty for the entire corporation. A.B. (1642-68), 8 June 1660, 208v.

[3] ibid., 25 June 1660, 209v.

[4] The Assembly ordered the voluntary contribution on 25 June and stipulated that the names of donors and the sums given should be recorded. By 28 July £735 had been collected and the city borrowed the remaining £265 from Aldermen Bendish and Wenman (£100 each) and Francis Norris (£65) without interest so that there would be no further delay. A congratulatory address was also written to accompany the gift. ibid., 25 June, 13 and 28 July, and 8 Aug. 1660, 209v, 210r-v, 211r.

[5] ibid., 8 Aug 1660, 211r.

[6] ibid., 8 Aug. and 21 Sept. 1660, 211r, 212r; M.C.B. (1654-66), 8 Sept. 1660, 130r. Apparently this committee was derelict in its duties, for on 6 January 1661/2 another committee was given the same task. A.B., 6 Jan. 1661/2, 224r. The word 'renounced' in red ink with the date 7 January 1661/2 may still be found throughout the pages of the Assembly Book between 1642 and 1660.

ordered the ministers in the city to give thanksgiving sermons in their parish churches the next Sunday.[1]

That such a profuse outpouring of loyalty should come from the very same magistrates who had ordered the defence of the city against Royalist uprising in 1655 and had offered an official and unsolicited declaration of appreciation to Oliver Cromwell early in 1658 might seem at least puzzling if not downright hypocritical. No doubt some of the aldermen elected during the Protectorate enthusiastically welcomed the Restoration. Others had come to accept monarchy as the best of the realistic alternatives which existed when Monck commenced his march into England. Moreover, the steps taken by the Norwich corporation in demonstrating loyalty to Charles were by no means exceptional if compared with those taken by other towns.[2] Nevertheless, the most plausible explanation for the sudden Royalism displayed by the magistracy lies in the desire of anxious aldermen to hold on to office. They were willing to make declarations, pass legislation, take oaths, and open their pocket-books precisely because they had no guarantees against Crown intervention.

The conditions established by the Convention Parliament for Charles's return were surprisingly limited and vague. In particular, no guarantees were extracted from Charles which provided municipal officeholders with any security of tenure. No doubt the Norwich magistrates hoped that the general amnesty that accompanied the Restoration in May would offer them protection, although the general pardon in the King's Declaration of Breda extended only to lives, liberty, and estates.[3] The arrival of Charles in England led the Commonwealthmen of some towns to resign their offices and in others, including Great Yarmouth, the local corporation conducted its own purge. But in Norwich the Commonwealth magistrates had no intention of leaving office and the corporation, on its own, was disinclined to provoke a local controversy by trying to force them out.[4] The Assembly did coerce Recorder Erasmus Earle to resign and Francis Cory was restored

---

[1] M.C.B. (1654–66), 12 Jan. 1660/1, 139ʳ.

[2] A useful description of the response of towns to the Restoration may be found in Shilling, 'Municipal Corporations', pp. 144–91.

[3] "Declaration of Breda", in Kenyon, ed., *Stuart Constitution*, pp. 357–8.

[4] Only one Norwich alderman, Nicholas Pointer, resigned. A.B. (1642–68), 8 Aug. 1660, 211ʳ.

to his old office in July, but no corresponding action was taken against the aldermen.[1]

The magistrates' reluctance to recruit Royalist magistrates or to purge their own chamber is seen in two problems which arose in the autumn of 1660. First, in September the magistrates chose George Steward to be sheriff. For men who otherwise appear to have been so eager to make a point of their loyalty to the new King, they did not make a very judicious choice. Steward had originally joined the Common Council in the purge elections of 1649, only three years after becoming a freeman. He served on several important committees until he was dropped from the Council in 1653.[2] The next year he joined in the petition against Hobart's election, rejoined the Council in 1656, and was dropped again the following year. Nor did he sign the Declaration to Monck. Shortly after his election in 1660, Steward made a nuisance of himself by rejecting the old sheriffs' oath and refusing to accompany Mayor Paine to the Cathedral on Sundays.[3] Somehow this situation came to the attention of the Privy Council, which promptly sent two letters to the mayor. The first insisted that all officeholders take the oaths prescribed by the ancient charters or else be dismissed, and the second demanded that Steward appear personally before the Privy Council within one week. The second problem which needed to be solved was to find some accommodation for the three surviving aldermen who had been ejected in the 1640s for Royalist proclivities.[4] By August the magistrates must have known how interested the Crown was in the restoration of excluded municipal magistrates, yet they took no action.[5] Finally, when two aldermanic vacancies opened in November, two of the three previously excluded aldermen were restored. This would seem to have been a good compromise: immediate restoration to positions created by attrition could satisfy the ejected aldermen without displacing the

[1] ibid., 18 and 25 June, and 28 July 1660, 208ᵛ, 209ᵛ, 210ᵛ.

[2] Steward was named to the committee for removing sequestered ministers, checking sequestration exactions, and securing the Cathedral for the city. ibid., 11 and 25 May 1649 and 13 May 1650, 81ᵛ, 82ᵛ, 98ʳ.

[3] M.C.B. (1654–66), 13 Oct. 1660, 133. The old oath required the sheriff to 'well and truly serve our sovereign lord the King'. N.N.R.O., *Mayor's Book*, pp. 126–8.

[4] They were John Osborne, Matthew Sotherton, and John Croshold.

[5] On 26 August, for example, the Crown directly intervened on behalf of ejected Royalists in Newcastle. See Shilling, 'Municipal Corporations', pp. 157–8.

Commonwealth aldermen. What is noteworthy is that it was the freemen of two wards, and not the magistrates, who took the initiative and proposed this solution.[1]

Evidently, the magistrates of Norwich in 1660 were not quite as Royalist as their declarations, oaths, and gifts indicated. The majority of them were not disposed, for example, to elect a Royalist or even a moderate sheriff. Nor did they encourage the freemen to restore the three evicted Royalist aldermen, much less purge the entire corporation. They clearly did not want the composition of the Court of Aldermen to be tampered with by either the Norwich Assembly or the Crown. They were able to protect their own position in the city and apparently hoped that their public professions of loyalty would appease the restored monarchy. They were mistaken. Prior to the late summer of 1660, the Crown displayed little desire to interfere in local town affairs. Then, during the autumn of 1660 and into 1661, it reacted sporadically and indecisively in response to individual cases,[2] and several towns, including Norwich, were singled out for special treatment. On 26 January 1660/1 a letter from Whitehall arrived in Norwich.[3] The purpose of the letter was to instruct the corporation to implement the Act of Indemnity passed the previous August. One provision of this Act was that persons who had given sentence of death in any of the High Courts of Justice since 1648 or had signed the warrant of execution for any person condemned in these courts were disallowed from holding public office or serving as a member of Parliament.[4] According to the Crown's information, there were some Norwich aldermen who fell into this net; but the Crown did not stop here. Going beyond the Act of Indemnity, the letter further ordered the corporation:

that forthwith you do not only restore such [Royalists] as have been removed in case they be living, but to proceed to new elections of others in their places in case they be dead and any disaffected persons be chosen in their rooms, and to take into consideration such elections as have been unduly made and to elect into their places such other persons as in your discretion you shall think most fit for our service . . .

[1] M.C.B. (1654–66), 27 and 31 Nov. 1660, 136r–v.
[2] Sacret, 'Municipal Corporations', pp. 238–40.
[3] S.P. Dom., Chas. II, 28/100: King Charles to City of Norwich, [21 January] 1660/1. The letter was also copied into the Assembly Book.
[4] *Statutes of the Realm* (London, 1963), V. 233: An Act of Free and General Pardon, Indemnity, and Oblivion.

Thus the full extent of the local purge was to be determined by the Norwich corporation.[1]

Three days after the letter arrived an Assembly was convened. By a vote of the seventeen magistrates and thirty-eight councilmen present, Robert Allen, John Andrews, Thomas Ashwell, William Davy, and William Rye were removed from the Court of Aldermen on the grounds that they had 'not been duly elected'.[2] Elections to fill the vacant seats were held in early February and passed without incident.[3] On 2 February the remodelled Mayor's Court ordered Aldermen Baret and Burman to appear before the Court and defend themselves against the charge that they were ineligible to continue in office owing to the Act of Indemnity.[4] Four days later Burman declared his innocence and stated his desire to continue as an alderman. Baret, however, refused to appear. The Mayor's Court was satisfied by Burman's testimony and gave Baret until the next city elections to answer the charge. In late February Aldermen Andrews and Davy, resolved to fight their expulsion, presented writs of restitution. The Assembly countered with the appointment of a committee to prepare a return to the writs and sent a letter to Charles explaining their position.[5] Both the letter and a draft of it have survived.[6] The King was informed that his instructions had been dutifully carried out and that the Assembly had also honoured a royal letter of 18 December which recommended William Watts for steward. A passage in the draft letter, omitted in the official letter, sheds further light on the proceedings against Burman and Baret: they had been members of 'an illegal and tyrannical high court of justice', but the Assembly could not prove that either of them had sentenced men to death. Thus, they were not summarily dismissed. By 6 April Baret had still not answered to the Mayor's Court, so he was removed from office and replaced.[7]

---

[1] Norwich was one of many towns to receive this request; a very similar letter to Kingston dated 25 February 1660/1 may be found in *C.S.P.D.*, Chas. II, 1660–1, p. 515.

[2] A.B. (1642–68), 29 Jan. 1660/1, 213ᵛ.

[3] ibid., 1 and 8 Feb. 1660/1, 214ʳ; M.C.B. (1654–66), 2 and 8 Feb. 1660/1, 140ᵛ, 141ʳ.

[4] M.C.B. (1654–66), 2 and 6 Feb. 1660/1, 140ᵛ, 141ʳ.

[5] A.B. (1642–68), 25 Feb. 1660/1, 215ʳ⁻ᵛ.

[6] S.P. Dom., Chas. II, 31/37: Corporation of Norwich to King Charles, 25 Feb. 1660/1; Tanner MSS., 311, fo. 60: Draft of a letter from the mayor and citizens of Norwich to the King, [February 1660/1].

[7] M.C.B. (1654–66), 6 Apr. 1661, 144ᵛ.

The corporation informed the King in February that the royal instructions to commence a purge 'hath much revived and cheered the spirits of us and other your loyal subjects, upon receipt whereof we presently put your Majesty's commands therein inserted in execution'. The members of the Assembly obviously wanted the Crown to think of them as dutiful and obedient subjects, but they had by no means applied the King's instructions as rigorously as their elaborate expressions of loyalty would suggest. With the restoration of John Croshold, all of the surviving aldermen removed from office during the 1640s had been put back into office. Yet, as Table 24 shows, the Assembly certainly could have removed more aldermen as 'unduly elected'. Not all of the aldermen who had risen to the Court owing to the ejection of previous aldermen were dismissed. Moreover, the Assembly could have interpreted 'unduly elected' to include all aldermen chosen during the period when the election ordinances and the Engagement were in effect.

If the intent of the King's letter was to obliterate the Commonwealth party completely, it was unsuccessful. If, on the other hand, it was meant to accelerate the declining influence of the Commonwealth party, it was a complete success. By September 1661 ten new aldermen had joined the Court of Aldermen within the space of one year. The number of pre-Restoration aldermen who had voted against Mingay in 1648 dropped from fourteen to six, the number who had supported the petition against Hobart in 1654 from six to one, and the number who had declined to join the Declaration to Monck in 1659/60 from nine to two. The men restored or elected to fill the seats were strong supporters of the Restoration. According to the draft letter of 25 February, the new aldermen were 'persons of great loyalty and affections to your Majesty's service'. The Royalist tide was running strong among the citizenry during the spring of 1661. In April, Alderman Christopher Jay and recently-restored recorder Francis Cory were elected to Parliament. A month later the freemen nominated and elected John Osborne to be mayor-elect. As the only surviving magistrate to be removed from office during the first purge in 1642/3, Osborne must have been a living symbol of Royalism. Owing to his advanced age, he petitioned the King in March to be spared from serving as mayor. In a letter to Mayor Paine, the King

TABLE 24: *The Court of Aldermen on 1 May 1660*

Alderman	Year Elected	Cause of Election	Voted Against Mingay in 1648	Signed 1654 M.P. Petition	Did Not Sign 1659/60 Monck Declaration	Departure From Court 1660–1664
Adrian Parmenter	1636	death	X			Corporation Act, 1662
Edmund Burman	1638	resignation	X			Corporation Act, 1662
Henry Watts	1642	death				
Samuel Puckle	1643	ejection	X	X	X	died in 1661
John Rayley	1643	death	X	X		
*Thomas Toft	1644	ejection	X		X	Corporation Act, 1662
Thomas Baret	1645	death	X	X	X	Act of Indemnity, 1661
Bernard Church	1646	death				
Richard Wenman	1648	death				
John Salter	1649	death			X	
†William Barnham	1649	ejection	X			Corporation Act, 1662
Robert Allen	1649	ejection	X		X	removed in 1660/1
William Davy	1649	ejection	X	X	X	removed in 1660/1
Thomas Ashwell	1649	ejection	X	X	X	removed in 1660/1
William Rye	1649	ejection	X		X	removed in 1660/1
Thomas Johnson	1649	death				died in 1660
John Andrews	1650	ejection	X		X	removed in 1660/1
John Man	1650	death	X			
Nicholas Pointer	1650	death	X	X	X	resigned in 1660
William Tooke	1652	death				
Roger Mingay	1654	death				died in 1660
Christopher Jay	1654	death				
Robert Holmes	1655	resignation				died in 1662
Joseph Paine	1655	death				

*Thomas Toft was originally elected by Mancroft Ward to replace ejected Alderman Alexander Anguish in 1643. For some unknown reason he does not appear on the list of aldermen for 1650, but he reappears in 1651 to replace deceased Alderman Samuel Brewster of Over-the-Water Ward.

†William Barnham was originally elected by Conesford Ward to replace ejected Alderman John Utting in 1648/9. For some unknown reason he does not appear on the list of aldermen for 1650, but reappears in 1651 to replace deceased Alderman Matthew Lindsay of Conesford Ward.

endorsed Osborne's request and recommended his own candidate.[1] The freemen and magistrates, however, were intent on electing Osborne whether he wanted to be elected or not. The candidate named by the King was nominated and elected the following year. A final sign of the demise of the Commonwealth party was an order of the Assembly passed in November 1661 to shut off funds for Thomas Allen's lectures.[2]

*   *   *

On both the national and local level, the Restoration settlement was not just the victory of Royalists over their Interregnum enemies; it was also a victory of Anglican-Royalists over their Interregnum allies, the Presbyterians. Both religiously and politically, the Presbyterians were worse off in 1665 under Charles than they had been in 1655 under Cromwell. Along with Puritans of all stripes, they fell victim to an intolerant and vengeful Cavalier Parliament determined to give Anglicanism a religious monopoly and to legislate harsh penalties for nonconformists who persisted in worshipping outside the state Church. Presbyterians in urban communities also fell victim to the Crown's plan to increase centralized control over the selection of urban officeholders and to ensure their loyalty to the state. Owing to the Corporation Act of 1661 and the misnamed Clarendon Code of subsequent years, the Presbyterians of English towns were not permitted to enter local politics or practise their religion. Since these measures had an immediate impact on Norwich and cast a long shadow over the politics of the city for the next three decades, they require some description and explanation.

Only a month before Charles set sail for Dover in 1660, the Presbyterians had good reason to believe that the new King's arrival would be their deliverance as well.[3] They had, after all, defiantly stood their ground against the army and Rump in 1659, warmly cheered on Monck (a moderate Presbyterian himself) during his fateful march, and dominated the restored Long

---

[1] *C.S.P.D.*, Chas. II, 1660–1, p. 548: King to Mayor, *et al.* of Norwich, 26 Mar. 1661.

[2] A.B. (1642–68), 6 Nov. 1661, 223ʳ. On the same day the Assembly agreed to present the bishop with a gift of two candlesticks at a cost of £15. 13s. 6d.

[3] A recent discussion of the disintegration of Puritan power after the Restoration may be found in Lacey, *Dissent*, pp. 3–70; Abernathy, *Presbyterians*, pp. 45 ff; J. R. Jones, 'Political Groups and Tactics in the Convention of 1660', *The Historical Journal*, vi (1963), 159–77.

Parliament which in late February took the first necessary steps to make the King's return possible. If they did not impose Presbyterianism themselves—and many in the House of Commons were determined to do precisely that in the last days before the dissolution of Parliament in March—they fully expected a grateful King to reward them either by establishing Presbyterianism or by adopting a comprehensive Anglicanism in which Presbyterians could find room for their system. They knew that Charles II, unlike his father, was not cemented in Anglicanism: he had actually agreed to accept the Solemn League and Covenant when seeking Scottish support in 1650. Moreover, the Presbyterians were encouraged by the Declaration of Breda which granted 'a liberty to tender consciences'. But as the months following the King's return passed, Presbyterian hopes gradually dimmed and then went out. Although they commanded a sizeable contingent if not a majority in the Convention Parliament, they were unable to legislate a religious settlement on the tolerant lines indicated in the Declaration of Breda. The King, who started his reign with no less than ten Presbyterian chaplains, was not the problem. Their failure was due in part to divisions within Presbyterian ranks, in part to bitter disunity between Presbyterians and Independents, and in part to the obstruction and ingenuity of High Church Anglicans who were as uncompromising in the 1660s as they had been in the 1630s. Whether a religious settlement acceptable to most moderate Puritans could have been achieved if the Presbyterians had been blessed with less intransigence and better leadership is academic. Less debatable is that the Presbyterians would never again have a similar opportunity after the Convention was dissolved in December.

The spring elections to the Cavalier Parliament were the decisive event leading to an Anglican religious settlement and the legal proscription of Puritanism. Having fought so many political battles against each other over the previous fifteen years, the Presbyterians and Independents had been slow to recognize that they were equally imperilled by the mounting strength of a renascent High Anglicanism. Nevertheless, an anti-Anglican party in the capital, aware of this danger, elected four nonconformists to Parliament in March. One Londoner informed a fellow nonconformist in Norwich that 'such men are needed to take down the pride of the bishops, who daily entrench on honest, godly ministers'.[1] The example of London, however, was rarely followed elsewhere. Armed with an overwhelming majority in Parliament, the Anglicans promptly commenced an assault on the few nonconformists in their midst.[2] On 13 May the House of Commons required all of its members to take the Anglican sacrament; four days later they declared the Solemn League and Covenant to be an unlawful oath and ordered it to be burned by the common hangman. After approving a number of Royalist bills, the House of Commons in mid-June heard the first reading of a bill designed to regulate corporations. The impetus for this controversial piece of legislation may well have come from the Crown and may have been political rather than religious in intent.[3] The Privy Council had encountered recurrent obstruction from some town corporations in its attempts to reinstate ejected Royalists and put out enemies of the King. The London parliamentary elections served further to convince the government that some policy must be formulated to reduce disaffected corporations to royal control. The initial reaction of the Crown was to consider the use of the prerogative to remodel municipal charters. But the early activities of the Cavalier Parliament, which was as Royalist and certainly more Anglican than the Crown itself, induced the government to turn to legislation instead.

The Act for the Well Governing and Regulating of Corporations was passed in December 1661.[4] Its purpose, as stated succinctly in the preamble, was to ensure 'that the succession in such corporations may be most probably perpetuated in the hands of persons well affected to His Majesty and the established government'. Although the act in its final form did not give the Crown everything it had originally wanted, it did provide the King with a temporary statutory authority to revolutionize the personnel of

---

[1] *C.S.P.D.*, Chas. II, 1660–1, p. 592: John Turin and Co. to James Denew, Norwich, 19 Mar. 1660/1. See also p. 127: Thomas Cooper to Thomas Everard, Norwich, 19 Mar. 1660/1.

[2] By one recent count, the Presbyterians and Congregationalists numbered between forty and fifty members in a House of 507 members. Lacey, *Dissent*, p. 30.

[3] This is the conclusion reached by Sacret, 'Municipal Corporations'. Recent studies have supplied additional details but have not challenged Sacret's interpretation. See Shilling, 'Municipal Corporations', pp. 177–8; Lacey, *Dissent*, pp. 34–7.

[4] *Statutes*, V. 321–3: An Act for the Well Governing and Regulating of Corporations.

corporations. The act may be considered in two parts: the series of new oaths to be required of all officeholders and the unprecedented powers of special commissioners named by the Crown to administer the act. All present and future town officials were required to take the oaths of supremacy and allegiance, declare that it was unlawful to take up arms against the King, subscribe to a disavowal of the Covenant, and testify to having taken the sacrament according to the rites of the Church of England during the preceding year. The Crown's commissioners were empowered to administer these oaths and remove from office any person who refused to accept them. Also, the commissioners were to see that all improperly ejected officeholders of the past two decades were restored. Their authority did not stop here. They could also remove from office any person they wished even if that person had complied or was willing to comply with all the oaths and declarations. Finally, all vacancies created either by the failure of officeholders to take any of the oaths or by dismissal at the hands of the commissioners were to be filled by these same commissioners. These appointments carried the same authority as if the new officeholders had been duly elected according to corporation charters. In short, the Crown through its commissioners could exclude and appoint anybody it pleased. The only limitation was that the powers of the commissioners were to expire on 25 March 1663. From that time forward the oaths were to be administered to new officeholders by the respective corporations.

The Corporation Act had less immediate impact in Norwich than in many other towns.[1] There are two reasons for this. The first is that in Norwich the previously ejected aldermen had already been returned to office and the number of objectionable magistrates had been reduced by the purge of 1660/1. In contrast, many other disaffected corporations either had been passed over by the Crown or had successfully evaded royal efforts to purge them. The second is that the rigour of local enforcement depended upon the zeal of the commissioners named by the Crown. Since these commissioners were almost always the leading Royalist gentry of the county, under the presidency of the lord lieutenant, the extent of their activities varied from county to county. The commissioners for Norfolk wielded

---

[1] For the enforcement of the Corporation Act and a list of the number of officials ejected in various corporations, see Shilling, 'Municipal Corporations', chap. VI and App. I.

a sharp axe in Yarmouth and yet, for reasons which are not clear, they were more lenient when they visited Norwich in July 1662.[1] Therefore, whereas more than half the magistrates of many corporations were purged, only four aldermen of Norwich were dismissed from office. Whether Edmund Burman, Thomas Toft, William Barnham, and Adrian Parmenter were evicted because they refused to take the oaths or for some other reason is not known. Nor can it be ascertained why the commissioners chose the replacements they did.[2] Presumably the magistrates who retained office took all the required oaths and subscribed against the Covenant, but even this is not certain. The Corporation Act specifically stated that the commissioners were to make entries of all oaths and subscriptions and deliver them to the town clerk of the corporation to be enrolled in the books and registers belonging to the city. However, the Norwich Assembly Book and Mayor's Court Book contain nothing of this sort and do not even mention the visit of the commissioners or the replacement of aldermen.

The Corporation Act was the most effective but by no means the only weapon used by the Crown to reduce towns to centralized control. Another was the remodelling of charters. In 1663, when the Norwich magistrates were first entrusted with enforcement of the Corporation Act, the city received a new charter. The product of two years of negotiation, this charter had originated in the corporation's desire to have the traditional liberties of the city confirmed by the new government. In late 1660 and early 1661 many towns voluntarily surrendered their charters to the Crown in the hope of currying the King's favour. The Norwich corporation, which had already gone to such lengths to impress Charles with its loyalty, was no exception. In December 1660 the Assembly named

[1] The commissioners were Lord Lieutenant Horatio Townshend, Thomas Richardson, John Knevet, Charles Mordaunt, Francis Cory, James de Grey, William Gawdy, Roger Spelman, Philip Woodhouse, Ralph Hare, Robert Kempe, William Doyly, Thomas Rant, E. Walpole, Thomas Townshend, and Bretts Bacon. Blomefield, *Norfolk*, III. 404–5. At Yarmouth, Townshend and his associates purged all the Independents and most, but not all, of the Presbyterians. *C.S.P.D.*, Chas. II, 1670, pp. 512–13: Sir Thomas Meadow to [Lord Townshend], 2 Nov. 1670. A Royalist and an Anglican, Townshend had almost completely dominated Norfolk elections to the Cavalier Parliament; he assured that the county and borough members were either Anglicans or extremely moderate Presbyterians. Abernathy, *Presbyterians*, p. 52.

[2] The commission chose James Long, Matthew Markham, Henry Woods, and Henry Watts, jr. to fill the vacancies. All of them had been sheriffs during the Interregnum with the exception of Watts, who became sheriff in 1664.

a committee to prepare a draft of a new charter; and they completed this task in the same week as the King's letter to remove improperly elected aldermen arrived in the city.[1] After the draft had been publicly displayed for a month, the Assembly approved it and borrowed £300 to defray expenses in obtaining the King's favour.[2] Before submitting it to the Crown, in late March the Assembly took the additional step of forwarding a copy to Henry Howard, no doubt in the belief that he would intercede at Court on their behalf.[3] Up to this point the Assembly was apparently enthusiastic over the prospect of a renewed charter, but this quickly changed. Because the draft of the charter requested by the members of the corporation has since been lost, the additions and alterations desired by them are not known. Clearly, however, they had not anticipated and did not want the kind of amendments proposed by the Crown in May 1661.

On 7 May, the day before the opening session of the Cavalier Parliament, Whitehall decided to establish its control over towns by inserting four specific clauses into all charters granted in the future.[4] The Crown would reserve to itself the first nomination of aldermen, the final choice of councilmen from nominations presented by the corporation, and the first and future appointment of recorders and town clerks. Finally, the election of borough members of Parliament would be restricted to the Common Council alone. The first three clauses would facilitate and accelerate the government's ongoing design to pack corporations. None of these provisions, by itself, represents a striking new departure: many corporations were already familiar with one or the other of them. What was new was the systematic application of all three provisions to all corporations. The fourth clause, which may well represent the government's alarmed reaction to the recent London parliamentary election, was the most innovative and, in conjunction with the three previous clauses, the most consequential. If successfully put into operation, this policy would have provided

---

[1] A.B. (1642–68), 6 Dec. 1660, and 23 Jan. 1660/1, 213r–v.

[2] ibid., 25 Feb. 1660/1, 215r.

[3] As early as the summer of 1660 the city had courted the favour of Henry Howard, son of the late Earl of Arundel, in gaining access to the Crown to present their voluntary gift. At that time Howard stated that he would take great satisfaction in being at the service of the city and standing up for their interests. Blomefield, *Norfolk*, III. 404; A.B. (1642–68), 26 Mar. 1661, 216r.

[4] The following is drawn from Sacret, 'Municipal Corporations', pp. 242 ff.

the Crown with an indirect but effective control over the election of a majority of the members of the House of Commons. The Crown's decision to proceed by statute rather than prerogative in the summer of 1661 did not mean that the government had abandoned entirely its policy of May. The Corporation Act was a triumph for the Crown, but only a partial triumph. What the King was not provided by statute, he could still seek to obtain in the granting of individual charters.

As soon as the May guidelines for new charters were known in Norwich, the Assembly hurriedly dispatched the town clerk to London and appointed a special charter committee.[1] In June the Assembly forwarded a petition concerning the charter to King Charles.[2] This petition has since been lost. There can be no doubt, however, that the corporation was opposed to the provisions established by Whitehall on 7 May. A document remains in the state papers which has every appearance of being a petition from Norwich defending the traditional liberties of the city.[3] Prepared at some time following the passage of the Corporation Act, the document lists the four proposed additions and then provides arguments against each in turn. The major line of reasoning consists of two points. First, the corporation was already Royalist and hence the proposed additions were unnecessary. Second, each of the provisions was a departure from ancient charter and injurious to the city's historical liberties. Indeed, by 1662 the officeholders of Norwich were preponderately if not exclusively Royalist and the proposed additions did constitute a breach with customary usage. Therefore, the document presents the statement of a local urban community which opposed the Crown not because the proposed charter revisions would displace many local officeholders or even change the political stance of the corporation, but because these changes would advance state centralization at the expense of local autonomy.

The defence against major charter revision provides some extremely interesting insights into seventeenth-century constitutional and political thinking in Norwich. In response to the first provision, the document points out that ejected Royalist aldermen

---

[1] A.B. (1642–68), 16 May 1661, 220ʳ.

[2] ibid., 16 June 1661, 220ᵛ.

[3] S.P. Dom., Chas. II, 36/85. The document states that it represents the views of 'them who agitate on the behalf of the city of Norwich for the obtaining of a charter. . . '.

had already been restored and unduly elected aldermen had been replaced by men 'well-affected to his Majesty'. Moreover, the Corporation Act empowered commissioners to remove 'those (if there yet be any) that are disaffected persons'. As for the Common Council, it also has been purged by the freemen, who 'in general are loyal to his Majesty and well-affected to the present government'.[1] These 'not rightly principled' councilmen would never have been elected in the first place had it not been for the parliamentary election ordinance passed 'in those times of defection'. Moreover, it was essential that the councilmen continue to be elected yearly by the freemen of the wards 'by reason of which choice the freemen are bound up by what is consented unto in Common Council by their representatives which if altered may be questionable'. The implication of this striking statement of representative freeman democracy is that if the citizens ceased to elect the councilmen, then they might not be subject to the decisions made by these councilmen in Assembly.[2] Third, the recorder and town clerk are and have always been chosen by the Assembly and Court of Aldermen respectively. Since both of these bodies were loyal to the King, the recorders and town clerks chosen by them would also be loyal to the King. In addition, these officials needed to be fully conversant with municipal affairs and live near or in Norwich: thus the corporation would be in a better position to appoint them than the Crown. Lastly, the document asserts that the election of members of Parliament belongs to the freemen by prescription. If they were to lose this right, considerable discontent would arise and the legality of the elections could be questioned. The document stops short of arguing that what applied to the Common Council also applied to Parliament; that is, that if the freemen ceased to elect members of Parliament, then they might not be bound by statutes made in Parliament. The shoe fitted, but was not put on.

Negotiations for a new charter proceeded slowly, but in the end

[1] The document does not seem to have overstated the case. In 1661 and 1662 a total of twenty-eight men who had never previously held political office were elected to the Common Council. Added to the thirteen new councilmen elected in 1660, this meant that fully two-thirds of the Council in 1662 consisted of men who had not been councilmen during the Civil War and Interregnum.

[2] The mayoral election of 1661 is especially interesting if viewed in this context. Possibly the freemen ignored the King's recommendation to put aside Osborne and elect Wenman because they did not want to establish the precedent of accepting Crown nominees for local office.

the corporation prevailed. By early July 1662 a tentative list of additions to the new charter was drawn up for the King's approval: no mention was made of the Crown's right to name or approve city officers.[1] A comparison of this list with the actual charter granted on 26 June 1663, reveals that with the exception of a few details the content of the charter was formulated by the summer of 1662.[2] The magistrates named in the charter included the four aldermen appointed by the Corporation Act commission, but no additional changes were made by the Crown.[3] Nor did the charter alter the procedure of electing officers other than to change the date of the election of sheriffs.[4] Most of the additions and revisions concerned clarification and extension of authority. Here the major change was that every alderman was to become a justice of the peace for the ward which elected him.[5] Since his duties were increased, it was necessary to ensure that each alderman was present to perform them. Hence a clause was added which required a magistrate who departed the city for the county to return within six months after written request to do so or be subject to a fine up to £100. If enforced, this addition would quickly eliminate the old problem of wealthy magistrates becoming absentee county gentry. Another old problem was also cleared up: by-laws passed by the Assembly would now need the consent of a majority of the councilmen. The Mayor's Court and Sheriffs' Court retained their previous membership and procedure, but their jurisdiction was increased. Also, restrictions on foreigners doing business in the city were significantly tightened.

With regard to the election of magistrates, the new charter sanctioned a restoration of old local procedures rather than the

---

[1] S.P. Dom., Chas. II, 57/32: Edw. Nichols at Whitehall to the King, 8 July 1662.

[2] N.N.R.O., Norwich charter of 1663. An English translation of the charter may be found in N.N.R.O., MS. 79: Benjamin Mackerell, *A History of Norwich*, II. 145–64.

[3] In the state papers there is a warrant dated 20 Mar. 1662/3 for the insertion of additional clauses into the charter; one of these reserved for the Crown the approval of the steward and town clerk. The clause, however, does not appear in the 1663 charter. *C.S.P.D.*, Chas II, 1663–4, p. 80.

[4] In the future, the magistrates were to choose their sheriff at any time between 24 June and 1 September and the freemen were to gather on the last Tuesday in August to choose the second sheriff; both were to be sworn in on 29 September.

[5] This addition was first recommended by the Assembly in May 1662. A.B. 1642–68), 26 May 1662, 229ᵛ.

adoption of a new system of Crown nominations and approvals. The reversion, however, went back to 1620 rather than 1642. For reasons which are not known, the 1663 charter made no reference to any of the seniority regulations passed in 1620 and later. The aldermen were to be chosen from among 'the most worthy and sufficient citizens' and not necessarily from among the sheriffs alone. The seniority ordinance for mayoral elections, passed in 1620 and repealed in 1644, was not restored. In practice, the freemen exercised this greater freedom of choice. In the twenty-one aldermanic contests held from 1660 to 1670, the freemen of all four wards dispensed on seven occasions with the former criterion of tenure in the shrievalty.[1] Although the new alderman would be a justice of the peace among the freemen who elected him, the freemen chose residents of their own ward in only eight of the twenty-one elections. Similarly, only three of the mayors from 1660 to 1670 were the senior alderman under the chair, and on three occasions the mayor-elect came from the bottom half of the seniority ladder. Therefore, the ironic outcome of the new charter was that the freemen were as involved in choosing local officeholders as they had been in 1640 and 1650, and even less restricted.

*   *   *

By the middle of 1663 the autonomy of the city was once again secure. During the preceding two years the Cavalier Parliament had passed legislation in an effort to make the corporation Anglican, and the Crown had used its prerogative to make it Royalist. Once the new charter had been deposited in the guild-hall and the authority of the Corporation Act commission had expired, direct intervention by the state came to a temporary halt. Nevertheless, the steps which had already been taken and the safeguards which would continue in operation might well have led contemporary observers of Norwich to believe that the corporation would remain Anglican-Royalist in the future. Of the aldermen of early 1660, ten had been purged from office, four had died, and one had resigned. The nine survivors and the newly-chosen aldermen had

---

[1] Twenty-eight men were promoted to the Court of Aldermen during this period, but three gained office by restitution and four were appointed by the Corporation Act commissioners. A complete list of these aldermanic elections and an analysis of them may be found in Evans, 'Political Elite of Norwich', pp. 255–7.

subscribed to the oaths of allegiance and supremacy, renounced the Covenant, taken the Anglican sacrament, and survived the scrutiny of the special commission. These magistrates were now left with the responsibility of keeping the corporation and city Anglican and Royalist. They were required to make sure that new officeholders took the oaths and made the declarations set forth in the Corporation Act. In addition, they would soon be given the task of enforcing the Conventicle and Five Mile Acts, which made it an offence to attend any service other than that prescribed by the Anglican Prayer Book and prohibited ejected ministers from approaching within five miles of any corporate town where they had previously exercised their calling.

The Cavalier Parliament must have been aware that its policy to legislate nonconformity out of existence could never be entirely successful, and certainly not in traditional Puritan pockets such as Norwich. This result was assured when Parliament rejected both the toleration desired by the Independents and the comprehensive Church craved by the Presbyterians. The Act of Uniformity of 1662 locked the Presbyterians as well as the Independents outside the Church of England; henceforth they would all be nonconformists. The statutes which constitute the Clarendon Code were exceedingly harsh. Perhaps some of the citizens of Norwich who found Puritanism so comfortable during the Interregnum now preferred Anglicanism to persecution. On the other hand, the Puritan community had already weathered one Anglican persecution in which their ministers had been ejected and their forms of worship prohibited. They had learned not only how to survive but how to thrive in the midst of persecution. They had set up conventicles in the late 1630s and they would do so again thirty years later. Throughout the 1660s conventicles attended by hundreds were held by ejected ministers; there were also secret meetings of Quakers, Independents, and Baptists in Norwich.[1] On one occasion in 1663 the deputy-lieutenants of the city raided a nonconformist meeting and discovered between two and three hundred persons present.[2]

Given the prevalence of nonconformity in Norwich, the question

---

[1] S. W. Carruthers, 'Norfolk Presbyterianism in the Seventeenth Century', *Norfolk Archaeology*, XXX (1952), 89–100.

[2] *C.S.P.D.*, Chas II, 1663–4, p. 333: Wm. Newell to Williamson, 9 Nov. 1663. See also 1666–7, p. 179: [Thomas Cory] to Williamson, 3 Oct. 1666.

at the time was whether or not the magistrates and the bishop would strictly enforce the Conventicle and Five Mile Acts. Before the acts had been passed, the magistrates had already developed a reputation for leniency. Writing from Norwich in 1663, William Newell noted that but three or four indictments in 400 were against nonconformists, but at Yarmouth 200 men were punished for not taking the sacrament.[1] In 1663/4 one John Leverington was brought before the Mayor's Court on the charge of holding a conventicle in his home. The magistrates made him promise not to hold or attend conventicles in the future and then released him.[2] The Conventicle Act of 1664 authorized the aldermen, serving in their capacities as justices of the peace, to roam their respective wards and break into private homes if they thought illegal conventicles were being held there. However, there is no evidence that they did so, or that they made a serious effort in other ways to persecute nonconformists. This was also true of Bishop Reynolds, who had come into prominence as a divine of Presbyterian leanings during the Civil War, but supported General Monck, accepted the religious settlement, and was consecrated in 1661.[3] As bishop of Norwich until 1676, he was as favourably disposed towards nonconformity as Wren had been opposed to it.[4]

Nonconformity not only remained strong in the city; it also seems to have been determined to make inroads into political office. The case of William Barnham is instructive. Barnham had been elected to the Court of Aldermen in the purges of 1648/9, served as mayor in 1652, and was elected to Richard Cromwell's Parliament and the Convention Parliament. A well-known Presbyterian, he was removed from office by the Corporation Act commission in 1662.[5] In November of 1664 James Long, appointed

---

[1] ibid., 1663–4, p. 298: William Newell to Mr. Muddiman, 12 Oct. 1663.

[2] M.C.B. (1654–66), 10 Feb. 1663/4, 209^{r-v}. See also ibid., 512: Wm. Newell to Muddiman, 11 Mar. 1663/4.

[3] *V.C.H.: Norfolk*, II. 297–8; Abernathy, *Presbyterians*, pp. 45, 62–3, 80.

[4] Reynolds even went so far as to ordain privately several known Presbyterians who had not subscribed to conformity. *C.S.P.D.*, Chas II. 1665–6, p. 40: Newell to Muddiman, 3 Nov. 1665.

[5] In 1656 the widely-known Puritan preacher Thomas Moor died. Some of his sermons were then published and dedicated to Barnham and others. He remained a nonconformist to his death in 1676. In his will he left £5 to each of twelve nonconformist 'outed' ministers. Blomefield, *Norfolk*, II. 425; N.N.R.O., Norwich Archdeaconry Court, Wills Proved, 1676–7, 96^r–102^r.

by the commissioners to replace Barnham for the ward of Conesford, applied for and was granted a discharge from the aldermanry.[1]
On 31 November the Conesford freemen went to the polls and
elected Barnham despite, or perhaps in spite of, the Corporation
Act. When the mayor requested Barnham to take the required
oaths, he replied that he was growing old and was no longer a resident of the city, hence he could not accept the election.[2] This
would seem to have been a pretext. The new charter contained a
clause that would allow the Assembly to fine an elected alderman
up to £200 for refusal to take the oaths as well as prevent him from
taking office. Moreover, the Assembly Book records that Barnham
simply refused to take the oaths.[3] In either case, the magistrates
did not press the matter and the Conesford freemen were ordered to
elect another alderman. Apparently the freemen and Barnham were
undaunted. Four years later Barnham was again elected to the
Court of Aldermen, this time by the freemen of Wymer.[4] Again
Barnham refused to take the oaths. This time the magistrates
revealed a striking lack of resolve. Indeed, two weeks after the
election they received a letter from the Privy Council explicitly
ordering them not to accept any person into office who would not
fulfil the requirements of the Corporation Act.[5] Thus Barnham
was once again forced to renounce office, although this time he
freely admitted that he would not renounce the Covenant.[6]

The Barnham affair reveals one of the two major flaws in the
Corporation Act. National legislation was only as effective as the
will of local magistrates was to enforce it. Presumably the freemen
of Conesford and Wymer would not have elected Barnham if they
had believed that the statute would be upheld. Although Barnham
was kept out of office, later events suggest that the magistrates had

---

[1] Long lived outside Norwich and had pointed out to the Mayor's Court in
1662 that he could not conveniently get into the city for meetings of the magistrates; his petition for discharge was probably on the grounds of his non-
residence. M.C.B. (1654–66), [18–23] Dec. 1662, 184ᵛ. Long was required to
pay £150 for his discharge. A.B. (1642–68), 16 Nov. 1664, 250ᵛ.

[2] M.C.B. (1654–66), 14 Jan. 1664/5, 237ʳ.

[3] A.B. (1642–68), 16 Jan. 1664/5, 261ʳ.

[4] ibid. (1668–1707), 21 Sept. 1668, 2ᵛ.

[5] M.C.B. (1666–7), 3 Oct. 1668, 89ᵛ. The Privy Council ordered a circular
letter to be addressed to the sheriffs of all counties concerning enforcement of
the Corporation Act on 28 September 1668. Sacret, 'Municipal Corporations',
pp. 254–5.

[6] M.C.B. (1666–7), 14 Nov. 1668, 93ᵛ. There is no record that Barnham was
fined for this admission.

been indulgent to the point of being remiss in applying the oaths to new officeholders during the 1660s. The major flaw in the Corporation Act, however, was that it did not screen 'occasional conformists' from taking office. 'Occasional conformity' for political purposes had been born in the House of Commons during the first months of the Cavalier Parliament. At that time many Presbyterian members concluded that they could reconcile their nonconformist beliefs and practices with an occasional observance of Anglican rites and ceremonies in order to save their seats; hence they agreed to accept the Anglican sacrament and renounce the Covenant. When the Act of Uniformity went into effect in 1662, many Presbyterian and even some Independent ministers were willing to make the necessary occasional accommodation with conformity.[1] With these examples to follow, it would seem that few nonconformists elected to the Norwich magistracy after 1661 scrupled to take the Anglican sacrament or renounce the Covenant as required by the Corporation Act. Barnham was an exception. For those nonconformists who agreed with Barnham, one route open to them was to compound from office to avoid the risk of election.[2] The number of nonconformists elected to the magistracy after 1662 is not known because there is no available test for identifying the occasional conformist from the Anglican. What is known is that when the issue of nonconformity occupied the centre of the political stage in Norwich in the 1670s, many of the magistrates elected in the 1660s either sided with the Dissenters or were sympathetic to their cause.

Politically, the decade from 1663 to 1673 was uncommonly tranquil if compared with the civic turmoil of the decades which came before and after. There are no signs of bitterly disputed elections, conflicts between the corporation and the citizens, or

---

[1] For the issue of occasional conformity, see Lacey, *Dissent*, chap. II.

[2] In some towns the Corporation Act proved to be a blessing to men who wished to escape office and also avoid compounding: all they needed to do was to refuse to take the oaths and they would be disabled from assuming office. This could not be done in Norwich because fines for refusal to take the oaths were set down in the new charter and they were higher than the fees for compounding. For some unknown reason, the number of men who compounded from office and the fees they paid to do so were much higher after 1660. Possibly some of these compounders were nonconformists who could not in good conscience assume office if it entailed taking the oaths, but it is also possible that the major reason for the rise was the desire of the magistrates to increase city revenues by electing men they knew would compound. See Evans, 'Political Elite of Norwich', pp. 384–9.

factional hostilities within the magistracy. Religious tension seems to have been minimal. By far the greatest interruption in daily affairs was the devastating plague of 1666, which took over two thousand lives and caused considerable unemployment and hardship.[1] Moreover, relations between the corporation and Whitehall remained good, and local enthusiasm for King Charles did not subside. In May 1669, for example, the magistrates put aside £10 for gunpowder to celebrate the King's birthday and the date of the Restoration.[2] The popularity of the Crown reached a peak in September 1671, when Charles and his queen visited Norwich and were provided with the most sumptuous hospitality the city could muster.[3] The corporation was given only three weeks notice, but no expense was spared in making lavish arrangements.[4] The great spectacle and a chance to catch a glimpse of the King attracted people from throughout the county to streets already crowded with Norwich citizens. Anglicans, who always considered themselves to be the true Royalists, flocked to greet their King. Nonconformists, who were suffering under the Second Conventicle Act passed in 1670, looked to the King as their only hope of relief. Their hopes were not misplaced. Six months later Charles issued his Declaration of Indulgence which suspended the penal laws against Catholics and Dissenters. Shortly afterwards the nonconformists became bolder in both their public worship and their defiance of the Corporation Act. As the passions of religious factions heated up, the years of civic harmony and stability came to an end.

Private nonconformist meetings were beind held regularly in at least seven Norwich houses when the Declaration of Indulgence was issued.[5] Yet the benefits nonconformists derived from the Declaration were limited, short-lived, and followed by Anglican

---

[1] The bills of mortality may be found in *C.S.P.D.*, Chas II, 1666–7, *passim*. The plague lasted from June to December and peaked in August with 203 fatalities in one week.

[2] M.C.B. (1666–77), 26 May 1669, 110ʳ.

[3] A detailed account of the King's arrival and stay in Norwich is provided in a etter from Thomas Corie to ?, 2 Oct. 1671 in Robert H. Hill, ed., *The Correspondence of Thomas Corie, Town Clerk of Norwich, 1664–1687* [Norfolk Rec. Soc., xxvii] (Norwich, 1956), pp. 32–6.

[4] A.B. (1668–1707), 4 Sept. 1671, 21ʳ; Blomefield estimates that the total expense approximated £900, but a large portion of this fell on Henry Howard, who entertained the King at the Duke's Palace. Blomefield, *Norfolk*, III. 413.

[5] Carruthers, 'Norfolk Presbyterianism', p. 98. The houses were located in St. Martin at Oak, St. Stephen, St. Peter Mancroft, St. John Maddermarket, St. Andrew, and two in St. Peter Hungate.

retaliation. The penal laws were suspended, yet the Dissenters were permitted to conduct public worship only in locations approved by the government, and nonconformist ministers were required to obtain official licences. Catholics could worship only in private homes. The Anglican Church would remain intact and could not be criticized. This limited toleration nevertheless went much too far to satisfy most Anglican ministers and members of Parliament. Soon after Parliament reconvened in February 1672/3, Charles was pressured into revoking the Declaration. The Anglicans in Norwich decided that the time was ripe to strike back and demand enforcement of the old laws against nonconformists. On 3 May 1673, the members of the Assembly ordered half a dozen councilmen to appear before them and take the required oaths.[1] At the next meeting one of the councilmen complied, but four others refused to renounce the Covenant and the sixth did not bother to attend.[2] Three of these councilmen had served in the Council between 1667 and 1670, which strongly implies that the magistrates were not rigorously enforcing the Corporation Act in the late 1660s, at least not with respect to councilmen.[3]

The problem of the delinquent councilmen was further complicated by the magistrates. On 9 July the Mayor's Court decided to write to one of these councilmen, John Dearsley, of their intention to make him sheriff for the coming year.[4] This might imply that the majority of the magistrates supported the Presbyterians. On the other hand, only one week after agreeing on Dearsley, the magistrates forwarded a petition to the King complaining of the difficulty in getting public officials to take the oath against the Covenant.[5] Early in August Dearsley and the other councilmen who refused to deny the Covenant were removed from the Council and replaced.[6] This still left the problem of Dearsley's election as

[1] A.B. (1668–1707), 3 May 1673, 36ᵛ.

[2] ibid., 16 June 1673, 37ʳ. They were John Barnham, John Dearsley, Hugh Bokenham, and Roger Salter. Thomas Lombe was absent despite the Assembly's order for his appearance. Barnham is known to have had Dissenter meetings at his home. Carruthers, 'Norfolk Presbyterianism', p. 98.

[3] Barnham served for Wymer in 1667 and 1668, Lombe for Over-the-Water in 1666 and 1668, and Salter for Over-the-Water in 1669.

[4] M.C.B. (1666–77), 9 July 1673, 247ᵛ.   [5] ibid., 19 July 1673, 249ʳ.

[6] A.B. (1668–1707), 4, 5, 6, 14 Aug. 1673, 37ᵛ. The Assembly Book gives the reason for their dismissal to be their refusal to declare against the Covenant. After this date the Assembly Book carefully noted that each newly-elected councilman took the oaths and renounced the Covenant, whereas previously the only comment was that new councilmen were sworn into the Common Council.

sheriff. To make matters even more difficult, in late August the freemen elected Hugh Bokenham, another one of the displaced councilmen, to be their sheriff.[1] The Mayor's Court reacted in curious fashion: they sent two letters, one to Henry Howard and the other to Robert Southwell, requesting them to ask their friends in the Privy Council what to do in case the sheriffs-elect would not satisfy the provisions of the Corporation Act on the day appointed for their swearing-in. They also inquired whether the King and Council would be favourable to a petition requesting authority to order new elections in the event of the sheriffs refusing the oaths.[2] The final outcome is not clear. The magistrates received a letter from the Privy Council in September informing them what to do with sheriffs-elect who refused to abjure the Covenant.[3] Although the contents of the Crown's instructions are unknown, Dearsley and Bokenham retained their offices and in neither of the corporation books is there evidence that they agreed on 29 September to the oaths which they had refused to accept in August.

The flow of nonconformists into office continued after 1673. Bokenham and Dearsley both returned to the Council after serving as sheriffs, this time without apparent obstruction. John Leverington, who had been tried in the Mayor's Court for holding conventicles as early as 1663/4, returned to the Council in 1675.[4] In 1674 Robert Cooke, who was later accused of holding conventicles, was elected sheriff by the magistrates. How many other Dissenters were elected to the corporation during these years cannot be ascertained, but clearly the freemen and the magistrates were sponsoring nonconformists to office with regularity. With nonconformist strength in local political office growing, the Dissenters became more open in their worship. By December 1674, conventicles were organized for Sundays in a location known as the Granaries. According to one report, the Presbyterians were 'valueing themselves much upon his Majesty's Indulgence and promise of liberty of meeting'.[5] After the first meeting, two private citizens,

---

[1] M.C.B. (1666–77), 26 Aug. 1673, 252[r]. On 30 August the magistrates confirmed their election of Dearsley.

[2] ibid.   [3] ibid., 24 Sept. 1673, 254[v].

[4] ibid. (1654–66), 10 Feb. 1663/4, 209[r]. Leverington had been councilman for Mancroft between 1668 and 1672.

[5] The following description of the conventicle controversy is taken from a letter from Thomas Corie to Sir Joseph Williamson, 14 Dec. 1674 in Hill, ed., *Corie Correspondence*, pp. 36–7. See also *C.S.P.D.*, Chas II, 1673–5, pp. 454, 468: Richard Bower to Williamson, 9 Dec. 1674, and same to same, 16 Dec. 1674.

John Fawcett and Jacob Robbins, made a formal complaint to Mayor Watts, who together with two other justices of the peace convicted the Dissenters but imposed no penalties upon them. This encouraged an even greater number of Dissenters to turn up at the Granaries the next Sunday. With more courage than wisdom, Fawcett appeared in person and attempted to disrupt the meeting. Violently attacked and beaten, he fled for the protection of Alderman Bendish's home with the Presbyterians chasing in hot pursuit. A minor riot followed. The magistrates dutifully reported the incident to the King, adding that they would exercise the law unless otherwise ordered. Nevertheless, no action against the Dissenters was taken.

Several years later Fawcett went hunting for bigger game. He brought a case against Mayor Thomas Chickering for not carrying out the law against conventicles.[1] This was, of course, the logical thing to do: if the magistrates would not persecute the Dissenters then he would prosecute the magistrates.[2] Fawcett's presentation however, was not enough to convince a jury and Chickering was acquitted. This must have discouraged Fawcett considerably, for one account of the trial mentions that he and his supporters were prepared to bring additional suits against other magistrates if he won this case. By 1678 nonconformists or sympathizers to their movement were so entrenched in local office that the corporation was described by the new Bishop Sparrow as 'the worst corporation I thought that I had met with'.[3] If the Anglicans wanted to reverse the nonconformist trend in the city, which by 1678 could only be accomplished by coercing or cashiering many magistrates, they would need the assistance of a powerful outside force. At precisely this moment their prayers were answered and such a person arrived on the scene.

[1] Tanner MSS., 396, fo. 37. Chickering was elected mayor in 1676. Since the mayor for 1677 is mentioned, the trial probably took place sometime in 1677.

[2] The Second Conventicle Act (1670) set a fine of £100 for a justice of the peace who knowingly failed to take action. Fawcett was no doubt aware that this act also contained a provision which granted one-third of the fine collected to those who gave information leading to conviction. Kenyon, ed., *Stuart Constitution*, pp. 383–6.

[3] Tanner MSS., 39, fo. 36: Bishop Sparrow to Archbishop Sancroft, 1678. Sparrow was translated from Exeter to Norwich on 28 Aug. 1676.

Whigs, Tories, and Civic Instability, 1678–1690

In the tranquil years of the 1660s and early 1670s Norwich achieved a degree of political stability unknown since the 1630s. Religious conflict between Anglicans and Dissenters was sporadic and at times heated, but it did not interfere with peaceful government until 1678. In that year the lord lieutenant of Norfolk, Robert Paston, forced the city to accept his son in a parliamentary by-election despite the determined opposition of the mayor and other magistrates. Eager to reduce nonconformist strength in the magistracy and to extend his personal influence over the corporation, Paston then attempted with only partial success to drive his opposition from office. Paston's incursions into civic life ignited the old fires of faction and strife, which were further fanned by the Whig–Tory controversy in Parliament over the Exclusion Bill. In Norwich the Tory party, aided by Paston, was able to win all of the elections to the Exclusion Parliaments, capture the Assembly, and use its majority here to provide highly partisan propaganda for the King. The city Whigs, however, were not completely routed. They utilized their own voting strength in two wards, managed to contest some aldermanic elections successfully, and maintained their large but minority position in the Court of Aldermen. The confrontation between the two parties came in 1682. Intent on surrendering the city charter to the Crown, the Tories and Robert Paston encountered the resolute obstruction of Whig aldermen supported by a number of moderates. After months of an intense political struggle which completely disrupted city government, the Tories and Paston prevailed.

The new charter granted by Charles eliminated the remaining Whigs from city government and solidified the hold of the Anglican–Tories on municipal affairs and offices. However, with the death of Paston and with the Whigs safely removed from the political arena, previously simmering differences between the extreme and moderate wings of the Tory party came to the boil in an acrimonious conflict over the choice of a recorder. Once again city government came to a grinding halt, but early in 1684 the moderates prevailed and the Tories were once again united. The coronation of James II was warmly greeted by the corporation and during 1685 and early 1686 the Norwich Tories enjoyed their halcyon days. For this brief period of little more than one year the city Common Council, the Court of Aldermen, the Church, and the Crown agreed on basic political and religious matters. The local Anglican–Tory hegemony, however, suffered from two weaknesses: it did not possess the overwhelming backing of the freemen and, more important, it could be overthrown by the Crown. In late 1686 James abandoned his former allies because of their resistance to his plan to grant toleration to Catholics. The supremacy of the Anglican–Tories in local communities which had been engineered by Charles, was now seen by James to be a barrier in his attempt to link the Crown with the Whig–Dissenters, produce a new majority in Parliament, and repeal the Test Acts and penal laws. Thus James demanded changes in the officeholders of corporations in early 1688 and Norwich had little choice but to acquiesce. Nevertheless, when the old charter was restored in October 1688 and the Convention Parliament convened, the Anglican–Tories reasserted their hold. The Revolution of 1688 is most notable for bringing about a restoration of local autonomy for Norwich.

*   *   *

The politico-religious situation in Norwich in the mid-1670s bears a striking similarity to that which had existed in the mid-1630s. Following years of sporadic and ineffective enforcement of the laws against nonconformity, the citizens who preferred their own forms of worship to the required liturgy and ceremony of the state Church were faced with the portent of a severe and relentless persecution. The threat came from three directions. The first was the new bishop of Norwich, who was more insistent upon conformity and more closely attached to the High Church party than his predecessor. Bishop Sparrow, however, was a moderate man who believed more in conversion than persecution; he was hardly another Bishop Wren. More ominous was the growing identification of the Crown with the persecution-minded Anglicans in and out of Parliament. During the 1660s and early 1670s, Charles II had clearly demonstrated his preference for a tolerant and more comprehensive Church. His attempts to establish a Declaration of

Indulgence in 1662/3 and 1672 had led many Dissenters to place their trust in the Crown. Royal policy changed abruptly during 1674 and 1675. In a complete realignment of political factions, Charles forged an alliance with the High Church party and repression of nonconformists became evident early in 1675. For the first time since the 1630s, the monarchy was linked with the Anglican Church and was calling for stricter persecution of those who refused to conform to it. By 1676 two relatively well-defined and organized national parties were discernible and the Dissenters, for political as well as religious reasons, had lined up with the opposition to the Crown. Nevertheless, the major threat to Norwich Dissenters in the late 1670s did not come from Crown and Church, as it had in the 1630s. It came from Lord Robert Paston.

A personal friend of King Charles, Robert Paston received numerous favours from the Crown.[1] The eldest son of Baronet William Paston, who suffered sequestration for his loyalty to Charles I,[2] Robert travelled abroad during the Commonwealth and returned in 1660 to be knighted. His passion was politics and his politics were the defence of the King and the Anglican Church. At his death an admirer described him as having lived by only one rule: to defend the King's prerogative as the best way to secure the lives and liberties of the people. Religion and politics dictated his choice of friends, according to this eulogist, to the point that 'they loved him not who did not love the King, they loved him not who did not love the Church, and his service to the King and Church he valued more than he did their love'.[3] His links with the Crown were to be cemented by the marriage of his eldest son William to Catherine Boyle, a natural daughter of Charles. William also became a loyal servant of the King and eventually held the position of Treasurer of the Household under James II. Up to 1676 Robert had been very successful: a member of Parliament for Castle Rising from 1661 to 1673 and a gentleman of the Privy Chamber in 1666/7, he was named a deputy-lieutenant for Norfolk in 1661, became second Baronet Paston upon the death of his father in 1662/3, and was created Viscount Yarmouth in 1673.

[1] *D.N.B.*, s.v. Robert Paston; R. W. Ketton-Cremer, *Norfolk Portraits* (1944), pp. 22–57.

[2] Ketton-Cremer, *Norfolk*, pp. 191–7.

[3] John Hildeyard, *A Sermon Preached at the Funeral of the Right Honorable Robert, Earl and Viscount Yarmouth* (London, 1683), pp. 21, 23.

His influence in Norfolk affairs was then augmented by his appointment as lord lieutenant on 6 March 1675/6.

From the moment he became lord lieutenant, Paston devoted his energies to securing town and county for the King, an endeavour that preoccupied him up to his death in 1682/3. His tireless zeal in pursuing his objectives made him a controversial man of ardent friends and inveterate enemies in both Norfolk and Norwich. He even owed his premier position in the county to a controversy. A parliamentary by-election in 1675 had led the Earl of Danby to dismiss Horatio Townshend as lord lieutenant and replace him with Paston. This caused a rupture in Norfolk society which quickly expanded into sharp factional strife as leading county families aligned themselves with Paston, Townshend, and Sir John Hobart, a county M.P. who supported the opposition in Parliament.[1] The rift between Court and country factions would, in a few years, assume the form of a bitter struggle between county Tories and Whigs. Paston's appointment had an equally divisive impact on Norwich. His chaplain reported that 'the fanatic party at Norwich are much dissatisfied and they say begin to cry out popery (God knows with how little reason).'[2] On the other hand, Lord Lieutenant Yarmouth described his reception in Norwich later in the same month 'as beyond expression, and had the King himself been there, he could not have been more honored than his commission'. He added that the streets were so crowded that his coach could barely move forward; the windows and balconies were crammed with people, and joyous shouting filled the city.[3] Determined to transform the city into an Anglican–Royalist stronghold, Lord Yarmouth quickly became the mainstay for citizens supporting the Crown and the Church. He also represented something else which had not been seen in Norwich in more than a century: a powerful county magnate intent on manipulating civic affairs.

The first test of Lord Yarmouth's influence in the city came with the death of M.P. Christopher Jay and the by-election to replace him in February 1677/8. Jay had been ailing for some years. As early as 1675 at least three candidates, including Aldermen

---

[1] For Norfolk politics during this period see J. R. Jones, 'The First Whig Party in Norfolk', *Durham University Journal*, new ser. XV. i. (1953), 13–21.

[2] *H.M.C., 6th Report*, Ingilby MSS., p. 375a: John Gough to Lady Yarmouth, 8 Mar. 1675/6.

[3] ibid., p. 375b: Lord Yarmouth to his wife, 31 Mar. 1676.

Adrian Paine and Robert Bendish, were actively campaigning for his seat on the assumption that Jay was lying on his deathbed.[1] A year later, in 1676, Lord Yarmouth put forward as his own candidate, his son William. By-elections throughout the country were feverishly contested between Court and opposition factions in the late 1670s and Yarmouth knew that his son's candidacy would surely meet some obstruction. Nevertheless, his supporters in the city informed him that 'the royal citizens do not question but he will carry it for the burgess of this town, but there is a fanatic crew that will oppose all things that's just and good; but blessed be God we outnumber them.'[2] Jay finally died on 22 August 1677, and Paston forces were still confident of victory.[3] William Paston was so sure of his election that he continued his travels around the county. But Lord Yarmouth, who as a seasoned veteran of county politics understood that having a majority of the qualified voters was no guarantee that the election would be won, spent most of September and October in Norwich managing his son's campaign.[4] By late October Yarmouth was satisfied with the way things were going and wrote to his wife: 'My son's business at Norwich I think is fixed beyond the power of any opposition that's now to be raised.'[5]

Suspicious and cautious though he was, Lord Yarmouth had seriously underestimated the determination of his opposition within Norwich. In December a majority of the Court of Aldermen, led by Dissenter magistrates, spurned William Paston and nominated their own candidate, Alderman Augustine Briggs.[6] The choice of Briggs, who was a moderate Anglican and who quickly declared his refusal to stand against William Paston, seems curious. The strategy of the magistrates is clear: nonconformists in Norfolk and elsewhere had previously been active and successful in

[1] ibid., p. 374b: John Gough to Lady Yarmouth, 26 Nov. 1675.

[2] ibid., p. 381b: Thomas Clayton to same, 28 Dec. 1676.

[3] ibid., p. 382b: Jo. Doughty to same, 22 Aug. 1677; pp. 382b–383a: John Fisher to same, 22 Aug. 1677.

[4] ibid., p. 383a: William Paston to same, 2 Sept. 1677. William was buoyant: 'My lord hath used his interest with very good success here at Norwich concerning my being burgess, so that I think there will be no dispute at all of it . . .'

[5] ibid., p. 383b: Lord Yarmouth to same, 22 Oct. 1677.

[6] ibid., p. 384b: John Gough to Lord Yarmouth, 17 Dec. 1677. An unknown chronicler labelled the anti-Paston group who nominated Briggs as 'the faction of Presbyterians, Independents, Anabaptists, and others'. N.N.R.O., Norwich MSS. 453.

supporting moderate Anglican candidates.[1] But supporting a man who refused to stand was novel. Nevertheless, armed with a reluctant candidate whose protestations they ignored, the magistrates decided to seek outside assistance and do a little election fixing of their own. To offset Lord Yarmouth, Mayor John Richer, the leader of the resistance to Paston's election, appealed to and received the influential backing of Lord Townshend and the Hobarts of Blickling.[2] Startled by the sudden course of events, William Paston hurried to Norwich to prevent division within his ranks and to reiterate his resolve to serve the Crown through thick and thin.[3] Perhaps more important, his father was working behind the scenes and arranged for his two sons to be made freemen by the Assembly on 11 January.[4] Satisfied that he had patched up whatever damage had been done, Lord Yarmouth wrote to his wife that 'we are in as good a position to our election as we can well wish; but in these matters lies and stories will be everyday put abroad.'[5]

With the election only several weeks away, the Dissenters, a majority of the magistrates, and Mayor Richer were desperate, but resourceful. In an unprecedented manoeuvre, at least as far as seventeenth-century Norwich is concerned, the Mayor's Court admitted over 300 men to the freedom of the city so that they could vote against Paston. They then set aside considerable sums of money to provide beer, wine, and entertainment for those voters who would join their side.[6] As the day of the election drew near, the ideological aspects came to the foreground: the contest had become nothing less than a struggle between those for and those against King and Church. Expecting violence, Lord Yarmouth confided to his wife: 'People are so bold in talking against

---

[1] Lacey, *Dissent*, p. 104.

[2] *H.M.C., 6th Report*, p. 384b: John Doughty to William Paston, 21 Dec. 1677.

[3] ibid., p. 384b: Lord Yarmouth to Lady Yarmouth and same to same, 21 and 28 Dec. 1677.

[4] N.N.R.O., A.B. (1668–1707), 11 Jan. 1677/8, 63^r.

[5] *H.M.C., 6th Report*, p. 384b: Lord Yarmouth to Lady Yarmouth, 14 Jan. 1677/8.

[6] Norwich MSS. 453. According to this source, 'the other side [was] not behind them in these undue practices' of providing beer and entertainment. Percy Millican has found that 362 men were granted their freedom in January 1677/8. Millican, ed., p. xvi. For a listing of the new freemen see N.N.R.O., M.C.B. (1677–95), 11, 12, and 16 Jan. 1677/8, 14^r-17^r. On 19 January the Mayor's Court agreed that no more freemen would be admitted until after the M.P. elections.

the government that if I have not some instructions to suppress them they will be as ready for action as words.'[1] In a tense and hostile atmosphere, the election was held on 18 February. The nonconformists and their sympathizers were led to the market-place by Mayor Richer and Mr. Hobart. Presbyterian Alderman Mark Cockey had been chosen to stand in for Augustine Briggs, who made good his refusal to oppose Paston. According to one of Paston's supporters, the 'Dutch and Scottish' Cockey was con-fronted by a bold, honest fellow who presented him with a rotten Dutch cheese.[2] The tally was taken. William Paston carried the day by more than three to one.[3]

Lord Yarmouth had suffered more anxiety at the hands of Mayor Richer and his nonconformist colleagues than he could endure. On the eve of the election he wrote to Whitehall that Norwich could be the most loyal town in England if a number of leading citizens, who 'infect a party with anti-monarchical principles', were removed from the city.[4] He was especially incensed with Richer, whom he characterized as the 'impudentest fanatic in the world'.[5] Convinced that he could perform a great service to his King, Church, and country and at the same time obtain his revenge, Yarmouth wrote to Danby following the election that he wished permission 'to purge this bench of the goats and keep the sheep'.[6] The problem was to find a legal pretext to force Dissenter magistrates from office. By March he had discovered the tech-nicality he was looking for and informed Whitehall of his plan of attack: in the past the magistrates had taken the oaths but had neg-lected to subscribe their declarations against the Covenant as required by the Corporation Act and thus they were ineligible to assume office. If the Privy Council would provide an order for the freemen to proceed to new elections, some ten or twelve undesirable

---

[1] *H.M.C., 6th Report*, p. 385a: Lord Yarmouth to Lady Yarmouth, 4 Feb. 1677/8. Lord Yarmouth took it upon himself to apprehend one person who claimed that Oliver Cromwell was a better bred man than the King and uttered other seditious statements. Apparently the man was affluent, which led Yarmouth to comment that he was 'worth the fleecing if not the hanging'.

[2] ibid., p. 385b: John Gough to same, 18 Feb. 1677/8.

[3] The vote given by Gough (ibid.) was 2,163 for Paston and 672 for Cockey; these figures are corroborated in Norwich MSS. 453.

[4] *C.S.P.D., Chas II, 1677–8*, p. 634: Lord Yarmouth to Secretary Williamson, 8 Feb. 1677/8.

[5] *H.M.C., 6th Report*, pp. 384b–385a: Lord Yarmouth to Lady Yarmouth, 21 Jan. 1677/8.

[6] ibid., p. 385b: same to Lord Danby, 20 Feb. 1677/8.

aldermen could be removed from office and replaced by men loyal to the Crown.[1] Somehow Mayor Richer and the magistrates got wind of what Yarmouth was up to. Their reaction was to call a special meeting of the Court of Aldermen, subscribe the declaration against the Covenant, and enter the fact that they had done so in the Mayor's Court Book.[2] Nevertheless, the Anglican–Royalists were undeterred. Beginning on 18 March the freemen went to the polls in the yearly elections and voted eleven aldermen out of office. Mayor Richer, who was one of the dismissed aldermen, promptly declared the elections void and refused to swear in the newly-elected aldermen.[3]

There was little Lord Yarmouth or the Royalist citizens of Norwich could do to counteract Mayor Richer. An appeal to the Mayor's Court or an attempt to make the Assembly approve a petition for Whitehall was obviously of no use. Lord Yarmouth, on his own, was also hamstrung, and lamented: 'The mayor and aldermen are very brisk, and I do suppose the brisker because they see I have yet nothing from London.'[4] When the Royalist cause seemed all but lost, Yarmouth's influence at Court suddenly paid out a handsome dividend. On 28 March the King sent Mayor Richer a letter demanding that he swear in the newly-elected aldermen immediately.[5] But Richer stood his ground and refused to obey the royal command. For this act of defiance he was ordered on 5 April to appear in person before the Privy Council.[6]

---

[1] *C.S.P.D., Chas II, 1678*, p. 45: Lord Yarmouth to Williamson, 15 Mar. 1677/8.

[2] N.N.R.O., List of Signatories Against the Solemn League and Covenant, 1677–8. The listings for 9 March contain seventeen aldermen, but the Mayor's Court Book lists nineteen aldermen who subscribed. The three aldermen whose names appeared on neither list were R. Hawes, J. Lowe, and R. Bendish. As a close friend of Lord Yarmouth, Bendish was not in danger of losing his seat. M.C.B. (1677–95), 10 and 20 Mar. 1677/8, 20^r. The 10 March entry was written between the lines, which suggests that it may well have been added after the elections were held.

[3] Norwich MSS. 453; *H.M.C., 6th Report*, p. 385b: Lord Yarmouth to Lady Yarmouth, 22 Mar. 1677/8. The details of the election controversy were reported immediately to Whitehall. *C.S.P.D., Chas II, 1677–8*, pp. 536–7.

[4] *H.M.C., 6th Report*, p. 385b: Lord Yarmouth to Lady Yarmouth, 25 Mar. 1678.

[5] *C.S.P.D., Chas II, 1678*, pp. 76–7: King Charles to John Richer, 28 Mar. 1678.

[6] Complete details of Richer's reactions to the King's letter were sent by Lord Yarmouth to the Privy Council. *H.M.C., 6th Report*, pp. 385b–386a: Williamson to Lord Yarmouth, 6 Apr. 1678

By this time the affair was well known throughout the county. Sir John Hobart hastily penned a letter to Whitehall requesting them to deal leniently with Richer. On the other side, the Duke of Norfolk sped to Norwich in hopes of reprimanding the mayor personally, but when he arrived in the city he was chagrined to discover that the mayor had already departed for London.[1] It was thirty years to the month since another Norwich mayor, John Utting, had been summoned to London under somewhat similar circumstances and Richer was no doubt fully aware of what had happened on that occasion.

The case of the 'New Elected Aldermen' against the mayor was short and straightforward.[2] The Corporation Act stated explicitly that all office-holders were to take the oaths and subscribe against the Covenant at the same time that they took other oaths or else their election was void. The ancient charters specified that the freemen should choose new aldermen at the yearly elections to fill any vacancies on the Bench. Therefore, when the ward electorates gathered to select councilmen, the mayor was told that the aldermen who had not subscribed against the Covenant were out of office, and that their seats should be filled by an immediate poll. Since the newly-elected aldermen were properly elected according to the statute and the charter, Mayor Richer had exceeded his authority in refusing to swear them in. In conclusion, the case of the 'New Elected Aldermen' switched from legal argument to political persuasion: 'the mayor and the ejected aldermen are very factious', whereas 'the new elected aldermen are great Royalists and good Churchmen'. A verdict against Richer would provide a useful precedent for future action against several other corporations in the same circumstances.

Against these accusations and for his failure to execute the King's demands, Richer and his attorneys appeared before the Privy Council on 24 April and presented their defence.[3] Concern-

---

[1] *C.S.P.D., Chas II, 1678*, p. 89: Sir John Hobart to Williamson, 2 Apr. 1678: *H.M.C., 6th Report*, p. 386a: Lord Yarmouth to Lady Yarmouth, 8 Apr. 1678.

[2] P.R.O., S.P. Dom., Chas II, 63/140. This document has mistakenly been shelved with the state papers of 1661–2. Another copy may be found in Bodleian, Tanner MSS., 311, fo. 15. The names of the newly-elected aldermen are not known.

[3] Notes of this meeting were kept by Secretary Williamson and are preserved in S.P. Dom., Chas. II, 366/513. Williamson's abbreviations and almost illegible writing make the document unreadable in parts and in other places his use of sentence fragments is incomprehensible. The most complete account of the

ing the election, the mayor contended that all the aldermen had declared if not subscribed against the Covenant. At the time of the last elections he had sought the advice of legal counsel and they had agreed that the aldermanic seats were not void.[1] Nor, the defence continued, could Mayor Richer swear in the newly-elected aldermen without violating the charters which he had sworn to uphold. Richer had summoned the freemen to elect councilmen but not aldermen, and the charters stated that there should be no election of aldermen without a public summons issued by the mayor for that purpose. The principle involved was that all freemen were eligible to vote in the election of aldermen and thus prior notice was essential for fair elections. At the last elections some of the citizens may have stayed at home unaware that aldermanic elections were taking place;[2] hence the election of the new aldermen was invalid. As for the contempt charge, Richer argued ingeniously that if he recognized the legitimacy of the elections then he himself would no longer be an alderman and would thus possess no authority to swear in new aldermen. When pressed by the Privy Council, however, the mayor fell back on the position that he preferred the advice of his lawyers in the county to the commands of the Crown.[3] After Richer had completed his presentation, the Privy Council deliberated and settled on a compromise.[4] The removal of the aldermen who had taken office without subscribing against the Covenant had been proper, but the election of new

---

[1] A strict, literal interpretation of the Corporation Act would not require subscription. The Act states that the commissioners were to have the officers 'take and subscribe' the declaration against the Covenant, yet 'from and after the expiration of the said respective commissions the said three oaths and declarations shall be from time to time administered' by the proper officials. *Statutes of the Realm* (London, 1963), V. 321–3: An Act for the Well Governing and Regulating of Corporations.

[2] Events proved Richer to be correct, for in the March elections he was himself voted out of office, but in the second elections a month later he retained his seat.

[3] Williamson thought this admission so remarkable that he underlined it in his notes.

[4] *C.S.P.D., Chas II, 1678*, pp. 131–2: Declaration in Council, 24 Apr. 1678. The Council obtained the opinion of the Attorney General and two Lord Chief Justices in handing down the decision. The Privy Council's concern for the legal aspects of the case and its willingness to find a judicious compromise rather than impose its will in favour of the Royalists is noteworthy. In March and April there was widespread apprehension among opposition leaders that Charles might try to make himself an absolute monarch.

March elections seen from the mayor's point of view is found in Tanner MSS., 68, fo. 13.

aldermen was unacceptable because the freemen had not been properly summoned. Therefore, new elections should be held immediately and Richer was to be released so that he could return to Norwich and preside over them.[1]

With the second civic elections of 1678 on 29 and 30 April, Lord Yarmouth had an opportunity to prove his contention that the majority of freemen adhered to the Anglican–Royalist party. Only those aldermen who had been certified by the Corporation Act commission in 1662 were spared from re-election.[2] As Table 25 shows, this gave immunity to nine aldermen, not all of whom were by any means Anglican–Royalists. The other fifteen aldermen, regardless of their religious affiliation, were subject to recall. If the majority of freemen in each of the four wards had supported Anglican–Royalist candidates, they could have decisively altered the ideological composition of the Court of Aldermen and as a by-product guaranteed that the mayoralty would be held by an Anglican–Royalist for at least the next decade.[3] But this did not happen. The freemen of Conesford were the first to vote at the guild-hall.[4] They reinstated Thomas Chickering, who had been accused the year before of not enforcing the Conventicle Act during his tenure as mayor; and replaced Roger Hawes with Hugh Bokenham, who had refused to declare against the Covenant in 1673. The Dissenters, in short, were provided with a vote of confidence by this ward. In Mancroft and Wymer, however, they seem to have suffered losses. Nine of the twelve aldermen of these wards went up for re-election: seven were dismissed and only two were confirmed in office. There is no way to determine what the politico-religious stances of these two confirmed and seven newly-elected aldermen were in 1678, but five years later seven of the nine were unquestionably Anglican–Royalists.[5] Over-the-Water, long a

---

[1] ibid., p. 136: 27 Apr. 1678; N.N.R.O., Norwich Mayor's Book MSS., 27 Apr. 1678, p. 46.

[2] This was not the case in the March election, when several magistrates who became aldermen before 1663 were displaced. Tanner MSS., 68, fo. 13.

[3] All of the aldermen elected to the Bench before 1663 had completed tenure in the mayoralty. Thus the eligible candidates for future mayoral elections would be determined by the 29–30 April elections.

[4] A.B. (1668–1707), 29 and 30 Apr. 1678, 66ᵛ.

[5] The city received a new charter in 1682/3 which removed from office all magistrates who were not Anglican–Royalists. Davy, Freeman, Gardiner, Helwys, Osborne, Parmenter, and Vynn were maintained in office and Crowe was dismissed. Shildrake compounded out of office in 1678/9.

TABLE 25: *The Court of Aldermen in early March 1678*

Results of second election, 1678

CONESFORD
  *Augustine Briggs (1660/1)
  Roger Hawes (1665)   replaced by Hugh Bokenham
  *Henry Watts, Jr. (1662)
  *Thomas Wisse (1660/1)
  *Henry Woods (1662)
  Thomas Chickering (1664/5)   confirmed in office

MANCROFT
  *John Man (1650)
  Thomas Thacker (1664)   replaced by Jehosaphat Davy
  Adrian Paine (1673)   replaced by Francis Gardiner
  Jehosaphat Davy (1677)   replaced by Leonard Osborne
  Henry Crowe (1667)   confirmed in office
  Richard Wenman (1664/5)   replaced by William Parmenter

WYMER
  Mark Cockey (1670)   replaced by Jeremiah Vynn
  John Wrench (1669)   replaced by Nicholas Helwys
  Robert Freeman (1677)   confirmed in office
  *Robert Bendish (1660/1)
  John Wigget (1668)   replaced by William Shildrake
  *John Lawrence (1661)

OVER-THE-WATER
  John Lowe (1676)   confirmed in office
  John Richer (1664/5)   confirmed in office
  *Bernard Church (1647)
  John Manser (1662/3)   confirmed in office
  *Henry Herne (1662)
  John Todd (1677)   replaced by Mark Cockey

*already served as mayor
( ) = date elected to aldermanry
Note: The fifteen aldermen elected after 1662 are italicized; they were required to run for office in late April 1678 to be either confirmed or replaced.

nonconformist centre, was the last ward to vote. It kept Mayor Richer in office and cashiered one alderman in order to restore Mark Cockey, the unsuccessful M.P. candidate who had been dismissed earlier in the day by the freemen of Wymer. If the outcome of the elections reflects the political attitude of a majority of the freemen in their respective wards, then it would seem that

Conesford and Over-the-Water were nonconformist strongholds, whereas Mancroft and Wymer were in the grip of Lord Yarmouth's faction.[1]

In the political commotion which attended the aldermanic elections and the mayoral contest held the following day, patterns of magisterial recruitment which had been observed earlier in the decade were neglected. For reasons which are not clear, in late 1672 the corporation agreed to revert to the old seniority system in nominating and electing mayors.[2] In each of the five elections prior to 1678 the senior alderman under the chair had been elevated. A corresponding change in the election of aldermen also dates from late 1672. During the 1660s neither tenure in the shrievalty nor residence in the ward needing a replacement were necessary credentials for aspirants to the Bench, yet each of the five aldermen chosen from 1672 to 1678 was a past or present sheriff and four of them lived in the ward which elected them.[3] The freemen departed from this formula in 1678: three of the seven new aldermen had never served in the shrievalty and two others were not residents of the ward which elected them.[4] The determination of the Privy Council that the seats of aldermen elected after 1662 were void was interpreted to mean that all of the aldermen elected during the previous sixteen years lost their seniority. Thus all of the mayoral candidates on 1 May dated their entrance into the aldermanry with the elections of 28 and 29 April, regardless of whether they were newly elected or restored. In this context, one could argue that the election of Jehosaphat Davy, who had served on the Bench for less than one year, was not a breach of the seniority principle.[5] To prevent future confusions, in June the Mayor's Court established the order of precedence for aldermen who had never been mayor. The formula adopted was to list the aldermen according to the day and time on which they had been

[1] This is a realignment of the situation of the 1640s. During the Civil War Mancroft and Conesford were Royalist whereas Wymer and Over-the-Water were Puritan strongholds and supported Parliament.

[2] M.C.B. (1677–95), 24 Dec. 1672, 227ᵛ; A.B. (1668–1707), 24 Feb. 1672/3, 33ʳ. See Evans, 'Political Elite of Norwich', pp. 265–6.

[3] Residence is determined by N.N.R.O., Poor Rate Books, 1659–80 MSS.

[4] Osborne, Gardiner, and Shildrake had never been sheriffs; Bokenham lived in Mancroft and was elected for Conesford, and Parmenter was a resident of Conesford and was elected for Mancroft.

[5] Davy was chosen alderman on 6 July 1677; confirmed aldermen Crowe, Cockey, and Lowe were elected in 1667, 1670, and 1676 respectively.

elected. That is, Hugh Bokenham of Conesford was listed first, followed by the aldermen representing Mancroft, Wymer, and Over-the-Water respectively.[1]

Had Lord Yarmouth's efforts been in vain? Did the second aldermanic elections convert the magistracy from a nonconformist to an Anglican–Royalist body? Bishop Sparrow was convinced, at least initially, that great gains had been made. Following the election of Davy, he wrote to Archbishop Sancroft: 'Norwich . . . is now much changed by our new choice of aldermen, which I hope will hold good, and by a new steward, an able lawyer and a hearty man to the Church . . . and by a very honest mayor, who promises me to be careful of his office, and to be ready to receive advice.'[2] He commenced another letter: 'I much rejoice that his Majesty is so well pleased with the good success of his regulation of our city.'[3] The election of Davy to succeed Richer provided the Anglican–Royalists with the first mayor in several years to hold their point of view. This was a definite advantage. Later in the year, for example, the Mayor's Court declared that the magistrates should receive the sacrament collectively at the Cathedral on the first Sunday in October, a decision which elated Bishop Sparrow.[4]

But Sparrow exaggerated the situation: the second elections may not have changed the balance of power within the magistracy. Only a few of the aldermen can be identified with one or other of the two factions on the basis of their actions in 1678. However, if their positions five years later may be taken as a gauge of their stance in 1678, then the Court of Aldermen seems to have been evenly split between nonconformists and their sympathizers on the one hand and Anglican–Royalists on the other.[5] Perhaps more to

---

[1] M.C.B. (1677–95), 15 June 1678, 24ᵛ. The order of precedence was Bokenham, Gardiner, Osborne, Crowe, Parmenter, Vynn, and Helwys, Freeman, Shildrake, Lowe, and Cockey. Gardiner, Osborne, Vynn, Helwys, and Shildrake had not completed tenure in the shrievalty.

[2] Tanner MSS., 39, fo. 36: Bishop Sparrow to Archbishop Sancroft, n.d.

[3] ibid., fo. 64: same to same, 15 July 1678.

[4] ibid., fo. 125: same to same, 14 Oct. 1678; M.C.B. (1677–95), 28 Aug. 1678, 30ᵛ. Sparrow does not mention which magistrates appeared, but he considered the unprecedented occasion as a gesture of loyalty to the Church.

[5] Thirteen of the fifteen newly-elected and confirmed aldermen were still members of the Bench in 1682/3. So also were five of the nine aldermen whose tenure dated from or before the Corporation Act commission and whose seats were safe in 1678. Five of the thirteen in the first group and two of the five in the second group were removed from office by the new charter of 1682/3. Of the six aldermen of 1678 who left office before 1682/3, at least one (Chickering) is

the point, events during the summer of 1678 suggest that Richer and his following remained a slight majority or, at least, a large minority in the Court of Aldermen. When the newly-elected and confirmed aldermen assembled on 30 April to subscribe against the Covenant, for example, all complied except Hugh Bokenham, who conveniently disappeared from the chamber just before the oaths and declarations were taken. Yet the magistrates did not declare his election void.[1] More positive evidence of the strength of the nonconformist group was manifested in July when the aldermen divided eleven to seven in favour of requesting Dissenter John Barnham to be their next sheriff.[2]

A rather bizarre episode in July involving the Presbyterian minister John Collins reveals how mistaken Bishop Sparrow was in his belief that the remodelled magistracy strongly supported the Church. At least as early as the parliamentary by-election, Lord Yarmouth was resolved to eject Collins from the ministry.[3] Bishop Sparrow had already assured him that proceedings would be commenced against Collins as soon as the election was over.[4] No action, however, seems to have been taken and Collins remained active in his opposition to the Anglican–Royalists. In July rumours reached Lord Yarmouth of a plot on Bishop Sparrow's life.[5] Taking the rumours seriously, he ordered Mayor Davy to issue warrants to the suspects and apprehend them; and one of them was Collins. The mayor complied. At a subsequent Quarter Session, to which all the justices of the peace had been summoned, only Alderman Robert

---

[1] Norwich MSS. 453; Signatories Against Solemn League and Covenant, 1677–8. Bokenham was finally prevailed upon to subscribe the declaration against the Covenant on 18 May 1678,

[2] M.C.B. (1677–95), 13 July 1678, 27ʳ. This was the only instance from 1620 to 1690 that the Mayor's Court Book recorded a vote on a prospective sheriff. Barnham then compounded out of office for £120. A.B. (1668–1707), 26 Aug. 1678, 68ᵛ.

[3] *H.M.C., 6th Report*, p. 385b: Lord Yarmouth to Lord Danby, 20 Feb. 1677 8.

[4] ibid., p. 385a: Lord Yarmouth to Lady Yarmouth, 8 Feb. 1677/8.

[5] *C.S.P.D., Chas II, 1678*, pp. 306–7: Lord Yarmouth to Williamson, 22 July 1678.

---

known to have supported Richer's group and the other five (Watts, Woods, Shildrake, Lawrence, and Herne) cannot be determined with certainty. Lastly, John Lowe, mayor in 1682, was not removed from office by the new charter even though he was not sympathetic to the Anglican–Tory cause. Thus, the magistracy of mid-1678 was composed of ten future Anglican–Tories, nine future Whigs, and five unknowns.

Bendish showed up. One of Lord Yarmouth's agents in the city observed that from this 'your lordship may judge how they stand affected to his Majesty's government'.[1] Despite this attempt to destroy him, Collins remained in the city and was one of the Dissenter leaders in the early 1680s. One Tory then described him as 'a man of some learning, which he employs in promoting Presbytery, and were he removed 'tis probable many of that sect would fall off'.[2]

*   *   *

From 1679 to 1682 national affairs were dominated by the exclusion crisis. In three successive Parliaments the Whig party attempted to overcome the determined opposition of the Crown and the Tory party, and pass legislation which would exclude James from the line of succession to the throne. The struggle should properly be viewed as a continuation of the prior conflict between 'Court' and 'country' interests in Parliament which had been heating up since 1674. After 1678, however, the rival camps were better disciplined and possessed more established leadership, the hostility between them was more pronounced, and the issues were more carefully defined and uncompromising. In addition, both parties recognized that parliamentary elections were crucial and thus they were better organized, more active, and less scrupulous than before in waging local electoral campaigns. A direct result of this was that the provinces, which had for the most part receded into local insularity during the long eighteen-year duration of the Cavalier Parliament, were increasingly drawn into national affairs by the fight of local Whigs and Tories for county and borough seats.

The intensity of the conflict in Norfolk and Norwich was perhaps unparalleled outside London. Partisan politics combining a mixture of local and national concerns and including fiercely contested parliamentary elections were already well advanced in the county and city before 1679, as has already been stressed. They became even more frenzied during the following years. Given Lord Yarmouth's fixation with national politics and his heavy-handed obsession with local political manipulation, this was to be expected.

---

[1] *H.M.C., 6th Report*, p. 386b: Thomas Corie to Lord Yarmouth, 22 July 1678.

[2] *C.S.P.D. Chas II, 1682*, pp. 54–6: no author, 2 Feb. 1681/2.

The focal points for county politics continued to be Lord Yarmouth, Lord Townshend, and John Hobart.[1] Differences of opinion on national political issues were marked, but it was the presence of long-standing family rivalries and jealous personal enmities which gave an added virulence to Norfolk politics.[2] Faction was so rife that defendents in Quarter Sessions were judged innocent or guilty on the basis of their political affiliation and county business meetings were reduced to little more than quarrelsome debates. Politics in Norwich were equally contentious, although the animating factor here was religion. The Privy Council was informed in 1681/2 that Norwich citizens could be divided into 'violent Tories and violent Whigs, as they are called, and the moderate men'.[3] Travelling through Norwich in 1681, Humphrey Prideaux commented: 'This town I find divided into two factions, Whigs and Tories ... and both contend for their way with the utmost violence. I do not believe that any place can afford of either part more vehement votaries to it than in this town.'[4] Even Bishop Sparrow found that his views were too moderate for the city's Anglican extremists. Writing to Sancroft in 1681/2, he complained that he was constantly confronted by many people clamouring against him for persecuting schismatics on the one hand and by others equally adamant that he 'proceed violently beyond the rules of law'.[5]

The use of the terms Whig and Tory by contemporaries in describing affairs in Norwich underlines the similarity of issues on the national scene and in the city. The Whig party in Parliament consisted of at least five diverse groups united on the central issue

---

[1] A report to the Privy Council in 1681/2 states that Lord Yarmouth led the Anglican-Tory group and 'such as are disaffected to the government herd themselves with Sir John Hobart, who having been one of Oliver's lords, still retains a respectful memory for his master and his cause, and, so to what appears, would stick at nothing to promote it again'. *C.S.P.D., Chas II, 1682*, pp. 54–6. The document is also reproduced in Mason, *History of Norfolk* (London, 1882–5), I. 367–8.

[2] Lord Townshend, for example, was politically neutral, but apparently joined Hobart through no other motivation than his resentment of being displaced as lord lieutenant by Lord Yarmouth, whom he considered socially inferior to himself.

C.S.P.D., Chas II, 1682, pp. 54–6.

[4] Edmund Maunde Thompson, ed., *Letters of Humphrey Prideaux, sometime dean of Norwich, to John Ellis, sometime undersecretary of state, 1674–1722*, [Camden Society] (1875) p. 90.

[5] Tanner MSS., fo. 228: Sparrow to Sancroft, 8 Feb. 1681/2.

of exclusion.[1] The Norwich Whigs cannot similarly be broken down into subgroupings owing to lack of information on the motivation of individual members, but most probably the largest portion of them would fall into the category referred to by J. R. Jones as 'old Presbyterians'. The unifying elements at the outset were nonconformity and resentment of Yarmouth's meddling. This is not to say that all Whigs were conventiclers, but they were sympathetic to them and attempted to prevent their persecution. On the other side, the Tories opposed nonconformity, resolutely buttressed Yarmouth's actions, and rallied to the Crown against the exclusionists. The rival groups in the city may properly be referred to as parties, not only because they were divided over religious and political issues, but also because the voting patterns in contested elections reveal electoral organization and management. Each party had an identifiable leader who maintained disciplined and organized voter support. For the Whigs this was Alderman John Man, the wealthiest man in town and an ex-Commonwealthman; for the Tories it was Lord Yarmouth himself, who lived only seven miles outside the gates of Norwich and kept in constant touch with his followers in the city.[2]

The dominant theme of these troubled years in Norwich was the triumph of the local Tory party and the extension of Lord Yarmouth's influence over the corporation. Yarmouth's first concern, of course, was to continue his control over parliamentary elections. He was successful in the city but not in the county. In May 1678, three months after the by-election triumph of William Paston, another city by-election was held to replace Francis Cory, deceased. Augustine Briggs, standing on his own rather than as a Dissenter candidate, won the election. Lord Yarmouth was especially pleased with Brigg's high praise for the Paston family in his victory speech.[3] The Cavalier Parliament was finally dissolved in

[1] J. R. Jones, *The First Whigs: The Politics of the Exclusion Crisis, 1678–1683* (London, 1961), pp. 9–19.

[2] *C.S.P.D., Chas II, 1682*, pp. 54–6. The twin issues of nonconformity and municipal independence from county control were the key factors in determining political alignments in other towns. See, for example, M. Mullett, 'The Politics of Liverpool, 1660–88', *Transactions of the Historic Society of Lancashire and Cheshire*, 124 (1972), 31–56.

[3] *H.M.C., 6th Report*, p. 386a: Lord Yarmouth to Lady Yarmouth, 17 May 1678. In 1681/2 Briggs was described as 'an honest old Cavalier' and leader of the moderate Tory faction. *C.S.P.D., Chas II, 1682*, pp. 54–6. Both Paston and Briggs received a triple 'vile' rating from Shaftesbury. K. H. D. Haley, 'Shaftesbury's Lists of the Lay Peers and Members of the Commons, 1677–8', *Bulletin of the Institute of Historical Research*, 43 (1970), 99.

January 1678/9 and in February the elections to what was to become the first of the three Exclusion Parliaments were held. Few of these elections were contested along party lines, but Norfolk and Norwich were an exception.[1] In the city the extreme Royalists started a movement to replace Briggs with a less moderate candidate, but this was deemed too risky, and abandoned.[2] In an extremely controversial county election, Yarmouth's two candidates outpolled Sir John Hobart, only to have the election voided by the House of Commons.[3] In a second election, Hobart prevailed. The County Whigs swamped Yarmouth's candidates in the August election of 1679 for the second Exclusion Parliament, but the Tory party in the city managed, once again, to return Briggs and Paston despite rumours circulated by their opposition that they were pensioners of the King.[4] Briggs and Paston were also successful in their bid for election to the short-lived Oxford Parliament of March 1681, although Hobart and Sir Peter Gleane, with Lord Townshend's assistance, soundly defeated the Tories for the county seats.[5]

The ability of the Norwich Tories to maintain a majority in the Assembly and to mobilize their strength here for partisan political purposes is as impressive as their unblemished record in parliamentary elections. A sign of their loyalty to Lord Yarmouth in 1678 was a successful defence against the writs of restitution filed by five of the aldermen ejected from office in the second elections of that year.[6] The Assembly also took action to ensure that the major officials chosen to assist the corporation were men loyal to

[1] Jones, *First Whigs*, p. 40.

[2] *H.M.C., 6th Report*, p. 387b: George Stebbing to Colonel Paston, 29 Jan. 1678/9; Jones, *First Whigs*, pp. 96–7.

[3] J. R. Jones, 'Restoration Election Petitions', *Durham University Journal*, new ser. 22 (1961), pp. 52–6.

[4] The Norwich election took place on 1 September 1679. Robert Paston was created Earl of Yarmouth in 1679 at his own request to prove that he was still in the King's favour despite the disgrace of Danby. The vote was Paston 1,415, Briggs 1,217, Alderman Adrian Paine 958, and Recorder Francis Bacon 838. *H.M.C., 7th Report*, Frere MSS. p. 532b: Edward L'Estrange to Lady Yarmouth 27 Aug. and 3 Sept. 1679; M.C.B. (1677–95), 27 Sept. 1679, 54^v-55^r; Jones, *First Whigs*, pp. 96–7.

[5] *C.S.P.D., Chas II*, 1682, p. 54.

[6] Aldermen Paine, Thacker, Todd, Wigget, and Wrench filed writs of restitution in May 1678. The Assembly fought the case in King's Bench to a successful conclusion in 1679. A.B. (1668–1707), 24 May and 11 Oct. 1678, and 16 June 1679, 68^r, 69^v, 74^r; Tanner MSS., 38, fo. 28: Mr. John Hobart to Sir John Hobart, 21 May 1679.

the lord lieutenant. By early 1680 Yarmouth could count on Town Clerk Thomas Corie and Steward John Norris to advance his interest, but Recorder Francis Bacon had proved to be an unwanted obstacle.[1] Bacon, who had previously been the city steward, was elevated in May 1678 following the death of recorder and M.P. Francis Cory.[2] In the summer of 1678, Bacon refused to assist Mayor Davy in investigating the case against John Collins; the following year he ran against William Paston in the parliamentry elections.[3] Twice before, in 1644 and 1660, the Assembly had removed the recorder from office for purely political reasons, and Bacon was an obvious target for the Tories. In May 1680 the Assembly voted him out, elevated Norris to the recordership, and made John Mingay the new steward.[4] Bacon succeeded in obtaining a writ of mandamus, but his efforts to gain restitution failed and the following year the Assembly took the unusual step of appointing Norris to a life tenure.[5]

As the debate on the exclusion issue spread from the halls of Parliament to the provinces in 1680 and 1681, the Assembly proclaimed its unequivocally Tory opinions on national affairs. Its first contribution to the propaganda struggle came in the aftermath of the decision by Charles to prorogue the second Exclusion Parliament (which was to begin in October 1679) before it had even assembled. Aware that the recent elections had strengthened their position, the Whig leaders organized local petitions demanding the meeting of Parliament and the preservation of the Protestant religion.[6] The revitalized Tories retaliated whenever they could with a purge of Whigs, especially the promoters of petitions, from local office. The procedure used in boroughs was to send orders to put the Corporation Act into execution. Possibly the Tories had in mind the purge of 1678 in Norwich as a desirable precedent and

[1] For Steward Norris see Bishop Sparrow's comment cited above. In 1681/2 Thomas Corie was labelled one of the 'violent Tories'. *C.S.P.D., Chas II, 1682,* p. 54. Corie had been town clerk since 1664 and Norris was appointed steward in May 1678.

[2] Norwich MSS. 453.

[3] *H.M.C., 6th Report,* p. 386b: Thomas Corie to Lady Yarmouth, 22 July 1678.

[4] A.B. (1668–1707), 11 and 18 May 1680, 79^v.

[5] ibid., 18 May, 3 and 21 June 1680, 6 and 21 June 1681, 80^r, 80^v, 90^v, 92^r; M.C.B. (1677–95), 15 May 1680, 66^v.

[6] For details see Jones, *First Whigs*, pp. 115 ff.

model. At the height of the Whig–Tory pamphlet warfare in the spring of 1680, the Assembly, possibly at Yarmouth's urging, sent its own petition to the King.[1] The address condemned 'all traitorous petitions imposing upon your Majesty against your royal prerogatives', and thanked the King for preserving their rights and liberties and 'for encouraging the execution of the laws against the adversaries and enemies of the Church of England'. The Assembly also heartily congratulated Charles on the safe return of his brother. The petition concluded with a declaration 'to maintain and defend your Majesty's person and government, your heirs and lawful successors to the utmost of our powers'.

The second Exclusion Parliament finally convened in October 1680, but was dissolved the following January before the Whigs had achieved their objectives. Bitterness between rival sides reached an intensity unknown since 1642 as Whigs and Tories quickly made preparations for elections to the Oxford Parliament. The Whig propaganda press attempted to convince voters that liberty, property, and religion were in peril; only the election of Whigs could save the country.[2] As a means of influencing parliamentary opinion after the election, Whig constituencies sent instructions to newly-elected members directing them to support Whig proposals and in particular to refuse grants of money until the Exclusion Bill had been passed.[3] The Tories quickly recognized the value of this propaganda technique and in emulation the Norwich Assembly sent its own instructions to Paston and Briggs.[4] Thanking them for their services in defending the King and the established government, the Assembly went on to state its approval of the 'punishing and suppressing [of] all seditious and scandalous libellers of his [Charles's] person and government'. As a pledge of loyalty and affection to the Crown, subsidies in whatever amount was requested by Charles should be granted unconditionally. The corporation hoped, however, that Charles would use the money to secure the country from popery and faction alike. William Paston wrote back that these instructions were shown to the King, who

[1] A.B. (1668–1707), 3 May 1680, 79ʳ. The address to Charles was sent in a letter to Lord Yarmouth.

[2] Jones, *First Whigs*, pp. 156–67.

[3] ibid., pp. 167–73; M. Dorothy George, 'Elections and Electioneering, 1679–1681', *English Historical Review*, 45 (Oct. 1930), 552 ff.

[4] A.B. (1688–1707), 24 Feb. 1680/1, 84ᵛ.

was very pleased and declared his intention of bestowing his royal favour on the city in the future.[1]

The dissolution of the Oxford Parliament, which lasted less than one month, was met with a mixture of disillusionment and scorn by the Whigs, but with unqualified joy by the Norwich corporation. The Assembly spelled out its attitude on a wide range of national issues in an extraordinary letter to the King on 3 May.[2] Charles was to be commended for maintaining the legitimate succession and the rights of the Crown 'against the arbitrary proceedings of the House of Commons'. The 'timely' dissolutions of past Parliaments was applauded, as was the King's refusal to sign Whig legislation. True to the initial Anglican–Royalist stance, popery and nonconformity were denounced in the same breath and vigorous execution of laws against both religious groups was prayed for. If the King were to summon another Parliament, the Assembly would exert its influence to elect M.P.s who 'shall readily and willingly support your Majesty's occasions'. In a repudiation of Whig rhetoric, the letter continued that 'the convening of Parliament to any place, managing, dissolving, or proroguing the same is the unquestioned right of your Majesty'. The Assembly concluded with the resolution that they would stand by the Crown and proper succession against 'all the popish plots and the vile attempts of all that retain their old Commonwealth principles (by which your father of blessed memory was barbarously murdered)'. Lord Yarmouth wrote to the corporation that the petition was read to the King at Windsor by Earl Conway and it was very gratefully received.[3] Nevertheless, a Whig-packed jury in Middlesex declared the address libellous and fined a printer for circulating copies of it.[4] The Norwich Assembly was incensed. In a vindication of its declaration, the Assembly charged that for anyone to find libel in the address was itself libellous. The sole motivation behind the

[1] William Paston to Norwich corporation, 5 Mar. 1680/1 in ibid., 16 Mar. 1680/1, 85ᵛ.

[2] Mayor, etc of Norwich to King Charles, 3 May 1681 in ibid., 3 May 1681, 89ʳ⁻ᵛ. The letter was not necessarily spontaneous, for on 8 April Yarmouth recommended that Norfolk send a loyal address to Charles. *H.M.C., 7th Report*, p. 533a: Lord Yarmouth to Edward L'estrange, 8 April 1681.

[3] Earl of Yarmouth to City of Norwich, 10 May 1681 in A.B. (1668–1707), 20 May 1681, 90ʳ. See also *H.M.C., 7th Report*, p. 533a: Earl of Yarmouth to Edward L'Estrange, 8 Apr. 1681.

[4] *C.S.P.D., Chas II, 1680–1*, p. 285: newsletter of 17 May 1681: Jones, *First Whigs*, pp. 186–7.

letter, the corporation asserted, was to publicize its obedience to Charles, his heirs and successors and to the established government in Church and state.[1]

The success of Lord Yarmouth's party in each of the five parliamentary elections from 1677/8 to 1682 and the strong Anglican–Royalist declarations of the corporation during this period would suggest that the supremacy of the Tories in the city was without serious challenge. Parliamentary election tallies, for example, favoured the Tories over the Whigs by a ratio of 3:2. These figures, however, may give a distorted impression of the relative numerical strength of the two parties in the city owing to the influence and energetic campaigning of Lord Yarmouth.[2] Contemporaries disagreed on which party was more numerous. In 1681/2 one observer concluded: 'the disaffected are but an inconsiderable party in the city, and have little influence in public business, the greater and governing part being firm to the King's interest.'[3] On the other hand, a visitor to Norwich in mid-1681 thought that the Whigs were 'more numerous, but the latter [Tories] carry all before them as consisting of the governing part of the town'.[4] The near parity between the two parties would explain how the Whigs could lose each of the parliamentary elections and yet capture three of the four mayoral contests after 1678. They also continued to elect new aldermen and this enabled them to maintain their strength in the Court of Aldermen.

The four mayoral elections from 1679 to 1682 do not conform with the seniority principle honoured during the 1670s and reveal a perplexing political inconsistency. The Mayor's Court had carefully defined the seniority of aldermen under the chair in June 1678 and Alderman Hugh Bokenham was placed at the top of the list. In 1679, however, Henry Crowe was elected mayor.

---

[1] M.C.B. (1677–1695), 28 May 1681, 89ʳ; A.B. (1668–1707), 6 June 1681, 90ᵛ–91ʳ.

[2] The unknown author of the report to the Privy Council commented: 'The Lord Lieutenant of the county has had a great interest in the city, and the choice of members of Parliament has been much influenced by him.' *C.S.P.D., Chas II, 1682*, pp. 54–6. Another and at times crucial factor in M.P. elections was, of course, the attitude of the sheriffs. Unfortunately, not enough is known about the eight sheriffs elected from 1678 to 1682 to permit generalizations. There is no evidence, however, that the sheriffs were improperly managing borough elections and the House of Commons did not question their returns.

[3] *C.S.P.D., Chas II, 1682*, pp. 54–6.

[4] Prideaux to ?, 17 Aug. 1681 in Thompson, ed., *Prideaux Letters*, p. 90.

Crowe's tenure on the Bench dated from 1667, which made him the senior alderman under the chair if the Mayor's Court readjustment of seniority was ignored. If this was the procedure to be followed, Mark Cockey would have become mayor in 1680, followed by John Lowe in 1681, yet Robert Freeman was chosen mayor in 1680. Departure from seniority may also be noted in the elections of Bokenham and Lowe in 1681 and 1682 respectively. Presumably the freemen dispensed with the rigidity of seniority in order to voice their political preference; this, at least, is what had occurred in somewhat similar circumstances during the early 1640s. If this was the case, the alternation of Whig and Tory mayors is difficult to account for. Jehosaphat Davy, mayor-elect in 1678, supported the Anglican–Royalist faction, yet Crowe proved to be a strong Whig, and Robert Freeman was a moderate Tory.[1] The Assembly Book unfortunately does not record the nominees for mayor in 1679 and 1680, and thus it is not possible to determine whether the freemen forced the magistrates to select a mayor who was affiliated with a particular political party, or whether the magistrates were given the opportunity to choose from two nominees of opposed political viewpoints. In 1681 and 1682, however, both nominees were Whigs or Whig sympathizers.[2]

The choice of mayor was of great importance in determining the policy of the magistracy towards nonconformity. In 1678 the magistrates had taken the Anglican sacrament in the Cathedral; in 1680, during the mayoralty of Freeman, they repeated this symbolic gesture and promised Bishop Sparrow that they would 'do their duties in curbing the pride of the Dissenters'.[3] There is no evidence of similar appearances by the mayor and his colleagues during the mayoralties of Crowe and Bokenham. Most important was that the mayor presided over the Mayor's Court and Quarter Sessions, and thus the persecution of nonconformists depended mostly on his attitude.[4] Accordingly, conventiclers were attacked relentlessly during the mayoralties of Davy and Freeman, but a

[1] Brit. Lib., Add MSS., 27448, fo. 74: W. Cecil and J. Houghton to Lord Yarmouth 5 June 1682.

[2] The freemen nominated Bokenham and Lowe in 1681 and Thomas Cooke and Lowe in 1682. Cooke was removed from office by the 1682/3 charter.

[3] Tanner MSS., 37, fo. 114: Sparrow to Sancroft, 11 Aug. 1680.

[4] Arthur J. Eddington, *The First Fifty Years of Quakerism in Norwich* (London, 1932), p. 99.

lenient policy was carried out by the Court under Crowe and Bokenham.[1]

The aldermanic elections of these four years reveal a definite pattern in which the politico-religious factor was critical. The freemen of the respective wards desired a resident ex-sheriff of their own political persuasion and, if no man with these three qualifications was available, then the freemen chose an ex-sheriff of their own political leaning from another ward. On the basis of the 1678 elections, Mancroft and Wymer would be expected to vote Tory and Over-the-Water and Conesford to vote Whig. This is precisely what happened. No elections were held in Mancroft during this period, but the freemen of Wymer elected William Helwys and William Salter in 1679 and 1681 respectively. Both were ex-sheriffs and Tories. Helwys was not a resident of Wymer, but at the time of his election in 1679 the only resident ex-sheriff in the ward was Whig Robert Cooke. Whig-dominated Over-the-Water had confirmed Richer and restored Cockey in 1678. In 1680 the ward elected another ejected alderman, John Wrench, who was a resident of Over-the-Water, and like Richer and Cockey, was soon to be dismissed from office by the Tories. Conesford had three elections between 1678 and early 1682. In 1679 the freemen chose resident ex-sheriffs Simon Wissiter and Thomas Cooke. In early 1682 the freemen went to the polls and, with no resident ex-sheriffs to choose from settled on Robert Cooke of Wymer. Wissiter died in 1682 and both Cookes found themselves out of office by 1683.

The election of Robert Cooke in April 1682 draws attention to the crucial role played by religion in the election of magistrates. The need for an election resulted from a petition to the Assembly dated 24 February 1681/2 and signed by twenty-five Conesford citizens who demanded the dismissal of Alderman Henry Woods from the Court.[2] One of the complaints against Woods was that he did not look after the poor, and more to the point that he willingly absented himself from his parish church just before the Anglican sacrament was administered. In addition, the petition charged that Woods associated with Dissenters and incited 'a con-

---

[1] N.N.R.O., Lieutenancy Order Book MSS., 26 Mar. 1679, 69v; *H.M.C. 14th Report*, Kenyon MSS., iv, newsletter of 13 Jan. 1680/1, 124–5. The latter states that at the last sessions over fifty dissenters were prosecuted upon the act against Catholics even though not a single Catholic was present. See also N.N.R.O., Return of Dissenters MSS.

[2] A.B. (1668–1707), 31 Mar. 1682, 95r–v.

tentious people to make it their business to stir up people . . . to the great offence of all regular and obedient subjects and to the encouragement of sectaries'. The Tory Assembly deemed this sufficient cause for dismissal and ejected Woods on 3 April.[1] Both parties were active in the ensuing campaign to elect Wood's replacement. The Whigs pushed the candidacy of Cooke. Before the election one Conesford resident told Cooke that his prospects would be much improved if only he would cease to attend conventicles.[2] At any rate, Cooke won the election held on 24 April. Five days later he was called before the Mayor's Court to answer the charge that he was a conventicler, which he denied.[3] Although three witnesses were brought forward to testify that Cooke had indeed been present at seditious meetings, Mayor Hugh Bokenham was satisfied with Cooke's statement and swore him in. The Conesford Tories then filed another petition similar to the earlier one against Woods; the Whigs countered with a petition of their own.[4] In the latter, Cooke's supporters claimed that he was legally elected by a majority of the voters present and hence the Tory petition requesting his dismissal was unwarranted. They added that the corporation should not concern itself with good citizens like Cooke when the real problem was to 'remove the great differences cast among them by the common enemy of Rome'. The Whigs prevailed and Cooke kept his seat—until he was ejected from office a year later.

* * *

By early 1681 Charles was convinced that a new royal policy was needed. Three times in the previous two years he had ordered parliamentary elections; each time the Whigs had returned in greater strength and with increased determination to force an Exclusion Bill on an equally determined and intransigent Crown. As long as exclusion remained the central issue, there was nothing to be gained from further attempts to work with Parliament. Thus, after the fruitless Oxford Parliament, Charles adopted a new strategy designed to strengthen royal government and simultaneously to obtain retaliation against his Whig opposition. One feature of this policy was the consolidation of royal influence over county govern-

[1] N.N.R.O., Mayor's Court Minute Book MSS., 3 Apr. 1682, 108ᵛ.
[2] M.C.B. (1677–95), 29 Apr. 1682, 108ᵛ.
[3] ibid.
[4] Tanner MSS., 311, fo. 58: no author, [May] 1682.

ment by purging local Whig officeholders and replacing them with Tories. The Crown also sought to bring the professional judiciary under far stricter royal control and to curb the effectiveness of Whig propaganda by a more rigid censorship of the Press. There were limits, however, on how far the Crown was prepared to go in reasserting its authority in these areas.[1] On the other hand, Whitehall was thorough and uncompromising when it came to the corner-stone of the new policy: an assault on the independence of municipal corporations.

The Crown's decision in 1681 and 1682 to focus its attention on towns is not surprising. Many of the corporations had become active Whig strongholds. With little supervision and even less interference from central government during the previous decade, local Whigs had used civic office to protect nonconformity and return Whigs to Parliament. In the words of the bishop of Exeter in mid-1681: 'Our corporations and boroughs, who have so great a share in the government, are nurseries of faction, sedition, and disloyalty . . .'[2] If all corporations were purged of Whigs and replaced by Tories, many of Charles's enemies would lose their local base of power and a more rigorous prosecution of the laws against the Dissenters could proceed.[3] Charles's ultimate goal, however, was not simply to establish royal control over local administration, but to use this control to obtain a more subservient Parliament. Three-quarters of the members of the House of Commons were returned by boroughs. In many of these boroughs the members of the corporation possessed the exclusive right to name M.P.s. Where they did not have the franchise themselves, they could exercise a considerable and possibly decisive influence on the wider electorate. In short, the compliant House of Commons which Charles had previously hoped to obtain by dissolving Parliament he would now attempt to secure by remodelling the governing bodies of corporations.

[1] For further discussion of the Crown's initiatives see J. R. Western, *Monarchy and Revolution* (London, 1972), Chap. 3.

[2] Bishop of Exeter to Archbishop Sancroft, cited in Lacey, *Dissent*, p. 152

[3] County Sheriffs were appointed by the Crown, but borough sheriffs were elected by the localities. They, or the recorders, were responsible for picking juries. Apparently in many boroughs Whig officials refused to prosecute men accused of inciting anti-Royalist riots or attending conventicles and the men indicted of these crimes were exonerated by hand-picked juries who refused to convict them. Jennifer Levin, *The Charter Controversy in the City of London, 1660–1688, and its Consequences* (London, 1969), pp. 7–8.

There were two alternatives available to the Crown in its drive to remodel corporations: in 1682 Charles abandoned the politically less controversial but also less effective in favour of the more drastic but ultimately more successful of the two options. In 1680 and 1681 the Privy Council attempted to breathe new life into the Corporation Act by ordering its strict enforcement. Confronted by royal command, corporations demonstrated their independence by deliberately ignoring the Council's orders.[1] Even if the act were enforced, it would be ineffective in removing from office the occasional conformists and the moderate Anglicans who had joined the opposition; and almost all of the Whig leaders were one or the other.[2] The futility of trying to coerce reluctant corporations to enforce a statute which would not produce the desired results even if it were enforced soon became apparent to the Crown. Therefore Whitehall turned to the more potent of its two weapons: the threat or actual use of *quo warranto* proceedings.[3] In a technical, legal sense, all liberties, jurisdictions, and authority held by a corporation were derived from royal charter. If the Crown concluded that the powers granted to a corporation had been misused or exceeded, it could demand that the corporation establish by what right (the literal meaning of *quo warranto*) such unwarranted powers were exercised. If the corporation could not prove its case in court, its charters were forfeited to the King. Since some minor or technical violation of charters could invariably be discovered by astute Crown attorneys, the mere threat of *quo warranto* proceedings was usually sufficient to induce corporations to surrender their charters without contest. In order to drive this point home to lesser corporations, the Crown successfully attacked the City of London in 1683 and forced it to submit. Once the surrendered charters reverted to the Crown, they could be revised and reissued. This permitted the Crown to name the present members of the corporation (and thus to carry out a purge) and also to perpetuate control over corporate bodies by the insertion of clauses which allowed the Crown to exercise a veto over future civic elections.

[1] J. R. Jones, *The Revolution of 1688 in England* (London, 1972), p. 44; Levin, *London Charter Controversy*, p. 11; Western, *Monarchy and Revolution*, p. 72.

[2] Lacey, *Dissent*, pp. 152–3.

[3] For the most complete discussion of the history and legal aspects of *quo warranto* during the reign of Charles II see Levin, *London Charter Controversy*, *passim*.

The new royal policy towards the corporations, devised and first implemented by Charles II and later utilized by James II, has recently received the scholarly attention which it deserves. To be sure, there were precedents for *quo warranto* actions initiated by the Crown against municipal corporations. Also, in many respects the 'new' policy was a reversion to the strategy contemplated by the Privy Council in 1661 prior to the Corporation Act.[1] Yet, the Crown's policy after 1682 was unprecedented. It was unprecedented in its systematic and open application to all corporations, in the imposition of royal restraints on the election of major civic office-holders which far exceeded anything which had ever been considered much less attempted before, and in the success with which the remodelling of corporations in fact led to a striking transformation in the political outlook of the House of Commons. As such, the submission of the corporations in the 1680s must be recognized as one of the central events leading up to the Revolution of 1688.[2] The Crown's attack on the corporations also provides a dramatic conclusion for the two major issues of seventeenth-century constitutional and political history. First, as J. R. Jones has stressed, it was the last serious attempt (and nearly successful attempt) of the monarchy to reduce the House of Commons to a subservient body and thus end the century-long struggle between King and Parliament in favour of the former. Second, as Stuart Prall has pointed out, the assault on enfranchized boroughs was the last of many attempts made by the Stuarts to restructure local government to their advantage and at the expense of local autonomy.[3] The stakes were indeed great.

Norwich might seem an unlikely place for an intense storm to develop over the surrender of the town's charter. The Crown would not be especially concerned about Norwich, since the local Tories had already gained the upper hand in the Assembly and the corporation had repeatedly and fervently denounced the Whigs

---

[1] Levin, for example, has stressed that the Crown desired 'to pursue boldly a course which it had been more tentatively following since the Restoration'. ibid., p. 16. Possible Cromwellian and early Restoration precedents of interference with borough charters with the intent of influencing M.P. elections are discussed in Chapter VI.

[2] This thesis is provided by J. R. Jones, who suggests: 'If slogans are permissible, "municipalize" is what those undertaking research in the period should be urged to do.' Jones, *Revolution*, p. 11.

[3] Stuart E. Prall, *The Bloodless Revolution: England, 1688* (New York, 1972), p. 80.

and exclusion. Moreover, there was no urgency to increase royal influence in a city which had sent two Tories to each of the Exclusion Parliaments. Lastly, a remodelling of the corporation would not assure future control over parliamentary elections because the franchise was held by the freemen and not by the corporation. The Crown was no doubt aware of the propaganda value which it would derive from having a provincial capital surrender its charter, but this was not enough to induce Whitehall to put pressure on the Norwich corporation during 1682. The Norwich Tories, for their part, might be expected to rest contentedly with the reality of local power and not risk a new disruption of city politics by forcing the charter issue. However, the city Tories were not interested in moderation. Their principal concern was to demonstrate their superiority over the local opposition and give further testimony of their loyalty to Charles. This they resolved to do by surrendering the charter early in 1682; that is, even before it was known what additions, if any, the Crown might make in regranting charters. Throughout they were urged on by Lord Yarmouth, who welcomed every opportunity to exhibit his local influence in the royal interest.

The origins of the Whig–Tory charter controversy in Norwich go back to the eve of the Oxford Parliament. At that time the Norwich Assembly coupled its public professions of loyalty to the King with the appointment of a charter committee.[1] The apparent assumption of the magistrates and councilmen was that they could capitalize on the city's good relations with the King to obtain a new or revised charter which would extend the corporation's privileges. No action was taken, but the committee continued to meet.[2] Then, in 1681/2, the Assembly decided to make a further public display of its support for the King. This led to the approval of another declaration. In this address the Assembly expressed its 'utmost abhorrence' of the Whig Association to the point of asserting that the Association was the contrivance of traitors.[3] A month later, in March, the city played host to Charles and shortly afterwards Secretary Jenkins was informed that the Norwich charter would

---

[1] A.B. (1668–1707), 16 Mar. 1680/1, 85ᵛ.
[2] M.C.B. (1677–95), 20 Sept. 1681, 99ʳ.
[3] A.B. (1668–1707), 6 Feb. 1681/2, 93ᵛ. The letter was addressed to King Charles, but was forwarded to Lord Yarmouth. On 24 February the corporation received a reply from Yarmouth containing Charles's pleasure with the declaration. For the Whig Association see Jones, *First Whigs*, pp. 145–7.

soon be surrendered.[1] For this purpose the Assembly enlarged the original committee on 31 March.[2] Nothing further was decided until the next Assembly meeting on 3 May, when the Assembly instructed the committee to meet twice weekly and encouraged all freemen to participate and make their opinions known. [3]

By the spring of 1682 the surrender of municipal charters was becoming a controversial issue in Norwich and elsewhere. Throughout the country charters were being scrutinized with the object of finding pretexts for forfeiture; local Tories were aided by lord lieutenants who used their influence to procure surrender.[4] Within Norwich, the Tories favoured an immediate vote in the Assembly to surrender the charter. They knew that they possessed a majority in the Common Council and they could count on the influential assistance of Lord Yarmouth. Paston was not about to be outdone by other lord lieutenants in manipulating boroughs, even though he had already convinced all Norwich Whigs and many moderates that he was willing to sacrifice the rights of the citizens in order to enhance his standing and prestige in the eyes of Charles.[5] The Norwich Whigs opposed surrender and had a tactical advantage. Under the leadership of Mayor Hugh Bokenham and with the support of moderate magistrates, the Whigs could prevent the Assembly from taking such a vote. If necessary, they could prevent the Assembly from meeting at all.[6] The Tories learned what they were up against on 22 May, when Bokenham was presented with a petition together with a letter from Lord Yarmouth requesting action on the charter. The mayor immediately called a meeting of the magistrates, in which Royalist Alderman Francis Gardiner

[1] *C.S.P.D., Chas II, 1682*, pp. 119, 141: Francis Gwyn to Secretary Jenkins, 12 Mar. 1681/2 and Jenkins to Earl of Conway, 25 Mar. 1682.

[2] A.B. (1668–1707), 31 Mar. 1682, 95^r.

[3] ibid., 3 May 1682, 98^v; notes on an Assembly meeting of 3 May taken by Thomas Corie in Hill, ed., *Corie Correspondence*, p.40

[4] David Ogg, *England in the Reign of Charles II* (Oxford, 1934), II. 634; J. H. Plumb, *The Growth of Political Stability in England, 1675–1725* (London, 1967), p. 55; see also Levin, *London Charter Controversy*, pp. 82–95.

[5] On 22 April, for example, Yarmouth told the corporation that he wanted the city to make a present of one thousand guineas to the Crown 'to lead the dance of other corporations'. *H.M.C., 7th Report*, p. 533b. The corporation took no action on this request.

[6] The situation is reminiscent of 1636 when a majority of the magistrates attempted to prevent the Puritan petition against Wren from being presented to the Puritan-dominated Assembly. The major difference is that in 1682 the mayor opposed Assembly action.

advised Bokenham to comply with Lord Yarmouth's desires. But Bokenham, in the words of Paston's agent in Norwich, 'replied that he should act by advice of his brethren which the writer supposes he said because he knows that the majority of the Bench are fanatics and would consequently oppose it'.[1] As had so frequently been the case in the past, the political conflict quickly took on constitutional overtones.

When it became clear to the Royalists in the city that the magistrates were stalling, they became impatient not only with Bokenham but also with Lord Yarmouth for not taking a more adamant stance. In late May they even went so far as to write to Yarmouth that they were beginning to question his loyalty to the Royalist party in the city.[2] Shaken to the marrow of his Tory bones, Yarmouth reacted more forcefully. On 26 May he received a letter from the mayor and other magistrates protesting that the delay was due to the weight of the matter and thus should not be taken as a personal insult. Yarmouth was not to be duped: three days later he wrote to the mayor that an immediate surrender would place the corporation in the great favour of the Crown whereas further procrastination might irritate the King.[3] In another letter to Bokenham he proposed that if the Assembly met immediately and surrendered the charter then he would personally intercede with Charles to make sure that everything the city desired in a new charter would be granted.[4] And he insisted on an immediate reply from the mayor. Paston's communications restored his leadership in the eyes of the city's Royalists and had a strong impact on the corporation. On 3 June Bokenham called the magistrates together to consider Yarmouth's letters.[5] He started the meeting by enjoining the aldermen to secrecy; but one of Yarmouth's agents managed to discover what transpired and provided him with an account. According to this source, several aldermen urged the mayor to call the Assembly into session and he refused. Nevertheless, Yarmouth's pressure had

[1] Add. MSS., 27448, fo. 64: J. Houghton to Yarmouth, 22 May 1682. Houghton added that Bokenham was determined 'positively not to call an Assembly'.

[2] ibid., fos. 64, 66: loyal citizens [of Norwich] to Yarmouth, 22 May 1682. Houghton observed that the declaration was so strongly worded that it caused dissension within the Royalist ranks and a number of them refused to sign. The original petition with signatories has been lost, but a copy of the text has survived.

[3] ibid., fos. 70–1: Yarmouth to Mayor of Norwich, 29 May 1682.

[4] ibid., fo. 61: same to same, 29 May 1682.

[5] M.C.B. (1677–95), 3 June 1682, 112ᵛ.

convinced several aldermen to switch sides. Reluctant to take a poll of the magistrates, Bokenham instructed four aldermen to draw up an appropriate reply.[1] The mayor, who had no intention of alienating Yarmouth personally, then rushed off a letter to him in which he again protested that the delay was due to the extreme importance of the matter.[2]

By mid-June regular city business requiring the attention of the Assembly was building up. More important, the mayor was required by charter to convene the Assembly before stepping down from office and permitting the new mayor to be sworn in. The inevitable confrontation came on 19 June. The Royalist magistrates and councilmen came armed with a letter from Lord Yarmouth demanding surrender and they were prepared to prevent the transaction of any ordinary business until the charter matter had been settled.[3] The Whigs appeared with an equally potent weapon: a petition signed by eight or nine hundred citizens demanding that the charter not be surrendered.[4] The central argument of the petition was that the freemen were obligated by their oaths to protect the liberties of the city and to this end they felt compelled to make their opinions known and stand by the mayor 'with their body and goods'. In a rather startling threat of public disorder or riot, the petitioners claimed that if necessary they were prepared to bring one thousand men to the market-place to back

[1] Add. MSS., 27448, fo. 74: W. Cecil and J. Houghton to Yarmouth, 5 June 1682. The four aldermen selected by Bokenham to write the reply were John Richer, Henry Crowe, Sheriff John Westhorpe, and Francis Gardiner. According to Cecil and Houghton, Gardiner had no desire to be part of this committee and Aldermen Robert Bendish and Robert Freeman absolutely refused to have anything to do with it.

[2] ibid., fo. 72: Mayor Bokenham to Lord Paston, 5 June 1682. Bokenham was careful to thank Yarmouth 'for the great goodness you have done the city'.

[3] There are three accounts of what happened in the Assembly: S.P. Dom., Chas. II, 419/117: some of the aldermen of Norwich to Lord Yarmouth, 25 June 1682; Add. MSS., 27448, fos. 78, 82: J. Houghton and W. Cecil to Yarmouth, 19 June 1682 and Thomas Corie to Yarmouth, 19 June 1682. Corie's letter may also be found in Hill, ed., *Corie Correspondence*, pp. 40–1.

[4] Both Houghton and Cecil's and Corie's letters list the number of signatories to be between 800 and 900; they also agree that many of the signatories were not freemen. Houghton and Cecil further claimed that some were drawn into it by lies and artifices. They also remarked that the petition was promoted by some forty men 'all of whom are fanatics and conventiclers (some of them old rebels)'. A later letter from a group of Royalist councilmen to William Paston stated that 803 men signed the petition and the first name on the list was Mr. Leverington 'who had the impudence to ride for Mr. Hobart against your lordship the last election'. Add. MSS., 27448, fo. 87: 26 June 1682.

them up. The Royalists in the Assembly demanded that the mayor reject the petition and punish its leaders, and to be sure, the petitioners' blatant use of intimidation gave Bokenham little choice but to reject it. He refused, however, to take punitive action against the petitioners. He also refused to allow the letter from Lord Yarmouth to be read, whereupon a number of councilmen challenged him. When it became clear that no business would be transacted until the letter was read, the mayor finally gave in. But he absolutely refused to allow a vote on surrendering the charter and in the midst of near pandemonium he dissolved the meeting. If the account of Yarmouth's agents is accurate, Bokenham must also have been impressed by the disaffection of three more moderates from the Whig camp and the near disaffection of others.[1]

The Royalist councilmen were extremely upset by the failure of 19 June Assembly meeting. Thirty-four of them, together with two aldermen and one of the sheriffs, immediately wrote to Lord Yarmouth of their disappointment.[2] The list of signatories reveals clearly that the wards which were electing Anglican–Tory aldermen between 1678 and 1682 were also electing Royalist councilmen: twenty-four of these thirty-four councilmen represented Mancroft and Wymer wards.[3] For their part, Mayor Bokenham and the Whigs also sent a letter to Yarmouth in which they indicated that their strength in the magistracy was more than adequate to counteract the Tory dominance of the Council.[4] The purpose of the letter was to deny that the mayor and other aldermen were the true instigators of the citizens' petition, which Lord Yarmouth's agents had alleged. On the other hand, the mayor and the sixteen aldermen signatories revealed a sympathetic posture towards the petitioners' motives. For example, they stressed the natural reluctance of the freemen voluntarily to deliver up all the immunities and franchises obtained by their ancestors. Moreover, they rather impertinently warned Lord Yarmouth to desist from strong-arm tactics: 'We have reason to believe that (upon sedate

[1] Houghton and Cecil noted that Aldermen Bendish, Davy, and Osborne had deserted the mayor's party and there were other members of the Bench who were wavering.

[2] ibid., fo. 80: Petition to Lord Yarmouth, 19 June 1682. The aldermen were Jeremy Vynn and William Helwys; the sheriff was William Salter.

[3] Over-the-Water also reflects an increase in Royalist strength. In 1681 seven new councilmen were elected and four of them signed this petition to Yarmouth.

[4] S.P. Dom., Chas. II, 419/117: Mayor and aldermen to Yarmouth, 28 June 1682.

and mature deliberation) your lordship will not either use or promote what may in the least tend to compulsion in a matter of this nature . . .' The letter was signed not only by the Whig magistrates but also by a number of moderates including Augustine Briggs, Thomas Wisse, William Parmenter, and Robert Freeman.[1] This would imply that Bokenham and the Whig magistrates were not behind the citizens' petition and that there was some genuine concern that heavy-handed interference by Lord Yarmouth might result in a riot in the city. In keeping with the political division of the wards, all twelve aldermen elected by Conesford and Over-the-Water signed this letter whereas the names of only five of the twelve aldermen for Mancroft and Wymer are included.

Within days of the controversial Assembly meeting, John Lowe was sworn in as the new mayor. Shortly afterwards, a delegation of Royalist councilmen paid him a visit in order to sound him out on the charter issues. Lowe treated them courteously, but when it came to the matter of calling an Assembly he was evasive and told them he would make up his mind within a week.[2] The delegation responded by telling the mayor that no city business would be transacted at any Assembly during his year in office until the charter had been surrendered. On 29 June Yarmouth was informed that there was little hope that Mayor Lowe would convene the Assembly and in private the mayor was attempting to persuade moderates to oppose the surrender.[3] The Royalist councilmen confirmed this opinion in a letter to Yarmouth the next day and mentioned for the first time the possibility of a *quo warranto* proceeding: 'if a *quo warranto* comes (which they [the Whigs] believe never will) they will not oppose it, but that's because they know they want [lack] power.'[4] Another friend of Lord Yarmouth wrote to him that nothing less than a *quo warranto* could force the magistrates to give up the charter.[5] In the meantime, the magistrates guarded their flank by holding a Mayor's Court session to hear charges that some aldermen had abetted the citizens' petition of

---

[1] The known Whigs who signed the petition included Bokenham, Church, Cockey, Robert Cooke, Crowe, Man, Richer, and Wrench. All of the ten aldermen removed from office by the 1682/3 charter signed this letter to Yarmouth.

[2] Add. MSS., 27448, fo. 85: Citizens of Norwich to Lord Yarmouth, 23 June 1682.

[3] ibid., fo. 89: W. Cecil to same, 29 June 1682.

[4] ibid., fo. 92: Citizens of Norwich to same, 30 June 1682.

[5] ibid., fo. 96: Edward L'estrange to same, 3 July 1682.

19 June and, although such accusations were presented, they concluded that no alderman was guilty.[1]

Lord Yarmouth was not quite ready to advocate *quo warranto* proceedings, which would have been tantamount to acknowledging that the local Tories, with his influential support, were unable to carry the day. But clearly some additional pressure was needed, so he wrote to Town Clerk Corie that if some action were not taken soon, he would inform Charles of the refusal of the last two mayors to call an Assembly.[2] Mayor Lowe and the magistrates still refused to budge. Stalemate had been reached, although Lowe did his best to appear impartial and put on the appearance of trying to resolve the impasse.[3] If Yarmouth wanted the surrender without *quo warranto* proceedings, it was becoming abundantly clear that he would have to leave London for Norwich and settle the issue himself. This, at least, was the blunt message of his agents in Norwich at the end of July.[4] Lord Yarmouth came to the same conclusion early in August and informed the mayor to prepare for his arrival.[5] On 11 August he rode through the city gates.[6] Thirteen days later an aldermanic election was held in Conesford and Philip Stebbing, a Royalist councilman who strongly favoured the surrender of the charter, won easily over the Whig and moderate candidates.[7] Since the Conesford freemen had consistently elected Whig aldermen, the last being the controversial choice of Robert Cooke the previous May, Lord Yarmouth was no doubt under-

[1] M.C.B. (1677–95), 5 July 1682, 114ᵛ.

[2] Lord Yarmouth to Thomas Corie, 29 June 1682 in Hill, ed., *Corie Correspondence*, p. 42.

[3] Lowe told the Tories he would call an Assembly when the heightened passions had cooled off. Later in July he proposed that the surrender of the charter be referred to a committee of aldermen and councilmen and that they be given a month for deliberation. The Tories thought this was a delaying tactic to allow the Assembly to transact urgent business without voting on the surrender. Add. MSS., 27448, fo. 106: Houghton and Cecil to Yarmouth, 21 July 1682.

[4] Houghton and Cecil wrote to Yarmouth that 'your presence here is highly desired. It is not doubted but that your presence will resolve the difficulty.' ibid., fo. 108: 28 July 1682.

[5] ibid., fo. 110: Yarmouth to Mayor Lowe, 3 Aug. 1682. Yarmouth also warned Lowe that popular petitions to the magistrates against surrender would not be allowed to prevent the Assembly from meeting.

[6] Accounts of Yarmouth's visit to Norwich may be found in *H.M.C., 7th Report*, p. 533b.

[7] Add. MSS., 27448, fos. 114–15: Lord Yarmouth to his wife, 23 August 1682. According to Yarmouth, the opposition was Michael Beverly and Augustine Briggs, jr., and Stebbing won by more than a hundred voices.

stating the case when he wrote to his wife that 'our being here was no disadvantage to Mr. Stebbing'. It was another matter, however, to coerce Mayor Lowe into calling an Assembly. Yet the Royalist tide was running strong with Yarmouth personally on the scene and, besides, time was now on their side.

By early September it had been four months since business had been conducted in an Assembly meeting. Yet the controversy was now coming to a conclusion because the charters required the Assembly to swear in new sheriffs. Lord Yarmouth was still in the city and was joined by his son William. Although there is no evidence of Paston interference in the sheriffs' elections, they may well have been instrumental in the elevation of Royalists, one of whom was Stebbing, by both the magistrates and the commons.[1] Ready to trim his sails to the changing wind, Mayor Lowe promised Lord Yarmouth on 6 September to convene the Assembly in the near future and permit the issue of surrender to come to a vote.[2] The Whigs were now getting desperate. A Mr. John Craddock of London rode into Norwich and claimed that he had a commission from the King to oppose the surrender of the charter, whereupon Yarmouth secured a written statement from Secretary Jenkins that no such commission had been issued. The King, although he did not wish to take sides, was 'satisfied that you [Yarmouth] have nothing in your view but the public good and (what is all the same) the service of the Crown'.[3] The freemen who opposed the surrender resorted to more traditional measures: on 18 September, the day on which Mayor Lowe committed himself publicly to call an Assembly three days later, a large and dangerous mob gathered near the old castle. According to the deputy-lieutenants, it took a company of armed men to disperse the 'unlawful' and 'riotous' meeting.[4] Finally, on 21 September the Assembly met and

[1] Stebbing was the choice of the magistrates and Lawrence Goodwin, elected by the commons, was a signatory of the 19 June petition to Yarmouth which supported the surrender of the charter.

[2] ibid., fo. 116: Lord Yarmouth to his wife, 6 Sept. 1682.

[3] ibid., fo. 120: same to Secretary Jenkins, 13 Sept. 1682; fos. 122, 123: John Fawcett to Viscount Hyde, 13 and 16 Sept. 1682; *C.S.P.D., Chas II, 1682,* p. 400: Jenkins to Lord Yarmouth, 16 Sept. 1682.

[4] Add. MSS., 27448, fo. 127: Lord Yarmouth to his wife, 18 Sept. 1682; N.N.R.O., Lieutenancy Order Book MSS., 18 Sept. 1682, 79ʳ. Yarmouth described his own reaction to the mayor's pledge to delay no longer: 'which is great news for me, for I have earlier today doubted that the Mayor would so consent. Now its past all doubt, since he has made oaths that no Christian can

immediately proceeded to vote by 40 to 22 to surrender the charter.[1]

The Earl of Yarmouth had waited long for his moment of glory. Secretary Jenkins quickly assured him that the King was aware of his efforts and was greatly pleased with the good news.[2] Not only was the charter surrender of good service to the Crown and considerable reputation to the Earl, but also, Jenkins added, the example of Norwich would be a great influence on other corporations. Norwich was the first major city and the first provincial capital to surrender its charter, and this happened over three months before the Crown went to court against the city of London,[3] Bishop Sparrow also rejoiced, believing that Yarmouth's triumph would provide favourable conditions in which the Church would flourish.[4] The Norwich Tories, however, stood to gain the most from the surrender and were perhaps the most jubilant. They would later claim that their sole motivation in the struggle had been to provide a demonstration of loyalty to Charles and not to further their own interests.[5] The magistrates who opposed surrender, however, had been convinced for months that the Tories were driven primarily by personal and local considerations, not the least of which was a desire to force the Whigs from office and occupy the resulting vacancies themselves.[6] Whatever the case, the vote to surrender the charter provided the Tories with an opportunity both to oust their opponents from office and also to guarantee a Tory monopoly of the corporation for the indefinite future. They had no intention of allowing this opportunity to slip by.

[1] A.B. (1668–1707), 21 Sept. 1682, 99ʳ. No breakdown of the vote is provided.

[2] *C.S.P.D., Chas II, 1682*, pp. 423–4: Secretary Jenkins to Lord Yarmouth, 23 Sept. 1682.

[3] Other corporations to receive charters prior to 1683 were Thetford, Hereford, Tavistock, Chard, Portsmouth, Derby, Andover, Nottingham, and Maidstone. Levin, *London Charter Controversy*, p. 109.

[4] Tanner MSS., 35, fo. 107: Sparrow to Sancroft, 11 Oct. 1682.

[5] A.B. (1668–1707), 2 July 1683, 104.

[6] In their letter to Lord Yarmouth in late June, the magistrates asserted that the party demanding surrender consisted of 'a very small (but angry) number of men, who upon joint piques to some persons amongst us, and to succeed them [the Whig magistrates] in their places' have pushed forward with their plans. S.P. Dom., Chas. II, 419/117.

break.' He also acknowledged the importance of the Royalist councilmen and stated: 'The Common Council has been most fair to me so that no business of the city could ever have passed until the charter was surrendered—but that might yet have been delayed till Easter all the same.'

Two matters needed to be resolved before a new charter could be issued by the Crown. One concerned additions to or revisions of the existent charters and the other involved a possible purge of the corporation. Both were at the discretion of the Crown in granting a new charter. As for the first, the assumption in Norwich was that Charles, eager to reward the city for its voluntary surrender, would grant whatever the corporation requested and would make no additions or alterations on his own. This led the Assembly, on the day the vote was taken, to appoint a committee of eight men, none of whom was a Whig or Whig sympathizer, to draw up a formal petition of surrender and to deliberate items to be requested in the new charter.[1] Indeed, on 22 September Secretary Jenkins wrote to Lord Yarmouth that Charles was prepared to bestow his favour on the city and 'if he retrench them in anything, it will only be in those things that do the community no good and yet breed disturbance to the public and are dangerous to the peace of the Kingdom.'[2] In keeping with the passive posture of the Crown, Jenkins further informed Yarmouth in a letter three days later that Charles was in no hurry and left the date of surrender completely to the corporation.[3]

In the belief, then, that they were under no pressure from Whitehall and that the new charter should not and would not result in any changes other than those petitioned for, the members of the Assembly convened again on 29 September. The Tory-dominated charter committee had not completed its task of drawing up a specific list of items to be inserted in the new charter, but they had drafted a formal address and petition to Charles, which the Assembly quickly approved.[4] Remarkably, the address contained a request that in the new charter the King should reserve for himself the approbation of all magistrates and councilmen elected in the future; officeholders objected to would not be sworn in and the citizens would then be obliged to choose other men who did meet the King's approval. Presumably the King would accept only

---

[1] The committee contained four aldermen and four councilmen. All the aldermen (Freeman, Bendish, Briggs, and Gardiner) maintained their seats in 1683. Of the councilmen, two (Nicholas Bickerdyke and John Lowe, not to be confused with Mayor John Lowe) were named aldermen in the new charter and the other two (John Atkinson and John Chapman) were confirmed in the Council.

[2] *C.S.P.D., Chas II, 1682*, pp. 423–4: Jenkins to Yarmouth, 23 Sept. 1682.

[3] Add. MSS., 27448, fo. 135: same to same, 26 Sept. 1682.

[4] A.B. (1668–1707), 29 Sept. 1682, 100^r.

Tory officeholders. Lord Yarmouth was surprised and startled by the willingness of the Assembly to sacrifice the traditional autonomy of the city. He informed Jenkins of the controversial clause 'which I thought might look a little harsh to have been therein and yet of great consequence to the King'.[1]

In early September rumours were circulating in the city that surrender of the charter would lead to a purge of the corporation. It was common for a royal charter to include a list of the officers of the corporation, as was the case with the charter received by Norwich in 1663. There was no obligation, however, for the new charter to name the current officeholders. Hence the surrender of a municipal charter carried with it a built-in opportunity for the Crown to remodel the corporation. Few Norwich citizens in 1682 doubted that surrender would involve some turnover, but it was not clear how thorough the purge would be. The Whig John Craddock, for example, had stated that handing up the charter would result in the removal of eighteen loyal aldermen and their replacement by men of little or no estate.[2] Anxious that such rumours might endanger arrangements for an Assembly vote on surrender, Lord Yarmouth immediately reassured moderate aldermen that officeholders loyal to the King would not be turned out.[3] What Yarmouth did not learn until October was that the task of drawing up the list naming the mayor, aldermen, and councilmen would, in the unambiguous words of the Privy Council, 'be left wholly by his Majesty to your Lordship'.[4]

During the remainder of October the charter committee, slightly enlarged and now including Mayor Lowe, continued to deliberate a list of items to be inserted in the new charter while Lord Yarmouth, extending his stay in Norwich, gave further thought to his choice of future officeholders. Apparently the revised committee was beginning to back away from its stance of 29 September. In late October Yarmouth was shown a copy of the proposed final petition, which omitted a plea for the King to assume a veto power over future civic elections.[5] Yarmouth, who was now of the opinion that such a plea was vital, wrote to Jenkins that he had managed to

---

[1] Add. MSS., 27448, fo. 139: Yarmouth to Jenkins, 2 Oct. 1682.

[2] ibid., fo. 151: John Fawcett to ? ; fo. 122: Fawcett to Viscount Hyde, 13 Sept. 1682.

[3] ibid., fo. 120: Yarmouth to Jenkins, 13 Sept. 1682.

[4] ibid., fo. 141: Jenkins to Yarmouth, 4 Oct. 1682.

[5] ibid., fo. 149: Yarmouth to his wife, 27 Oct. 1682.

persuade the committee to reconsider.[1] Nevertheless, the situation had become so touchy that he did not deem it 'prudent or safe' to inform the committee of his choice of future officeholders; rather, he would send a list directly to the King. Three days later the Assembly met for the first time since 29 September and approved a final list of fifteen requests for the King.[2] The petition not only made no mention of increasing royal authority over elections, but also asked the King to include in the new charter the names of the present mayor, aldermen, recorder, steward, and town clerk. On 4 November Mayor Lowe headed a delegation to London to negotiate a new charter with the Crown.[3] In mid-December it was still not clear what the final form of the charter would be and speculation continued about whether the purge would be mild or thorough. Although Craddock was still in town and had become a hero to some citizens, Lord Yarmouth was informed that the city was quiet.[4]

Whitehall agreed upon a new charter for Norwich in February, drew it up in March, and sent it to Norwich early in April.[5] In anticipation, the magistrates made arrangements for an extravagant dinner, bonfires, and the ringing of church bells to welcome William Paston and the charter;[6] but many of the magistrates and citizens had little to celebrate. Mayor Lowe and Sheriffs Stebbing and Goodwin retained their offices, but ten aldermen were removed by the new charter.[7] Eight of these men represented Conesford and Over-the-Water. Every alderman elected by these

---

[1] ibid., fo. 147: same to Jenkins, 27 Oct. 1682.

[2] A.B. (1668–1707), 30 Oct. 1682, 100^v–101^r. Among the additions were such items as authorizing a deputy-mayor to call Assembly meetings during sickness of the mayor, permitting the mayor and sheriffs to be sworn in their homes if they could not make it to the guild-hall, and obligating tradesmen who were not freemen to hold office if elected.

[3] M.C.B. (1677–95), 4 Nov. 1682, 120^r.

[4] Add. MSS., 27448, fo. 167: W. Cecil to Yarmouth, 18 Dec. 1682.

[5] *C.S.P.D., Chas II, 1683 (Jan.-June)*, p. 71: Warrant for a charter, 11 Feb. 1682/3; Norwich MSS. 453, 7 Apr. 1683.

[6] M.C.B. (1677–95), 31 Mar. 1683, 127^r. The feast featured two Westphalia hams, two tongues, salmon, sturgeon with olives and anchovies, loin of veal, loin of beef, two forequarters of lamb, two dishes of lobster, and plenty of wine and beer.

[7] The dismissed aldermen were Bokenham, Church, Cockey, R. Cooke, T. Cooke, Crowe, Man, Manser, Richer, and Wrench. The men who replaced them were Beverly, Bickerdyke, Blofield, Brady, Goodwin, Guybon, Lowe, Morley, Postle, and Warkehouse. N.N.R.O., Norwich charter of 22 Mar. 1682/3, fo. 1.

wards since 1677 was removed. In contrast, none of the aldermen elected after 1677 by the freemen of Mancroft and Wymer lost his seat.[1] Since the Common Council had been so strongly Royalist since 1678 and had given Lord Yarmouth such needed assistance in the surrender of the charter, a far less dramatic change in its personnel might have been expected. Although the Assembly omits the annual list of councilmen for the years 1680 to 1682, a fairly accurate listing for 1682 may be compiled from entries in the Assembly Book recording the swearing into office of new councilmen. This indicates that sixteen councilmen were removed by the new charter and, predictably, the wards most affected were Conesford and Over-the-Water.[2] The June petition favouring the surrender of the charter had been signed by thirty-four councilmen; twenty-six of these men continued in the Council and five were elevated to the aldermanry. Of the twenty-six councilmen who did not sign the petition, only twelve retained office in 1683.

The purge of Whig magistrates did not significantly alter the social and economic composition of the Court of Aldermen. The fundamental issues which divided the Whigs and the Tories in the later 1670s and 1680s were, as in the 1640s, religious and political in character and again there are no signs that deeper social or economic motivations were involved. Of the magistrates who held office from 1678 to 1683, thirteen may be identified as Whigs and twenty-one as Tories.[3] The magistrates of both parties represented a diversity of family backgrounds and they cannot be distinguished on this basis. One curious difference between Whig and Tory magistrates was that seven of the twenty-one Tories were grocers whereas none of the thirteen Whigs practised this trade. Grocers were the backbone of the parliamentary-Puritan party during the Civil War, yet grocers also formed the leadership of the

[1] John Man and Henry Crowe, both representing Mancroft, were among those ejected, but in 1678 both were ineligible for replacement since they had joined the Bench before 1663.

[2] Conesford and Over-the-Water lost nine out of twenty-four councilmen, whereas only six out of thirty-six councilmen for Mancroft and Wymer were removed.

[3] The Whigs were Bokenham, Chickering, Church, Cockey, R. Cooke, T. Cooke, Crowe, Lowe (ex-mayor), Man, Manser, Richer, Wrench, and Woods. The Tories (this includes the appointments made by the charter) were Bendish, Beverly, Bickerdyke, Blofield, Brady, Briggs, Davy, Freeman, Gardiner, Goodwin, Guybon, W. Helwys, Lowe, Morley, Osborne, Parmenter, Postle, Salter, Stebbing, Vynn, and Warkehouse.

Anglican–Royalist party in the late 1670s and 1680s. Other trades were divided: seven Whig and four Tory magistrates were worsted weavers, two Whigs and three Tories were brewers, two Whigs and one Tory were merchants, one Whig and one Tory were mercers, and one Whig and one Tory were drapers.[1] A comparison of the wealth of the magistrates cannot be made without a complete subsidy dating from this period, and none is known to have survived.[2] Thus the prediction of Craddock that surrender of the charter would bring men of lower financial status to the magistracy cannot be measured. However, there were no later assertions that this had occurred and most of the new Tory magistrates were later elected to the Court of Aldermen in free elections held in 1689. Although the majority of freemen in Conesford and Over-the-Water were Whig in sympathy whereas the freemen of Mancroft and Wymer consistently elected Tories, the Whig and Tory magistrates were drawn from all four wards.[3]

The purge was only the first step in Charles's plan to gaurantee the loyalty of the corporation. The second was to make sure that the city's officeholders would continue to remain loyal to the Crown in the future. To this end the provisions of the Corporation Act, including the officeholding criteria of accepting the Anglican sacrament, the oaths of allegiance and supremacy, and the subscription against the Covenant, were incorporated into the new charter. Whitehall was aware that this, by itself, was not sufficient. So the Crown altered the old charter and provided life tenure to the newly-approved councilmen, recorder, steward, and town clerk. More important, the Crown added clauses to the charter which were designed to give the King the authority to control the future choice of officeholders without destroying completely the traditional system of civic elections. All future officeholders were to be chosen according to the procedures used during the past seven years, but these newly-elected officials were not to take the oaths and be sworn into office until twenty-eight days after the

[1] The remaining four Tory magistrates were a haberdasher, an ironmonger, a millener, and a wool comber. See Chapter II, Table 6 and Evans, 'Decline of Oligarchy', p. 72.

[2] Partial returns for the Royal Aid of 1689, covering four parishes, are in the N.N.R.O., but they include only four of the Whig and four of the Tory magistrates.

[3] Of the Whig magistrates, two resided in Conesford, two in Mancroft, four in Wymer, and five in Over-the-Water. Of the Tories, three lived in Conesford, six in Mancroft, seven in Wymer, and five in Over-the-Water.

election. During this period the King could declare any elected person or persons to be unfit for office and not to be sworn in, whereupon additional elections would be held until a suitable man was chosen. There was still the possibility that the Crown might misjudge a prospective officeholder or that a once-loyal officeholder might later turn against the Crown. This possible loophole was closed with a clause that permitted the King and his successors to declare any man unable to continue in office, remove him by the royal seal without opportunity for protest, and require a new election to fill his office. Since the charter was a direct grant from the King to the corporation, all of the above powers were within the scope of the royal prerogative and did not require the sanction of Parliament, nor could Parliament question their authority.

Robert Paston did not live to witness the arrival of the charter; he died early in March. At his funeral his chaplain John Hildeyard delivered a sermon praising the Earl's loyalty to King and Church and recounting his labours with the city of Norwich:

I will be his asserter, that great was his love to the ancient, loyal, and honorable corporation of Norwich, because the members of that body (generally speaking) loved the King . . . I am sure they found him [Yarmouth] their friend, and maugre the blasts of calumny, the new charter shall remain a token of it. I must say, he spared no cost, no pains, as they themselves can witness, to make the world believe that he loved them . . . Nay, his very sleep, to my knowledge, was often broken to find out ways how best to serve them[1]

In his rigid support for King and Church, Lord Yarmouth had made many friends and many enemies in the city. He had influenced M.P. elections and declarations of the Assembly and he had provided the major impetus in two purges of the corporation within five years. Above all, he more than any other man was responsible for the surrender of the charter. The Norwich Tories were thankful both to Yarmouth for his intercessions and to Charles for the new charter. In July 1683 the reconstituted Assembly wrote to the King:

We have been censored by factious and capricious men for being extravagantly royal in some of our late proceedings, but if it were possible to be guilty of expressing allegiance and gratitude to your sacred Majesty, we would study to acquire the virtue and honor of such extravagancy.[2]

[1] Hildeyard, *Sermon*, p. 27.   [2] A.B. (1668–1707), 2 July 1683, 104.

The immediate result of the new charter was that the Assembly was monopolized by Tories and would remain Tory as long as it pleased the Crown. In a larger constitutional sense, the new charter meant the loss of the city's ancient right to hold free and unobstructed elections and to determine its own governors. The Norwich Tories of 1682 were not only aware that this might occur, they had requested such an alteration and expressed gratitude to the King once it had taken place. As a later chronicler correctly observed, the Assembly voted their venerable charter to Charles without either the King's command or any forfeiture whatsoever, which amounted to 'a wonder in this age and a riddle in the next'.[1] The new charter in time would become the symbol of monarchical oppression and unwanted external interference. As a consequence, the reputation of the Crown as well as the memory of Lord Yarmouth was severely damaged.

*　　　*　　　*

The death of Robert Paston and the arrival of the charter did not bring political tranquillity to Norwich. The new charter, which resolved one controversy, was the cause of another quarrel, which might have been averted had it not been for Lord Yarmouth's death. This time the Whigs were not involved; they had been reduced to political obscurity by the new charter. Rather, the conflict involved a split between moderates and extremists within the triumphant Royalist ranks. Disunity within the Tory party was a problem which had concerned Lord Yarmouth and Bishop Sparrow for some time. Manifestations of internal dissension went back at least to the 1678/9 elections to the first Exclusion Parliament, when an effort was made to replace M.P. Briggs with a more extreme candidate. The report to the Privy Council in 1681/2 on Norwich politics was careful to distinguish the 'mad Tories' from the moderates, who were led by Briggs and 'who are for the present government both in Church and State, but go soberly and quietly to work'.[2] Whig opposition, Yarmouth's leadership, and the charter issue helped to preserve a sense of common purpose amongst Tories. With the removal of the unifying presence of Yarmouth and the common enemy overthrown, the smouldering hostility between the two Royalist groups came to the surface early in 1683.

---

[1] Tanner MSS., 396, fo. 38: no author, no date, but written by a person who approved Mayor Richer's actions in 1678.

[2] *C.S.P.D., Chas II, 1682*, pp. 54–6.

As a result, faction feuding disrupted civic life for the duration of the year and once again civic government came to a standstill.

The rift between moderate and extreme Tories was both religious and political in nature. Sparrow wrote to Archbishop Sancroft in January 1682/3 that he considered himself and his adherents to be loyal supporters of Lord Yarmouth, but they were moderates compared to the Royalist fanatics in the city who were 'so hot and eager that nothing will please them unless it is done by their methods'. Sparrow added that these extremists, led by Sheriff Philip Stebbing and the indefatigable anti-Dissenter John Fawcett, even went so far as to have a libel against Sparrow signed by several hundred citizens and delivered to the bishop.[1] In the meantime, the Tory extremists conducted their own ruthless campaign against Dissent within the city. Within six months of their election to the shrievalty, Stebbing and Lawrence Goodwin established a well-deserved reputation as merciless persecutors of nonconformists with a special animus for Quakers.[2] In the spring of 1683 the extremists focused on a new enemy and a new cause: they now opposed William Paston and his appointment to the recordership in the new charter.

The first skirmishes in the conflict were fought during the winter of 1682–3. On 23 December ten members of the Mayor's Court, at the instigation of Mayor Lowe, decided to send a letter to Lord Yarmouth expressing their appreciation of his assistance in the surrender affair and stating their willingness to accept his son as recorder if he were to be named to that office in the new charter.[3] That the mayor and his fellow aldermen, who had gone to such lengths to thwart Yarmouth and obstruct the surrender of the charter during the summer of 1682, should take such action seems almost incredible. In a later explanation to the Privy Council in the summer of 1683, the next mayor (a Tory extremist) described the affair as a Machiavellian plot. Using 'all the malice and art imaginable', Mayor Lowe connived with other aldermen, two-thirds of whom were described as 'violent opposers of the surrender', and concocted the 'evil design'. Fully aware that the

[1] Tanner MSS., 35, fo. 117: Sparrow to Sancroft, 24 Jan. 1682/3.
[2] N.N.R.O., Return of Dissenters MSS., 1682–3; *C.S.P.D., Chas II, 1683 (Jan.–June), passim.* Known Quakers were imprisoned in the most deplorable conditions.
[3] M.C.B. (1677–95), 23 Dec. 1682, 123ʳ; Add. MSS., 27448, fo. 170: Mayor and others of Norwich to Yarmouth, 23 Dec. 1682.

appointment of recorders was a power vested in the Assembly and
that the mayor and nine aldermen could not act on behalf of the
entire corporation, they nevertheless hoped that the appointment
of William Paston would create dissension within the city, drive a
wedge between the Pastons and the true Royalists, and discourage
other corporations from surrendering their charters.[1] Whether the
devious motivations attributed to Mayor Lowe and his followers
by the mayor of 1683 were correct or not cannot be known. What
the next mayor obscured was that although two-thirds of these
aldermen had not given their full support for surrender, the great
majority of them were moderate Tories rather than Whigs.
Indeed, five of these ten signatories owed their seats to the intervention of Lord Yarmouth and the second aldermanic elections of
1678.[2] Perhaps these moderates merely wished to protect their seats
by flattering Lord Yarmouth when the latter was making his final
decision on the officeholders to be named in the new charter.
Possibly they genuinely desired William Paston to be recorder in
the hope that he would favour the moderates in their conflict with
the extremists.

Whatever the true motivation of Lowe and his followers was, the
petition to Lord Yarmouth certainly created consternation among
the Tory extremists. Their problem was exasperated by Yarmouth's
agents in Norwich, who were inclined to view the petition as a
genuine display of loyalty and courtesy to their lord and who were
baffled by the opposition to it by Stebbing and other extremists.[3]
In an effort to explain their position and block the nomination of
Paston, the extremists on the charter committee held an emergency session on 1 January and eight of its members sent their own
letter to Paston.[4] Their first and central argument was that the

---

[1] *C.S.P.D., Chas II, 1683 (July–Sept)*, p. 257: Mayor William Helwys to
Secretary Jenkins, 6 Aug. 1683.

[2] The 23 December petitioners to Yarmouth were Lowe, Church, Cockey,
Davy, Freeman, Gardiner, N. Helwys, Osborne, Parmenter, and Vynn. Lowe,
Church, Cockey, Freeman, Helwys, and Parmenter had signed the 28 June
petition to Yarmouth, but only Church and Cockey were removed from office by
the new charter. One of Yarmouth's agents also noted that the petition had the
blessing of Augustine Briggs. Add. MSS., 27448, fo. 171: J. Houghton to
Yarmouth, 25 Dec. 1682.

[3] ibid., fo. 174: Wm. Cecil to Lady Yarmouth, 27 Dec. 1682. Houghton wrote
to Yarmouth that Mayor Lowe 'behaves himself very well'.

[4] S. P. Dom., Chas. II, 422/1: Committee for charter to William Paston, 1 Jan.
1682/3; Add. MSS., 27448, fo. 177. The subscribers included Sheriff Stebbing
and Aldermen Bendish, W. Helwys, and Salter.

Assembly had always possessed the right to elect recorders; for William Paston to be named recorder in the charter without the approval of the Assembly would 'be looked upon as a great infringement of the privileges of this city'. They were fully aware that a number of towns would be compelled to accept a Crown-appointed recorder but, the letter protested, this treatment was designed for Whig-dominated corporations and Norwich did not deserve to be placed in that category. Finally, if the traditional right of the Assembly to elect recorders and other officials was overridden, the arguments of the Whigs against surrender would seem to be justified and other corporations would be reluctant to follow Norwich's example. About the same time as this letter was sent, a majority of the charter committee wrote a letter to Lord Yarmouth to remind him of his and the King's promise that 'no diminution of our ancient privileges or franchises were intended, but rather an augmentation thereof by new grants'.[1] They wanted the items petitioned for by the Assembly, 'to which instructions we do adhere and to no other'.

That the Tory extremists in general and the charter committee in particular should assume the pose of champions of the traditional privileges of the city lies between the ironic and the ridiculous. They more than anyone else had been insistent and active in forcing the voluntary and unconditional surrender of the charter in the first place, and they formed a majority in the charter committee which drew up the September petition inviting the King to assume a veto power over local elections. The simple fact of the matter is that they did not want William Paston to be recorder. Why they did not want him is not clear, but the most plausible explanation is that they found him, like Sparrow, too moderate for their tastes. Their motives were political and possibly religious, but their public justifications were couched in constitutional and legal terms. For them to adopt this stance is not surprising. The seventeenth-century mind masked motives of political expediency behind an outward guise of legal rectitude whenever possible, even if the legal argument was strained, based on technicality, or, as in this case, obviously self-serving. In this vein Town Clerk Thomas Corie, one of the ringleaders of the extremist faction, unabashedly if hypocritically advised Yarmouth in December not to tamper

---

[1] S. P. Dom., Chas. II, 422/2: Committee for charter to Lord Yarmouth, [1 January] 1682/3.

with the rights of the city.[1] In the days following Lord Yarmouth's death in early March, Corie suspected that William Paston would still be named recorder and then, as the new Lord Yarmouth, would name a deputy to serve in his place. He noted that this would be an additional violation of custom and sure to displease the corporation, which was already suspicious that the new charter would make an encroachment upon their privileges.[2]

The arrival of the new charter in April confirmed the fears of the Tory extremists: Paston was listed as the recorder and was provided with life tenure. Since he had no desire to take up residence in Norwich, he instructed the Mayor's Court to locate a fit person to act as deputy-recorder. The magistrates were unsuccessful in their search, whereupon a number of aldermen ordered Town Clerk Corie to inform Paston that any nominee recommended by him would be acceptable.[3] This initiative, like that of 23 December was taken without the approval of the Common Council. As events were to prove, a majority of the councilmen not only objected to Paston naming a deputy-recorder but they also refused to acknowledge the appointment of Paston himself as recorder. The extremists were further encouraged by the mayoral election of 1 May. William Helwys and William Salter, both of whom had served on the charter committee and had opposed the appointment of Paston, were nominated by the freemen; Helwys was selected mayor-elect. The inevitable confrontation did not come until an Assembly meeting on 19 July. Letters patent under the Great Seal empowering the Earl of Yarmouth to name a deputy-recorder were read, together with the Earl's appointment of Samuel Warkehouse, Esq. to fill the position.[4] The Assembly declared this an infringement of the anxient liberties of the city and contrary to the new charter. On the pretext that William Paston had not taken the usual

---

[1] Corie to Yarmouth, 18 Dec. 1682 in Hill, ed., *Corie Correspondence*, pp. 42–3. Corie wrote: 'I beg leave to mind your lordship what his Majesty was pleased to say at the rendition of our charter, that he intended not any diminution of the rights of our city; I am sure your lordship intends it not.' On 27 October Corie was a member of the delegation which visited Yarmouth and was persuaded to reintroduce the King's veto powers into the surrender petition.

[2] ibid., p. 43.

[3] Corie to William Paston, second Earl of Yarmouth, 18 Apr. 1683 in ibid., pp. 43–4.

[4] Minutes of an Assembly meeting of 19 July 1683 in ibid., p. 44; A.B. (1668–1707), 19 July 1683, 104ʳ. A copy of the transactions may also be found in *C.S.P.D., Charles II, 1683 (July–Sept.)*, p. 165.

oath of recorder but rather one drawn up by John Hildeyard, the Assembly, in a defiant mood, named a committee to pay the Earl a visit and persuade him to resign the recordership.[1] If the committee was successful then a new recorder would be elected by the Assembly; if it was unsuccessful then an address would be sent to the King.

The new Lord Yarmouth reacted to his opposition within the corporation just as his father might have done: in early August he took his case directly to the King and the Privy Council. Charles was sympathetic and adamant that Paston should receive no further indignity from the city. Nevertheless, he desired to hear the corporation's side of the story before announcing his royal will.[2] As commanded by the Privy Council, Mayor Helwys provided a defence of his and the Assembly's actions.[3] He emphatically denied that either he or the corporation wished to embarrass Yarmouth and indeed they had zealously promoted the lord's 'real interest' on all occasions. Helwys then traced the history of the conflict from the previous December, vilifying the aldermen who sponsored Paston for the recordership and arguing that the Assembly alone possessed the authority to name a recorder. Furthermore, he refused to swear in Warkehouse, first because Paston had sworn to an improvised recorder's oath, and second because neither the new charter nor any of the old charters gave a recorder the authority to appoint a deputy. On 19 July the Assembly endorsed his decision. Thus rested the mayor's case. In 1678 the Privy Council had been reluctant to punish a Dissent-sympathizing mayor who had thwarted a Lord Yarmouth and had claimed that in doing so he was upholding the law as stipulated by charter. In 1683 the Council could hardly deny a Royalist extremist who similarly had thwarted a Lord Yarmouth and took the same stand. Thus the Council's insistence on supporting William Paston in early August melted at the suggestion in late August that a compromise be reached with the Lord Keeper acting as mediator.[4]

---

[1] The committee was dominated by former members of the charter committee and included Aldermen Bendish and Salter.

[2] *C.S.P.D., Chas II, 1683 (July–Sept)*, p. 143: Jenkins to Yarmouth, 2 Aug. 1683.

[3] ibid., pp. 245, 257–8: same to Mayor of Norwich, 2 Aug. 1683 and Mayor Helwys to Jenkins, 6 Aug. 1683.

[4] ibid., pp. 288, 292, 333.

As the days of September passed and no immediate resolution was in sight, the struggle between Paston's adherents and opponents in the city approached boiling point. Neither the moderates nor the extremists were very pleased with the situation, but both sides were intransigent. As in 1682, the controversy resulted in a deadlock in which the Assembly was prevented from meeting. The mayor and a majority of councilmen opposed Paston and presumably wanted the Assembly to meet and elect a new recorder. But the charter required that an Assembly must possess a quorum of thirteen aldermen and the moderate magistrates were able to prevent this quorum by boycotting Assembly meetings. Finally, on 23 September, Mayor Helwys, seven aldermen, both sheriffs, and thirty-seven councilmen drew up a petition to Charles attacking the moderate aldermen.[1] The central complaint was that Helwys had summoned no fewer than seven Assemblies at which at least thirty-eight councilmen appeared, but a cabal of twelve aldermen refused to attend. These twelve 'evil minded men' were then accused of opposing the surrender of the charter in 1682 and, more recently, of allowing persons outside the city to dictate their actions (possibly a reference to Lord Yarmouth). The city desperately needed both a recorder and Assemblies, but William Paston was totally unacceptable. The King had already been informed of the reasons why this was the case and, in particular, the invitation made to Paston by eight or nine aldermen 'neither was nor is of more validity than the man in the moon'. Not to be outdone, the moderate aldermen and other citizens in support of Paston drew up a counter-petition and forwarded it to the King.[2] Their argument was that the Earl of Yarmouth, maligned by the mayor and his followers, had every right to be recorder and was named in the charter. They implored the King to take some action against 'the ambitious and sinister designs of some particular restless and discontented men who are daily threatening and fomenting differences and animosities in this corporation'.

Both factions claimed that they represented the true Royalist party and that their adversaries were disturbers of the peace and opposed to the interests of the Crown. The signatories of the

---

[1] S. P. Dom., Chas. II, 432/90: Mayor and Sheriffs of Norwich to Jenkins, 23 Sept. 1683.

[2] ibid., 432/91: Justices, aldermen, common councilmen, and freemen of Norwich to King Charles, [September] 1683.

petitions reveal that both sides were indeed Royalist and that there had been very little shift in their leadership since the previous December.[1] Of the eight original petitioners to Lord Yarmouth who were still in office, seven continued to support William Paston in September. This included ex-mayor Lowe and all of the five aldermen who had been elevated to office in the second elections of 1678; also prominent was the name of Augustine Briggs. In opposition to Paston were all eight members of the charter committee who had attempted to prevent his nomination in early January. Philip Stebbing, identified the previous February as one of the two leaders of the extremist party, signed this petition; John Fawcett, the other extremist leader, was given the honour of taking it up to London. The new charter benefited both factions equally: of the ten new aldermen, four joined the petition against Paston, four signed the petition for him, and two abstained. Conspicuously absent from both petitions were the Whigs, who were *persona non grata* to both Royalist groups. If either of the two factions had associated itself with the Whigs, the other faction would certainly have stressed this point in their petition to the Crown. So one wonders in vain what the Whigs thought about the recordership struggle.

The two petitions did not have any noticeable impact on the King, who was still unwilling to favour one faction or the other. The impasse continued through October and November. Not until 7 December did the Assembly meet again, for the first time since July.[2] The dispute over Paston and Warkehouse, however, was not resolved and the bitterness between the two factions continued unabated. A curious clash between Alderman Nicholas Helwys and his brother, Mayor William Helwys, testifies to the ill feeling which persisted. For over one and a half years the two brothers had

---

[1] The aldermen opposed to Paston were Bendish, Bickerdyke, Goodwin, W. Helwys, Lowe, Stebbing, Salter, and Warkehouse. In favour of Paston were Beverly, Brady, Briggs, Freeman, Gardiner, Guyborn, N. Helwys, ex-mayor Lowe, Morley, Osborne, Parmenter, and Vynn. Blofield, Davy, Postle, and Wisse were presumably neutral.

[2] *C.S.P.D., Chas II, 1683–4*, pp. 57, 93: Helwys to Jenkins, 24 Oct. 1683 and same to same, 16 Nov. 1683; A.B. (1668–1707), 7 Dec. 1683, 105ʳ⁻ᵛ. The purpose of the December meeting was to read two letters from the King ordering the courts to continue in operation even though Norwich had neither a recorder nor a steward. The recent charter intended to make Robert Davy, Esq. the new steward but mis-spelled his name as Davis, whereupon Davy refused to serve. In one of the two letters Charles told the city that they should re-elect Davy. ibid., p. 119: King Charles to Norwich corporation, 28 Nov. 1683.

stood on opposite sides of the political fence.[1] One day in February 1683/4 Nicholas called his brother a fool who would not remain mayor for long. William retaliated by calling an Assembly in which the councilmen voted thirty-four to seventeen to remove Nicholas from the aldermanry for using uncivil language towards the mayor.[2] Nicholas refused to accept this decision and violently forced his way into the next meeting of the Mayor's Court without the permission of his brother.[3] The Mayor's Court Book records that no further business was transacted at this meeting.

During the spring of 1684 the Royalists finally worked out their differences. What broke the log-jam is unknown, but Lord Yarmouth and the moderates prevailed. On 1 April Warkehouse was sworn in as deputy-recorder and the Assembly ordered all entries in the Assembly Book which dishonoured the Earl of Yarmouth to be obliterated.[4] At the same meeting it was also decided to write William Paston a humble letter assuring him that the sole cause for the delay was uncertainty over the power and authority of a deputy-recorder. In addition, the Assembly requested Paston's pardon for the unfavourable words spoken against him in the past. Two weeks later, the September petitioners against Paston issued a retraction: they acknowledged that their petition had been written in a fit of passion, they were now satisfied that the magistrates supporting Paston were loyal men, and they wished the petition to be forgotten. On the other side, the moderate aldermen apologized for calling their antagonists hot-headed and self-interested.[5] This did not, however, settle the bad blood between the Helwys brothers. Nicholas obtained a writ of mandamus to be returned to office, but on 30 April the Assembly voted twenty-five to twenty-three against his restoration.[6] Not to be denied, Nicholas managed to be re-elected to the aldermanry by

---

[1] In 1682 William signed the petition to Lord Yarmouth supporting the immediate surrender of the charter, but Nicholas signed the magistrates' letter to Yarmouth which sympathized with the freemen's attempt to block surrender In late 1682 Nicholas joined Mayor Lowe in the invitation to Yarmouth to name his son recorder; William, a member of the charter committee, joined in the petition against Paston's nomination. Finally, Nicholas subscribed the September petition for Paston whereas Mayor William organized the petition against Paston.

[2] A.B. (1668–1707), 25 Feb. 1683/4, 106ᵛ.

[3] M.C.B. (1677–95), 1 Mar. 1683/4, 150ᵛ.

[4] A.B. (1668–1707), 1 Apr. 1684, 106ᵛ.

[5] ibid., 14 Apr. 1684, 107ᵛ.

[6] ibid., 30 Apr. 1684, 108ᵛ.

the freemen of Wymer on 1 May and the same day he was nominated together with Henry Brady, another alderman who had supported Paston, for the mayoralty.¹ The Common Council could do
nothing but look on as the Court of Aldermen chose Nicholas
Helwys to be mayor-elect.

With the reconciliation of spring 1684, the two branches of the
Royalist party were once again united and in complete command of
the city. They held in common that Charles was the defender of
Englishmen's rights and liberties and the preserver of the established Church, and they viewed the Whig exclusionists as traitorous leftovers from the 1640s and 1650s who were constantly
plotting rebellion and civil war.² When Charles died in 1684/5, the
corporation wrote to King James that 'never had subjects more
reason to mourn for the death of a king than we'.³ They then
thanked God that James succeeded to the throne despite all the
'wicked contrivances of the haters of monarchy' and swore:

to spend all we have even to the last drop of our blood in defense of your
Majesty's royal person, crown, and dignity, the government in Church
and State as by law established, and for the preservation of the succession in the right line against all pretenders whatsoever.

As a token of their appreciation the Assembly vowed that they
would use all their power and influence to have M.P.s elected who
would be acceptable to James.⁴ The members of the Assembly did
not speculate, however, on what they would do in the event of
their new-beloved monarch combining with the Dissenters and the
equally-despised Catholics to attack the monopoly of local office
held by Tories and undermine their beloved Church of England.
They would soon learn that their loyalty was conditional.

*   *   *

James II opened his reign in a stronger position than any of his
Stuart predecessors.⁵ His former enemies, the Whigs, were in utter

¹ M.C.B. (1677–95), 1 May 1684, 152ᵛ.
² A good statement of the Anglican-Royalist point of view in the early 1680s in
Norwich may be found in William Smith, *A Sermon Preached in the Cathedral
Church of Norwich* (London, 1683).
³ A.B. (1668–1707), 12 Feb. 1684/5, 112ʳ. James was proclaimed in the city on
11 Feb. 1684/5. M.C.B. (1677–95), 167ᵛ. The address from Norwich was one of
151 messages of congratulation sent to James from the boroughs. Jones, *Revolution*, p. 47.
⁴ A.B. (1668–1707), 24 Feb. 1684/5, 112ʳ.
⁵ The most suggestive of recent reinterpretations of the events leading up to
and through the Revolution of 1688 is Jones *Revolution*.

disarray. Totally lacking in organization and leadership, the Whigs had been reduced from an effective political party to a collection of individuals wielding minimal influence. When Parliament convened in May 1685 for the first time since the Oxford Parliament four years before, only about forty Whigs were present. The charter campaign had been a great success: only one definite Whig was returned from the fifty-one corporations which had been granted new charters by Charles. The Anglican–Tories who filled the House of Commons were enthusiastic in their support of the new King. James helped the honeymoon along by adopting moderate policies, stressing his respect for the religion, liberty, and property of his subjects, and exhibiting a special regard for the Anglican Church. In response, the Tory Parliament, coming to believe that its own interests were identical with those of the Crown, displayed an unprecedented generosity in providing James with the luxury of complete financial independence. The failure of Monmouth's Rebellion in the summer of 1685 increased James's popularity and left him with virtually no political opposition. Not until the late autumn of 1685 did James slowly begin to introduce measures designed to strengthen the authority of the Crown and to improve the position of his fellow Catholics. When the Anglican–Tories offered polite and reluctant resistance, James increasingly applied pressure. By mid-1686, when the Court of Ecclesiastical Commission was created, the previous ardour of the Anglican–Tories had cooled considerably and the House of Commons was drifting further and further into opposition.

The Anglican–Tories who held sway over Norwich were just as elated in 1685 and early 1686 as their counterparts at Westminster. Following the crushing of Monmouth's Rebellion, for example, the magistrates ordered a great celebration.[1] For the King's birthday in October they arranged an extravagant display of loyalty: church bells rang all day and bonfires blazed all night.[2] Following Bishop Sparrow's death in May 1685, William Lloyd was translated to Norwich. Cordial relations between the Anglican magistrates and the new bishop were established and by the following February the magistrates were regularly attending the Cathedral services.[3]

[1] M.C.B. (1677–95), 9 July 1685, 186r.
[2] Tanner MSS., 31, fo. 217: Bishop Lloyd to Archbishop Sancroft, 16 Oct. 1685.
[3] ibid., fo. 273: Lloyd to Sancroft, 22 Feb. 1685/6.

Apparently, however, not all the magistrates were adequately pious. One evening after a dinner with the magistrates, Lloyd pointed out to his guests how strange it was for them to come to church every Sunday and then for some of them to turn their backs on the blessed sacrament. A few days later the mayor called the aldermen together and an order was passed that the magistrates go to the Cathedral and take the sacrament with appropriate devotion. They did so. To the delight of the Anglican citizens, Lloyd organized a mass confirmation open to all townsmen in late February and early March 1685/6.[1] With the eager assistance of the magistrates, the confirmation was successful beyond Lloyd's fondest dreams. The bishop was especially pleased that so many of those confirmed were 'the substantial people of this city' and included three aldermen with their wives and family. On one day alone he confirmed over 1,600 persons in the Cathedral over a five and a half hour period, which led him to report to Sancroft that he had never been so tired during his life and rarely so happy.[2]

In 1685 the Anglican–Tories of Norwich were pleased with their King, their Parliament, their Church, and their corporation; they witnessed and applauded the demise of their opposition on the national level and in Norwich. At no point during the preceding seventy years had a Norwich politico-religious group experienced a similar appreciation of national and local conditions. Not only did they monopolize all levels of civic government; they had guarantees provided by the charter that they would continue to do so in the future regardless of the opinions of the citizenry. From 1683 to 1685 the names of all newly-elected officials were dutifully reported to the Crown for approval. It was unthinkable, at least in 1685, that James would ever abandon the Anglican–Tories and he could use his veto power to keep them in office indefinitely. Actually, in the short run there was little need for the King's veto. Nominees for the mayoralty were restricted to aldermen, all of whom were Anglican–Tories approved by the first Lord Yarmouth. The freemen elected one of the sheriffs, but in practice their choice was limited. Seven of the men named to the Court of Aldermen in the charter had not previously served as sheriff. They were, of course,

---

[1] ibid., fo. 276: same to same, 1 Mar. 1685/6.

[2] ibid., fo. 293: same to same, 10 Mar. 1685/6. On the other hand, only a week later Lloyd complained to the magistrates about a fair which was to be held on Good Friday and asked them to prohibit it. He doubted that they would accept his request because 'I know that present profit is a prevailing argument with tradesmen.' ibid., fo. 295: same to same, 19 Mar. 1685/6.

eager to become sheriffs so that they could be eligible for the
mayoralty. The result was that each of the ten sheriffs elected from
1683 to 1687 was an alderman.[1] The freemen were also restricted in
the choice of councilmen because the men named in the charter
were given a life tenure. In April 1685 the Mayor's Court decided
that the charter provided life tenure for only those councilmen
named in the charter itself and that all men elected since 1683 would
be subject to annual elections.[2] No reason for this decision is
given, but there were obvious drawbacks to life tenure for councilmen. In March 1686 the Assembly dismissed one councilman for
non-residence and non-appearance and three others for 'having
failed in their estates'.[3] The new arrangement allowed the freemen
to choose some representatives, but by 1687/8 they could consider
only about one-third of the councilmen, who still had to pass the
scrutiny of the King.[4]

With the freeman vote so heavily restricted, it is difficult to tell
whether the Anglican–Tories enjoyed the support of the citizenry
or were artificially maintained in power by the new constitutional
arrangement. During the four years prior to the new charter the
Tories had won all Common Council and M.P. elections, but an
episode early in 1686 suggests that many of the freemen disapproved of them strongly enough to challenge the corporation and
the Crown. The confrontation was sparked off by a decision of the
Assembly to settle an old score with ex-mayor John Lowe by
removing him from office.[5] On 28 March, only weeks after Bishop

---

[1] The non-sheriff aldermen named in the charter were Beverly, Bickerdyke,
Blofield, Guybon, Lowe, Morley, and Warkehouse. The remaining three sheriffs,
Augustine Briggs, jr., Richard Brockden, and John Ward, were elected to the
aldermanic Court before they became sheriffs. All of the elected sheriffs went
through the process of approval by the King.

[2] M.C.B. (1677–95), 4 Apr. 1685, 180^r. At this date forty-nine of the councilmen listed in the charter were still in office.

[3] A.B. (1668–1707), 26 Mar. 1686, 122^v.

[4] On 15 April 1685, the freemen elected four councilmen to replace those who
had died and confirmed in office seven councilmen who had joined the Council
since 1682/3. The names of all eleven were then sent to the Duke of Norfolk for
the King's approval. ibid., 15 Apr. 1685, 181^r. In 1687/8 thirty-seven councilmen still enjoyed a life tenure and of the twenty-three additions to the Council
since 1683 only one, Edward Clark of Wymer, had been removed from office by
the 1682/3 charter.

[5] ibid., 26 Mar. 1686, 122^v. No reason for the dismissal was given other than
that Lowe was 'not capable to serve in his place'. The previous October the
Assembly had written to Lord Yarmouth and the Duke of Norfolk concerning
Lowe, but to what purpose is unknown.

Lloyd's mass confirmations, the freemen of Over-the-Water, a ward with a long tradition of Dissent, went to the polls and elected John Wrench to replace Lowe.[1] Whether the voters were reacting to the conformity campaign or the Assembly's treatment of Lowe or both is not known, but their choice of Wrench is curious. Ex-alderman Wrench had been ejected from the Court by the Anglican–Royalist citizens of Wymer in 1678, re-elected by Over-the-Water in 1680, and removed a second time by the new charter. The Crown, again for reasons which are not known, did not void the election and the Mayor's Court, after waiting the maximum allowable twenty-eight days, finally swore Wrench in.

The Wrench affair became more controversial on 1 May when a large number of citizens went to the guild-hall with the intention of both nominating and electing Wrench to the mayoralty. A later petition sent by the Assembly to Whitehall provides details of what happened next.[2] Before the freemen proceeded to vote, the Mayor's Court ordered that the seniority ordinance of 1620 was to be observed.[3] According to this ordinance the freemen should have confined their nominations to the aldermen with greatest seniority who had not been mayor. Instead, they nominated Wrench and ex-mayor Robert Bendish, and some present then admitted that Bendish was nominated for the sole purpose of forcing the magistrates to select Wrench. After a long debate, the magistrates voided both nominees on the grounds that Bendish was ineligible and Wrench was the 'youngest' alderman. Actually, Wrench was the youngest alderman only if his tenure prior to the new charter was completely discounted: he had first been elected to the Court in late 1669, a full eight years before any other alderman under the chair. Nevertheless, the magistrates stuck by their decision and ordered the freemen to nominate new candidates or at least someone other than Bendish, and the freemen refused. By this time it was getting late, so the mayor and Court went home.[4] Two days later the Assembly met and approved *ex post facto* the Mayor's Court order putting the 1620 ordinance into effect. They then sent

[1] M.C.B. (1677–95), 28 Mar. 1686, 197ᵛ.

[2] Petition of Mayor, etc. of Norwich to King James, 3 May 1686 in A.B. (1668–1707), 3 May 1686, 124ᵛ–125ʳ.

[3] Seniority in the nomination of mayors had not been observed in 1683, 1684, or 1685. The order of the Mayor's Court was thus tailored to the situation.

[4] Norwich MSS. 453, entry for 1 May 1686.

their petition to James and a letter to the Duke of Norfolk requesting his support.[1]

James rather predictably agreed with the magistrates and the
Assembly. He declared that the behaviour of the freemen was
against royal authority and repugnant to the peace and good
government of the city, and instructed the corporation to hold a
second election as soon as possible.[2] The freemen dutifully appeared on the last day in May, nominated William Salter and
Philip Stebbing, and the magistrates selected Salter as the senior
alderman of the two.[3] John Wrench, thoroughly disgusted, requested the Assembly to approve his immediate resignation from
the Court of Aldermen, which the Assembly did for a fine of
£50.[4]

Norwich seems to have been calm during the autumn and early
winter months of 1686 while a cataclysmic shift in royal policy was
slowly taking place. James still hoped that the Anglicans and
Tories could be persuaded to co-operate in the project of obtaining
toleration for Catholics, but he was increasingly aware that they
would not budge. The new royal strategy, set in motion in 1686/7,
was to repudiate the Crown's traditional and natural allies and
establish links with its former enemies, the Whigs and Dissenters.
The King's bold gamble was twofold: first, that the inducement
of religious toleration for nonconformists as well as Catholics
would be adequate to erase traditional anti-Catholicism and whatever bitter emotions remained from the exclusion crisis and,
second, that the new political alliance would prove strong enough
to form a working majority in a new Parliament and would repeal
the Test Acts and penal laws. The first major bid for Whig–
Dissenter support was made in early April, when the King issued
the First Declaration of Indulgence suspending the Test Acts and
penal laws.

The reaction of the Norwich Anglican–Tories to the political

[1] A.B. (1668–1707), 3 May 1686, 124ʳ.

[2] King James to corporation of Norwich, 22 May 1686 in ibid., 125ʳ. The
letter is included in *C.S.P.D., Chas II, 1686–7*, p. 136.

[3] M.C.B. (1677–95), 31 May 1686, 200ʳ. The final irony is that Salter, the
magistrates' candidate, was third in seniority.

[4] A.B. (1668–1707), 2 and 14 June 1686, 125ᵛ, 126ᵛ. The Assembly also sent
letters of appreciation to the Duke of Norfolk and James, thanking them for
their assistance. The freemen of Over-the-Water waited two months before they
were summoned to elect a replacement for Wrench, and then chose John Ward.
M.C.B. (1677–95), 5 Aug. 1686, 204ʳ.

realignment is unknown. Since their control of the corporation depended upon the support of the Crown, they must have been alarmed. They must also have been alarmed by the prompt resurgence of Catholicism in the city. Within a month of the Declaration, the Catholics in Norwich petitioned the corporation for the use of the Dutch Chapel for public services, but at the same time the Dutch Congregation filed their own petition with the Assembly to keep the chapel.¹ By a vote of forty-two to four the Assembly turned down the Catholics' request. Eventually the two petitions were brought to the attention of James. He did not want to alienate the Dutch Congregation, but he was sympathetic to the plight of the city Catholics, who could not afford to construct their own chapel. Thus he instructed the corporation to leave the chapel in the hands of the Dutch Congregation, but recommended that the Catholics be provided with a meeting place.² The Assembly consented and gave the Catholics the lease of the Granaries, where nonconformists had once held their meetings. During the winter of 1687/8, when the city received confirmation that the Queen was pregnant and would provide James with a Catholic heir, the local Catholics became confident and bold.³ Lloyd wrote to Sancroft that they held frequent meetings, publicly scoffed at the penal laws, and even drew up articles against a sermon delivered by Lloyd which they may have intended for the dreaded Ecclesiastical Commission.⁴

No permanent solution to the issue of religious toleration could be based on the suspending power of the Crown's prerogative alone, and no one knew this better than James. What was needed was legislative action, which in turn required a co-operative House of Commons. In short, James would have to create a new parliamentary majority, consisting of Whigs and Dissenters. This project, announced by the Declaration of Indulgence, confirmed by the dissolution of the Tory Parliament in July 1687, and then accelerated in its implementation by the pregnancy of Queen Mary in November, ultimately led to a systematic and unprecedented

---

¹ A.B. (1668–1707), 9 May 1687, 132ᵛ–133ʳ. The Dutch Congregation had rented this chapel from the corporation since the reign of Queen Elizabeth.

² Henry Bedingfield on behalf of James II to the Norwich corporation in ibid., 23 Aug. 1687, 134ᵛ.

³ M.C.B. (1677–95), 28 Jan. 1687/8, 224ᵛ. The Mayor's Court ordered bells to be rung and declared a day of thanksgiving.

⁴ Tanner MSS., 29, fo. 133, Lloyd to Sancroft, 6 Feb. 1687/8.

royal intervention in the constituencies in order to obtain a sub-servient Parliament. The campaign to pack Parliament, which was perhaps the most important domestic policy leading to the Revolution of 1688 but which has only recently received scholarly emphasis, rather predictably focused on the municipalities.[1] Charles II had demonstrated how remodelling the corporations could produce a Tory Parliament; James would now re-model the corporations to obtain a Whig majority. In one respect James's project was actually less problematic than that confronted by his brother: whereas Charles had to force the surrender of borough charters, James needed merely to utilize the authority to purge cor-porations which was explicitly provided for the Crown by these charters.

The regulation of corporations, following on the heels of a purge of country justices of the peace and deputy-lieutenants, com-menced in January 1687/8 and continued for four months. In early February Bishop Lloyd, distraught by the replacement of six 'honest' men by six 'Independents' in Great Yarmouth, anticipated a similar change in Norwich.[2] The magistrates, convinced that their days in office were numbered, proudly marched to the Cathedral for the Anglican sacrament so that all might know that they were about to suffer for their loyalty to the Church.[3] The royal order arrived on 30 March, only days before the annual elections.[4] By authority of the recent charter, ten alderman and nineteen council-men were displaced. The identity of the men removed and the fact that so few aldermen and councilmen lost their seats is at first sur-prising. Apparently no alderman was immune: one of the ejected had been an alderman since 1661, three owed their seats to the second election of 1678, three were named in the new charter, and the remainder were promoted at normal elections from 1679 to 1685.[5] Nor did the recordership feud and the division between moderates and extremists have any known impact: both of the

---

[1] See Jones, *Revolution*, chap. 6. Professor Jones observes that this campaign 'represented the most deliberate, methodical, and elaborate attempt that had been made at any time during the century to subordinate the localities to the center' (p. 130).

[2] Tanner MSS., 29, fo. 133: Lloyd to Sancroft, 6 Feb. 1687/8.

[3] ibid., fo. 135: same to same, 20 Feb. 1687/8.

[4] Order of King James to Norwich corporation, 26 Mar. 1688 signed by the Earl of Sunderland in A.B. (1668–1707), 30 Mar. 1688, 139r–v.

[5] The displaced aldermen were Bendish, Beverly, Bickerdyke, Briggs jr., Brockden, Gardiner, Goodwyn, N. Helwys, W. Helwys, and Osborne.

Helwys brothers, for example, found themselves out of office.[1] Since eight of the ten aldermen and all of the nineteen councilmen had been elected by the wards of Conesford and Mancroft, the impression is that this was only the first stage of what would ultimately be a thorough purge. This approach was not unique to Norwich: at least a dozen other towns experienced a series of purges as part of a deliberate policy of the Crown.

The royal warrant of 30 March did not leave the city with the freedom to elect replacements. The new charters of 1682 to 1687 usually gave the Crown the authority to remove officeholders at will but not to fill the resulting vacancies with its own nominees. In order to circumvent local elections a number of towns, including Norwich, were issued additional charters.[2] These allowed the Crown to appoint men to the empty seats and these new officers were to be spared from taking the required oaths. Although the legality of the process was extremely dubious, it proved remarkably successful. The new magistrates and councilmen for Norwich, according to one account, were 'sectaries or that way inclined'.[3] Although a number of the appointees, such as John Dearsley, Robert Cooke, and John Wrench, had long been associated with the Dissenters and Whigs, few of the Whig-exclusionist leaders were returned to office. John Man, John Richer, and Mark Cockey, for example, were passed over in favour of new men. Six of the ten appointees had not previously been members of the Bench; thirteen of the nineteen councilmen had never served in the Council and none of the remaining six had been evicted from office by the 1682/3 charter.[4] The exclusion of the Whig leadership of 1682 is curious but not surprising. Elsewhere in England, many moderate Dissenters opposed to a repeal of the Test Acts had drifted into alliance with moderate Anglicans in 1687/8 and this coalition became stronger in the spring of 1688.[5] Whether some of

[1] Four of the ejected aldermen had opposed William Paston and three had supported him.

[2] Robert H. George, 'The Charters Granted to English Parliamentary Corporations in 1688', *English Historical Review*, 55 (Jan. 1940). 47–56. This topic needs a complete examination.

[3] Norwich MSS. 453.

[4] The new aldermen were J. Barnham, W. Barnham, Leverington, Dearsley, Seaman, and Wenn. Only three (Dearsley, Leverington, and Seaman) had previously been sheriffs and none of these men were councilmen at any time during the 1680s. The restored aldermen were R. Cooke, T. Cooke, Wigget, and Wrench.

[5] See Lacey, *Dissent*, chaps. IX, X.

the Whig magistrates of 1682 were excluded because they had joined such a coalition or whether the royal agents responsible for remodelling simply distrusted these former opponents to the Crown is not known. No evidence has been found which reveals the existence of an Anglican–Dissenter alliance of local moderates at any time during 1688, but the extant evidence is too scanty to preclude such a possibility. On the other hand, the Crown's appointees for Norwich conform to a general policy adopted by Whitehall in which prominent Whigs were deliberately shunned in favour of men with less personal standing in their community. Tax records are insufficient to determine the financial status of the new officeholders, but there was considerable talk in Norwich about new alderman Thomas Seaman, who had to borrow horses to be of proper appearance at the assizes.[1]

The reaction of Norwich citizens to the royal order is difficult to ascertain. Although there is no surviving correspondence or descriptions of civic life in April which might shed light on this issue, the clear impression is that the majority of freemen either welcomed the change or at least were not willing to mount any opposition. In the yearly elections held in early April, the wards confirmed all of James's appointees in office without incident. During the same month the special agents appointed by the Crown to investigate the political state of boroughs visited the city. Their return for Norwich states that if a parliamentary election were held, the approximately 1,500 freemen would elect Alderman Barnham, 'a popular man and a Dissenter', and Alderman Cooke, a man 'in whom the city have a great confidence'.[2] Both were among James's recent appointees. Finally, on 1 May the freemen threw seniority to the winds and nominated John Wrench and John Dearsley for the mayoralty. The magistrates chose Wrench. Only two years before, in 1686, the Assembly had vigorously blocked his nomination for mayor; but in 1688 the Assembly made no protest and politely refunded the £50 demanded of Wrench at the time of his resignation in 1686.[3] The absence of Assembly opposition to the remodelling and Whig–Dissenter resurgence is

---

[1] M. Chamberlayne to Mr. Windham, 6 Aug. 1688 in *Norfolk Archaeology*, 24 (1932), 15–7.

[2] Bodleian, Rawlinson MSS. A139B, cited in Mason, *History of Norfolk*, I. 378–9. For the activities of James's agents in the cities see Jones, *Revolution*, chap. 6 and Plumb, *Political Stability*, pp. 57–60.

[3] M.C.B. (1677–95), 1 May 1688, 233ᵛ; A.B. (1668–1707), 3 May 1688, 142ᵛ.

not surprising. If the corporation proved resistant the Crown could either implement the second stage of the purge or, as it had done in some towns, initiate *quo warranto* actions. Nevertheless, the half-purged corporation balked when it came to honouring an order from James to provide the freedom to thirty-eight Quakers without requiring them to take the traditional freeman's oath.[1] By a vote of thirty-nine to eight the Assembly refused the order, but then sent a petition to James and wrote letters to the Duke of Norfolk, the Earl of Yarmouth, and the Earl of Sunderland explaining their decision.[2] Moreover, in late September Bishop Lloyd was convinced that in the forthcoming M.P. elections for Norfolk, Norwich alone would return men loyal to the Church.[3]

As Prince William's ships awaited the Protestant wind in October 1688, James made a desperate bid for popular support by dissolving the Ecclesiastical Commission, cancelling the approaching M.P. elections, and annulling the charters arising from forfeits and surrenders earlier in the decade. The arrival in Norwich on 29 October of the royal proclamation restoring the old charters of the city led to the immediate restoration of magistrates evicted by the 1682/3 charter. A number of old Whigs, including Man, Richer, and Cockey, were thus back in office, but they were not back in power and they enjoyed little local support. Of the nineteen aldermen of 1682 who were still alive in 1688, eight were evicted Whigs and eleven were Tories continued in office by the 1682/3 charter. City elections were held during the last three days of October to replace the five aldermen who had died in the interim.[4] Whatever popularity James and the local Whigs possessed in April had considerably diminished by late October. All of the King's aldermanic appointees of March were passed over whereas three men evicted by the royal order were returned by the freemen.[5] In

[1] James II to corporation of Norwich, 13 July 1688 in A.B. (1668–1707), 25 July 1688, 144^v; Eddington, *Quakerism*, pp. 259–61. James was on close personal terms with William Penn and in April 1686 had issued circular letters to justices of the peace to omit Quakers from execution of the penal laws.

[2] A.B. (1668–1707), 25 July, 1 Aug. 21 Sept. 1688, 145^r–147^r.

[3] Tanner MSS., 28, fo. 183: Lloyd to Sancroft, 26 Sept. 1688.

[4] The five deceased aldermen were Briggs, Church, Crowe, Parmenter, and W. Helwys. M.C.B. (1677–95), 29, 30, 31 Oct. 1688, 242^{r-v}.

[5] Augustine Briggs, jr. was elected to replace his father, Brocken for Crowe, Bickerdyke for Parmenter, Ward for Helwys, and Blofield for Church. Briggs, jr., Brockden, and Bickerdyke had been removed by James in March. Bickerdyke and Blofield were originally named to the aldermanry by the 1682/3 charter.

mid-November, after William of Orange had landed in England and the initial reluctance of many Englishmen to endorse his campaign began to disappear, Common Council elections were held in Norwich. The councilmen removed by the 1682/3 charter were not automatically restored, presumably because councilmen, unlike aldermen, did not possess a life tenure. In a further rebuff of the King and the local Whigs and Dissenters, only five of the nineteen councilmen named by James in March were able to maintain office, whereas eleven councilmen ejected in March were restored.

William's unopposed march to London signalled the end of James's brief reign. The Duke of Norfolk, accompanied by 300 knights and gentlemen, rode into Norwich on 1 December and declared for a free government and Parliament. The Norwich citizenry responded with joyous acclamation.[1] A week later mobs burned and pillaged houses of Catholics and demolished the Catholic chapel.[2] An entire regiment was needed to quell the disturbance. The downfall of the Norwich Catholics was later followed by the political retirement of several leading Whig magistrates. Aldermen Mark Cockey and John Manser resigned in February; John Man and John Richer were dismissed from office in August for refusing to take the oaths prescribed by the Act for Abrogating the Oaths of Supremacy and Allegiance.[3] By the end of 1689 the city was once again under the unchallenged sway of the Anglican–Tories. Six aldermen were elected in 1689, and five of them had previously been named to the Court by Charles six years before.[4] By the end of the year, three-quarters of the magistrates were men named to the Bench in the 1682/3 charter. The political preference of the Norwich freemen was clear. And yet, since urban politics in England had become so closely identified

[1] *H.M.C.*, Lothian MSS., 134; also appears in B. Cozens-Hardy, ed., *Norfolk Lieutenancy Journal, 1676–1701* [Norfolk Record Society, XXXII] (Norwich, 1961), pp. 94–5.

[2] Norwich MSS. 453, entry for 7 Dec. 1688; Lieutenancy Order Book MSS., 15 and 16 Dec. 98^{r-v}. See also Russell J. Kerr and Ida C. Duncan, eds., *The Portledge Papers* (London, 1928), p. 56.

[3] M.C.B. (1677–95), 6 Feb. 1688/9 and 16 Aug. 1689, 247, 254^v–255^r; N.N.R.O Oaths of Allegiance to William and Mary, 1689–1701. No reason is provided for the resignations of Cockey and Manser. Man and Richer were the only aldermen who refused to take the oaths. In September five councilmen were replaced for the same reason. M.C.B. (1677–95), 19 Sept. 1689, 256^{r-v}.

[4] The five new men originally appointed by Charles in 1682/3 were Beverly, Goodwin, Guybon, Postle, and Warkehouse; the exception was John Leverington, who first entered the aldermanry by mandate of James II in March 1688.

with national politics and parties, the citizens must have suspected that the political complexion of the corporation would ultimately be resolved not in Norwich but at Whitehall and Westminster.

The Revolution of 1688 and its immediate aftermath brought to an end twelve years of continuous and chronic political instability in Norwich. No fewer than fifty-nine men at one time or another served as aldermen from 1677 to 1690. Forty-five aldermen lost their seats in the successive purges. John Wrench had the unique distinction of having been appointed to the Court four times, of being forced from office three times, and of having served three different wards in the space of twelve years. Faction and party strife dominated city life. The roots of the turmoil lay in the religious differences between Dissenter and Anglican, but the instability in city government would never have become so acute but for the attempts first of Lord Yarmouth and then of Charles and James to control the corporation for their own purposes. In the end, the Whig–Dissenter interest in Norwich was rejected. Their loss paralleled Whig–Dissenter defeat in the Convention Parliament on the vital issues of corporation and religious settlement. In the months following James's flight to France, the Dissenters anxiously looked forward to comprehension and toleration and, in particular, to a repeal of the penal laws and a removal of the religious tests barring them from office.[1] The Toleration Act did bring some relief, but comprehension and other Dissenter objectives were dashed in the faction fighting that came to characterize parliamentary activity. On one issue the Anglican–Tories were adamant: they would not give up their legal monopoly of local office. An all-out effort by Whigs and Dissenters in 1689/90 to amend the Corporation Act and to force Anglican–Tories from office by disqualifying those men from office who had collaborated with the Crown in the surrender of charters proved unsuccessful.[2] The Corporation Act of 1661, which had figured so prominently in the political life of Norwich, remained in effect.

[1] Lacey, *Dissent*, pp. 231–43.
[2] Henry Horwitz, 'The General Election of 1690', *The Journal of British Studies*, XI (1971), 77–91.

Conclusion

The people also, for natural and civil parts, are genuinely of quick apprehension and sound understanding, and are courteous, affable, and friendly, but yet somewhat self-conceited, and given too much to disorders.

> Anonymous description of
> seventeenth-century Norwich
> townsmen.[1]

The Revolution of 1688 and its immediate aftermath brought to an end a period of chronic constitutional, political, and religious instability which extended back to 1620. This turmoil is in striking contrast to the comparative tranquillity and insularity which marked Elizabethan and early Jacobean Norwich. The politics of the city during this earlier period flowed from year to year with only minor disruption; the disputes which did flare up usually involved personal or family feuds and were confined within the corporation. Moreover, Norwich townsmen had revealed little interest in affairs beyond the city walls and communications to and from Whitehall were infrequent.[2] After 1620, however, conflict and controversy were more often the norm than the exception. In each of the seven decades from 1620 to 1690 at least one major confrontation within the town and corporation took place. During these critical moments, the emergence of electoral political politicized townsmen at large, who on occasion attempted to influence the corporation directly by petition or mob activity. Within the Mayor's Court and Assembly, rival factions vied for control and were often willing to revise election regulations or evict the opposition from office in order to strengthen their position. This strife was considerably influenced and exacerbated by the injection of national issues into local politics and by the intervention of extramural authorities into local politics.

The political experience of each seventeenth-century English

---

[1] N.N.R.O., Norwich MSS. 453, unknown writer, n.d. The hand is clearly of the seventeenth century and the chronicle from which this quote comes terminates in the early eighteenth century.

[2] The historian of Tudor Norwich has pointed out that in this period 'the government of Norwich was carried out in an atmosphere of almost studied calm'. Pound, 'Tudor and Stuart Norwich', p. 153.

city was different. In every case it was conditioned by a multiplicity of factors which, in combination, made each town unique. Nevertheless, in its concern for national politics and issues and in the nature of its internal political turmoil, Norwich bears a closer resemblance to London than to the other provincial capitals. Why was this the case? The answer lies in the confluence of factors which shaped the political life of Norwich. One was the decline of town oligarchy. If the city had been governed by a small and closed élite consisting of men linked by family ties, engaged in a few prestigious trades, empowered to recruit its membership by co-optation and unrestricted by an Assembly, we may assume that there would have been greater agreement on religious and political matters and, consequently, less conflict within the corporation.[1] But this was not the case. Moreover, there was in Norwich a large and active citizenry which possessed the constitutional right to participate in electoral politics and had in fact exercised this right in opposition to the magistracy prior to 1640. Politics in many towns were limited to the corporation, but not in Norwich. A third factor was the continuing presence of nonconformity, whose membership included many of the most prominent citizens. This assured that every religious issue was also a political and corporate issue. Fourth, the city was interested in and influenced by events in the city of London. This was due to the close personal and business connections of Norwich merchants with the national capital, the presence in both cities of politicized religious groups in contact with each other and undergoing a common experience, and an awareness of the similarity of political institutions and procedures in London with those in Norwich. A fifth factor which separates the experience of Norwich from other towns concerns the nature of Norfolk politics and the attitude of the bishop of Norwich.

The two periods when crisis was most acute in the city were the 1640s and the 1680s. A comparison of these two periods reveals numerous similarities and thus stresses the continuity of conflict both in the issues involved and in the manner in which political groups responded to changing national and local circumstances. In both periods the conflict grew out of a prior local controversy

---

[1] With reference to 1640, Professor Zagorin has noted: 'Every important town without exception was ruled by a small and virtually self-perpetuating body of such men, for the urban constitutions were invariably oligarchical, vesting the substance of power in organs little subject to popular check or dismissal.' Zagorin, *Court and Country*, p. 126. Norwich, then, is at least one exception.

involving religious issues. In the 1630s the Puritans strengthened a local religious structure responsive to their own needs and practised forms of worship unauthorized by an unacceptable to the Anglican Church; in the 1670s the Dissenters of Norwich successfully evaded the Corporation Act and the statutes against nonconformity. Both the Puritans of the 1630s and the Dissenters of the 1670s looked to the city magistrates, some of whom were leaders of the nonconformist movements, for protection against persecution. Political upheaval was then precipitated by the attempt of an outside authority to intervene in city affairs; in 1636 Bishop Wren tried to stamp out Puritanism and in 1678 Lord Lieutenant Paston was determined to force Dissenter aldermen and their sympathizers from office. Neither attempt was entirely successful and left a residue of lingering friction and resentment within the corporation and the city.

The stage was thus set for the conflict between Royalists and parliamentary-Puritans in the 1640s and Whigs and Tories in the 1680s. The prior local controversies were quickly transformed into local crises by the election of new parliaments in 1640 and 1679 and the association of religious conformity with the Crown and nonconformity with the parliamentary opposition in the national confrontation which followed. As the previous local controversies were suddenly inflamed and enlarged, the leaders of the old politico-religious factions in Norwich became the leaders of new politico-religious parties. Both the Royalists and parliamentary-Puritans and the Tories and Whigs after them were divided on essentially ideological issues in which the factor of religion was omnipresent and frequently paramount. In both periods the struggle involved efforts to manipulate the electorate and election procedures in accordance with what appears to have been preconceived strategy. In both periods the successful party engineered the removal of their opposition from office and altered electoral regulations to guarantee the future election of men of their own party. In both periods the parties linked their movement to either Whitehall or Westminster and their continuation in power depended upon the vicissitudes of the struggle between Crown and Parliament. In both periods the resolution of the national struggle was decisive also for the local conflict, and the side which emerged victorious nationally also triumphed locally.

Given the emphasis on provincial urban insularity in recent

studies of other seventeenth-century towns, it must be questioned whether these politico-religious upheavals in Norwich were really religious and ideological in character, or whether the rhetoric merely cloaked a deeper hostility between conflicting socio-economic groups. The evidence which remains clearly indicates the former. First, there are no hints of underlying social or economic grievances in any of the documents. Secondly, fragmentary evidence of voting patterns suggests that the religious affiliation of candidates could be an important factor in municipal elections, whereas it is impossible to trace electoral patterns based on social or economic factors. Again, the triumph of neither the parliamentary-Puritans in the 1640s nor the Tories in the 1680s altered the social composition of the magistracy or the social and economic criteria for political recruitment. Finally, an examination of the major protagonists of both parties in both periods reveals that it is impossible to differentiate the one from the other in terms of either wealth, occupation, or social background.

The determination of local communities to preserve autonomy from the encroachment of outside forces is now generally recognized as one of the salient themes of seventeenth-century English history.[1] Just as the Stuart monarchy was extremely sensitive to assaults on the royal prerogative and as the House of Commons was jealous of parliamentary privilege and liberty, so also local communities were obstinate in protecting their traditional independence.[2] This was apparently true of both county and urban establishments. A serious threat to this autonomy was posed by the centralizing tendencies of the state; this included not only the Crown, but also Parliament in the midst of the Civil Wars and the major-generals of the Protectorate. But for many towns the greater danger lay closer to home: in the domineering inclinations of neighbouring magnates and, in those towns with active nonconformist groups, the attacks of crusading bishops. A summary of the intervention of outside forces in Norwich affairs and the reaction of the

[1] For example, Everitt, *Change in the Provinces*, *passim*; Prall, *Bloodless Revolution*, p. 80; Underdown, *Somerset*, *passim*.
[2] Ivan Roots has used the term 'localism' to describe these local attachments; it was a 'stubborn local patriotism backed by living traditions of provincial independence and was to be found throughout the realm'. Ivan Roots, 'The Central Government and the Local Community', in Ives, ed., *The English Revolution*, p. 37.

city and corporation to this intervention therefore deserves close attention.

Conflict between the Cathedral and the corporation during the seventeenth century was predictable. Conditions which had already given rise to friction in the sixteenth century remained substantially unaltered after 1600. Throughout the century Norwich possessed deep-rooted and thriving parochial communities animated by nonconformist ministers and resolved to practise their forms of worship despite the threat of persecution. At the east end of town resided the bishop of Norwich, who was responsible for the enforcement of uniformity. The bishop's task was complicated by the close association of nonconformity with the corporation, which was established during the sixteenth century, survived the Restoration, and continued until the corporation was remodelled in 1683. Up to 1640, harmony between the Cathedral and corporation was disrupted whenever the bishop was determined to persecute Puritans and to withstand the resistance which the corporation was sure to mount. Thus Bishop Harsnet aroused considerable enmity and Bishop Wren strained relations to breaking point. Post-Restoration relations between the bishops and town government were much improved. If not always cordial towards each other, they were rarely hostile. This was in part due to the so-called Clarendon Code, which made the corporation rather than the bishop responsible for the prosecution of nonconformity. It was also due to a change in the attitude among the bishops. Reynolds was known for his tolerance of nonconformity. Sparrow and Lloyd were concerned with reducing Dissent, but their approach was to encourage conversion and to support Anglican groups within the city rather than to intervene directly and forcefully as Wren had done.

The struggle to maintain independence from powerful lords and county gentry figures prominently in the history of almost all early-modern provincial towns. The success of the town in preserving autonomy usually depended upon its size and political structure on the one hand and the social composition of the neighbouring county on the other. Here Norwich was doubly fortunate. As a large provincial capital in which oligarchy was declining and free-man participation in politics was strong, the city would have been difficult for county magnates to control. Until the last quarter of the century, moreover, Norwich was never challenged by this type of outside interference. The last lord to hold sway over Norwich politics was Thomas Duke of Norfolk, who was executed for treason in 1752.[1] From his death until the appearance of Robert Paston a century later, the county lacked a single dominant peer. During this interval county society was run by a group of some twenty families who lived together harmoniously and who have been characterized as parochial, clannish, and insular.[2] In addition, during the Civil War and Interregnum there was no known divergence of opinion between the city and the county which might otherwise have encouraged friction and intervention. Thus Paston's attempt to control M.P. elections, remodel the corporation, manipulate civic elections, influence the transactions of the Assembly, and surrender the city charter was unprecedented in living memory. Other cities confronted a similar challenge to local independence at this time: the Crown utilized the services of other lord lieutenants to control boroughs in a manner reminiscent of the Protectorate's use of the major-generals. Only the death of Paston in 1683 and the restoration of old charters in 1688 could assure Norwich citizens that they were once again free from county domination.

On five separate occasions after 1640 the central government attempted to regulate city politics: Parliament from 1647–50, the Protectorate in 1656, the Restoration monarchy from 1661–3, the Crown in the period following the exclusion crisis, and James II in 1688. The circumstances which led to intervention and the motives of the central government in doing so were similar. In each case the government was reacting to a previous confrontation with a parliamentary opposition which had been able to block government programmes and policies or had stood as a challenge to the authority of the executive. The desire of the government in each case was to secure the loyalty of Norwich and other corporations and, through this control, to increase support for the government and its policies on the national level. What changed was the willingness of the government to expand upon previous precedent and make ever deeper inroads on local independence in order to gain its ends.

Prior to the Civil War the Privy Council took an active interest in

---

[1] For the Duke's relations with Norwich see Smith, *County and Court*, chap. II.

[2] Owens, 'Norfolk', pp. 31–8.

Norwich affairs, but it did not intervene unless invited to do so by
the corporation. Conformity campaigns launched by bishops were
supported by the Crown, but the latter made no effort to tamper
with the personnel of the corporation or with electoral procedures
for recruiting officeholders. The first step in this direction was
taken by the House of Commons before and after the second Civil
War. The methods adopted here were a locally-conducted purge
of magistrates who had actively opposed Parliament, the imposition of political eligibility tests for electors and candidates, and the
use of loyalty oaths for present and future officeholders. The disruption of municipalities which occurred during the short-lived
rule of the major-generals depended upon the rigour of each major-
general and where and how he chose to concentrate his activities.
With some corporations this entailed a purge, an attempt to restructure politics following a forced surrender of the charter, and direct
involvement in parliamentary and civic elections. The full extent
of Major-General Haynes's dealings with Norwich is not clear,
but apparently he did not push for a surrender of the charter or
attempt a purge. The restored Crown made use of all of the above
precedents during its first three years: the Norwich corporation was
ordered to purge itself of 'disaffected' men, a new set of religious
and political oaths were required of officeholders, the surrender of
the charter was demanded and a new charter issued, and special
commissioners were appointed to regulate corporations personally.
The principle upon which this policy was based was that if sufficient actions were taken and proper safeguards established at the
time, there would be no need for direct supervision in the indefinite future. As such, the Crown's policy proved unsuccessful in the
long run. Thus, when the Crown once again turned to municipal
corporations in the 1680s, the decision was made to construct
charter-sanctioned guarantees of unlimited and indefinite royal
authority over the personnel of Norwich and other town governments. James II did little to enlarge royal authority over corporations, but he demonstrated in extremely controversial fashion the
powers which by this point resided in the Crown.

The citizens and corporation of Norwich were rarely united in
their opposition to external intervention. In almost every instance
the local faction which stood to benefit encouraged and welcomed
this intervention and the faction which stood to lose put up stren-
uous opposition. The reaction of the corporation was then deter-

mined by which of the two groups had the upper hand in the Court of Aldermen and Assembly. A majority of magistrates were unwilling to take a strong stance against Bishop Wren in 1636, but they were outflanked by a Puritan majority in the Assembly. In 1648 and 1649 the Independents of Norwich supported parliamentary ordinances designed to reduce conservative and Royalist influence in the corporation; local resistance took the form of a major riot. In the first years of the Restoration the Presbyterian-dominated corporation carried out royal instructions to eject Commonwealthmen from office, but then fought against further royal and parliamentary measures which would have diminished their own control over the corporation. City Tories co-operated with Paston in the latter's struggle with city Whigs. They also initiated the campaign to surrender voluntarily the charter, requested the Crown to assume increased power over the corporation, and formally thanked King Charles for the new charter. The Whigs put up vigorous resistance to Paston and the surrender of the charter, but they registered no complaints in 1688 when James used the authority provided by the new charter to turn out Tory officeholders and replace them with Dissenters.[1]

The lack of a strong and united reaction within the city and corporation against all forms of external intervention is not surprising. The groundwork was prepared by the decline of oligarchy in the early Stuart period and by the rise to political office of many men born outside the city. Presumably a closed corporation dominated by closely-knit and long-established families would have been more sensitive and opposed to outside interference. Moreover, factions within the corporation had already established the precedent of tampering with the constitution and personnel of government for partisan political purposes before local political autonomy was violated. In 1620 a majority of the magistrates

[1] J. R. Jones has argued that local Whig parties allied themselves with interests which stood for municipal independence against both county gentry and Crown. Stuart Prall has suggested that a principal concept in the Tory point of view was local control of the provinces against additional centralizing tendencies of the Crown. Jones, *Revolution* pp. 44, 139–40, 154–6; Prall, *Bloodless Revolution*, pp. 55–6. If the Tories did champion local control of provincial England, they were thinking solely of rural as distinct from urban England. The Norwich Tories exhibited no interest in municipal independence. As for the Norwich Whigs, they seem to have supported local autonomy when they were the victims of external intervention from 1678 to 1683, but not when they were on the receiving end in 1688.

invited the Crown to impose an alteration in election procedures which would serve their own ends. Further adjustments were made in 1627 and again the corporation appealed to Whitehall for support. In 1641 the Puritans in the corporation, under no external prodding, voided the seniority principle in mayoral elections and two years later ejected active Royalists from the magistracy. Thus by 1648 Norwich citizens had already witnessed the association of partisan politics involving national as well as local issues with purges and manipulation of electoral regulations. The only new ingredients to be added in the next four decades were that the central government intervened more forcefully and without invitation although, as pointed out, there was always some group within the city wbich warmly greeted intervention. Local autonomy ceased to be an important concern of politico-religious groups. They were more concerned with their own political hegemony in the city and with the triumph of the national faction and issues which they supported.

Sources Consulted

All of the manuscripts and printed materials used in the preparation of this work are provided in complete form in the footnotes. However, many of these sources deal solely with Norwich and thus are unfamiliar to most historians. For this reason a separate listing is included here. The most important manuscripts on Norwich are in the Norfolk and Norwich Record Office. The only complete catalogue to this collection is an augmented edition of W. Hudson and J. C. Tingey, eds., *A Revised Catalogue of the Records of the City of Norwich* (Norwich, 1898) now in the reading room of the Norfolk and Norwich Record Office. An indispensable collection of secondary materials is in the local history section of the Norwich Central Library. An augmented edition of *Bibliotheca Norfolciensis, A Catalogue of the Writings of Norfolk Men and Works Relating to Norfolk in the Library of J. J. Colman* (Norwich, 1896) is difficult to use but invaluable.

MANUSCRIPT SOURCES

1. *Norfolk and Norwich Record Office*

   Municipal corporation and judicial series :
   Norwich Assembly Books of Proceedings, 4 vols., 1585–1707.
   Norwich Mayor's Court Books of Proceedings, vols. 15–25, 1615–95. Vols. 17, 18, 19, and 21 are Court minute books from 1628–44, which sometimes contain information not transcribed in vols. 16 (1624–34) and 20 (1634–46). Vol. 22 (1646–54) has been lost.
   Norwich Enrolled Deeds, 1616–90. To be used with Docket Book of Enrolments, 1509–1776.
   Norwich Quarter Sessions Minute Books, 1602–18, 1629–90.
   Norwich Sheriffs' Tourns, 1672–88, 1689–1702 (incomplete).
   Lieutenancy Order Books, 1662–1704.

   Norwich assessments and rates :
   Subscriptions for Regaining Newcastle, 1643. Also published in *Norfolk Archeology*, XVIII, 149–60.
   Assessment for Maintaining Forces of Sir Thomas Fairfax, 1645.
   Parochial Collections for the Rivers and Streets, 1648.

Poor Rate Books, 1659–80 (incomplete).

Assessment of the City of Norwich for Disbanding the King's Forces, 1660.

Rate for Repair of the Walls, 1665.

Militia Assessments, 1665 (incomplete).

Assessments for the Royal Aid of 1689 (incomplete).

Probate records, 1620–1730:

Norwich Consistory Court:

Register Books of Wills Proved, 1620–52, 1660–1730.

(See T. F. Barton and M. A. Farrow, compilers, *Index of Wills Proved in the Consistory Court of Norwich, 1604–1750* 2 vols., Norfolk Record Society Publications, xxviii (1958) and xxxiv (1964).

Administration Act Books, 1620–5, 1628–9, 1639–40, 1641–6, 1666–88. (Original indexes only.)

Inventories, 1620–1730, numerous gaps. (Typewritten lists by T. F. Barton.)

Norfolk Archdeaconry Court:

Register Books of Wills Proved, 1620–1730 with gaps. (Original indexes only.)

Administration Act Books are non-existent, but original bonds exist for 1672–85, 1687–1730. (Original indexes only.)

Inventories are non-existent until 1728.

Norwich Archdeaconry Court:

Register Books of Wills Proved, 1620–52, 1652–1730. (Original indexes only.)

Administration Act Books, 1624–6, 1632–7, 1660–80. (Original indexes only.)

Inventories, 1674–5, 1682–92, 1700–1, 1706–30. (Typewritten lists, but not indexed.)

Peculiar Court of the Dean and Chapter of Norwich:

Register Books of Wills Proved, 1620–52, 1660–1730. (Original index only.)

Administration Act Books are non-existent.

Inventories are non-existent.

Parish registers on microfilm in N.N.R.O.:

St. Peter Southgate (1558–1812)

St. Ethelred (1665–1812)

St. Julian (1589–1812)

St. Peter Permountergate (1538–1812)

St. John Sepulchre (1632–1812)

St. Peter Mancroft (1538–1812)

St. Stephen (1538–1812)

St. Benedict (1608–1812)
St. Lawrence (1558–1812)
St. Gregory (1571–1812)
St. John Maddermarket (1558–1711)
St. Andrew (1558–1812)
St. Michael at Plea (1558–1696)
St. Peter Hungate (1596–1689)
St. Simon and St. Jude (1539–1753)
St. George Tombland (1538–1812)
St. Martin at Palace (1558–1812)
St. Mary Coslany (1557–1812)
St. Michael Coslany (1558–1812)
St. Augustine (1558–1800)
St. Paul (1614–1812)
St. Saviour (1555–1812)
St. Clement (1538–1812)
St. Edmund (1550–1812)

Other manuscripts:

Books of St. George's Company, 1602–1729.
Certificate of the Mayor, etc. Concerning the Fee Farm Rent, 1650.
Charter of 1663.
Charter of 1683.
Differences Between the Dean and Chapter and the City, 1630s.
Liber Albus.
List of Signatories Against the Solemn League and Covenant, 1677–1718.
Mayor's Book or Book of Oaths.
Muster Rolls and Assessments for Maintaining Forces, 17th century, Norwich MS. 453.
Notes on the Mayors of Norwich, 1404–1896, MS. 4499.
Oaths of Allegiance to William and Mary, 1689–1701.
Papers Concerning Various Norwich Offices.
Petition of Bishop Harsnet to the King against the Encroachments of the Citizens, 1619–28.
Solemn League and Covenant with Names of Signatories, 1643 (incomplete).
Various Accounts and Correspondence Relating to Norwich, 1642–50.

2. *Public Record Office*

State Papers, Domestic Series: James I–James II.
Privy Council Registers, 1613–31.
Returns into Chancery of Members of Parliament, C 219/43.

3. *British Museum*
   Additional Manuscripts:
   22619, 22620 (manuscript collections relating to Norwich, 1633–70).
   27448 (correspondence of Lord Yarmouth, 1680s).
   12525 (Benjamin Mackerell, *The Monumental Inscriptions Fenestral and Other Arms in the Parish Churches of the City of Norwich*, 1723).

4. *Bodleian Library, Oxford:*
   Tanner MSS. (For these very important manuscripts, see *Catalogi codicum Manuscriptorum Bibliotecae Bodleiannae, Pars Quarta, Codices Viri Admodum Reverendi Thomae Tanner*, Oxford, 1862.)

5. *Somerset House, London* (probate records of the Prerogative Court of Canterbury)
   Register Books of Wills Proved, 1620–1730. (See *Index Library*, 1620–1700.)
   Administration Act Books, 1620–1730. (Indexed only for 1649–1700.)
   Inventories were not available at the time of this study.

PRINTED SOURCES

1. *National government series:*
   Acts of the Privy Council (1613–31 in bound volumes, London, 1929f.; 1631–7 from microcard reproduction series; 1637–45 from facsimile reproduction).
   Calendar of Charter Rolls, 6 vols., London, 1916.
   Calendar of Inquisitions Post Mortem Preserved in the Public Record Office, 12 vols., London, 1904–39.
   Calendar of the Proceedings of the Committee for Compounding, 1643–1660, 5 vols., London, 1889–92.
   Calendar of State Papers, Domestic Series: James I–James II, London, 1858 f.
   Journals of the House of Commons.
   Journals of the House of Lords.
   Statutes of the Realm, London, 1963.

2. *Norfolk Record Society Publications* (vols. 15, 21, and 28 were also used and are included elsewhere in this bibliography):
   BRADFER-LAWRENCE, H. L., *Norwich Subscriptions to a Voluntary Gift of 1662*, i, 1931, 69–86.
   CAMPLING, Arthur, *East Anglian Pedigrees*, xiii, 1940.
   ——, and A. W. Hughes CLARK, eds., *The Visitation of Norfolk, anno domini 1664*, iv and v, 1934. See also G. H. HOLLEY, *Observations and Comments on the Visitation of Norfolk, 1664*, xxvii, 1956, 61–89.

COZENS-HARDY, B., ed., *Old Meeting House, Norwich, and Great Yarmouth Independent Church*, xxii, 1951, 1–39.

HILL, Robert H., ed., *The Correspondence of Thomas Corie, Town Clerk of Norwich, 1664–1687*, xxvii, 1956, 7–58.

MILLICAN, Percy and Winifred M. RISING, eds., *An Index of Indentures of Norwich Apprentices enrolled with the Norwich Assembly, Henry VII to George II*, xxix, 1959.

SACHSE, William L., ed., *Minutes of the Norwich Court of Mayoralty, 1630–1631*, xv, 1942.

SCHOFIELD, Bertram, ed., *The Knyvett Letters, 1620–1644*, xx, 1949.

3. *Historical Manuscripts Commission Reports*:
   4th Report, House of Lords MSS.
   6th Report, Ingilby MSS.
   7th Report, Frere MSS.
   10th Report, Appendix 2, Gawdy MSS.
   13th Report, Portland MSS.
   14th Report, Kenyon MSS.
   Lothian MSS.

4. *Thomason Tracts, British Library* (listed by order of Thomason Tract no.):

669. f. 6 (54)   *To the Lords. The Petition of Many Thousands of the Inhabitants of Norwich*, London, 16 July 1642, printed for George Tomlinson and R.C.

E. 112. (16)   *Joyfull Newes from Norwich wherein is declared how the Earle of Lindsey endeavored to raise a party against the Parliament . . .*, London, 17 August 1642, printed for T. Rider.

E. 114. (15)   *Newes from the Citie of Norwich*, London, 26 August 1642, printed for Th. Clapham.

E. 114. (27)   *A True and Exact Relation of the Present estate of the City of Norwich, made known to the High and Honorable Court of Parliament; by way of Petition . . .*, London, 27 August 1642, printed for D. Bradley.

E. 140. (17)   L., T., *True Newes from Norwich. Being a certaine relation how that the Cathedrall Blades of Norwich . . . did put themselves into a posture of defence, because that the Apprentices of Norwich would have pulled down their Organs*, London, 1641, printed for Benjamin Allen and I.B.

E. 147. (1).   *Foure Wonderfull, Bloudy, and Dangerous Plots discovered: from Norwich, where a Train of Papists had conspired the firing of the Citie . . .*, London, 1642, printed for John Gilbert.

E. 179. (10)   *Bloody Newes from Norwich : or, a True relation of a bloody attempt of the Papists in Norwich to consume the whole city by fire,* London, 1641, printed for John Greensmith.

E. 351. (4)   T., S., *Truth Vindicated from the unjust accusations of the Independent Society in the City of Norwich,* London, 1646, printed by Th. Harper for Gifford Galton.

E. 351. (7)   *Vox Populi, or the people's cry against the clergy,* London, 1646, printed by Tho. Paine for John Pounset.

E. 355. (13)   *An Hue and Cry after Vox Populi; or, an Answer to a libellous Pamphlet styled Vox Populi, reviling the Magistracy and Ministry of Norwich,* London, 25 September 1646, printed for Edward Martin, in Norwich.

E. 358. (4)   *Vox Norwici, or the Cry of Norwich vindicating their Ministers from the lying Libell intitled Vox Populi,* London, 1646, printed for William Frankling and sold by Richard Tomlins.

E. 411. (6)   Carter, John, *The Nail hit on the head : and Driven into the City and Cathedral Wall of Norwich,* 17 June 1644, and *The Wheel Turned by a voice from the throne of Glory Described in a Sermon At the Greenyard in Norwich, upon the Guild-day,* 22 June 1647, in Carter, *The Nail and the Wheel. Both described in two several sermons in the Greenyard at Norwich,* London, 1647, printed by J. Macock for M. Spark.

E. 437. (12)   S., T., *A Letter from Norwich of the Blowing up of the Magazine there,* London, 25 April 1648.

E. 438. (6)   *A True Relation of the Late Great Mutiny which was in the City and County of Norwich, 24 April,* London, April 1648, printed for George Whittington.

E. 447. (6)   *The Attestation of the Ministers of Norfolk and Suffolk, in vindication of the truths of Jesus Christ and prosecution of the Solemn Covenant,* London, 9 June 1648.

E. 544. (5)   *Certain Queries Humbly presented in way of Petition by many Christian People throughout the County of Norfolk and the City of Norwich to the Lord General and Council of War,* London, 1649, printed for Giles Calvert.

5. *Other Printed Sources:*

ABBOTT, W. C., ed., *The Writings and Speeches of Oliver Cromwell,* 4 vols., Cambridge, 1934–47.

BELL, Robert, ed., *Memorials of the Civil War,* 2 vols., London, 1849.

BIRCH, Thomas, ed., *A Collection of State Papers of John Thurloe,* 7 vols., London, 1742.

BLISS, James and William SCOTT, eds., *The Works of William Laud,* 7 vols., Oxford, 1847–60.

CAMDEN, William, *Britannia,* trans. Philemon Holland, London, 1637.

CARY, Henry, ed., *Memorials of the Great Civil War in England, 1642–52,* 2 vols., London, 1842.

DASHWOOD, Revd. G. H., *The Visitation of Norfolk in the Year 1563,* 2 vols., Norwich, 1878.

DE BEER, E. S., ed., *The Diary of John Evelyn,* 6 vols., Oxford, 1955.

Dictionary of National Biography, 63 vols., 1885–1900.

FIRTH, C. H. and R. S. RAIT, eds., *Acts and Ordinances of the Interregnum, 1642–1660,* 3 vols., London, 1911.

FULLER, Thomas, *The Worthies of England,* ed. John Freeman, London, 1952.

HARRINGTON, Sir John, *Nugae Antiquae,* ed. T. Clark, 2 vols., London, 1804.

HILDEYARD, John, *A Sermon Preached at the Funeral of the Right Honorable Robert, Earl and Viscount Yarmouth,* London, 1683.

HUDSON, William and J. C. TINGEY, eds., The *Records of the City of Norwich,* 2 vols., Norwich, 1906–10.

JAY, George Branwhite, *The First Parish Register of St. George Tombland, 1538–1707,* Norwich, 1891.

KEMP, William, *Kemp's Nine Daies Wonder,* Camden Society Publication, London, 1840.

KENYON, J. P., *The Stuart Constitution,* Cambridge, 1966.

L'ESTRANGE, John and William RYE, *Calendar of the Freemen of Norwich, 1317–1603,* London, 1888.

LE STRANGE, Hamon and Walter RYE, eds., *An Address from the Gentry of Norfolk and Norwich to General Monck in 1660,* Norwich, 1913.

MILLICAN, Percy, ed., *The Register of the Freemen of Norwich, 1548–1713: A Transcript,* Norwich, 1934.

MORRIS, C., ed., *The Journeys of Ceila Fiennes,* London, 1947.

Newes from Norwich; or, an Exact Relation . . . , London, 1647 (copy available in Local History Section, Norwich Central Library).

Norwich Mercury, 22–29 August 1752.

NOTESTEIN, Wallace, ed., *The Journal of Sir Simonds D'Ewes*, New Haven, 1923.

A Perfect Diurnal of some passages in Parliament and the Daily Proceedings of the Army under his Excellency the Lord Fairfax from Monday the 24th April till Monday the 1 of May 1648, London, 1648, reprinted in John L'Estrange, ed., *Eastern Counties Collectanae*, Norwich, 1872–3.

RUSHWORTH, John, *Historical Collections*, 8 vols., London, 1721.

RUTT, J. T., ed., *Diary of Thomas Burton, Esquire*, 4 vols., London, 1828.

RYE, Walter, ed., *The Norwich Rate Book, Easter 1633 to Easter 1634*, 1903.

——, *The Visitations of Norfolk, 1563, 1589, and 1613*, Harleian Society Publication, 32, London, 1891.

THOMPSON, Edmund Maunde, ed., *Letters of Humphrey Prideaux*, Camden Society Publication, London, 1875.

WILSON, Thomas, *The State of England anno Dom. 1600*, ed. F. J. Fisher, Camden Miscellany XVI, 3rd ser., LII, London, 1936.

WOOD, Anthony à, *Athenae Oxonienses*, 2 vols., London, 1691.

WREN, Matthew, *Parentalia*, 1750.

SELECTED SECONDARY WORKS

ABERNATHY, George R., Jr., *The English Presbyterians and the Stuart Restoration, 1648–1663*, Transactions of the American Philosophical Society, new ser. LV, pt. 2, Philadelphia, 1965.

ALLEN, Bruce Halliday, 'The Administrative and Social Structure of the Norwich Merchant Class, 1485–1660', unpublished Ph.D. thesis, Harvard University, 1951.

ALLISON, K. J., 'The Norfolk Worsted Industry in the Sixteenth and Seventeenth Centuries', *Yorkshire Bulletin*, XII. 2 (1960), 73–83, XIII. 1 (1961), 61–77.

——, 'The Wool Supply and the Worsted Cloth Industry in Norfolk in the Sixteenth and Seventeenth Centuries', unpublished Ph.D. thesis, University of Leeds, 1955.

AYLMER, G. E., ed., *The Interregnum: The Quest for Settlement, 1646–1660*, London, 1972.

BAYNE, A. D., *A Comprehensive History of Norwich*, Norwich, 1869.

BLAKELY, E. T., *History of the Manufactures of Norwich*, Norwich, 188?

BLOMEFIELD, Francis, *An Essay Towards a Topographical History of the County of Norfolk*, 11 vols., London, 1805–10.

BRENNER, Robert, 'The Civil War Politics of London's Merchant Community', *Past and Present*, 58 (Feb. 1973), 53–107.

BROWNE, John, *History of Congregationalism and Memorials of the Churches in Norfolk and Suffolk*, London, 1877.

BRUNTON, D. and D. H. PENNINGTON, *Members of the Long Parliament*, Cambridge, Mass., 1954.

CARRUTHERS, S. W., 'Norfolk Presbyterianism in the Seventeenth Century', *Norfolk Archaeology*, XXX (1952), 89–100.

CLARK, Peter and Paul SLACK, eds., *Crisis and Order in English Towns 1500–1700*, London, 1972.

COLEMAN, D. C., 'An Innovation and its Diffusion: The "New Draper-ies"', *Economic History Review*, 2nd ser. XXII (1969), 417–29.

CORFIELD, Penelope, 'A Provincial Capital in the Late Seventeenth Century: The Case of Norwich', in Clark and Slack, eds., *Crisis and Order*, pp. 263–310.

COZENS-HARDY, Basil and Ernest A. KENT, *The Mayors of Norwich 1403–1835*, Norwich, 1938.

CROSS, Claire, 'The Church in England, 1646–1660', in Aylmer, ed., *Interregnum*, pp. 99–120.

DAVIES, Godfrey, *The Restoration of Charles II, 1558–1660*, Oxford, 1955.

EDDINGTON, Arthur J., *The First Fifty Years of Quakerism in Norwich*, London, 1932.

EVANS, John T., 'The Decline of Oligarchy in Seventeenth-Century Norwich', *Journal of British Studies*, XIV (Nov. 1974), 46–76.

——, 'The Political Elite of Norwich, 1620–1690: Patterns of Recruit-ment and the Impact of National Affairs', unpublished Ph.D. thesis, Stanford University, 1971.

EVERITT, Alan, *Change in the Provinces: The Seventeenth Century*, Leicester, 1969.

FARNELL, J. E., 'The Usurpation of Honest London Householders: Barebone's Parliament', *English Historical Review*, 82 (1967), 24–46.

GRASSBY, Richard, 'The Personal Wealth of the Business Community in Seventeenth-Century England', *Economic History Review*, 2nd ser. XXIII, 2 (Aug. 1970), 220–34.

HARDACRE, Paul H., *The Royalists During the Puritan Revolution*, The Hague, 1956.

HENDERSON, B. L. K., 'The Commonwealth Charters', *Transactions of the Royal Historical Society*, 3rd ser. VI (1912), 129–62.

HEXTER, J. H., 'The Problem of the Presbyterian Independents', *American Historical Review*, 44 (1938–9), 29–49.

HIRST, Derek, *The Representative of the People?*, Cambridge, 1975.

HOLMES, Clive, *The Eastern Association in the English Civil War*, Cambridge, 1974.

HOSKINS, W. G., *Local History in England*, London, 1959.

HOWELL, Roger, Jr., *Newcastle-upon-Tyne and the Puritan Revolution*, Oxford, 1967.

IVES, E. W., ed., *The English Revolution, 1600–1660*, London, 1968.

JONES, J. R., *The First Whigs: The Politics of the Exclusion Crisis, 1678–1683*, London, 1961.

——, *The Revolution of 1688 in England*, London, 1972.

KAPLAN, Lawrence, 'English Civil War Politics and the Religious Settlement', *Church History*, 41 (1972), 307–25.

KEELER, M. F., *The Long Parliament 1640–1641, A Biographical Study*, Philadelphia, 1954.

KETTON-CREMER, R. W., *Norfolk in the Civil War*, Hamden, Conn., 1970.

KING, Peter, 'Bishop Wren and the Suppression of the Norwich Lecturers', *Historical Journal*, XI. 2 (1968), 237–54.

KINGSTON, Alfred, *East Anglia and the Great Civil War*, London, 1897.

LACEY, Douglas R., *Dissent and Parliamentary Politics in England, 1661–1689*, New Brunswick, 1969.

LANG, R. G., 'Social Origins and Social Aspirations of Jacobean London Merchants', *Economic History Review*, 2nd ser. XXVII. 1 (Feb. 1974), 28–47.

LASLETT, Peter, *The World We Have Lost*, New York, 1965.

LEVIN, Jennifer, *The Charter Controversy in the City of London, 1660–1688, and its Consequences*, London, 1969.

MACCAFFREY, Wallace T., *Exeter, 1540–1640*, Cambridge, Mass., 1958.

MASON, R. H., *History of Norfolk*, 2 vols., London, 1882–5.

OWENS, Gary Lynn, 'Norfolk, 1620–1640: Local Government and Central Authority in an East Anglian County', unpublished Ph.D. thesis, University of Wisconsin, 1970.

PAGE, William, ed., *The Victoria History of the County of Norfolk*, 2 vols., London, 1906.

PEARL, Valerie, 'London's Counter-Revolution', in Aylmer, ed., *Interregnum*, pp. 29–56.

——, *London and the Outbreak of the Puritan Revolution*, London, 1961.

PLUMB, J. H., 'The Growth of the Electorate in England from 1600 to 1715', *Past and Present*, 45 (Nov. 1969), 90–116.

——, *The Growth of Political Stability in England, 1675–1725*, London, 1967.

POUND, John F., 'An Elizabethan Census of the Poor', *University of Birmingham Historical Journal*, VIII. 2 (1962), 135–61.

——, 'The Elizabethan Corporation of Norwich', unpublished M.A. thesis, University of Birmingham, 1962.

——, 'Government and Society in Tudor and Stuart Norwich, 1525–1675', unpublished Ph.D. thesis, University of Leicester, 1975.

——, 'The Social and Trade Structure of Norwich, 1525–1575', *Past and Present*, 34 (July 1966), 49–69.

PRALL, Stuart E., *The Bloodless Revolution: England, 1688*, New York, 1972.

Roots, Ivan, 'Cromwell's Ordinances: The Early Legislation of the Protectorate', in Aylmer, ed., *Interregnum*, pp. 147, 157.

——, *The Great Rebellion, 1642–1660*, London, 1966.

Sacret, J. H., 'The Restoration Government and Municipal Corporations', *English Historical Review*, 45 (1930), 232–59.

Seaver Paul S. *The Puritan Lectureships: The Politics of Religious Dissent 1560–1642*, Stanford, 1970.

Sharpe Reginald R., *London and the Kingdom*, 3 vols., London, 1894.

Shaw, W. A., *A History of the English Church during the Civil Wars and Under the Commonwealth 1640–1662*, 2 vols., 1900.

Shilling, William A. Hayden, 'The Central Government and the Municipal Corporations in England, 1642–1663', unpublished Ph.D. thesis, Vanderbilt University, 1970.

Shipps, Kenneth, 'Lay Patronage of East Anglian Puritan Clerics in Pre-Revolutionary England', unpublished Ph.D. thesis, Yale University, 1971.

Smith, A. Hassell, *County and Court: Government and Politics in Norfolk, 1558–1603*, Oxford, 1974.

Stone, Lawrence, 'Social Mobility in England, 1500–1700', *Past and Present*. 33 (Apr. 1966), 16–55.

Tait, James, 'The Common Council of the Borough', *English Historical Review*, 46 (1931), 1–29.

Underdown, David, *Pride's Purge: Politics in the Puritan Revolution*, Oxford, 1971.

——, 'A Case Concerning Bishops' Lands: Cornelius Burges and the Corporation of Wells', *English Historical Review*, 78 (1963), 21–3.

——, *Somerset in the Civil War and Interregnum*, Newton Abbot, 1973.

——, 'Settlement in the Counties, 1653–1658', in Aylmer, ed., *Interregnum*, pp. 116–82.

Wedgwood, C. V., *The King's War, 1641–1647*, Manchester, 1958.

Weinbaum, Martin, *British Borough Charters, 1307–1660*, Cambridge, 1943.

Western, J. R., *Monarchy and Revolution*, London, 1972.

Wrigley, E. A., 'A Simple Model of London's Importance in Changing English Society and Economy, 1650–1750', *Past and Present*, 37 (July 1967), 44–70.

——, 'Mortality in Pre-Industrial England: the Example of Colyton, Devon, Over Three Centuries', *Daedalus* (Spring 1968), 546–80.

Zagorin, Perez, *The Court and the Country*, London, 1969.

Index